ISIS UNVEILED

ARYAN THEOSOPHICAL PRESS
Point Loma, California

ISIS UNVEILED

A MASTER-KEY

TO THE

MYSTERIES OF ANCIENT AND MODERN

SCIENCE AND THEOLOGY

BY

H. P. BLAVATSKY

"Cecy est un livre de bonne Foy."— MONTAIGNE

VOL. II — THEOLOGY

SECTION I

THIRD POINT LOMA EDITION — REVISED

THE ARYAN THEOSOPHICAL PRESS
POINT LOMA, CALIFORNIA
1919

Copyright 1877 by J. W. Bouton

New and Revised Edition
Copyright 1919 by Katherine Tingley

The Author
Dedicates these volumes
to the
Theosophical Society
which was founded at New York, A.D. 1875,
to study the subjects on which they treat

TABLE OF CONTENTS

VOLUME TWO

THE 'INFALLIBILITY' OF RELIGION

SECTION I

CHAPTER I — THE CHURCH: WHERE IS IT?

CHAPTER II — CHRISTIAN CRIMES AND HEATHEN VIRTUES

CHAPTER III — DIVISIONS AMONGST THE EARLY CHRISTIANS

CHAPTER IV — ORIENTAL COSMOGONIES AND BIBLE RECORDS

CHAPTER V — MYSTERIES OF THE KABALA

CHAPTER VI — ESOTERIC DOCTRINES OF BUDDHISM PARODIED IN CHRISTIANITY

CONTENTS

SECTION II

CHAPTER VIII — JESUITRY AND MASONRY

CHAPTER IX — THE VEDAS AND THE BIBLE

CHAPTER X — THE DEVIL-MYTH

CONTENTS

CHAPTER XI — COMPARATIVE RESULTS OF BUDDHISM AND CHRISTIANITY

CHAPTER XII — CONCLUSIONS AND ILLUSTRATIONS

AUTHOR'S PREFACE TO VOLUME II

WERE it possible, we would keep this work out of the hands of many Christians whom its perusal would not benefit, and for whom it was not written. We allude to those whose faith in their respective churches is pure and sincere, and those whose sinless lives reflect the glorious example of that Prophet of Nazareth, by whose mouth the spirit of truth spake loudly to humanity. Such there have been at all times. History preserves the names of many as heroes, philosophers, philanthropists, martyrs, and holy men and women; but how many more have lived and died, unknown but to their intimate acquaintance, unblessed but by their humble beneficiaries! These have ennobled Christianity, but would have shed the same luster upon any other faith they might have professed — for they were higher than their creed. The benevolence of Peter Cooper and Elizabeth Thompson, of America, who are not orthodox Christians, is no less Christ-like than that of the Baroness Angela Burdett-Coutts, of England, who is one. And yet, in comparison with the millions who have been accounted Christians, such have always formed a small minority. They are to be found at this day, in pulpit and pew, in palace and cottage; but the increasing materialism, worldliness and hypocrisy are fast diminishing their proportionate number. Their charity and simple, child-like faith in the infallibility of their Bible, their dogmas, and their clergy, bring into full activity all the virtues that are implanted in our common nature. We have personally known such God-fearing priests and clergymen, and we have always avoided debate with them, lest we might be guilty of the cruelty of hurting their feelings; nor would we rob a single layman of his blind confidence, if it alone made possible for him holy living and serene dying.

An analysis of religious beliefs in general, this volume is in particular directed against theological Christianity, the chief opponent of free thought. It contains not one word against the pure teachings of Jesus, but unsparingly denounces their debasement into pernicious ecclesiastical systems that are ruinous to man's faith in his immortality and his God, and subversive of all moral restraint.

We cast our gauntlet at the dogmatic theologians who would enslave both history and science; and especially at the Vatican, whose despotic pretensions have become hateful to the greater portion of enlightened Christendom. The clergy apart, none but the logician, the investigator, the dauntless explorer should meddle with books like this. Such delvers after truth have the courage of their opinions.

ISIS UNVEILED

PART TWO — RELIGION

CHAPTER I

"Yes, the time cometh, that whosoever killeth you will think that he doeth God service."— *John*, xvi, 2

"Let him be ANATHEMA . . . who shall say that human Sciences ought to be pursued in such a spirit of freedom that one may be allowed to hold as true their assertions even when opposed to revealed doctrine."— *Oecumenical Council of 1870*

"GLOUC.— The Church! Where is it?"— *1 King Henry VI*, I, i

IN the United States of America sixty thousand (60,428) men are paid salaries to teach the Science of God and His relations to His creatures.

These men contract to impart to us the knowledge which treats of the existence, character, and attributes of our Creator; His laws and government; the doctrines we are to believe and the duties we are to practise. Five thousand (5141) of them,[1] with the prospect of 1273 theological students to help them in time, teach this science according to a formula prescribed by the Bishop of Rome, to five million people. Fifty-five thousand (55,287) local and traveling ministers, representing fifteen different denominations,[2] each contradicting the other upon more or less vital theological questions, instruct, in their respective doctrines, thirty-three million (33,500,000) other persons. Many of these teach according to the canons of the cis-Atlantic branch of an establishment which acknowledges a daughter of the late Duke of Kent as its spiritual

---

1. These figures are copied from the *Religious Statistics of the United States for the year 1871.*

2. These are: The *Baptists, Congregationalists, Episcopalians,* Northern *Methodists,* Southern *Methodists,* Methodists *various,* Northern *Presbyterians,* Southern *Presbyterians,* United *Presbyterians,* United *Brethren, Brethren in Christ, Reformed Dutch, Reformed German, Reformed Presbyterians, Cumberland Presbyterians.*

head. There are many hundred thousand Jews; some thousands of
Orientals of all kinds; and a very few who belong to the Greek Church.
A man at Salt Lake City, with nineteen wives and more than one hundred children and grandchildren, is the supreme spiritual ruler over
ninety thousand people, who believe that he is in frequent intercourse
with the gods — for the Mormons are Polytheists as well as Polygamists,
and their chief god is represented as living in a planet they call Colob.

The God of the Unitarians is a bachelor; the Deity of the Presbyterians, Methodists, Congregationalists, and the other orthodox Protestant sects a spouseless Father with one Son, who is identical with Himself. In the attempt to outvie each other in the erection of their sixty-two
thousand and odd churches, prayer-houses, and meeting-halls, in which
to teach these conflicting theological doctrines, $354,485,581 have been
spent. The value of the Protestant parsonages alone, in which are
sheltered the disputants and their families, is roughly calculated to
approximate $54,115,297. Sixteen million (16,179,387) dollars are,
moreover, contributed every year for the current expenses of the Protestant denominations only. One Presbyterian church in New York cost a
round million; a Catholic altar alone, one-fourth as much!

We will not mention the multitude of smaller sects, communities, and
extravagantly original little heresies in this country which spring up one
year to die out the next, like so many spores of fungi after a rainy day.
We will not even stop to consider the alleged millions of Spiritualists;
for the majority lack the courage to break away from their respective
religious denominations. These are the back-door Nicodemuses.

And now with Pilate let us inquire, What is truth? Where is it to be
searched for amid this multitude of warring sects? Each claims to be
based upon divine revelation, and each to have the keys of the celestial
gates. Is any one of them in possession of this rare truth? Or, must we
exclaim with the Buddhist philosopher, "There is but one truth on earth,
and it is unchangeable: and this is — that there is *no* truth on it!"

Though we have no disposition whatever to trench upon the ground
that has been so exhaustively gleaned by those learned scholars who have
shown that every Christian dogma has its origin in a heathen rite, still the
facts which they have exhumed, since the enfranchisement of science, will
lose nothing by repetition. Besides, we propose to examine these facts
from a different and perhaps rather novel point of view: that of the old
philosophies as esoterically understood. These we have barely glanced
at in our first volume. We will use them as the standard by which to
compare Christian dogmas and miracles with the doctrines and phenomena of ancient magic, and the modern 'New Dispensation,' as Spiritualism is called by its votaries. Since the materialists deny the phenom-

ena without investigation, and since the theologians in admitting them offer us the poor choice of two palpable absurdities — the Devil and miracles — we can lose little by applying to the theurgists, and they may actually help us to throw a great light upon a very dark subject.

Professor A. Butlerof of the Imperial University of St. Petersburg remarks in a recent pamphlet, entitled *Mediumistic Manifestations*, as follows: "Let the facts [of modern spiritualism] belong if you will to the number of those which were more or less known by the ancients; let them be identical with those which in the dark ages gave importance to the office of Egyptian priest or Roman augur; let them even furnish the basis of the sorcery of our Siberian Shaman; . . . let them be all these, and if they are *real facts*, it is no business of ours. All the facts in nature *belong to science*, and every addition to the store of science enriches instead of impoverishes her. If humanity has once admitted a truth, and then in the blindness of self-conceit denied it, to return to its realization is a step forward and not backward."

Since the day when modern science gave what may be considered the death-blow to dogmatic theology by assuming the ground that religion was full of mystery, and mystery is unscientific, the mental state of the educated class has presented a curious aspect. Society seems from that time to have been ever balancing itself upon one leg on an unseen tight-rope stretched from our visible universe into the invisible one; uncertain whether the end hooked on faith in the latter might not suddenly break and hurl it into final annihilation.

The great body of nominal Christians may be divided into three unequal portions: materialists, spiritualists, and Christians proper. The materialists and spiritualists make common cause against the hierarchical pretensions of the clergy; who, in retaliation, denounce both with equal acerbity. The materialists are as little in harmony as the Christian sects themselves — the Comtists, or, as they call themselves, the Positivists, being despised and hated to the last degree by the schools of thinkers, one of which Maudsley honorably represents in England. Positivism, be it remembered, is that 'religion' of the future about whose founder even Huxley has made himself wrathful in his famous lecture, *The Physical Basis of Life;* and Maudsley felt obliged, in behalf of modern science, to express himself thus: "It is no wonder that scientific men should be anxious to disclaim Comte as their law-giver, and to protest against such a king being set up to reign over them. Not conscious of any personal obligation to his writings, conscious how much, in some respects, he has misrepresented the spirit and pretensions of science, they repudiate the allegiance which his enthusiastic disciples would force upon them, and which popular opinion is fast coming to think a natural one. They do well in thus making a timely assertion of independence; for if it be not done soon, it will soon be too late to be done well." [3] When a materialistic doctrine is repudiated so strongly by two such materialists as Huxley and Maudsley, then we must think indeed that it is absurdity itself.

Among Christians there is nothing but dissension. Their various churches represent every degree of religious belief, from the omnivorous credulity of blind faith to a condescending and high-toned deference to the Deity which thinly masks an evident conviction of their own deific wisdom. All these sects believe more or less in the immortality of the soul. Some admit the intercourse between the two worlds as a fact; some entertain the opinion as a sentiment; some positively deny it; and only a few maintain an attitude of attention and expectancy.

Impatient of restraint, longing for the return of the dark ages, the Romish Church frowns at the *diabolical* manifestations, and indicates what she would do to their champions had she but the power of old. Were it not for the self-evident fact that she herself is placed by science on trial, and that she is handcuffed, she would be ready at a moment's notice to repeat in the nineteenth century the revolting scenes of former days. As to the Protestant clergy, so furious is their common hatred toward spiritualism, that as a secular paper very truly remarks: "They seem willing to undermine the public faith in all the spiritual phenomena of the past as recorded in the *Bible*, if they can only see the pestilent modern heresy stabbed to the heart." [4]

Summoning back the long-forgotten memories of the Mosaic laws, the Romish Church claims the monopoly of miracles and of the right to sit in judgment over them, as being the sole heir thereto by direct inheritance. The *Old Testament*, exiled by Colenso, his predecessors and contemporaries, is recalled from its banishment. The prophets, whom his Holiness the Pope condescends at last to place, if not on the same level with himself, at least at a less respectful distance,[5] are dusted and cleaned. The memory of all the diabolical abracadabra is evoked anew. The blasphemous *horrors* perpetrated by Paganism, its

---

3. H. Maudsley: *Body and Mind;* lect. on 'The Limits of Philosophical Inquiry.'
4. Boston *Sunday Herald*, November 5, 1876.
5. See the self-glorification of the present Pope in the work entitled, *Speeches of Pope Pius IX*, by Don Pasquale di Franciscis; and the famous pamphlet of that name by the Rt. Hon. W. E. Gladstone (reviewed in his *Rome and the Newest Fashions in Religion:* London, 1875). The latter quotes from the work named the following sentence pronounced by the Pope: "My wish is that all governments should know that I am speaking in this strain. . . . And I have *the right* to speak, *even more than Nathan the prophet to David the king, and a great deal more than Ambrose had to Theodosius"*!!

phallic worship, thaumaturgical wonders wrought by Satan, human sacrifices, incantations, witchcraft, magic, and sorcery are recalled; and
DEMONISM is confronted with *spiritualism* for mutual recognition and
identification. Our modern demonologists conveniently overlook a few
insignificant details, among which is the undeniable presence of heathen
phallicism in the Christian symbols. A strong spiritual element of this
worship may be easily demonstrated in the dogma of the Immaculate
Conception of the Virgin Mother of God; and a physical element
equally proved in the fetish-worship of the holy *limbs* of Sts. Cosmo
and Damiano at Isernia, near Naples; a successful traffic in which
ex-votos in wax was carried on by the clergy annually, until barely
a century ago.[6]

We find it rather unwise on the part of Catholic writers to pour out
their vials of wrath in such sentences as these: "In a multitude of
pagodas, the phallic stone, ever and always assuming, like the Grecian
betylos, the brutally indecent form of the *lingam* . . . the *Mahâ-Deva.*"[7]
Before casting slurs on a symbol whose profound metaphysical meaning
is too much for the modern champions of that religion of sensualism
par excellence, Roman Catholicism, to grasp, they are in duty bound
to destroy their oldest churches, and change the form of the cupolas
of their own temples. The Mahody of Elephanta, the Round Tower of
Bhagalpur, the minarets of Islam — either rounded or pointed — are the
originals of the *campanile* column of San Marco at Venice, of Rochester
Cathedral, and of the modern Duomo of Milan. All of these steeples, tur-
rets, domes, and Christian temples are the reproductions of the primitive
idea of the *lithos,* the upright phallus. "The western tower of St. Paul's
Cathedral, London," says the author of *The Rosicrucians,* "is one of the
double *lithoi* placed always in front of every temple, Christian as well as
heathen."[8] Moreover, in all Christian Churches, "particularly in Protestant churches, where they figure most conspicuously, the two tables of
stone of the Mosaic Dispensation are placed over the altar, side by side,
as a united stone, the tops of which are rounded. . . . The right stone is
masculine, the left *feminine.*" Therefore neither Catholics nor Protestants have a right to talk of the 'indecent forms' of heathen monuments,
so long as they ornament their own churches with the symbols of the
Lingam and Yoni, and even write the laws of their God upon them.

Another detail not redounding very particularly to the honor of the
Christian clergy might be recalled in the word Inquisition. The torrents

---

6. Cf. C. W. King: *The Gnostics, etc.;* R. P. Knight:
   Worship of Priapus, p. 3, *sq.;* and other works.
7. Des Mousseaux: *Les hauts phén. de la magie,* p. 24.
8. Hargrave Jennings: *The Rosicrucians,* II, i; 3rd ed.

of human blood shed by this *Christian* institution, and the number of its human sacrifices, are unparalleled in the annals of Paganism. Another still more prominent feature in which the clergy surpassed their masters, the 'heathen,' is *sorcery*. Certainly in no Pagan temple was black magic, in its real and true sense, more practised than in the Vatican. While strongly supporting exorcism as an important source of revenue, they neglected magic as little as the ancient heathen. It is easy to prove that the *sortilegium*, or sorcery, was widely practised among the clergy and monks so late as the last century, and is practised occasionally even now.

Anathematizing every manifestation of occult nature outside the precincts of the Church, the clergy — notwithstanding proofs to the contrary — call it "the work of Satan," "the snares of the fallen angels," who "rush in and out from the bottomless pit," mentioned by John in his Kabalistic *Revelation*, "from whence arises a smoke as the smoke of a great furnace." "*Intoxicated by its fumes, around this pit are daily gathering millions of Spiritualists, to worship at 'the Abyss of Baal.'* "

More than ever arrogant, stubborn, and despotic, now that she has been nearly upset by modern research, not daring to interfere with the powerful champions of science, the Latin Church revenges herself upon the unpopular phenomena. A despot without a victim is a word void of sense; a power which neglects to assert itself through outward, well-calculated effects, risks being doubted in the end. The Church has no intention of falling into the oblivion of the ancient myths, or of suffering her authority to be too closely questioned. Hence she pursues, as well as the times permit, her traditional policy. Lamenting the enforced extinction of her ally, the Holy Inquisition, she makes a virtue of necessity. The only victims now within reach are the Spiritists of France. Recent events have shown that the meek spouse of Christ never disdains to retaliate on helpless victims.

Having successfully performed her part of *deus ex machinâ* from behind the French Bench, which has not scrupled to disgrace itself for her, the Church of Rome sets to work and shows in the year 1876 what she can do. From the whirling tables and dancing pencils of profane Spiritualism, the Christian world is warned to turn to the divine 'miracles' of Lourdes. Meanwhile the ecclesiastical authorities utilize their time in arranging for other more easy triumphs, calculated to scare the superstitious out of their senses. So, acting under orders, the clergy hurl dramatic, if not very impressive anathemas from every Catholic diocese; threaten right and left; excommunicate and curse. Perceiving, finally, that her thunderbolts directed even against crowned

heads fall about as harmlessly as the Jovian lightnings of Offenbach's
Calchas, Rome turns about in powerless fury against the victimized
protégés of the Emperor of Russia — the unfortunate Bulgarians and
Servians. Undisturbed by evidence and sarcasm, unbaffled by proof,
'the lamb of the Vatican' impartially divides his wrath between the
liberals of Italy, "the impious whose breath has the stench of the
sepulcher," [9] the "schismatic Russian *Sarmates*," and the heretics and
spiritualists, "who worship at the bottomless pit where the great
Dragon lies in wait."

Mr. Gladstone went to the trouble of making a catalog of what he
terms the "flowers of speech," disseminated through these Papal discourses. Let us cull a few of the chosen terms used by this vice-regent of
Him who said that, "whosoever shall say, *Thou fool*, shall be in danger of
hell-fire." They are selected from authentic discourses. Those who
oppose the Pope are "wolves, Pharisees, thieves, liars, hypocrites, drop-
sical, children of Satan, of perdition, of sin and corruption, satellites
of Satan in human flesh, monsters of hell, demons incarnate, stinking
corpses, men issued from the pits of hell, traitors and Judases led by the
spirit of hell, children of the deepest pits of hell," etc., etc.; the whole
piously collected and published by Don Pasquale di Franciscis, whom
Gladstone has, with perfect propriety, termed, "an accomplished professor of *flunkeyism* in things spiritual." [10]

Since his Holiness the Pope has such a rich vocabulary of invectives
at his command, why wonder that the Bishop of Toulouse did not scruple
to utter the most undignified falsehoods about the Protestants and Spiritualists of America — people doubly odious to a Catholic — in his address
to his diocese: "Nothing," he remarks, "is more common in an era of
unbelief than to see a *false revelation substitute itself for the true one*,
and minds neglect the teachings of the Holy Church, to devote themselves to the study of divination and the occult sciences." With a fine
episcopal contempt for statistics, and strangely confounding in his memory the audiences of the revivalists Moody and Sankey and the patrons
of darkened *séance*-rooms, he makes the unwarranted and fallacious assertion that "it has been proven that Spiritualism, in the United States,
has caused one-sixth of all the cases of suicide and insanity." He says
that it is not possible that the spirits "teach either an exact science,
because they are lying demons, or a useful science, because the character
of the word of Satan, like Satan himself, is sterile." He warns his dear

---

9. Don Pasquale di Franciscis: *Discorsi del Sommo Pontefice Pio IX*, I, p. 341.
10. W. E. Gladstone: *Rome and the Newest Fashions in Religion*,
p. 154 (Speeches of Pope Pius IX): London, 1875.

collaborateurs that "the writings in favor of Spiritualism are under the ban"; and he advises them to let it be known that "to frequent spiritual circles with the intention of accepting the doctrine, is to apostatize from the Holy Church, and assume the risk of excommunication"; finally, says he, "Publish the fact that the teaching of no spirit should prevail against that of the pulpit of Peter, which is the teaching of the Spirit of God Himself"!!

Aware of the many false teachings attributed by the Roman Church to the Creator, we prefer disbelieving the latter assertion. The famous Catholic theologian, Tillemont, assures us in his work that "all the illustrious Pagans are condemned to the eternal torments of hell, *because* they lived before the time of Jesus, and, therefore, could not be benefited by the redemption"!! He also assures us that the Virgin Mary personally testified to this truth over her own signature in a letter to a saint. Therefore this is also a revelation — "the Spirit of God Himself" teaching such charitable doctrines.

We have also read with great advantage the topographical descriptions of *Hell and Purgatory* in the celebrated treatise of that name by a Jesuit, the Cardinal Bellarmine. A critic found that the author, who gives the description from a *divine* vision with which he was favored, "appears to possess all the knowledge of a land-measurer about the secret tracts and formidable divisions of the bottomless pit." Justin Martyr having actually committed to paper the heretical thought that after all Socrates might not be altogether fixed in hell,[11] his Benedictine editor criticises this too-benevolent father very severely. Whoever doubts the Christian charity of the Church of Rome in this direction is invited to peruse the *Censure* of the Sorbonne on Marmontel's *Bélisaire*. The *odium theologicum* blazes in it on the dark sky of orthodox theology like an aurora borealis — the precursor of God's wrath according to the teaching of certain medieval divines.

We have attempted in the first part of this work to show by historical examples how completely men of science have deserved the stinging sarcasm of the late Professor De Morgan, who remarked of them that "they wear the priest's cast-off garb, dyed to escape detection." The Christian clergy are in like manner attired in the cast-off garb of the *heathen* priesthood; acting diametrically in opposition to their *God's* moral precepts, but nevertheless sitting in judgment over the whole world.

When dying on the cross, the martyred Man of Sorrows forgave his enemies. His last words were a prayer in their behalf. He taught his disciples to curse not, but to bless, even their foes. But the heirs of

---

11. Cf. *2 Apology*, §§ 7, 9.

St. Peter, the self-constituted representatives on earth of that same meek
Jesus, unhesitatingly curse whoever resists their despotic will. Besides,
was not the 'Son' long since crowded by them into the background?
They make their obeisance only to the Dowager Mother, for — according
to their teaching — again through 'the direct Spirit of God,' she alone
acts as a mediatrix. The Oecumenical Council of 1870 embodied the
teaching into a dogma, to disbelieve which is to be doomed forever to
the 'bottomless pit.' The work of Don Pasquale di Franciscis is positive
on that point; for he tells us that, as the Queen of Heaven owes to the
present Pope "the finest gem in her coronet," since he has conferred
on her the unexpected honor of becoming suddenly immaculate, there is
nothing she cannot obtain from her Son for "her Church." [12]

Some years ago certain travelers saw in Bari, Italy, a statue of the
Madonna, arrayed in a flounced pink skirt over a swelling *crinoline!*
Pious pilgrims who may be anxious to examine the regulation wardrobe
of their God's mother may do so by going to Southern Italy, Spain, and
Catholic North and South America. The Madonna of Bari must still
be there — between two vineyards and a *locanda* (gin-shop). When last
seen, a half-successful attempt had been made to clothe the infant Jesus;
they had covered his legs with a pair of dirty, scollop-edged pantaloons.
An English traveler having presented the 'Mediatrix' with a green
silk parasol, the grateful population of the *contadini*, accompanied by the
village-priest, went in procession to the spot. They managed to stick
the sunshade, opened, between the infant's back and the arm of the
Virgin which embraced him. The scene and ceremony were both solemn
and highly refreshing to our religious feelings. For there stood the
image of the goddess in its niche, surrounded with a row of ever-burning
lamps, the flames of which, flickering in the breeze, infect God's pure air
with an offensive smell of olive oil. The Mother and Son truly represent
the two most conspicuous idols of *Monotheistic* Christianity!

For a companion of the idol of the poor *contadini* of Bari, go to the
rich city of Rio de Janeiro. In the Church of the Domo da Candelaria,
in a long hall running along one side of the church, there might be seen
a few years ago another Madonna. Along the walls of the hall there is
a line of saints, each standing on a contribution-box, which thus forms a
fit pedestal. In the center of this line, under a gorgeously rich canopy
of blue silk, is exhibited the Virgin Mary leaning on the arm of Christ.
'Our Lady' is arrayed in a very *décolleté* blue satin dress with short

12. *Speeches of Pope Pius IX*, II, pp. 325, 394, by Don Pasquale di Franciscis; Gladstone's *Rome and the Newest, etc.;* Draper's *Conflict between Religion and Science,*
and other works.

sleeves, showing to great advantage the snow-white, exquisitely-molded neck, shoulders, and arms. The skirt, of blue satin with an over-skirt of rich lace and gauze puffs, is as short as that of a ballet-dancer; hardly reaching the knee, it exhibits a pair of finely-shaped legs covered with flesh-colored silk tights and blue satin French boots with very high red heels! The blonde hair of this 'Mother of God' is arranged in the latest fashion, with a voluminous *chignon* and curls. As she leans on her Son's arm, her face is lovingly turned toward her Only-Begotten, whose dress and attitude are equally worthy of admiration. Christ wears an evening dress-coat with swallow-tail, black trousers, and low-cut white vest; varnished boots, and white kid gloves, *over one of which* sparkles a rich diamond ring, worth many thousands we must suppose — a precious Brazilian jewel. Above this body of a modern Portuguese dandy is a head with the hair parted in the middle; a sad and solemn face, and eyes whose patient look seems to reflect all the bitterness of this last insult flung at the majesty of the Crucified.[13]

The Egyptian Isis was also represented as a Virgin-Mother by her devotees, and as holding her infant son, Horus, in her arms. In some statues and *basso-rilievos*, when she appears alone she is either completely nude or veiled from head to foot. But in the Mysteries, in common with nearly every other goddess, she is entirely veiled from head to foot, as a symbol of a mother's chastity. It would not do us any harm were we to borrow from the ancients some of the poetic sentiment in their religions, and the innate veneration they entertained for *their* symbols.

It is but fair to say at once that the last of the *true* Christians died with the last of the direct apostles. Max Müller forcibly asks: "How can a missionary in such circumstances meet the surprise and questions of his pupils, unless he may point to that seed,[14] and tell them what Christianity was meant to be; unless he may show that, like all other religions, Christianity, too, has had its history; that the Christianity of the nineteenth century is not the Christianity of the Middle Ages, and that the Christianity of the Middle Ages was not that of the early Councils; that the Christianity of the early Councils was not that of the Apostles, and that what has been said by Christ, that alone was well said?"[15]

Thus we may infer that the only characteristic difference between modern Christianity and the old heathen faiths is the belief of the former in a personal devil and in hell. "The Aryan nations had no Devil," says Max Müller. "Pluto, though of a somber character, was a very

---

13. The fact is given to us by an eye-witness who has visited the church several times, a Roman Catholic, who felt perfectly *horrified*, as he expressed it.
14. Referring to the seed planted by Jesus and his apostles.
15. *Chips from a German Workshop*, I, xxv-xxvi, preface.

respectable personage; and Loke [the Scandinavian], though a mischiev-
ous person, was not a fiend. The German goddess, Hell, too — like
Proserpina — had once seen better days. Thus, when the Germans were
indoctrinated with the idea of a real Devil, the Semitic Satan or Diabolus,
they treated him in the most good-humored manner." [16]

The same may be said of hell. Hades was quite a different place from
our region of 'eternal damnation,' and might be termed rather an intermediate state of purification. Neither does the Scandinavian *Hel* or
Hela imply either a state or a place of punishment; for when Frigga,
the grief-stricken mother of Balder, the white god, who died and found
himself in the dark abodes of the shadows (Hades), sent Hermod, a son
of Thor, in quest of her beloved child, the messenger found him in the
inexorable region — alas! but still comfortably seated on a rock, and
reading a book. [17] The Norse kingdom of the dead is moreover situated
in the higher latitudes of the Polar regions; it is a cold and cheerless
abode, and neither the gelid halls of Hela nor the occupation of Balder
present the least similitude to the blazing hell of eternal fire and the
miserable 'damned' sinners with which the Church so generously peoples
it. Neither is it the Egyptian *Amenti*, the region of judgment and
purification; nor the *Honderah* — the abyss of darkness of the Hindûs;
for even the fallen angels hurled into it by Śiva are allowed by Parabrahman to consider it as an intermediate state, in which an opportunity
is afforded them to prepare for higher degrees of purification and redemption from their wretched condition. The Gehenna of the *New Testament* was a locality outside the walls of Jerusalem; and in mentioning
it Jesus used but an ordinary metaphor. Whence then came the dreary
dogma of hell, that Archimedean lever of Christian theology, with which
they have succeeded in holding in subjection the numberless millions of
Christians for nineteen centuries? Assuredly not from the Jewish
Scriptures, and we appeal for corroboration to any well-informed Hebrew
scholar.

The only suggestion of something approaching hell in the *Bible* is
Gehenna or Hinnom, a valley near Jerusalem, where was situated Tophet,
a place where a fire was perpetually kept for sanitary purposes. The
prophet Jeremiah informs us that the Israelites used to sacrifice their
children to Moloch-Hercules on that spot; and later we find Christians
quietly replacing this divinity by their god of *mercy* whose wrath will
not be appeased, unless the Church sacrifices to him her unbaptized
children and sinning sons on the altar of 'eternal damnation'!

Whence then did the divines learn so well the conditions of hell, as

---

16. *Chips, etc.*, II, p. 233.   17. Mallet: *Northern Antiquities*, p. 448.

actually to divide its torments into two kinds, the *poena damni* and *poena sensus*, the former being the privation of the beatific vision; the latter the *eternal* pains *in a lake of fire and brimstone?* If they answer us that it is in the *Apocalypse* (xx, 10), we are prepared to demonstrate whence the theologist John himself derived the idea, "And *the devil* that deceived them was cast into the lake of fire and brimstone, where *the beast* and the false prophet are and shall be tormented day and night for ever and ever," he says. Laying aside the esoteric interpretation that the "devil" or tempting demon meant our own earthly body, which after death will surely dissolve in the *fiery* or ethereal elements,[18] the word 'eternal' by which our theologians interpret the words 'for ever and ever' does not exist in the Hebrew language, either as a word or meaning. There is no Hebrew word which properly expresses *eternity;* םלוע, *oulam,* according to Le Clerc, only imports a time whose beginning or end is not known.[19] While showing that this word does not mean *infinite* duration, and that in the *Old Testament* the word *forever* only signifies a long time, Archbishop Tillotson has completely perverted its sense with respect to the idea of hell-torments. According to his doctrine, when Sodom and Gomorrah are said to be suffering 'eternal fire,' we must understand it only in the sense of that fire "not being extinguished till both cities were entirely consumed." But, as to hell-fire the words must be understood in the strictest sense of infinite duration. Such is the decree of the learned divine. For the duration of the punishment of the wicked must be proportionate to the eternal happiness of the righteous. So he says, "These" (speaking of the wicked) "shall go away εἰς κόλασιν αἰώνιον into *eternal* punishment; but the righteous εἰς ζωὴν αἰώνιον into life eternal." [20]

The Reverend T. Swinden,[21] commenting on the speculations of his predecessors, fills a whole volume with unanswerable arguments, tending to show that the locality *of Hell is in the sun.* We suspect that the reverend speculator had read the *Apocalypse* in bed, and had the nightmare in consequence. There are two verses in the *Revelation of John* reading thus: "And the fourth angel poured out his vial upon the sun; and power was given unto him to scorch men with fire. And men were scorched with great heat, and blasphemed the name of God." [22] This is simply Pythagorean and Kabalistic allegory. The idea is new neither with the above-mentioned author nor with John. Pythagoras placed the "sphere of purification in the sun," which sun, with its sphere, he more-

---

18. Ether is both *pure* and *impure* fire. The composition of the latter comprises all its visible forms, such as the 'correlation of forces' — heat, flame, electricity, etc. The former is the *Spirit* of Fire. The difference is purely alchemical.

19. Cf. Gesenius: *A Hebrew and English Lexicon, s. v.* 'Oulam.'

20. John Tillotson: *Sermon* 35.   21. Cf. Tobias Swinden: *Inquiry into the Nature and Place of Hell:* London, 1727.   22. *Revelation,* xvi, 8-9.

over locates in the middle of the universe,[23] the allegory having a double meaning: 1. Symbolically, the central, spiritual sun, the Supreme Deity. Arrived at this region every soul becomes purified of its sins, and unites itself forever with its spirit, having previously suffered throughout all the lower spheres. 2. By placing the sphere of *visible* fire in the middle of the universe, he simply taught the heliocentric system which appertained to the Mysteries, and was imparted only in the higher degree of initiation. John gives to his Word a purely kabalistic significance, which no 'Fathers,' except those who had belonged to the Neo-Platonic school, were able to comprehend. Origen understood it well, having been a pupil of Ammonious Saccas; therefore we see him bravely denying the perpetuity of hell-torments. He maintains that not only men, but even devils (by which term he meant disembodied human sinners), after a certain duration of punishment shall be pardoned and finally restored to heaven.[24] In consequence of this and other such heresies Origen was, as a matter of course, exiled.

Many have been the learned and truly inspired speculations as to the locality of hell. The most popular were those which placed it in the center of the earth. At a certain time, however, skeptical doubts which disturbed the placidity of faith in this highly-refreshing doctrine arose in consequence of the meddling scientists of those days. As a Mr. Swinden in the last century observed, the theory was inadmissible because of two objections: 1st, that a fund of fuel or sulphur sufficient to maintain so furious and constant a fire could not be there supposed; and, 2nd, that it must want the nitrous particles in the air to sustain and keep it alive. "And how," says he, "can a fire be eternal, when, by degrees, the whole substance of the earth must be consumed thereby?"[25]

The skeptical gentleman had evidently forgotten that centuries ago St. Augustine solved the difficulty. Have we not the word of this learned divine that hell, nevertheless, *is* in the center of the earth, for "God supplies the central fire with air *by a miracle?*" The argument is unanswerable, and so we will not seek to upset it.[26]

The Christians were the first to make the existence of Satan a dogma of the Church. And once that she had established it, she had to struggle for over 1700 years for the repression of a mysterious force which it was her policy to make appear of diabolical origin. Unfortunately, in manifesting itself, this force invariably tends to upset such a belief by the ridiculous discrepancy it presents between the alleged cause

---

23. Aristotle mentions Pythagoreans who placed the sphere of fire in the sun, and named it *Jupiter's Prison*. See *De coelo*, lib. II.

24. August.: *The City of God*, xxi, xvii; Orig.: *De princ.*, I, vi.

25. *Demonologia*, p. 289: London, 1831.   26. Swinden: *Op cit.*, p. 75.

and the effects. If the clergy have not over-estimated the real power
of the 'Arch-Enemy of God,' it must be confessed that he takes mighty
precautions against being recognised as the 'Prince of Darkness' who
aims at our souls. If modern 'spirits' are devils at all, as preached
by the clergy, then they can only be those "poor" or "stupid devils"
whom Max Müller describes as appearing so often in the German and
Norwegian tales.

Notwithstanding this, the clergy fear above all to be forced to relinquish this hold on humanity. They are not willing to let us judge of the
tree by its fruits, for that might sometimes force them into dangerous di-
lemmas. They refuse likewise to admit, with unprejudiced people, that
the phenomena of Spiritualism have unquestionably spiritualized and re-
claimed from evil courses many an indomitable atheist and skeptic. But,
as they confess themselves, what is the use of a Pope, if there be no Devil?

And so Rome sends her ablest advocates and preachers to the rescue
of those perishing in 'the bottomless pit.' Rome employs her cleverest
writers for this purpose — albeit they all indignantly deny the accusation
— and in the preface to every book put forth by the prolific Des Mousseaux, the French Tertullian of our century, we find undeniable proofs of
the fact. Among other certificates of ecclesiastical approval, every
volume is ornamented with the text of a certain original letter addressed
to the very pious author by the world-known Father Ventura de Raulica,
of Rome. Few are those who have not heard this famous name. It is the
name of one of the chief pillars of the Latin Church, the ex-General of the
Order of the Theatins, Consultor of the Sacred Congregation of Rites,
Examiner of Bishops, and of the Roman Clergy, etc., etc., etc. This
strikingly characteristic document will remain to astonish future generations by its spirit of unsophisticated demonolatry and unblushing sincerity. We translate a fragment verbatim, and by thus helping its
circulation hope to merit the blessings of Mother Church:[27]

"MONSIEUR AND EXCELLENT FRIEND:

"The greatest victory of Satan was gained on that day when he succeeded in making himself denied.

"To demonstrate the existence of Satan, is to re-establish *one of the fundamental
dogmas of the Church*, which serve as a basis for Christianity, and without which it would
be but a name. . . .

"Magic, mesmerism, magnetism, somnambulism, spiritualism, spiritism, hypnotism
. . . are only other names for SATANISM.

"To bring out such a truth and show it in its proper light, is to unmask the enemy;
it is to unveil the immense danger of certain practices, *reputed innocent;* it is to deserve
well in the eyes of humanity and of religion.

"FATHER VENTURA DE RAULICA"

---

27. *Les hauts phénomènes de la magie*, p. iv.

A—men!

This is an unexpected honor indeed, for our American 'controls' in general, and the innocent 'Indian guides' in particular. To be thus introduced in Rome as princes of the Empire of Eblis, is more than they could ever hope for in other lands.

Without in the least suspecting that she was working for the future welfare of her enemies — the spiritualists and spiritists — the Church, some twenty years since, in tolerating Des Mousseaux and de Mirville as the biographers of the Devil, and giving her approbation thereto, tacitly confessed the literary copartnership.

M. the Chevalier Gougenot Des Mousseaux, and his friend and collaborateur, the Marquis Eudes de Mirville, to judge by their long titles, must be aristocrats *pur sang*, and they are, moreover, writers of no small erudition and talent. Were they to show themselves a little more parsimonious of double points of exclamation following every vituperation and invective against Satan and his worshipers, their style would be faultless. As it is, the crusade against the enemy of mankind was fierce, and lasted for over twenty years.

What with the Catholics piling up their psychological phenomena to prove the existence of a personal devil, and the Count de Gasparin, an ancient minister of Louis Philippe, collecting volumes of other facts to prove the contrary, the spiritists of France have contracted an everlasting debt of gratitude toward the disputants. The existence of an unseen spiritual universe peopled with invisible beings has now been demonstrated beyond question. Ransacking the oldest libraries, they have distilled from the historical records the quintessence of evidence. All epochs, from the Homeric ages down to the present day, have supplied their choicest materials to these indefatigable authors. In trying to prove the authenticity of the miracles wrought by Satan in the days preceding the Christian era, as well as throughout the Middle Ages, they have simply laid a firm foundation for a study of the phenomena in our modern times.

Though an ardent, uncompromising enthusiast, Des Mousseaux unwittingly transforms himself into the tempting demon, or — as he is fond of calling the Devil — the "serpent of *Genesis.*" In his desire to demonstrate in every manifestation the presence of the Evil One, he only succeeds in demonstrating that Spiritualism and magic are no new things in the world, but very ancient twin-brothers, whose origin must be sought for in the earliest infancy of ancient India, Chaldæa, Babylonia, Egypt, Persia, and Greece.

He proves the existence of 'spirits,' whether these be angels or devils, with such a clearness of argument and logic, and such an amount

of evidence, historical, irrefutable, and strictly authenticated, that little
is left for spiritualist authors who may come after him. How unfortunate
that the scientists, who believe neither in devil nor spirit, are more than
likely to ridicule M. Des Mousseaux's books without reading them, for
they really contain so many facts of profound scientific interest!

But what can we expect in our own age of unbelief when we find
Plato, over twenty-two centuries ago, complaining of the same? "Me,
too," says he, in his *Euthyphron*, "when I say anything in the public
assembly concerning divine things, *and predict to them* what is going to
happen, they ridicule as mad; and although *nothing that I have predicted
has proved untrue*, yet they envy all such men as we are. However, we
ought not to heed, but pursue our own way."

The literary resources of the Vatican and other Catholic repositories
of learning must have been freely placed at the disposal of these modern
authors. When one has such treasures at hand — original manuscripts,
papyri, and books pillaged from the richest heathen libraries; old treatises on magic and alchemy; and records of all the trials for witchcraft,
and sentences for the same to rack, stake, and torture — it is mighty easy
to write volumes of accusations against the Devil. We affirm on good
grounds that there are hundreds of the most valuable works on the
occult sciences, which are sentenced to eternal concealment from the
public, but are attentively read and studied by the privileged who
have access to the Vatican Library. The laws of nature are the same
for heathen sorcerer as for Catholic saint; and a 'miracle' may be
produced as well by one as by the other, without the slightest intervention of God or devil.

Hardly had the manifestations begun to attract attention in Europe,
than the clergy commenced their outcry that their traditional enemy had
reappeared under another name, and 'divine miracles' also began to
be heard of in isolated instances. First they were confined to humble
individuals, some of whom claimed to have them produced through the
intervention of the Virgin Mary, saints and angels; others — according
to the clergy — began to suffer from *obsession* and *possession;* for the
Devil must have his share of fame as well as the Deity. Finding that,
notwithstanding the warning, the *independent*, or so-called spiritual phenomena went on increasing and multiplying, and that these manifestations threatened to upset the carefully-constructed dogmas of
the Church, the world was suddenly startled by extraordinary intelligence. In 1864 a whole community became possessed of the Devil.
Morzine, and the awful stories of its demoniacs; Valleyres, and the
narratives of its well-authenticated exhibitions of sorcery; and those
of the Presbytère de Cideville, curdled the blood in Catholic veins.

Strange to say, the question has been asked over and over again, why the 'divine' miracles and most of the obsessions are so strictly confined to Roman Catholic dioceses and countries? Why is it that since the Reformation there has been scarcely one single divine 'miracle' in a Protestant land? Of course, the answer we must expect from Catholics is, that the latter are peopled by *heretics*, and abandoned by God. Then why are there no more Church-miracles in Russia, a country whose religion differs from the Roman Catholic faith but in external forms of rites, its fundamental dogmas being identically the same, except as to the emanation of the Holy Ghost? Russia has her accepted saints and thaumaturgical relics, and miracle-working images. The St. Mitrophaniy of Voroneg is an authenticated miracle-worker, but his miracles are limited to healing; and though hundreds upon hundreds have been healed *through faith*, and though the old cathedral is full of magnetic effluvia, and whole generations will go on *believing* in his power, and some persons will always be healed, still no such miracles are heard of in Russia as the Madonna-walking, and Madonna letter-writing, and statue-talking of Catholic countries. Why is this so? Simply because the emperors have strictly forbidden that sort of thing. The Czar, Peter the Great, stopped every spurious 'divine' miracle with one frown of his mighty brow. He declared he would have *no false* miracles played by the holy *icones* (images of saints), and they disappeared forever.[28]

There are cases on record of isolated and independent phenomena exhibited by certain images in the last century; the latest was the bleeding of the cheek of an image of the Virgin, when a soldier of Napoleon cut her face in two. This miracle, alleged to have happened in 1812, in the days of the invasion by the 'grand army,' was the final farewell.[29]

---

28. Dr. Stanley: *Lectures on the Hist. of the Eastern Church*, p. 407; lect. xiii.

29. In the government of Tambov, a gentleman, a rich landed proprietor, had a curious case happen in his family during the Hungarian campaign of 1848. His only and much-beloved nephew, whom, having no children, he had adopted as a son, was in the Russian army. The elderly couple had a portrait of his — a water-color painting — constantly, during the meals, placed on the table in front of the young man's usual seat. One evening as the family, with some friends, were at their early tea, the glass over the portrait, without any one touching it, was shattered to atoms with a loud explosion. As the aunt of the young soldier caught the picture in her hand she saw the forehead and head besmeared with blood. The guests, in order to quiet her, attributed the blood to her having cut her fingers with the broken glass. But, examine as they would, they could not find the vestige of a cut on her fingers, and no one had touched the picture but herself. Alarmed at her state of excitement the husband, pretending to examine the portrait more closely, cut his finger on purpose, and then tried to assure her that it was his blood and that, in the first excitement, he had touched the frame without any one remarking it. All was in vain, the old lady felt sure that Dimitry was killed. She began to have masses said for him daily at the village church, and arrayed the whole

But since then, although the three successive emperors have been pious
men, their will has been respected, and the images and saints have
remained quiet, and hardly been spoken of except as connected with
religious worship. In Poland, a land of furious ultramontanism, there
were, at different times, desperate attempts at miracle-doing. They
died at birth, however, for the argus-eyed police were there; a Catholic
miracle in Poland, made public by the priests, generally meaning political
revolution, bloodshed, and war.

Is it then not permissible at least to suspect that if in one country
divine miracles may be arrested by civil and military law, and in another
they *never occur*, we must search for the explanation of the two facts in
some natural cause, instead of attributing them to either god or devil?
In our opinion — if it is worth anything — the whole secret may be
accounted for as follows. In Russia the clergy know better than to
bewilder their parishes, whose piety is sincere and faith strong without
miracles; they know that nothing is better calculated than the latter to
sow seeds of distrust, doubt, and finally of skepticism which leads directly to atheism. Moreover the climate is less propitious, and the magnetism of the average population too positive, *too healthy*, to call forth
independent phenomena; and fraud would not answer. On the other
hand, neither in Protestant Germany, nor England, nor yet in America,
since the days of the Reformation, has the clergy had access to any of
the Vatican secret libraries. Hence they are all but poor hands at the
magic of Albertus Magnus.

As for America being overflowed with sensitives and mediums, the
reason for it is partially attributable to climatic influence and especially
to the physiological condition of the population. Since the days of the
Salem witchcraft, 200 years ago, when the comparatively few settlers had
pure and unadulterated blood in their veins, nothing much had been
heard of 'spirits' or 'mediums' until 1840.[30] The phenomena then
first appeared among the ascetic and exalted Shakers, whose religious
aspirations, peculiar mode of life, moral purity, and physical chastity,
all led to the production of independent phenomena of a psychological
as well as physical nature. Hundreds of thousands, and even millions

---

household in deep mourning. Several weeks later, an official communication was received
from the colonel of the regiment, stating that their nephew was killed by a fragment
of a shell which had carried off the upper part of his head.

30. Executions for witchcraft took place, not much later than a century ago, in other
of the American provinces. Notoriously there were negroes executed in New Jersey by
burning at the stake — the penalty denounced in several States. Even in South Caro-
lina, in 1865, when the State government was 'reconstructed' after the Civil War, the
statutes inflicting death for witchcraft were found to be still unrepealed. It is not a
hundred years since they have been enforced to the murderous letter of their text.

of men from various climates and of different constitutions and habits, have, since 1492, invaded North America, and by intermarrying have substantially changed the physical type of the inhabitants. In what country in the world do the women's constitutions bear comparison with the delicate, nervous, and sensitive constitutions of the female portion of the population of the United States? We were struck on our arrival in the country with the semi-transparent delicacy of skin of the natives of both sexes. Compare a hard-working Irish factory girl or boy with one from a genuine American family. Look at their hands. One works as hard as the other; they are of equal age, and both seemingly healthy; and yet, while the hands of the one, after an hour's soaping, will show a skin little softer than that of a young alligator, those of the other, notwithstanding constant use, will allow you to observe the circulation of the blood under the thin and delicate epidermis. No wonder, then, that while America is the conservatory of sensitives, the majority of its clergy, unable to produce divine or any other miracles, stoutly deny the possibility of any phenomena except those produced by tricks and juggling. And no wonder also that the Catholic priesthood, who are practically aware of the existence of magic and spiritual phenomena, and believe in them while dreading their consequences, try to attribute the whole to the agency of the Devil.

Let us adduce one more argument, if only for the sake of circumstantial evidence. In what countries have 'divine miracles' flourished most, been most frequent and most stupendous? Catholic Spain and Pontifical Italy, beyond question. And which, more than these two, has had access to ancient literature? Spain was famous for her libraries; the Moors were celebrated for their profound learning in alchemy and other sciences. The Vatican is the storehouse of an immense number of ancient manuscripts. During the long interval of nearly 1500 years they have been accumulating, from trial after trial, books and manuscripts confiscated from their sentenced victims, to their own profit. The Catholics may plead that the books were generally committed to the flames; that the treatises of famous sorcerers and enchanters perished with their accursed authors. But the Vatican, if it could speak, could tell a different story. It knows too well of the existence of certain closets and rooms, access to which is had but by the very few. It knows that the entrances to these secret hiding-places are so cleverly concealed from sight in the carved frame-work and under the profuse ornamentation of the library-walls, that there have even been Popes who lived and died within the precincts of the palace without ever suspecting their existence. But these Popes were neither Sylvester II, Benedict IX,

John XX, nor the VIth and VIIth Gregory; nor yet the famous Borgia of toxicological memory. Neither were those who remained ignorant of the hidden lore friends of the sons of Loyola.

Where, in the records of European Magic, can we find cleverer enchanters than in the mysterious solitudes of the cloister? Albertus Magnus, the famous Bishop and conjurer of Ratisbon, was never surpassed in his art. Roger Bacon was a monk, and Thomas Aquinas one of the most learned pupils of Albertus. Trithemius, Abbot of the Spanheim Benedictines, was the teacher, friend, and confidant of Cornelius Agrippa; and while the confederations of the Theosophists were scattered broadcast about Germany, where they first originated, assisting one another, and struggling for years for the acquirement of esoteric knowledge, any person who knew how to become the favored pupil of certain monks, might very soon be proficient in all the important branches of occult learning.

This is all in history and cannot be easily denied. Magic, in all its aspects, was widely and nearly openly practised by the clergy till the Reformation. And even he who was once called the 'Father of the Reformation' — the famous John Reuchlin,[31] author of the *Mirific Word* and friend of Pico di Mirandola, the teacher and instructor of Erasmus, Luther, and Melancthon — was a kabalist and occultist.

The ancient *sortilegium*, or divination by means of *sortes* or lots — an art and practice now decried by the clergy as an abomination, designated by *Stat. 10 Jac.* as felony, and by *Stat. 12 Caroli II* excepted out of the general pardons, on the ground of being *sorcery*[32] — was widely practised by the clergy and monks. Nay, it was sanctioned by St. Augustine himself, who does not "disapprove of this method of learning futurity, provided it be not used for worldly purposes." More than that, he confesses having practised it himself.[33]

Aye; but the clergy called it *sortes sanctorum*, when it was they who practised it; while the *sortes praenestinae*, succeeded by the *sortes Homericae* and *sortes Virgilianae*, were abominable *heathenism*, the worship of the Devil, when used by any one else.

Gregory de Tours informs us that when the clergy resorted to the *sortes* their custom was to lay the *Bible* on the altar, and to pray the Lord that He would discover His will, and disclose to them futurity in one of the verses of the book.[34] Gilbert de Nogent writes that in his days

---

31. *Vide* the title-page on the English translation of Mayerhoff's *Reuchlin und seine Zeit*, Berlin, 1830. *The Life and Times of John Reuchlin, or Capnion, the Father of the German Reformation*, by F. Barham, London, 1843.

32. Lord Coke: 3 *Institutes*, fol. 44.   33. *Epistle II to Januarius*, § 37.

34. *Histoire des François, de S. Grégoire, évêque de Tours*, II, 37; V, 14, etc.: Paris, 1668.

(about the twelfth century) the custom was, at the consecration of bishops, to consult the *sortes sanctorum*, thereby to learn the success and fate of the episcopate. On the other hand, we are told that the *sortes sanctorum* were condemned by the Council of Agde in 506. In this case again we are left to inquire in which instance the infallibility of the Church has failed. Was it when she prohibited that which was practised by her greatest saint and patron, Augustine, or in the twelfth century, when it was openly and with the sanction of the same Church practised by the clergy for the benefit of the bishop's elections? Or must we still believe that in both of these contradictory cases the Vatican was inspired by the direct 'spirit of God'?

If any doubt that Gregory of Tours approved of a practice that prevails to this day, more or less, even among strict Protestants, let them read this: "Leudastus, Earl of Tours, who was for ruining me with Queen Fredegonde, coming to Tours, big with evil designs against me, I withdrew to my oratory under a deep concern, where I took the *Psalms*. . . . My heart revived within me when I cast my eyes on this of the seventy-seventh *Psalm:* 'He caused them to go on with confidence, whilst the sea swallowed up their enemies.' Accordingly, the count spoke not a word to my prejudice; and leaving Tours that very day, the boat in which he was, sunk in a storm, but his skill in swimming saved him."

The sainted bishop simply confesses here to having practised a bit of sorcery. *Every mesmerizer knows the power of will during an intense desire bent on any particular subject.* Whether in consequence of 'coincidence' or otherwise, the opened verse suggested to his mind revenge by drowning. Passing the remainder of the day in "deep concern," and possessed by this all-absorbing thought, the saint — it may be unconsciously — exercises his will on the subject; and thus while imagining in the accident the hand of God, he simply becomes a sorcerer exercising his magnetic will which reacts on the person feared; and the count barely escapes with his life. Were the accident decreed by God the culprit would have been drowned; for a simple bath could not have altered his malevolent resolution against St. Gregory had he been very intent on it.

Furthermore we find anathemas fulminated against this lottery of fate, at the council of Vannes, which forbids "all ecclesiastics, under pain of excommunication, to perform that kind of divination, or to pry into futurity, by looking into any book, or writing, whatsoever." The same prohibition is pronounced at the councils of Agde in 506, of Orleans in 511, of Auxerre in 578, and finally at the council of Aenham in 1009; the last condemning "sorcerers, witches, diviners, such as occasioned death by magical operations, and who practised fortune-telling by the holy-book lots"; and the joint complaint of the clergy against de Garlande, their bishop at Orleans, and addressed to Pope Alexander III, concludes in this manner: "Let your apostolical hands put on strength to *strip naked* the iniquity of this man, that the curse prognosticated on the d₁v of his consecration may overtake him; for the gospels being opened on the altar *according to custom*, the first words were: *and the young man, leaving his linen cloth, fled from them naked*." [35]

Why then roast the lay magicians and consulters of books, and canonize the ecclesiastics? Simply because the medieval as well as the modern phenomena, manifested through laymen, whether produced through occult knowledge or happening independently, upset the claims of both the Catholic and Protestant Churches to divine miracles. In the face of reiterated and unimpeachable evidence it became impossible for the former to maintain successfully the assertion that seemingly miraculous manifestations by the 'good angels' and God's direct intervention could be produced exclusively by her chosen ministers and holy saints. Neither could the Protestant Church well maintain on the same ground that miracles had ended with the apostolic ages. For, whether of the same nature or not, the modern phenomena claimed close kinship with the biblical ones. The magnetists and healers of our century came into direct and open competition with the apostles. The Zouave Jacob, of France, had outrivaled the prophet Elijah in recalling to life persons who were seemingly dead; and Alexis the somnambulist, mentioned by Mr. Wallace in his work,[36] was, by his lucidity, putting to shame apostles, prophets, and the Sibyls of old. Since the burning of the last witch the great Revolution of France, so elaborately prepared by the league of the secret societies and their clever emissaries, had blown over Europe and awakened terror in the bosom of the clergy. Like a destroying hurricane, it had swept away in its course that best ally of the Church, the Roman Catholic aristocracy. A sure foundation was now laid for the right of individual opinion. The world was freed from ecclesiastical tyranny by opening an unobstructed path to Napoleon the Great, who had given the deathblow to the Inquisition. This great slaughter-house of the Christian Church — wherein she butchered in the name of the Lamb all the sheep arbitrarily declared scrofulous — was in ruins, and she found herself left to her own responsibility and resources.

---

35. Translated from the original document in the Archives of Orleans, France; also see 'Sortes and Sortilegium,' in *Demonologia;* and *Lettres de Peter de Blois*, Paris, 1667.
36. *Miracles and Modern Spiritualism*, p. 65; De Mirville: *Des esprits*, tome I, p. 7, sq.: Paris, 1853.

So long as the phenomena had appeared only sporadically, she had always felt herself powerful enough to repress the consequences. Superstition and belief in the Devil were as strong as ever, and Science had not yet dared publicly to measure her forces with those supernatural Religion. Meanwhile the enemy had slowly but surely gained ground. All at once it broke out with an unexpected violence. 'Miracles' began to appear in full daylight, and passed from their mystic seclusion into the domain of natural law, where the profane hand of Science was ready to strip off their sacerdotal mask. Still for a time the Church held her position, and with the powerful help of superstitious fear checked the progress of the intruding force. But, when in succession appeared mesmerists and somnambulists, reproducing the physical and mental phenomenon of ecstasy, hitherto believed to be the special gift of saints; when the passion for the turning tables had reached in France and elsewhere its climax of fury; when the leaning toward psychography — alleged spiritual — from a simple curiosity had developed itself and settled into an unabated interest, and finally ebbed into religious mysticism; when the echoes aroused by the first raps of Rochester, crossing the oceans, spread until they were re-percussed from nearly every corner of the world — then, and only then, the Latin Church was fully awakened to a sense of danger. Wonder after wonder was reported to have occurred in the spiritualist-circles and the lecture-rooms of the mesmerists; the sick were healed, the blind made to see, the lame to walk, the deaf to hear. J. R. Newton in America, and Du Potet in France, were healing the multitude without the slightest claim to divine intervention. The great discovery of Mesmer, which reveals to the earnest inquirer the mechanism of nature, mastered as if by magical power organic and inorganic bodies.

But this was not the worst. A more direful calamity for the Church occurred in the evocation from the upper and nether worlds of a multitude of 'spirits,' whose private bearing and conversation gave the direct lie to the most cherished and profitable dogmas of the Church. These 'spirits' claimed to be the actual entities in a disembodied state of fathers, mothers, sons, and daughters, friends and acquaintances, of the persons viewing the weird phenomena. The Devil seemed to have no objective existence, and this struck at the very foundation upon which the chair of St. Peter rested.[37] Not a 'spirit' except the

37. There were two chairs of the titular apostle at Rome. The clergy, frightened at the uninterrupted evidence furnished by scientific research, at last decided to confront the enemy, and we find the *Chronique des Arts* giving the cleverest, and at the same time most *Jesuitical*, explanation of the fact. According to their story, "The *increase* in the number of the faithful decided Peter upon making Rome henceforth the center of his action. The cemetery of Ostrianum was too distant and would *not suffice for*

mocking mannikins of Planchette would confess to the most distant
relationship with the Satanic majesty, or accredit him with the gover-
norship of a single inch of territory. The clergy felt their prestige
growing weaker every day, as they saw the people impatiently shaking
off, in the broad daylight of truth, the dark veils with which they
had been blindfolded for so many centuries. Then finally fortune.
which previously had been on their side in the long-waged conflict
between theology and science, deserted to their adversary. The help
of the latter to the study of the occult side of nature was truly precious
and timely, and science has unwittingly widened the once narrow
path of the phenomena into a broad highway. Had not this conflict

---

the reunions of the Christians. The motive which had induced the apostle to confer
on *Linus and Cletus* successively the episcopal character, in order to render them capable of sharing the solicitudes of a church whose extent was to be without limits, led
naturally to a multiplication of the places of meeting. The particular residence of Peter
was therefore fixed at Viminal; and there was established that mysterious Chair, the
symbol of power and truth. The august seat which was venerated at the Ostrian Catacombs was not, however, removed. Peter still visited this cradle of the Roman Church
and often, without doubt, exercised his holy functions there. A *second* Chair, expressing
the same mystery as the first, was set up at Cornelia, and it is this which has come down
to us through the ages."

Now so far from it being possible that there ever were two genuine chairs of this
kind, the majority of critics show that Peter never was at Rome at all; the reasons
are many and unanswerable. Perhaps we had better begin by pointing to the works
of Justin Martyr. This great champion of Christianity writing in the early part
of the second century *in Rome,* where he fixed his abode, eager to get hold of the
least proof in favor of the truth for which he suffered, seems *perfectly unconscious of
St. Peter's existence!!*

Neither does any other writer of any consequence mention him in connexion with
the Church of Rome, earlier than the days of Irenaeus, who set himself to invent
a new religion drawn from the depths of his imagination. We refer the reader anxious
to learn more to the able work of Mr. George Reber, entitled *The Christ of Paul.*
The arguments of this author are conclusive. The above article in the *Chronique des
Arts* speaks of the *increase* of the faithful to such an extent that Ostrianum could not
contain the number of Christians. Now if Peter was at Rome at all — runs Mr. Reber's
argument — it must have been between the years A. D. 64 and 69; for at 64 he
was at Babylon, from whence he wrote epistles and letters to Rome, and at some
time between 64 and 68 (the reign of Nero) he either died a martyr or in his bed, for
Irenaeus makes him deliver the Church of Rome, together with Paul (!?) (whom he
persecuted and quarreled with all his life), into the hands of *Linus,* who became bishop
in 69 (see Reber's *Christ of Paul,* p. 122). We will treat of the subject more fully in
chapter iii.

Now we ask in the name of common sense, how could the *faithful* of Peter's Church
increase at such a rate, when Nero trapped and killed them like so many mice during
his reign? History shows the few Christians fleeing from Rome, wherever they could,
to avoid the persecution of the emperor, and the *Chronique des Arts* makes them increase and multiply! "Christ," the article goes on to say, "willed that this visible
sign of the doctrinal authority of his vicar should also have its portion of immortality;
one can follow it from age to age in the documents of the Roman Church." Tertullian
formally attests its existence in his book *De praescr. haeret.,* xxxvi. Eager to learn
everything concerning so interesting a subject, we should like to be shown when did
Christ WILL anything of the kind? However: "Ornaments of ivory have been fitted

culminated in the nick of time, we might have seen reproduced ●n a miniature scale the disgraceful scenes of the episodes of Salem witchcraft and of the nuns of Loudun. As it was the clergy were muzzled.

But if science has unintentionally helped the progress of the occult phenomena, the latter have reciprocally aided science herself. Until the days when newly-reincarnated philosophy boldly claimed its place in the world, there had been but few scholars who had undertaken the difficult task of studying comparative theology. This science occupies a domain heretofore penetrated by few explorers. The necessity which it involved of being well acquainted with the dead languages naturally limited the number of students. Besides there was less popular need for it so long as people could not replace the Christian orthodoxy by something more tangible. It is one of the most undeniable facts of psychology, that the average man can as little exist out of a religious element of some kind, as a fish out of the water. The voice of truth, "a voice stronger than the voice of mighty thunderings," speaks to the inner man in the nineteenth century of the Christian era, as it spoke in the corresponding century B. C. It is a useless and unprofitable task to offer to humanity the choice between a future life and annihilation. The only chance that remains for those friends of human progress who seek to establish for the good of mankind a faith, henceforth stripped entirely of superstition and dogmatic fetters, is to address them in the words of Joshua: "Choose you this day whom ye will serve; whether the gods which your fathers served

---

to the front and back of the chair, but only on those parts repaired with acacia-wood. Those which cover the panel in front are divided into three superimposed rows, each containing six plaques of ivory, on which are engraved various subjects, among others the 'Labors of Hercules.' Several of the plaques were wrongly placed, and seemed to have been affixed to the chair at a time when the remains of antiquity were employed as ornaments, without much regard to fitness." This is the point. The article was written simply as a clever answer to several facts published during the present century. Bower, in his *History of the Popes* (II, p. 7), narrates that in the year 1662, while cleaning one of the chairs, "the 'Twelve Labors of Hercules' unluckily appeared engraved upon it," after which the chair was removed and another substituted. But in 1795 when Bonaparte's troops occupied Rome, the chair was again examined. This time there was found the Mohammedan confession of faith, in Arabic letters: "There is no Deity but Allah, and Mohammed is his apostle." (See appendix to *Ancient Symbolic Worship*, by H. M. Westropp and C. Staniland Wake.) In this appendix Prof. Alexander Wilder very justly remarks as follows: "We presume that the Apostle of the Circumcision, as Paul, his great rival, styles him, was never at the Imperial City, nor had a successor there, not even in the ghetto. The 'Chair of Peter,' therefore, is *sacred* rather than apostolical. Its sanctity proceeded, however, from the esoteric religion of the former times of Rome. The hierophant of the Mysteries probably occupied it on the day of initiations, when exhibiting to the candidates the *Petroma* (stone tablet containing the last revelation made by the hierophant to the neophyte for initiation)."

that were on the other side of the flood, or the gods of the Amorites, in whose land ye dwell." [38]

"The science of religion," wrote Max Müller in 1860, "is only just beginning. . . . During the last fifty years the authentic documents of the most important religions in the world *have been recovered in a most unexpected and almost miraculous manner.* We have now before us the canonical books of Buddhism; the Zend *Avesta* of Zoroaster is no longer a sealed book; and the hymns of the *Rig-Veda* have revealed a state of religions anterior to the first beginnings of that mythology which in Homer and Hesiod stands before us as a mouldering ruin." [40]

In their insatiable desire to extend the dominion of blind faith, the early architects of Christian theology had been forced to conceal, as much as it was possible, the true sources of the same. To this end they are said to have burned or otherwise destroyed all the original manuscripts on the Kabala, magic, and occult sciences upon which they could lay their hands. They ignorantly supposed that the most dangerous writings of this class had perished with the last Gnostic; but some day they may discover their mistake. Other authentic and as important documents will perhaps reappear in a "most unexpected and almost miraculous manner."

There are strange traditions current in various parts of the East — on Mount Athos and in the Desert of Nitria, for instance — among

---

38. Joshua, xxiv, 15.

39. One of the most surprising facts that have come under our observation, is that students of profound research should not couple the frequent recurrence of these "unexpected and almost miraculous" discoveries of important documents, at the most opportune moments, with a premeditated design. Is it so strange that the custodians of 'Pagan' lore, seeing that the proper moment had arrived, should cause the needed document, book, or relic to fall as if by accident in the right man's way? Geological surveyors and explorers even as competent as Humboldt and Tschudi, have not discovered the hidden mines from which the Peruvian Incas dug their treasure, although the latter confesses that the present degenerate Indians have the secret. In 1839 Perring, the archaeologist, offered the sheik of an Arab village two purses of gold, if he would help him to discover the entrance to the hidden passage leading to the sepulchral chambers in the North Pyramid of Dahshûr. But though his men were out of employment and half-starved, the sheik proudly refused to "sell the secret of the dead," promising to show it *gratis*, when *the time would come for it*. Is it then impossible that in some other regions of the earth are guarded the remains of that glorious literature of the past, which was the fruit of its majestic civilization? What is there so surprising in the idea? Who knows but that as the Christian Church has unconsciously begotten free thought by reaction against her own cruelty, rapacity, and dogmatism, the public mind may be glad to follow the lead of the Orientalists, away from Jerusalem and towards Ellora; and that then much more will be discovered that is now hidden?

40. *Chips from a German Workshop,*
I, p. 373; 'Semitic Monotheism.'

certain monks, and with learned Rabbis in Palestine, who pass their lives in commenting upon the *Talmud*. They say that not all the rolls and manuscripts, reported in history to have been burned by Caesar, by the Christian mob, in 389, and by the Arab General Amru, perished as it is commonly believed; and the story they tell is the following: At the time of the contest for the throne, in 51 B. C., between Cleopatra and her brother Dionysius Ptolemy, the Bruchion, which contained over seven hundred thousand rolls, all bound in wood and *fire-proof* parchment, was undergoing repairs, and a great number of the original manuscripts, considered among the most precious, and which were not duplicated, were stored away in the house of one of the librarians. As the fire which consumed the rest was but the result of accident, no precautions had been taken at the time. But they add that several hours passed between the burning of the fleet, set on fire by Caesar's order, and the moment when the first buildings situated near the harbor caught fire in their turn; and that all the librarians, aided by several hundred slaves attached to the museum, succeeded in saving the most precious of the rolls. So perfect and solid was the fabric of the parchment, that while in some rolls the inner pages and the wood-binding were reduced to ashes, of others the parchment binding remained unscorched. These particulars were all written out in Greek, Latin, and the Chaldaeo-Syriac dialect, by a learned youth named Theodas, one of the scribes employed in the museum. One of these manuscripts is alleged to be preserved till now in a Greek convent; and the person who narrated the tradition to us had seen it himself. He said that many more will see it and learn where to look for important documents when a certain prophecy will be fulfilled; adding, that most of these works could be found in Tatary and India.[41] The monk showed us a copy of the original, which, of course, we could read but poorly, as we claim but little erudition in the matter of dead languages. But we were so particularly struck by the vivid and picturesque translation of the holy father, that we perfectly remember some curious paragraphs, which run, as far as we can recall them, as follows: — "When the Queen of the Sun (Cleo-

41. An after-thought has made us fancy that we can understand what is meant by the following sentences of *Moses of Chorene:* "The ancient Asiatics," says he, "five centuries before our era — and especially the Hindûs, the Persians, and the Chaldaeans, had in their possession a quantity of historical and scientific books. These works were partially borrowed, partially translated in the Greek language, mostly since the Ptolemies had established the Alexandrian library and encouraged the writers by their liberalities, so that the Greek language became the deposit of all the sciences" (*History of Armenia*). Therefore the greater part of the literature included in the 700,000 volumes of the Alexandrian Library was due to India and her next neighbors.

patra) was brought back to the half-ruined city, after the fire had
devoured the *Glory of the World;* and when she saw the mountains
of books — or rolls — covering the half-consumed steps of the *estrada;*
and when she perceived that the inside was gone and the indestructible
covers alone remained, she wept in rage and fury, and cursed the
meanness of her fathers who had grudged the cost of the real Pergamos
for the inside as well as the outside of the precious rolls." Further,
our author, Theodas, indulges in a joke at the expense of the queen
for believing that nearly all the library was burned; when, in fact,
hundreds and thousands of the choicest books were safely stored in
his own house and those of other scribes, librarians, students, and
philosophers.

No more do sundry very learned Copts scattered all over the East
in Asia Minor, Egypt, and Palestine believe in the total destruction
of the subsequent libraries. For instance they say that out of the
library of Attalus III of Pergamus, presented by Antony to Cleopatra,
not a volume was destroyed. At that time, according to their assertions, from the moment that the Christians began to gain power
in Alexandria — about the end of the fourth century — and Anatolius,
Bishop of Laodicea, began to insult the national gods, the Pagan
philosophers and learned theurgists adopted effective measures to preserve the repositories of their sacred learning. Theophilus, a bishop,
who left behind him the reputation of a most rascally and mercenary
villain, was accused by one named Antoninus, a famous theurgist
and eminent scholar of occult science of Alexandria, with bribing the
slaves of the Serapion to steal books which he sold to foreigners at
great prices. History tells us how Theophilus had the best of the
philosophers, in A. D. 389; and how his successor and nephew, the
no less infamous Cyril, butchered Hypatia. Suidas gives us some
details about Antoninus, whom he calls Antonius, and his eloquent
friend Olympus, the defender of the Serapion. But history is far
from being complete in the miserable remnants of books, which, crossing
so many ages, have reached our own learned century; it fails to give
the facts relating to the first five centuries of Christianity which are
preserved in the numerous traditions current in the East. Unauthenti-
cated as these may appear, there is unquestionably in the heap of
chaff much good grain. That these traditions are not oftener communicated to Europeans is not strange, when we consider how apt
our travelers are to render themselves antagonistic to the natives
by their skeptical bearing and, occasionally, dogmatic intolerance.
When exceptional men like some archaeologists, who knew how to
win the confidence and even friendship of certain Arabs, are favored

with precious documents, it is declared simply a 'coincidence.' And yet there are widespread traditions of the existence of certain subterranean and immense galleries, in the neighborhood of Ishmonia — the 'petrified City,' in which are stored numberless manuscripts and rolls. For no amount of money would the Arabs go near it. At night, they say, from the crevices of the desolate ruins, sunk deep in the unwatered sands of the desert, stream the rays from lights carried to and fro in the galleries by no human hands. The Afrits study the literature of the antediluvian ages, according to their belief, and the Jinn learn from the magic rolls the lesson of the following day.

The *Encyclopaedia Britannica* [earlier editions], in its article on Alexandria, says: "When the temple of Serapis was demolished . . . the valuable library was *pillaged* or destroyed; and *twenty* years afterwards [42] the *empty shelves* excited the regret . . . etc." But it does not state the subsequent fate of the *pillaged* books.

In rivalry of the fierce Mary-worshipers of the fourth century, the modern clerical persecutors of liberalism and 'heresy' would willingly shut up all the heretics and their books in some modern Serapion and burn them alive.[43] The cause of this hatred is natural. Modern research has more than ever unveiled the secret. "Is not the worship of saints and angels now," said Bishop Newton, years ago, "in all respects the same that the worship of demons was in former times? The name only is different, the thing is identically the same . . . the very same temples, the very same images, which were once consecrated to Jupiter and the other demons, are now consecrated to the Virgin Mary and the other saints . . . almost the whole of Paganism is converted and applied *to Popery*."

Why not be impartial and add that a good portion of it was adopted by Protestant religions also?

Even the apostolic designation *Peter* is from the Mysteries. The hierophant or supreme pontiff bore the Chaldaean title פתר, *peter*, or interpreter. The names *Ptah*, Peth'r, the residence of Balaam, Patara, and Patras, the names of oracle-cities, *pateres* or *pateras* and, perhaps,

---

42. Bonamy, in *La bibliothèque d'Alexandrie*, says "*thirty* years later." But the Presbyter P. Orosius, who was an eye-witness, says "twenty years" (*Hist. adv. paganos*, vi, 15, p. 421).

43. Since the above was written, the spirit here described has been beautifully exemplified at Barcelona, Spain, where the Bishop Fray Joachim invited the local spiritualists to witness a formal burning of spiritualistic books. We find the account in a paper called *The Revelation*, published at Alicante, which sensibly adds that the performance was "a caricature of the memorable epoch of the Inquisition."

Buddha,[44] all come from the same root. Jesus says: "Upon this *petra* I will build my Church, and the gates [or rulers] of Hades shall not prevail against it"; meaning by *petra* the rock-temple, and metaphorically, the Christian Mysteries; the adversaries to which were the old mystery-gods of the underworld, who were worshiped in the rites of Isis, Adonis, Atys, Sabazius, Dionysus, and the Eleusinia. No *apostle* Peter was ever at Rome; but the Pope, seizing the scepter of the *Pontifex Maximus*, the keys of Janus and Cybele, and adorning his Christian head with the cap of the *Magna Mater*, copied from that of the tiara of *Brahmâtma*, the Supreme Pontiff of the Initiates of old India, became the successor of the Pagan high priest, the real Peter-Roma, or *Petroma*.[45]

The Roman Catholic Church has two far mightier enemies than the 'heretics' and the 'infidels'; and these are — Comparative Mythology and Philology. When such eminent divines as the Rev. James Freeman Clarke go so much out of their way to prove to their readers that "Critical Theology from the time of Origen and Jerome . . . and the Controversial Theology during fifteen centuries, has not consisted in accepting on authority the opinions of other people," but has shown, on the contrary, much "acute and comprehensive reasoning," we can but regret that so much scholarship should have been wasted in attempting to prove that which a fair survey of the history of theology upsets at every step. In these 'controversies' and critical treatment of the doctrines of the Church one can certainly find any amount of "acute reasoning," but far more of a still acuter sophistry.

Recently the mass of cumulative evidence has been re-enforced to an extent which leaves little, if any, room for further controversy. A conclusive opinion is furnished by too many scholars to doubt the fact that India was the *alma mater*, not only of the civilization, arts, and sciences, but also of all the great religions of antiquity — Judaism, and hence Christianity, included. Herder places the cradle of humanity in India, and shows Moses as a clever and relatively *modern* compiler of the ancient Brâhmanical traditions: "The river which encircles the country (India) is the sacred Ganges, which all Asia considers as the paradisaical river. There, also, is the biblical Gihon, which is none else but the Indus. The Arabs call it so unto this day, and the names of the countries watered by it are yet existing among the Hindûs."[46] Jacolliot claims to have translated every ancient palm-leaf manuscript which he had the fortune

---

44. E. Pococke gives the variations of the name Buddha as: Bud'ha, Buddha, Booddha, Boutta, Pout, Pote, Pto, Pte, Phthe, Phtha, Phut. etc., etc. See *India in Greece*, appendix, p. 397.
45. The tiara of the Pope is also a perfect copy of that of the Dalai-Lama of Tibet.
●   46. See his *Ideen zur Geschichte der Menschheit*, bk. X, ch. 6, in *Ausgewählte Werke*, p. 828: 1844.

of being allowed by the Bráhmanas of the pagodas to see. In one of his translations we found passages which reveal to us the *undoubted origin of the keys* of St. Peter, and account for the subsequent adoption of the symbol by their Holinesses, the Popes of Rome.

He shows us on the testimony of the *Agrushada Parikshai,* which he freely translates as "the *Book of Spirits*" (Pitris), that centuries before our era the *initiates* of the temple chose a Superior Council, presided over by the *Brahmátma* or supreme chief of all these *Initiates;* that this pontificate could be exercised only by a Bráhmana who had reached the age of eighty years; [47] and that the *Brahmátma* was sole guardian of the mystic formula, *résumé* of every science, contained in the three mysterious letters,

A
U M

which signify *creation, conservation,* and *transformation.* He alone could expound its meaning in the presence of initiates of the third and supreme degree. Whosoever among these initiates revealed to a profane a single one of the truths, even the smallest of the secrets entrusted to his care, was put to death. He who received the confidence had to share his fate.

"Finally, to crown this able system," says Jacolliot, "there existed a word even superior to the mysterious monosyllable — A U M, and which rendered him who came into the possession of its key nearly the equal of Brahmâ himself. The *Brahmátma* alone possessed this key, and transmitted it in a sealed casket to his successor.

"This unknown word, of which no human power could, even today, when the Bráhmanical authority has been crushed under the Mongolian and European invasions, today, when each pagoda has its *Brahmátma,*[48] *force the disclosure,* was engraved in a golden triangle and preserved in a sanctuary of the temple of Asgartha, whose *Brahmátma* alone held the keys. He also bore upon his tiara *two crossed keys* supported by two kneeling Bráhmanas, symbol of the precious deposit of which he had the keeping. This word and this triangle were engraved upon the tablet of the ring that this religious chief wore as one of the signs of his dignity; it was also framed in a golden sun on the altar, where every morning the Supreme Pontiff offered the sacrifice of the *sarvamedha,* or sacrifice to all the forces of nature." [49]

---

47. It is the traditional policy of the College of Cardinals to elect, whenever practicable, the new Pope from among the oldest. The hierophant of the Eleusinia was likewise always an old man, and unmarried.

48. This is not correct.   49. *Le spiritisme dans le monde,* pp. 27-28.

Is this clear enough? And will the Catholics still maintain that it was the Bráhmanas of 4000 years ago who copied the ritual, symbols and dress of the Roman Pontiffs? We should not feel in the least surprised.

Without going very far back into antiquity for comparisons, if we only stop at the fourth and fifth centuries of our era, and contrast the so-called 'heathenism' of the third Neo-Platonic Eclectic School with the growing Christianity, the result may not be favorable to the latter. Even at that early period, when the new religion had hardly outlined its contradictory dogmas; when the champions of the bloodthirsty Cyril knew not themselves whether Mary was to become 'the Mother of God,' or rank as a 'demon' in company with Isis; when the memory of the meek and lowly Jesus still lingered lovingly in every Christian heart, and his words of mercy and charity still vibrated in the air, even then the Christians were outdoing the Pagans in every kind of ferocity and religious intolerance.

And if we look still farther back, and seek for examples of true *Christism*, in ages when Buddhism had hardly superseded Bráhmanism in India, and the name of Jesus was only to be pronounced three centuries later, what do we find? Which of the holy pillars of the Church has ever elevated himself to the level of religious tolerance and noble simplicity of character of some of the heathen? Compare for instance the Hindû Aśoka, who lived 300 B. C., and the Carthaginian St. Augustine, who flourished three centuries after Christ. According to Max Müller, this is what is found engraved on the rocks of Girnar, Dhauli, and Kapurdigiri:

"Piyadasi, the king beloved of the gods, desires that the ascetics *of all creeds* might reside in all places. All these ascetics profess alike the command which people should exercise over themselves, and the purity of the soul. *But people have different opinions and different inclinations.*" [49a]

And here is what Augustine wrote after his baptism: "Wondrous depth of thy words! whose surface, behold! is before us, inviting to little ones; yet are they a wondrous depth, O my God, a wondrous depth! It is awful to look therein; an awfulness of honor, and a trembling of love. The enemies [read Pagans] thereof I *hate* vehemently; Oh *that thou wouldst slay them* with thy two-edged sword, that they might no longer be enemies to it; for *so do I love to have them slain.* . . ." [50]

Wonderful spirit of Christianity; and that from a Manichaean converted to the religion of one who even on his cross prayed for his enemies!

49a. *Chips, etc.*, I, p. 253.   50. Augustine: *Confessions*, bk. XII; quoted by Prof. Draper in *Conflict between Religion and Science*, ch. ii, pp. 60-61.

Who the enemies of the 'Lord' were, according to the Christians, is not difficult to surmise; the few inside the Augustinian fold were His new children and favorites, who had supplanted in His affections the sons of Israel, His 'chosen people.' The rest of mankind were His natural foes. The teeming multitudes of heathendom were proper food for the flames of hell; the handful within the Church communion, 'heirs of salvation.'

But if such a proscriptive policy was just, and its enforcement was 'sweet savor' in the nostrils of the 'Lord,' why not scorn also the Pagan rites and philosophy? Why draw so deeply from the wells of wisdom, dug and filled up to brim by the same heathen? Or did the fathers, in their desire to imitate the chosen people whose time-worn shoes they were trying to fit upon their feet, contemplate the re-enaction of the spoliation-scene of the *Exodus?* Did they propose, in fleeing from heathendom as the Jews did from Egypt, to carry off the valuables of its religious allegories, as the 'chosen ones' did the gold and silver ornaments?

It certainly does seem as if the events of the first centuries of Christianity were but the reflexion of the images thrown upon the mirror of the future at the time of the Exodus. During the stormy days of Irenaeus, the Platonic philosophy, with its mystical submersion into Deity, was not so obnoxious after all to the new doctrine as to prevent the Christians from helping themselves to its abstruse metaphysics in every way and manner. Allying themselves with the ascetical *therapeutae* — forefathers and models of the Christian monks and hermits — it was in Alexandria, let it be remembered, that they laid the first foundations of the purely Platonic trinitarian doctrine. It became the Plato-Philonean doctrine later, and such as we find it now. "Plato considered the divine nature under the three-fold modification of the *First Cause*, the reason or *Logos*, and the soul or spirit of the universe. The three archical or original principles," says Gibbon,[51] "were represented in the Platonic system as three gods, united with each other by a mysterious and ineffable generation." Blending this transcendental idea with the more hypostatic figure of the *Logos* of Philo — whose doctrine was that of the oldest Kabala, and who viewed the King Messiah, as the metatron, or 'the angel of the Lord,' the *Legatus* descended in flesh, but not the *Ancient of Days* Himself [52]— the Christians clothed Jesus, the son of Mary, with this mythical representation of the Mediator for the fallen race of Adam. Under this unexpected garb his personality was all but lost. In the modern Jesus of the Christian Church we find the ideal of the imaginative

---

51. *Decline and Fall of the Roman Empire*, ch. xxi.
- 52. *Zohar*, Comment. on *Gen.*, xl, 10; *Kabbala denud.*, I, p. 528.

Irenaeus, not the adept of the Essenes, the obscure reformer from Galilee. We see him under the disfigured Plato-Philonean mask, not as when the disciples heard him on the mount.

So far then the heathen philosophy had helped them in the building of the principal dogma. But when the theurgists of the third Neo-Platonic school, deprived of their ancient Mysteries, strove to blend the doctrines of Plato with those of Aristotle, and by combining the two philosophies added to their theosophy the primeval doctrines of the Oriental Kabala, then the Christians from rivals became persecutors. Once that the metaphysical allegories of Plato were being prepared to be discussed in public in the form of Grecian dialectics, all the elaborate system of the Christian trinity would be unraveled and the divine prestige completely upset. The eclectic school, reversing the order, had adopted the inductive method; and this method became its death-knell. Of all things on earth, logic and reasonable explanations were the most hateful to the new religion of mystery; for they threatened to unveil the whole groundwork of the trinitarian conception; to apprise the multitude of the doctrine of emanations, and thus destroy the unity of the whole. It could not be permitted, and it was not. History records the *Christ*-like means that were resorted to.

The universal doctrine of emanations, adopted from time immemorial by the greatest schools which taught the kabalistic, Alexandrian, and Oriental philosophers, gives the key to that panic among the Christian fathers. That spirit of Jesuitism and clerical craft, which prompted Parkhurst, many centuries later, to suppress in his *Hebrew Lexicon* the true meaning of the first word of *Genesis*, originated in those days of war against the expiring Neo-Platonic and eclectic school. The fathers had decided to pervert the meaning of the word *daimon*,[53] and they dreaded above all to have the esoteric and true meaning of the word *Rasit* unveiled to the multitudes; for if once the true sense of this sentence, as well as that of the Hebrew word *asdt* (translated in the Septuagint 'angels,' while it means emanations),[54] were understood rightly, the mystery of the Christian trinity would have crumbled, carrying in its downfall the new religion into the same heap of ruins with the ancient Mysteries. This is the true reason why dialecticians, as well as Aristotle himself, the 'prying philosopher,' were ever obnoxious to Christian theology. Even Luther, while on his work of reform, feeling the ground insecure under his feet, notwithstanding that the dogmas had been reduced by him to their simplest expression, gave full vent to his

53. "The beings which the philosophers of other peoples distinguish by the name 'daemons,' Moses names 'angels,' " says Philo Judaeus.—*De gigant.*, § 2; *De mundo*, § 3.

54. *Deuteronomy*, xxxiii, 2, אשדת is translated 'fiery law' in the English Bible.

fear and hatred of Aristotle. The amount of abuse he heaped upon the memory of the great logician can only be equaled — never surpassed — by the Pope's anathemas and invectives against the liberals of the Italian government. Collected, they might easily fill a copy of a new encyclopaedia with models for monkish diatribes.

Of course the Christian clergy can never become reconciled to a doctrine based on the application of strict logic to discursive reasoning. The number of those who have abandoned theology on this account has never been made known. They have asked questions and been forbidden to ask them; hence, separation, disgust, and often a despairing plunge into the abyss of atheism. The Orphean views of Aether as chief *medium between* God and created matter were likewise denounced. The Orphic Aether recalled too vividly the *Archaeus*, the Soul of the World, and the latter was in its metaphysical sense as closely related to the emanations, being the first manifestation — Sephira, or Divine Light. And when could the latter be more feared than at that critical moment?

Origen,[55] Clemens Alexandrinus,[56] Chalcidius,[57] Methodius,[58] and Maimonides,[59] on the authority of the *Targum* of Jerusalem, the orthodox and greatest authority of the Jews, held that the first two words in the book of *Genesis* — B-RASIT — mean *Wisdom*, or the *Principle;* and that the idea of these words meaning '*in the beginning*' was never held but by the profane, who were not allowed to penetrate any deeper into the esoteric sense of the sentence. Beausobre,[60] and after him Godfrey Higgins, have demonstrated the fact. "All things," says the Kabala, "are derived from one great Principle, and this principle is the *unknown* and *invisible* God. From Him a substantial power immediately proceeds, which is the *image of God*, and the source of all subsequent emanations. This second principle sends forth, by the *energy* (or *will* and *force*) of emanation, other natures, which are more or less perfect, according to their different degrees of distance in the scale of emanation from the First Source of existence, and which constitute different worlds or orders of being, all united to the eternal power from which they proceed. *Matter is nothing more than the most remote effect of the emanative energy* of the Deity. The material world receives its form from the immediate agency of powers far beneath the First Source of Being. . . ." [61] Beausobre, after citing St. Augustine the Manichaean, says: "And if by *Rasit* we understand the *active Principle* of the creation, instead of its *beginning*, in such a case we will clearly perceive that Moses never meant to say

55. *De princ.*, III, v.   56. *Strom.*, VI, v.   57. *Comm. in Timaeum.*
    58. Frag., 'Things Created,' § 8, ap. Photius, *Bibliotheca.*
59. *Moreh Nebûkhîm*, II, 30; p. 274.   60. *Hist. crit. du Manichéisme, etc.*,
I, p. 291 (liv. VI, i).   61. A. Rees: *Cyclopaedia*, art. 'Kabala.'

that heaven and earth were the first works of God. He only said that
God created heaven and earth *through the Principle*, who is His Son. It
is not the *time* he points to, but to the immediate author of the creation."
Angels, according to Augustine, were created *before* the firmament, and
according to the esoteric interpretation, the heaven and earth were created after that, evolving from the *second* Principle or the Logos — the
creative Deity. "The word *principe*," says Beausobre,[62] quoting Augustine,[63] "does not mean that the heaven and earth were created before
anything else, for, to begin with, the *angels* were created before that; but
that God did everything through His Wisdom, which is His *Verbum*, and
which the Christian *Bible* named the *Beginning*," thus adopting the exoteric meaning of the word abandoned to the multitudes. The Kabala —
the Oriental as well as the Jewish — shows that a number of *emanations*
(the Jewish Sephiroth) issued from the *First* Principle, the chief of which
was *Wisdom*. This Wisdom is the Logos of Philo, and Michael, the
chief of the Gnostic Eons; it is the Ormazd of the Persians; *Minerva*,
goddess of wisdom, of the Greeks, who emanated from the head of
Jupiter; and the second Person of the Christian Trinity. The early
Fathers of the Church had not much call to exert their imagination;
they found a ready-made doctrine that had existed in every theogony for
thousands of years before the Christian era. Their trinity is but the trio
of Sephiroth, the first three kabalistic *lights* of which Moses Nachmanides
says, that "*they have never been seen by any one;* there is not any defect
in them, nor any disunion." The first eternal number is the Father, or
the Chaldaean primeval, invisible and incomprehensible *chaos*, out of
which proceeded the *Intelligible* one — the Egyptian Ptaḥ, or "the
Principle of Light — not the light itself, and the Principle of Life,
though himself *no* life." The *Wisdom* by which the Father created the
heavens is the *Son*, or the kabalistic androgynous Adam Kadmon.
The Son is at once the male *Rā*, or Light of Wisdom, Prudence or *Intelligence*, Sephira, the female part of Himself; while from this dual being
proceeds the third emanation, the Binah or Reason, the second Intelligence — the Holy Ghost of the Christians. Therefore strictly speaking
there is a Tetraktys or quaternary, consisting of the Unintelligible
First monad and its triple emanation, which properly constitutes our
Trinity.

How then avoid perceiving at once that had not the Christians purposely disfigured in their interpretation and translation the Mosaic
Genesis to fit their own views, their religion, with its present dogmas,
would have been impossible? The word Rasit, once taught in its true
sense of the *Principle* and not the *Beginning*, and the anathematized doc-

---

62. *Loc. cit.*   63. *The City of God*, XI, xxxii.

trine of emanations accepted, the position of the second trinitarian personage becomes untenable. For if the angels are the *first* divine emanations from the Divine Substance, and were in existence *before* the Second Principle, then the anthropomorphized *Son* is at best an emanation like themselves, and cannot be God *hypostatically* any more than our visible works are ourselves. That these metaphysical subtleties never entered into the head of the honest-minded, sincere Paul, is evident; as it is furthermore evident, that like all learned Jews he was well acquainted with the doctrine of emanations and never thought of corrupting it. How can any one imagine that Paul identified the *Son* with the *Father*, when he tells us that God made Jesus "a *little lower* than the angels" (*Hebrews*, ii, 9) and a *little higher* than Moses! "For this MAN was counted worthy of more glory than Moses" (*Hebrews*, iii, 3). Of what or how many forgeries, interpolated later in the *Acts*, the Fathers are guilty, we know not; but that Paul never considered Christ more than a man "full of the Spirit of God" is but too evident: "In the *archē* was the *Logos*, and the Logos was adnate to the *Theos*."

Wisdom, the first emanation of Ain-Soph; the Protogonos, the Hypostasis; the Adam Kadmon of the Kabalist; the Brahmâ of the Hindû; the Logos of Plato; and the "*Beginning*" of St. John — are all the Rasit, ראשית, of the *Book of Genesis*. If rightly interpreted it overturns, as we have remarked, the whole elaborate system of Christian theology, for it proves that behind the *creative* Deity there was a HIGHER god, a planner, an architect; and that the former was but His executive agent — a simple POWER!

They [the Christians] persecuted the Gnostics, murdered the Philosophers, and burned the Kabalists and the Masons; and when the day of the great reckoning arrives, and the light shines in darkness, what will they have to offer in the place of the departed, expired religion? What will they answer, these pretended monotheists, these worshipers and *pseudo*-servants of the one living God, to their Creator? How will they account for this long persecution of those who were the true followers of the grand Megalistor, the supreme great master of the Rosicrucians, the FIRST of masons? "For he is the Builder and Architect of the Temple of the universe; He is the *Verbum Sapienti*." [64]

"Every one knows," wrote the great Manichaean of the third century, Faustus, "that the evangels were written neither by Jesus Christ,

---

64. "The altogether mystic coloring of Christianity harmonized with the Essene rules of life and opinions, and it is not improbable that Jesus and John the Baptist were initiated into the Essene Mysteries, to which Christianity may be indebted for many a form of expression; as indeed the community of Therapeutae, an offspring of the Essene order, soon belonged wholly to Christianity" (I. M. Jost: *The Israelite Indeed*, I, 411 — quoted by the author of *Sôd, the Son of the Man*, p. 62).

nor his apostles, but long after their time by some unknown persons, who,
judging well that they would hardly be believed when telling of things
they had not seen themselves, headed their narratives with the names of
the apostles or of disciples contemporaneous with the latter." [65]

Commenting upon the subject, A. Franck, the learned Hebrew
scholar of the Institute and translator of the Kabala, expresses the same
idea. "Are we not authorized," he asks, "to view the Kabala as a
precious remnant of religious philosophy of the Orient, which, transported into Alexandria, got mixed with the doctrine of Plato, and under
the usurped name of Dionysius the Areopagite, bishop of Athens, converted and consecrated by St. Paul, was thus enabled to penetrate into
the mysticism of the medieval ages?" [66]

Says Jacolliot: "What is then this religious philosophy of the Orient,
which has penetrated into the mystic symbolism of Christianity? We answer: This philosophy, the traces of which we find among the Magians,
the Chaldaeans, the Egyptians, the Hebrew kabalists and the Christians, is none other than that of the Hindû Brâhmanas, the sectarians of
the *pitris*, or the spirits of the invisible worlds which surround us." [67]

But if the Gnostics were destroyed, the *Gnosis*, based on the secret
science of sciences, still lives. It is the earth which helps the woman,
and which is destined to open her mouth to swallow up medieval Christianity, the usurper and assassin of the great master's doctrine. The
ancient Kabala, the Gnosis, or traditional *secret* knowledge, has never
been without its representatives in any age or country. The trinities of
initiates, whether passed into history or concealed under the impenetrable veil of mystery, are preserved throughout, and impressed upon the
ages. They are known as Moses, Aholiab, and Bezaleel, the son of Uri,
the son of Hur, as Plato, Philo, and Pythagoras, etc. At the Transfigura-
tion we see them as Jesus, Moses, and Elias, the three Trismegisti; and
three kabalists, Peter, James, and John — whose *revelation* is the key to
all wisdom. We found them in the twilight of Jewish history as Zoroaster, Abraham, and Terah, and later as Henoch, Ezekiel, and Daniel.

Who of those who ever studied the ancient philosophies — who
understand intuitively the grandeur of their conceptions, the boundless
sublimity of their views of the Unknown Deity — can hesitate for a
moment to give the preference to their doctrines over the incomprehensible, dogmatic and contradictory theology of the hundreds of
Christian sects? Who that ever read Plato and fathomed his τὸ Ὄν,

---

65. *Faustus, ap. August.*, xxxii, 2; xxxiii, 3; cf. Beausobre: *Hist. crit. du Manich.*, I, p. 297.
66. *La Kabbale*, IIIme part., ch. iv, p. 257: Paris, 1892, 3rd ed. The words "converted
and consecrated by St. Paul" may have been in earlier editions, but are not in 3rd.
67. *Le spiritisme, etc.*, p. 215.

"*whom no person has seen except the Son*," can doubt that Jesus was a disciple of the same secret doctrine which had instructed the great philosopher? For, as we have shown before now, Plato never claimed to be the inventor of all that he wrote, but gave credit for it to Pythagoras, who, in his turn, pointed to the remote East as the source whence he derived his information and his philosophy. Moreover, it is undeniable that the theologies of all the great nations dovetail together and show that each is a part of "one stupendous whole." Like the rest of the initiates we see Plato taking great pains to conceal the true meaning of his allegories. Every time the subject touches the greater secrets of the Oriental Kabala, secrets of the true cosmogony of the universe and of the *ideal*, pre-existing world, Plato shrouds his philosophy in the profoundest darkness. His *Timaeus* is so confused that no one but an *initiate* can understand the secret meaning. And Mosheim [68] thinks that Philo has filled his works with passages directly contradicting each other for the sole purpose of concealing the true doctrine. For once we see a critic on the right track.

And this very trinitarian idea, as well as the so bitterly denounced doctrine of emanations, whence their remotest origin? The answer is easy, and every proof is now at hand: in the sublime and profoundest of all philosophies, that of the universal 'Wisdom-Religion,' the first traces of which historical research now finds in the old pre-Vedic religion of India. As the much-abused Jacolliot well remarks, "It is not in the religious works of antiquity, such as the *Vedas*, the Zend *Avesta*, the *Bible*, that we have to search for the exact expression of the ennobling and sublime beliefs of those epochs." [69]

"The holy primitive syllable, composed of the three letters [A—U—M], in which is contained the Vedic *Trimûrti* [Trinity], must be kept secret, like another triple Veda," says *Manu*, in book xi, *śloka* 266.

Svayambhû is the unrevealed Deity; it is the Being existent through and of itself; it is the central and immortal germ of all that exists in the universe. Three trinities emanate and are blended in it, forming a Supreme *unity*. These trinities, or the triple *Trimûrti*, are: the *Nara, Nârî*, and *Virâj* — the *initial* triad; the *Agni, Vâyu*, and *Surya* — the *manifested* triad; Brahmâ, Vishnu, and Siva, the *creative* triad. Each of these triads becomes less metaphysical and more adapted to the vulgar intelligence as it descends. Thus the last becomes but the symbol in its concrete expression; the necessarianism of a purely meta-

---

68. Note in Cudworth's *True Intellectual System*, II, p. 324: London, 1845.
69. L. Jacolliot: *Le spiritisme dans le monde*, p. 13.

physical conception. Together with *Svayambhú*, they are the ten *Sephi-roth* of the Hebrew kabalists, the ten Hindû *Prajápatis* — the Ain-Soph of the former, answering to the great *Unknown*, expressed by the mystic A U M of the latter.

Says Franck, the translator of the Kabala:

"The ten Sephiroth are divided into *three classes;* each of them presenting to us the divinity *under a different aspect,* the whole still remaining an *indivisible Trinity.*

"The first three Sephiroth are purely intellectual or metaphysical; they express the absolute identity of existence and thought, and form what the modern kabalists called the intelligible world — which is the first manifestation of God.

"The three that follow make us conceive God in one of their as-pects, as the identity of goodness and wisdom; in the other they show to us, in the Supreme good, the origin of beauty and magnificence [in the creation]. Therefore, they are named the *virtues,* or the *sensible world.*

"Finally, we learn, by the last three Sephiroth, that the Universal Providence, that the Supreme artist is also *absolute Force,* the all-powerful cause, and that, at the same time, this cause *is the generative element of all that is.* It is these last Sephiroth that constitute the *natural world,* or nature in its essence and in its *active* principle, *na-tura naturans.*" [70]

This kabalistic conception is thus proved identical with that of the Hindû philosophy. Whoever reads Plato and his dialog *Timaeus,* will find these ideas as faithfully echoed by the Greek philosopher. Moreover the injunction of secrecy was as strict with the kabalists, as with the initiates of the Adyta, and the Hindû *yogis.*

"Close thy mouth, lest thou shouldst speak of *this* [the mystery], and thy heart, lest thou shouldst think aloud; and if thy heart has escaped thee, bring it back to its place, for such is the object of our alliance." [71]

"This is a secret which gives death: close thy mouth lest thou shouldst reveal to the vulgar; compress thy brain lest something should escape from it and fall outside" (*Agrushada-Parikshai*).

Truly the fate of many a future generation hung on a gossamer thread in the days of the third and fourth centuries. Had not the Emperor sent in 389 to Alexandria a rescript — which was forced from him by the Christians — for the destruction of every idol, our own century would never have had a Christian mythological Pantheon of its own. Never

---

70. Franck: *La Kabbale,* IIme part., ch. iii: 1892.
71. *Sepher Yetzirah* (Book of Creation), I, § 8.

did the Neo-Platonic school reach such a height of philosophy as when nearest its end. Uniting the mystic Theosophy of old Egypt with the refined philosophy of the Greeks; nearer to the ancient Mysteries of Thebes and Memphis than they had been for centuries; versed in the science of soothsaying and divination, as in the art of the Therapeutists; friendly with the acutest men of the Jewish nation, who were deeply imbued with the Zoroastrian ideas, the Neo-Platonists tended to amalgamate the old wisdom of the Oriental Kabala with the more refined conceptions of the Occidental Theosophists. Notwithstanding the treason of the Christians, who saw fit for political reasons after the days of Constantine to repudiate their tutors, the influence of the new Platonic philosophy is conspicuous in the subsequent adoption of dogmas, the origin of which can very easily be traced to that remarkable school [of Neo-Platonism]. Though mutilated and disfigured, they still preserve a strong family likeness, which nothing can obliterate.

But if the knowledge of the occult powers of nature opens the spiritual sight of man, enlarges his intellectual faculties, and leads him unerringly to a profounder veneration for the Creator, on the other hand ignorance, dogmatic narrow-mindedness, and a childish fear of looking to the bottom of things, invariably leads to fetish-worship and superstition.

When Cyril, the bishop of Alexandria, had openly embraced the cause of Isis, the Egyptian goddess, and had anthropomorphized her into Mary, the mother of God; and the trinitarian controversy had been begun; from that moment the Egyptian doctrine of the emanation of the creative God out of Emepht [71a] began to be tortured in a thousand ways, until the Councils had agreed upon the adoption of it as it now stands — the disfigured Ternary of the kabalistic Solomon and Philo! But as its origin was yet too evident, the *Word* was no longer called the 'Heavenly man,' the *primal* Adam Kadmon, but became the Logos — Christ — and was made as old as the 'Ancient of the Ancient,' his father. The *concealed* WISDOM became identical with its emanation, the DIVINE THOUGHT, and had to be regarded as co-equal and co-eternal with its first manifestation.

If we now stop to consider another of the fundamental dogmas of Christianity, the doctrine of atonement, we may trace it as easily back to heathendom. This corner-stone of a Church which had believed herself built on a firm rock for long centuries, is now excavated by science, and proved to have come from the Gnostics. Professor Draper shows it as hardly known in the days of Tertullian, and as having "*originated* among the Gnostic heretics.'' [72] We will not permit ourselves to contra-

---

71a. Cf. A. Kircher: *Sphinx Mystagoga*, p. 52: Amstelodami, 1676.
72. *Conflict between Religion and Science*, p. 224.

dict such a learned authority, further than to state that it *originated* among them no more than did their 'anointed' Christos and Sophia. The former they modeled on the original of the 'King Messiah,' the male principle of wisdom, and the latter on the third Sephiroth, from the Chaldaean Kabala,[73] and even from the Hindû Brahmâ and Sarasvatî,[74] and the Pagan Dionysus and Demeter. And here we are on firm ground, if it were only because it is now proved that the *New Testament* never appeared in its complete form, such as we find it now, till 300 years after the period of apostles,[75] and the *Zohar* and other kabalistic books are found to belong to the first century before our era, if not to be far older still.

The Gnostics entertained many of the Essenean ideas; and the Essenes had their 'greater' and 'minor' Mysteries at least two centuries before our era. They were the *Isarim* or *Initiates*, the descendants of the Egyptian hierophants, in whose country they had been settled for several centuries before they were converted to Buddhistic monasticism by the missionaries of King Aśoka, and amalgamated later with the earliest Christians; and they existed, probably, before the old Egyptian temples were desecrated and ruined in the incessant invasions of Persians, Greeks, and other conquering hordes. The hierophants had their *atonement* enacted in the Mystery of Initiation ages before the Gnostics, or even the Essenes, had appeared. It was known among hierophants as the BAPTISM OF BLOOD, and was considered not as an atonement for the 'fall of man' in Eden, but simply as an expiation for the past, present, and future sins of ignorant but nevertheless polluted mankind. The hierophant had the option of offering either his pure and sinless life as a sacrifice for his race to the gods whom he hoped to rejoin, or an animal victim. The former [mode of expiation] depended entirely on his own will. At the last moment of the solemn 'new birth,' the initiator passed 'the word' to the initiated, and immediately after that the latter had a weapon placed in his right hand, and was ordered *to strike*.[76] This is the true origin of the Christian dogma of atonement.

---

73. See *Zohar; Kabbala denudata; Siphra Dtzeniuthah*, the oldest book of the Kabalists; and Milman: *History of Christianity*, pp. 212-215, original edition, 1840.

74. Milman: *op. cit.*, p. 280. The *Kurios* and *Kora* are mentioned repeatedly by Justin Martyr; see *1 Apol.*, ch. 64, etc.

75. See Olshausen: *Biblical Commentary on New Testament*, Introduction, § 1: New York, 1857-60.

76. There is a wide-spread *superstition* (?), especially among the Slavonians and Russians, that the *magician* or wizard cannot die before he has passed the 'word' to a successor. So deeply is it rooted among the popular beliefs, that we do not imagine there is a person in Russia who has not heard of it. It is quite easy to trace the origin

Verily the 'Christs' of the pre-Christian ages were many. But they died unknown to the world, and disappeared as silently and as mysteriously from the sight of man as Moses from the top of Pisgah, the mountain of Nebo (oracular wisdom), after he had laid his hands upon Joshua, who thus became "full of the spirit of wisdom" (*i. e.*, *initiated*).

Nor does the Mystery of the Eucharist pertain to Christians alone. Godfrey Higgins proves that it was instituted many hundreds of years before the 'Paschal Supper,' and says that "the sacrifice of bread and

---

of this 'superstition' to the old Mysteries which had been for ages spread all over the globe. The ancient *Variago-Rouss* had his Mysteries in the North as well as in the South of Russia; and there are many relics of the by-gone faith scattered in the lands watered by the sacred Dnieper, the baptismal Jordan of all Russia. No *Znáchar* (the knowing one) or *Koldoun* (sorcerer), male or female, can die in fact before he has passed the mysterious word to some one. The popular belief is that unless he does that he will linger and suffer for weeks and months, and were he even finally to get liberated, it would be only to wander on earth, unable to quit its region unless he finds a successor even after death. How far the belief may be verified by others we do not know, but we have seen a case which, for its tragical and mysterious *dénoument*, deserves to be given here as an illustration of the subject in hand. An old man, of over one hundred years of age, a peasant-serf in the government of S——, having a wide reputation as a sorcerer and healer, was said to be dying for several days, and still unable to die. The report spread like lightning, and the poor old fellow was shunned by even the members of his own family, as the latter were afraid of receiving the unwelcome inheritance. At last the public rumor in the village was that he had sent a message to a colleague less versed than himself in the art, and who, although he lived in a distant district, was nevertheless coming at the call, and would be on hand early on the following morning. There was at that time on a visit to the proprietor of the village a young physician who, belonging to the famous school of *Nihilism* of that day, laughed outrageously at the idea. The master of the house, being a very pious man, and but half inclined to make so cheap of the 'superstition,' smiled — as the saying goes — but with one corner of his mouth. Meanwhile the young skeptic, to gratify his curiosity, had made a visit to the dying man, had found that he could not live twenty-four hours longer, and, determined to prove the absurdity of the 'superstition,' had taken means to detain the coming 'successor' at a neighboring village.

Early in the morning a company of four persons, comprising the physician, the master of the place, his daughter, and the writer of the present lines, went to the hut in which was to be achieved the triumph of skepticism. The dying man was expecting his liberator every moment, and his agony at the delay became extreme. We tried to persuade the physician to humor the patient, were it for humanity's sake. He only laughed. Getting hold with one hand of the old wizard's pulse, he took out his watch with the other, and remarking in French that all would be over in a few moments, remained absorbed in his professional experiment. The scene was solemn and appalling. Suddenly the door opened, and a young boy entered with the intelligence, addressed to the doctor, that the *koum* was lying dead drunk at a neighboring village, and, according to *his orders*, could not be with "grandfather" till the next day. The young doctor felt confused, and was just going to address the old man, when, as quick as lightning, the Znáchar snatched his hand from his grasp and raised himself in bed. His deep-sunken eyes flashed; his yellow-white beard and hair streaming round his livid face made him a dreadful sight. One instant more, and his long, sinewy arms were clasped round the physician's neck, as with a supernatural force he drew the doctor's head closer and closer to his own face, where he held him as in a vise, while *whispering* words inaudible to us in his ear. The skeptic struggled to free himself, but before he had time to make one

wine was common to many ancient nations." [77] Cicero mentions it in
his works, and wonders at the strangeness of the rite. There had been
an esoteric meaning attached to it from the first establishment of the
Mysteries, and the Eucharistia is one of the oldest rites of antiquity.
With the hierophants it had nearly the same significance as with the
Christians. Ceres was *bread*, and Bacchus was *wine;* [78] the former
meaning regeneration of life from the seed, and the latter — the grape —
the emblem of wisdom and knowledge; the accumulation of the spirit
of things, and the fermentation and subsequent strength of that esoteric
knowledge being justly symbolized by wine. The mystery related to
the drama of Eden; it is said to have been first taught by Janus, who
was also the first to introduce in the temples the sacrifices of 'bread'
and 'wine' in commemoration of the 'fall into generation' as the symbol
of the 'seed.' "I am the true vine, and my Father is the husbandman,"
says Jesus, alluding to the secret knowledge that could be imparted
by him. "I will drink no more of the fruit of the vine, until that day
that I drink it new in the kingdom of God."

The festival of the Eleusinian Mysteries began in the month of Boe-
dromion, which corresponds with the month of September, the time of
grape-gathering, and lasted from the 15th to the 22nd of the month,
seven days. [79] The Hebrew festival of the Feast of Tabernacles began
on the 15th and ended on the 22nd of the month of Ethanim, which
Dunlap shows as derived from Adonim, Adonia, Attenim, Ethanim; [80]
and this feast is named in *Exodus* (xxiii, 16) the feast of *ingathering*.
"All the men of Israel assembled themselves unto King Solomon at the
feast in the month Ethanim, which is the *seventh* month." [81]

Plutarch thinks the feast of the booths to be the Bacchic rites, not
the Eleusinian. Thus "Bacchus was directly called upon," he says.
The *Sabazian* worship was *Sabbatic;* the names Evius, or Hevius, and

---

effective motion the work had evidently been done; the hands relaxed their grasp, and
the old sorcerer fell on his back — a corpse! A strange and ghostly smile had settled on
the stony lips — a smile of fiendish triumph and satisfied revenge; but the doctor looked
paler and more ghastly than the dead man himself. He stared round with an expression
of terror difficult to describe, and without answering our inquiries rushed out wildly from
the hut, in the direction of the woods. Messengers were sent after him, but he was
nowhere to be found. About sunset a report was heard in the forest. An hour later
his body was brought home, with a bullet through his head, for the skeptic had blown
out his brains!
    What made him commit suicide? What magic spell of sorcery had the 'word' of
the dying wizard left on his mind? Who can tell?

77. *Anacalypsis;* also Tertullian: *De praescr. haer.*, xl.
78. Cicero: *On the Nature of the Gods*, iii, 16.
79. Anthon: *Dict. Gk. and Rom. Ant.*, 'Eleusinia.'
80. *Sôd, Myst. of Adoni*, p. 71.   81. *1 Kings*, viii, 2.

Luaios are identical with *Hivite* and *Levite*. The French name Louis
is the Hebrew *Levi;* Iacchus again is Iao or Jehovah; and Baal or Adon,
like Bacchus, was a phallic god. "Who shall ascend into the hill [the
high place] of the Lord?" asks the holy king David, "who shall stand in
the place of his *Kadushu* קרש"? (*Psalms*, xxiv, 3). Kadesh may mean in
one sense to *devote, hallow, sanctify*, and even to initiate or to set apart;
but it also means the ministers of lascivious rites (the Venus-worship)
and the true interpretation of the word Kadesh is bluntly rendered in
Deuteronomy, xxiii, 17; *Hosea*, iv, 14; and *Genesis*, xxxviii, from verses
15 to 22. The 'holy' Kadeshuth of the *Bible* were identical as to the
duties of their office with the nautch-girls of the later Hindû pagodas.
The Hebrew *Kadeshim* or galli lived "by the house of the Lord, where
the women wove hangings for the grove," or bust of Venus-Astarte, says
verse the seventh in the twenty-third chapter of *2 Kings*.

The dance performed by David round the ark was the 'circle-dance'
said to have been prescribed by the Amazons for the Mysteries. Such
was the dance of the daughters of Shiloh (*Judges*, xxi, 21, 23 *et passim*),
and the leaping of the prophets of Baal (*1 Kings*, xviii, 26). It was
simply a characteristic of the Sabaean worship, for it denoted the motion
of the planets round the sun. That the dance was a Bacchic frenzy is
apparent. Sistra were used on the occasion, and the taunt of Michal and
the king's reply are very expressive. "The king of Israel uncovered himself before his maid-servants as one of the *vain* [or debauched] fellows
shamelessly uncovereth himself." And he retorts: "I will play [act
wantonly] before יהוה, and I will be yet more vile than this, and I will
be base in my own sight." [82] When we remember that David had so-
journed among the Tyrians and Philistines, where their rites were common; and that indeed he had conquered that land away from the house
of Saul, by the aid of mercenaries from their country, the countenancing
and even, perhaps, the introduction of such a Pagan-like worship by the
weak 'psalmist' seems very natural. David knew nothing of Moses, it
seems, and if he introduced the Jehovah-worship it was not in its monotheistic character, but simply as that of one of the many gods of the
neighboring nations — a tutelary deity to whom he had given the preference, and chosen among "all other gods."

Following the Christian dogmas seriatim, if we concentrate our attention upon one which provoked the fiercest battles until its recognition,
that of the Trinity, what do we find? We meet it, as we have shown,
northeast of the Indus; and tracing it to Asia Minor and Europe, recognise it among every people who had anything like an established religion.

---

82. *2 Sam.*, vi, 20-22.

It was taught in the oldest Chaldaean, Egyptian, and Mithraïtic schools. The Chaldaean Sun-god, Mithra, was called 'Triple,' and the trinitarian idea of the Chaldaeans was a doctrine of the Akkadians, who themselves belonged to a race which was the first to conceive a metaphysical trinity. According to Rawlinson, the Chaldaeans are a tribe of the Akkadians, who lived in Babylonia from the earliest times. They were Turanians, according to others, and instructed the Babylonians in the first notions of religion. But these same Akkadians, who were they? Those scientists who would ascribe to them a 'Turanian' origin, make of them the inventors of the cuneiform characters; others call them Sumerians; others again make their language, of which (for very good reasons) no traces whatever remain — Kasdean, Chaldaic, Proto-Chaldaean, Kasdo-Scythic, and so on. The only tradition worthy of credence is that these Akkadians instructed the Babylonians in the Mysteries, and taught them the sacerdotal or *Mystery*-language. These Akkadians were then simply a tribe of the Hindû-Brâhmanas, now called Aryans — their vernacular language, the Sanskrit [83] of the Vedas; and their sacred or Mystery-language, that which, even in our own age, is used by the Hindû fakirs and initiated Brâhmanas in their magical evocations.[84] It has been from time immemorial and still is employed by the initiates of all countries; and the Tibetan lamas claim that it is in this tongue that appear the mysterious characters on the leaves and bark of the sacred Kounboum.

Jacolliot, who took such pains to penetrate the mysteries of the Brâhmanical initiation, in translating and commenting upon the *Agrushada-Parikshai* confesses the following:

"It is pretended also, without our being able to verify the assertion, that the magical evocations were pronounced in a particular language, and that it was forbidden, under pain of death, to translate them into vulgar dialects. The rare expressions that we have been able to catch like — *L'rhom, h'hom, sh'hrum, sho'rhim*, are in fact most curious, and do not seem to belong to any known idiom." [85]

Those who have seen a fakir or a lama reciting his *mantras* and conjurations, know that he never pronounces the words audibly when preparing for a phenomenon. His lips move, but none will ever hear the

---

83. Let us remember in this connexion that Col. Vans Kennedy has long ago declared his opinion that Babylonia was once the seat of the Sanskrit language and of Brâhmanical influence (*Researches into the Nature and Affinity of Ancient and Hindu Mythology*).

84. "The *Agrushada-Parikshai*, which discloses, to a certain extent, the order of initiation, does not give the formula of evocation," says Jacolliot, and he adds that, according to some Brâhmanas, "these formulae were never written, they were and still are imparted in a whisper in the ear of the adepts" ("*mouth to ear, and the word at low breath*," say the Masons).— *Le spiritisme dans le monde*, p. 108.   85. *Ibid.*

terrible formula pronounced, except in the interior of the temples, and then in a cautious whisper. This, then, was the language now respectively baptized by every scientist, and according to his imaginative and philological propensities, Kasdeo-Semitic, Scythic, Proto-Chaldaean, and the like.

Scarcely two of even the most learned Sanskrit philologists are agreed as to the true interpretation of Vedic words. Let one put forth an essay, a lecture, a treatise, a translation, a dictionary, and straightway all the others fall to quarreling with each other and with him as to his sins of omission and commission. Professor Whitney, greatest of American Orientalists, says that Professor Müller's notes on the *Riĝ Veda Sanhitâ* "are far from showing that sound and thoughtful judgment, that moderation and economy which are among the most precious qualities of an exegete." [86] Professor Müller angrily retorts upon his critics that "not only is the joy embittered which is the inherent reward of all *bona fide* work, but selfishness, malignity, aye, *even untruthfulness*, gain the upper hand, and the healthy growth of science is stunted." He differs "in many cases from the explanations of Vedic words given by Professor Roth" in his *Sanskrit Dictionary*, and Professor Whitney shampoos both their heads by saying that there are, unquestionably, words and phrases "as to which both alike will hereafter be set right."

In volume i of his *Chips*, Professor Müller stigmatizes all the *Vedas* except the *Rik*, the *Atharva-Veda* included, as "theological twaddle," while Professor Whitney regards the latter as "the most comprehensive and valuable of the four collections, next after the *Rik*." [87] To return to the case of Jacolliot. Professor Whitney brands him as a "bungler and a humbug," and, as we remarked above, this is the very general verdict. But when *La Bible dans l'Inde* appeared, the Société Académique de Saint Quentin requested M. Textor de Ravisi, a learned Indianist, ten years Governor of Karikal, India, to report upon its merits. He was an ardent Catholic, and bitterly opposed Jacolliot's conclusions where they discredited the Mosaic and Catholic revelations; but he was forced to say: "Written with good faith, in an easy, vigorous, and passionate style, of an easy and varied argumentation, the work of M. Jacolliot is of absorbing interest . . . a learned work on known facts and with familiar arguments." [88]

Enough. Let Jacolliot have the benefit of the doubt when such very imposing authorities are doing their best to show up each other as incompetents and literary journeymen. We quite agree with Professor Whitney that "the truism, that [for European critics?] it is far easier to

86. *Oriental and Linguistic Studies*, p. 138.   87. *Ibid.*, pp. 147, 3.
88. L. Jacolliot: *Christna et le Christ*, p. 339.

pull to pieces than to build up, is nowhere truer than in matters affecting the archaeology and history of India." [89]

Babylonia happened to be situated on the way of the great stream of the earliest Hindû emigration, and the Babylonians were one of the first peoples benefited thereby. [90] These Khaldi were the worshipers of the Moon-god, Deus-Lunus, from which fact we may infer that the Akkadians — if such must be their name — belonged to the race of the Kings of the Moon, whom tradition shows as having reigned in *Prayâga* — now Allahâbâd. With them the trinity of Deus-Lunus was manifested in the three lunar phases, completing the quaternary with the fourth, and typifying the death of the Moon-god in its gradual waning and final disappearance. This death was allegorized by them, and attributed to the triumph of the genius of evil over the light-giving deity; as the later nations allegorized the death of their Sun-gods, Osiris and Apollo, at the hands of Typhon and the great Dragon Python, when the sun entered the winter solstice. Babel, Arach, and Akkad are names of the sun. The Chaldaean *Oracles* are full and explicit upon the subject of the Divine Triad. [91] "A triad of Deity shines forth throughout the whole world, of which a Monad is the head," admits the Reverend Dr. Maurice.

"For from this Triad, in the bosoms, are all things governed," says a Chaldaean oracle. [92] The *Phōs*, *Pur*, and *Phlox*, of Sanchoniathon, [93] are Light, Fire, and Flame, three manifestations of the Sun who is *one*. Bel-Saturn, Jupiter-Bel, and Bel or Baal-Chom are the Chaldaean trinity; [94] "The Babylonian Bel was regarded in the Triune aspect of Belitan, Zeus-Belus [the mediator] and Baal-Chom who is Apollo Chomaeus." [95] "This was the Triune aspect of the 'Highest God,' who is, according to Berosus, either El [the Hebrew], Bel, Belitan, Mithra, or Zeroana, and has the name πατήρ, 'the Father.' " [96] The Brahmâ, Vishnu, and Śiva, [97] corresponding to Power, Wisdom, and Justice, which answer in their turn to Spirit, Matter, Time, and the Past, Present, and Future, can be found

---

89. W. D. Whitney: *Oriental and Linguistic Studies*, p. 98.

90. Jacolliot seems to have very logically demonstrated the absurd contradictions of some philologists, anthropologists, and Orientalists, in regard to their *Akkado-* and *Semito-*mania. "There is not, perhaps, much of good faith in their negations," he writes. "The scientists who invent Turanian peoples know very well that in *Manu* alone there is more of veritable science and philosophy than in all that this pretended Semitism has hitherto furnished us with; but they are the slaves of a path which some of them are following the last fifteen, twenty, or even thirty years. . . . We expect, therefore, nothing of the present. India will owe its reconstitution to the scientists of the next generation" (*La genèse de l'humanité*, pp. 60-61).

91. Cory: *Anct. Frag.*, pp. 239-280.   92. Lydus: *De mens.*, 20.

93. Cory: *Anct. Frag.*, p. 6.   94. Movers: *Die Phöniz.*, I, p. 263.

95. *Ibid.*, I, p. 189.   96. Dunlap: *Spirit-Hist. Man*, p. 281.

97. Śiva is not a god of the *Vedas*, strictly speaking. When the *Vedas* were written, he held the rank of *Mahâ-Deva*, or Bel, among the gods of aboriginal India.

in the temple of Gharipuri; thousands of dogmatic Brâhmanas worship these attributes of the Vedic Deity, while the severe monks and nuns of Buddhistic Tíbet recognise but the sacred trinity of the three cardinal virtues: *Poverty, Chastity,* and *Obedience,* professed by the Christians, practised by the Buddhists and some Hindûs alone.

The Persian triplicate Deity also consists of three persons, Ormazd, Mithra, and Ahriman.[98] It is that principle, of which the author of the *Chaldaic Summary* saith, "*They conceive there is one principle of all things, and declare it to be one and good.*"[99] The Chinese idol Sanpao consists of three equal in all respects;[100] and the Peruvians "supposed their Tanga-tanga to be one in three, and three in one," says Faber.[101] The Egyptians have their Emepht, Eikton, and Ptah;[102] and the triple god seated on the Lotus can be seen in the St. Petersburg Museum, on a medal of the Northern Tatars.[103]

Among the Church dogmas which have most seriously suffered of late at the hands of the Orientalists, the last in question stands conspicuous. The reputation of each of the three personages of the anthropomorphic godhead as an original revelation to the Christians through Divine will, has been badly compromised by inquiry into its predecessors and origin. Orientalists have published more about the similarity between Brâhmanism, Buddhism, and Christianity than was strictly agreeable to the Vatican. Draper's assertion that "Paganism was modified by Christianity, Christianity by Paganism,"[104] is being daily verified. "Olympus was restored, but the divinities passed under other names," he says, treating of the Constantine period. "The more powerful provinces insisted on the adoption of their time-honored conceptions. Views of the trinity in accordance with the Egyptian traditions were established. Not only was the adoration of Isis under a new name restored, but even her image, standing on the crescent moon, reappeared. The well-known effigy of that goddess with the infant Horus in her arms has descended to our days, in the beautiful artistic creations of the Madonna and child."

But a still earlier origin than the Egyptian and Chaldaean can be assigned to the Virgin 'Mother of God,' Queen of Heaven. Though

---

98. Plutarch: *On Isis and Osiris.*   99. Gallaeus: *Summ. Chald.* (Pselli expos.), in Appx. (p. 111) to *Sib. oracula:* Amsterdam, 1689.
100. Navarette: *Tratados hist., etc., de China,* bk. II, ch. x.   101. *On the Origin of Pagan Idolatry.*   102. Iambl.: *De myst.,* VIII, 3; cf. Isis Unv., I, pp. 146-7, 157, 256.
103. Faber: *Dissertation on the Cabiri,* I, p. 315, note.
104. *Confl. betw. Rel. and Science,* p. 52. Isis and Osiris are said, in the Egyptian sacred books, to have appeared (i. e., been worshiped) on earth later than Thoth, the *first* Hermes, called Trismegistus, who wrote all their sacred books according to the command of God or by 'divine revelation.' The companion and instructor of Isis and Osiris was Thoth, or Hermes II, who was an incarnation of the celestial Hermes.

Isis is also by right the Queen of Heaven, and is generally represented carrying in her hand the Crux Ansata composed of the mundane cross and of the *Stauros* of the Gnostics, she is a great deal younger than the celestial virgin, Neith. In one of the tombs of the Pharaohs — that of Rameses — in the valley of Biban-el-Muluk in Thebes, Champollion junior discovered a picture, according to his opinion the most ancient ever yet found. It represents the heavens symbolized by the figure of a woman bedecked with stars. The birth of the Sun is figured by the form of a little child, issuing from the bosom of its 'Divine Mother.' [105]

In the *Book of Hermes*, *Pymander*, is enunciated in distinct and un-equivocal sentences the whole trinitarian dogma accepted by the Christians. "That light I am," says Pymander, the DIVINE THOUGHT. "I am the *nous* or intelligence; and I am thy god; and I am far older than the humid principle which escapes from the shadow. I am the germ of thought, the resplendent WORD, the SON of God. Think that what thus sees and hears in thee, is the *Verbum* of the Master, it is the Thought, which is God the Father." "The celestial ocean, the AETHER, which flows from east to west, is the Breath of the Father, the life-giving Principle, the HOLY GHOST!" "For they are not at all separated, and their union is LIFE." [106]

Ancient as may be the origin of Hermes, lost in the unknown days of Egyptian colonization, there is yet a far older prophecy, directly relating to the Hindû Krishna, according to the Brâhmanas. It is to say the least strange that the Christians claim to base their religion upon a prophecy of the *Bible* which exists nowhere in that book. In what chapter or verse does Jehovah, the 'Lord God,' promise Adam and Eve to send them a Redeemer who will save humanity? "I will put enmity between thee and the woman," says the Lord God to the serpent, "and between thy seed and her seed; it shall bruise thy head, and thou shalt bruise his heel."

In these words there is not the slightest allusion to a Redeemer, and the subtlest of intellects could not extract from them, as they stand in the third chapter of *Genesis*, anything like that which the Christians have contrived to find. On the other hand, in the traditions and in *Manu*, Brahmâ promises directly to the first couple to send them a Savior who will teach them the way to salvation.

"It is from the lips of a messenger of Brahmâ, who will be born in Kurukshetra, Matsya, and the land of Pañchâla, also called Kanyâ-kubja [mountain of the Virgin], that all men on earth will learn their duty," says *Manu* (II, *slokas* 19 and 20).

---

105. Champollion-Figeac: *Égypte ancienne*, p. 104.   106. L. Ménard: *Hermès Trismégiste*, I, ch. i. The penultimate sentence is from another Hermetic work.

The Mexicans call the Father of their Trinity Yzona, the Son Bacab, and the Holy Ghost Echvah, "and say they received it [the doctrine] from their ancestors." [107] Among the Semitic nations we can trace the trinity to the prehistorical days of the fabled Sesostris, who is identified by more than one critic with Nimrod, "the mighty hunter." Manetho makes the oracle rebuke the king, when the latter asks, "Tell me, O thou strong in fire, who before me could subjugate all things? and who shall after me?" And the oracle saith thus: "First God, then the Word, and then 'the Spirit.' " [108]

In the foregoing lies the foundation of the fierce hatred of the Christians toward the 'Pagans' and the theurgists. Too much had been *borrowed;* the ancient religions and the Neo-Platonists had been laid by them under contribution sufficiently to perplex the world for several thousand years. Had not the ancient creeds been speedily obliterated, it would have been found impossible to preach the Christian religion as a New Dispensation, or the direct Revelation from God the Father, through God the Son, and under the influence of God the Holy Ghost. As a political exigence the Fathers had — to gratify the wishes of their rich converts — instituted even the festivals of Pan. They went so far as to accept the ceremonies hitherto celebrated by the Pagan world in honor of the *God of the gardens,* in all their primitive *sincerity.* [109] It was time to sever the connexion. Either the Pagan worship and the Neo-Platonic theurgy, with all ceremonial of magic, must be crushed out forever, or the Christians become Neo-Platonists.

The fierce polemics and single-handed battles between Irenaeus and the Gnostics are too well known to need repetition. They were carried on for over two centuries after the unscrupulous Bishop of Lyons had uttered his last religious paradox. Celsus, the Neo-Platonist, and a disciple of the school of Ammonius Saccas, had thrown the Christians into perturbation, and even had arrested for a time the progress of proselytism by successfully proving that the original and purer forms of the most important dogmas of Christianity were to be found only in the teachings of Plato. Celsus accused them of accepting the worst superstitions of Paganism, and of interpolating passages from the books of the Sibyls without rightly understanding their meaning. The accusations were so just and the facts so patent, that for a long time no Christian writer had ventured to answer the challenge. Origen, at the fervent request of his friend Ambrosius, was the first to take the defense in

107. Lord Kingsborough: *Antiquities of Mexico,* p. 165.
108. Joannes Malala: *Hist. Chronica,* I, iv: Oxford, 1691. .
109. P. Knight: *Worship of Priapus,* p. 171, *sq.;* edit. 1865.

hand, for having belonged to the same Platonic school of Ammonius he was considered the most competent man to refute the well-founded charges. But his eloquence failed, and the only remedy that could be found was to destroy the writings of Celsus.[110] This could be achieved only in the fifth century, when copies had been taken from this work, and many were those who had read and studied them. If no copy of it has descended to our present generation of scientists, it is not because there is none extant at present, but for the simple reason that the monks of a certain Oriental church on Mount Athos will neither show nor confess they have one in their possession.[111] Perhaps they themselves do not even know the value of the contents of their manuscripts, on account of their great ignorance.

The dispersion of the Eclectic school had become the fondest hope of the Christians. It had been looked for and contemplated with intense anxiety. It was finally achieved. The members were scattered by the

---

110. The Celsus above mentioned, who lived between the second and third centuries, is not Celsus the Epicurean. The latter wrote several works against magic, and lived earlier during the reign of Hadrian.

111. We have the facts from a trustworthy witness, one having no interest in inventing such a story. Having injured his leg in a fall from the steamer into the boat in which he was to land at the Mount, he was taken care of by these monks, and during his convalescence, through gifts of money and presents, became their greatest friend and finally won their entire confidence. Having asked for the loan of some books, he was taken by the Superior to a large cellar in which they keep their sacred vessels and other property. Opening a great trunk, full of old musty manuscripts and rolls, he was invited by the Superior to "amuse himself." The gentleman was a scholar, and well versed in Greek and Latin. "I was amazed," he says, in a private letter, "and had my breath taken away on finding, among these old parchments so unceremoniously treated, some of the most valuable relics of the first centuries hitherto believed to have been lost." Among others he found a half-destroyed manuscript, which he is perfectly sure must be a copy of the 'True Doctrine,' the λόγος ἀληθής of Celsus, out of which Origen quoted whole pages. The traveler took as many notes as he could on that day, but when he came to offer to the Superior to purchase some of these writings he found, to his great surprise, that no amount of money would tempt the monks. They did not know what the manuscripts contained, nor "did they care," they said. But the "heap of writing," they added, was transmitted to them from one generation to another, and there was a tradition among them that these papers would one day become the means of crushing the "Great Beast of the Apocalypse," their hereditary enemy, the Church of Rome. They were constantly quarreling and fighting with the Catholic monks, and among the whole "heap" they knew that there was a "holy" relic which protected them. They did not know which, and so in their doubt abstained. It appears that the Superior, a shrewd Greek, understood his bévue and repented of his kindness, for first of all he made the traveler give him his most sacred word of honor, strengthened by an oath he made him take on the image of the Holy Patroness of the Island, never to betray their secret, and never to mention at least the name of their convent. And finally, when the anxious student who had passed a fortnight in reading all sorts of antiquated trash before he happened to stumble over some precious manuscript, expressed the desire to have the key that he might "amuse himself" with the writings once more, he was very naïvely informed that the "key had been lost" and that they did not know where to look for it. And thus he was left to the few notes he had taken.

hand of the monsters Theophilus, Bishop of Alexandria, and his nephew Cyril — the murderer of the young, the learned, and the innocent Hypatia! [112]

With the death of the martyred daughter of Theon the mathematician, there remained no possibility for the Neo-Platonists to continue their school at Alexandria. During the life-time of the youthful Hypatia her friendship and influence with Orestes, the governor of the city, had assured the philosophers security and protection against their murderous enemies. With her death they had lost their strongest friend. How much she was revered by all who knew her for her erudition, virtues, and noble character, we can infer from the letters addressed to her by Synesius, Bishop of Ptolemais, fragments of which have reached us. "My heart yearns for the presence of your divine spirit," he wrote in 413 A.D., "which more than anything else could alleviate the bitterness of my fortunes." At another time he says: "Oh, my mother, my sister, my teacher, my benefactor! My soul is very sad. The recollection of my children I have lost is killing me. . . . When I have news of you and learn, as I hope, that you are more fortunate than myself, I am at least only half-unhappy."

What would have been the feelings of this most noble and worthy of Christian bishops, who had surrendered family and children and happiness for the faith into which he had been attracted, had a prophetic vision disclosed to him that the only friend that had been left to him, his "mother, sister, benefactor," would soon become an unrecognisable mass of flesh and blood, pounded to jelly under the blows of the club of Peter the Reader — that her youthful, innocent body would be cut to pieces, "the flesh scraped from the bones" by oyster-shells, and the rest of her cast into the fire by order of the same Bishop Cyril he knew so well — Cyril, the CANONIZED Saint!! [113]

There has never been a religion in the annals of the world with such a bloody record as Christianity. All the rest, including the traditional fierce fights of the 'chosen people' with their next of kin, the idolatrous tribes of Israel, pale before the murderous fanaticism of the alleged followers of Christ! Even the rapid spread of Mohammedanism before the

112. See the historical romance of Canon Kingsley, *Hypatia*, for a highly picturesque account of the tragical fate of this young martyr.

113. We beg the reader to bear in mind that this is the same Cyril who was openly accused of simony, dishonesty, and the prostitution of his office to personal ends, and whom Neander (*Hist. Chr. Rel. and Church*, IV, p. 133, *sq.*) pictures as violent, tyrannical, a hypocrite and liar. Isidor, bishop of Pelusium, in a letter addressed to Cyril himself (I, ep. 370) wrote: "Let not the punishment, which you deem it necessary to inflict on mortal men *on account of personal grievances*, fall upon the living church. Prepare not the way for perpetual divisions of the church under the *pretense of piety*." Such was one of the first Christian saints — and the founder of the Trinity — as he appears on the pages of history.

conquering sword of the Islam prophet is a direct consequence of the
bloody riots and fights among Christians. It was the intestine war
between the Nestorians and Cyrilians that engendered Islamism; and
it is in the convent of Basra that the prolific seed was first sown by
Bahira, the Nestorian monk. Freely watered by rivers of blood, the
tree of Mecca has grown till we find it in the present century overshadowing nearly two hundred millions of people. The recent Bulgarian
atrocities are but the natural outgrowth of the triumph of Cyril and the
Mariolaters.

The cruel, crafty politician, the plotting monk, glorified by ecclesiastical history with the aureole of a martyred saint; the despoiled philosophers, the Neo-Platonists, and the Gnostics, daily anathematized by
the Church all over the world for long and dreary centuries; the curse of
the unconcerned Deity hourly invoked on the magian rites and theurgic
practice, and the Christian clergy themselves using *sorcery* for ages;
Hypatia, the glorious maiden-philosopher, torn to pieces by the Christian
mob; and such as Catherine de Médicis, Lucrezia Borgia, Joanna of
Naples, and the Isabellas of Spain, presented to the world as the faithful
daughters of the Church, some even decorated by the Pope with the
order of the 'Immaculate Rose,' the highest emblem of womanly purity
and virtue, a symbol sacred to the Virgin-mother of God! — such are the
examples of human justice! How far less blasphemous appears a total
rejection of Mary as an immaculate goddess, than an idolatrous worship
of her accompanied by such practices.

In the next chapter we shall present a few illustrations of sorcery,
as practised under the patronage of the Roman Church.

CHAPTER II

"They undertake by scales of miles to tell
The bounds, dimensions, and extent of hell;

Where bloated souls in smoky durance hung
Like a Westphalia gammon or neat's tongue,
To be redeemed with masses and a song."
— OLDHAM: *Satires upon the Jesuits:* 1679

"*York.*—But you are more inhuman, more inexorable —
O, ten times more — than tigers of Hyrcania."—*3 Henry VI*, I, iv

"*War.*—And hark ye, Sirs; because she is a maid
Spare for no faggots, let there be enow:
Place barrels of pitch upon the fatal stake."—*1 Henry VI*, V, iv

IN that famous work of Bodin on sorcery [114] a frightful story is told about Catherine de Médicis. The author was a learned publicist who, during twenty years of his life, collected authentic documents from the archives of nearly every important city of France, to make up a complete work on sorcery, magic, and the power of various 'demons.' To use an expression of Éliphas Lévi,[115] his book offers a most remarkable collection of "bloody and hideous facts; acts of revolting superstition, arrests, and executions of stupid ferocity. 'Burn everybody!' the Inquisition seemed to say — 'God will easily sort out His own!' Poor fools, hysterical women, and idiots were roasted alive without mercy for the crime of 'magic.' But at the same time how many great culprits escaped this unjust and sanguinary *justice!* This is what Bodin makes us fully appreciate."

Catherine the pious Christian — who has so well deserved in the eyes of the Church of Christ for the atrocious and never-to-be-forgotten massacre of St. Bartholomew's Day — the Queen Catherine kept in her service an apostate Jacobin priest. Well versed in the 'black art,' so fully patronized by the Medici family, he had won the gratitude and protection of his pious mistress through his unparalleled skill in killing people at a distance by torturing with various incantations their wax *simulacra.* The process has been described over and over again, and we scarcely need repeat it.

Charles was lying sick of an incurable disease. The queen-mother, who had everything to lose in case of his death, resorted to necromancy

---

114. *La démonomanie, ou traité des sorciers:* Paris, 1580 (often reprinted).
115. *Dogme et rituel de la haute magie,* Rit., ch. xv.

and consulted the oracle of the 'bleeding head.' This infernal operation required the decapitation of a child who must be possessed of great beauty and purity. He had been prepared in secret for his first communion by *the chaplain* of the palace, who was apprised of the plot, and at midnight of the appointed day, in the chamber of the sick man and in presence only of Catherine and a few of her confederates, the 'devil's mass' was celebrated. Let us give the rest of the story as we find it in one of Lévi's works: "At this mass, celebrated before the image of the demon having under his feet a reversed cross, the sorcerer consecrated two wafers, one black and one white. The white was given to the child, whom they brought clothed as for baptism, and who was murdered upon the very steps of the altar immediately after his communion. His head, separated from the trunk by a single blow, was placed all palpitating upon the great black wafer which covered the bottom of the paten, then placed upon a table where some mysterious lamps were burning. The exorcism then began, and the demon was charged to pronounce an oracle, and reply by the mouth of this head to a secret question that the king dared not speak aloud, and that had been confided to no one. Then a feeble voice, a strange voice, which had nothing of human character about it, made itself audible in this poor little martyr's head." [116] The sorcery availed nothing; the king died, and — Catherine remained the faithful daughter of Rome!

How strange that Des Mousseaux, who makes such free use of Bodin's materials to construct his formidable indictment against spiritualists and other sorcerers, should have overlooked this interesting episode!

It is a well-attested fact that Pope Sylvester II was publicly accused by Cardinal Benno with being a sorcerer and an enchanter. The brazen 'oracular head' made by his Holiness was of the same kind as the one fabricated by Albertus Magnus. The latter one was smashed to pieces by Thomas Aquinas, not because it was the work of or inhabited by a 'demon,' but because the spook who was fixed inside by mesmeric power talked incessantly, and his loquacity prevented the eloquent saint from working out his mathematical problems. These heads and other talking statues, trophies of the magical skill of monks and bishops, were facsimiles of the 'animated' gods of the ancient temples. The accusation against the Pope was proved at the time. It was also demonstrated that he was constantly attended by 'demons' or 'spirits.' In the preceding chapter we have mentioned Benedict IX, John XX, and the VIth and VIIth Gregory, who were all known as magicians. The last named Pope moreover was the famous Hildebrand, who was said to have been so expert at "shaking lightning out of his sleeve" — an expression

---

116. *Dogme et rituel, etc.,* loc. cit.

which the venerable spiritualistic writer, Mr. Howitt, thinks "was the origin of the celebrated thunder of the Vatican." [117]

The magical achievements of the Bishop of Ratisbon, and those of the 'angelic doctor' Thomas Aquinas, are too well known to need repetition; but we may explain further how the 'illusions' of the former were produced. If the Catholic bishop was so clever in making people believe on a bitter winter night that they were enjoying the delights of a splendid summer day, and in causing the icicles hanging from the boughs of the trees in the garden to seem like so many tropical fruits, the Hindû magicians also practise such psychological powers unto this very day, and claim the assistance of neither god nor devil. Such 'miracles' are all produced by the same human power that is inherent in every man, if he only knew how to develop it.

At about the time of the Reformation, the study of alchemy and magic had become so prevalent among the clergy as to produce great scandal. Cardinal Wolsey was openly accused before the court and the privy-council of confederacy with a man named Wood, a sorcerer, who said [on the authority of one William Neville, an inmate of the Cardinal's house] that "*My Lord Cardinale had suche a rynge that whatsomevere he askyd of the Kynges grace that he hadd yt;*" adding that "*Master Cromwell, when he . . . was servaunt in my lord cardynales housse,*" [was reported to owe his advancement to such arts and to his association with Wood, who further acknowledged himself to have] "*rede many bokes and specyally the boke of Salamon . . . and studied mettells and what vertues they had after the canon of Salamon.*" This case, with several others equally curious, is to be found among the Cromwell papers in the Record Office of the Rolls House. [118]

A priest named William Stapleton was arrested as a conjurer during the reign of Henry VIII, and an account of his adventures is still preserved in the Rolls House records. The Sicilian priest whom Benvenuto Cellini calls a necromancer, became famous through his successful conjurations, and was never molested. The remarkable adventure of Cellini with him in the Colosseum, where the priest conjured up a whole host of devils, is well known to the reading public. The subsequent meeting of Cellini with his mistress, as predicted and brought about by the conjurer, at the precise time fixed by him, is to be considered, as a matter of course, a 'curious coincidence.' [119] In the latter part of the sixteenth century there was hardly a parish to be found in which the priests did not study magic and alchemy. The practice of exorcism 'in imitation of Christ,' who by the way never used exorcism at all, led the clergy to devote them-

117. *Hist. of the Supernatural,* I, p. 483.
118. Thos. Wright: *Narr. of Sorcery and Magic,* I, pp. 203-4.   119. *Ibid.,* I, p. 219, *sq.*

selves openly to 'sacred' magic in contradistinction to black art, of which
latter crime were accused all those who were neither priests nor monks.

The occult knowledge gleaned by the Roman Church from the once
fat fields of theurgy she sedulously guarded for her own use, and sent to
the stake only those practitioners who 'poached' on her lands of the
Scientia Scientiarum, and those whose sins could not be concealed by the
friar's frock. The proof of this lies in the records of history. "In the
course of fifteen years only, between 1580 to 1595, and only in the single
province of Lorraine, the President Remigius burned 900 witches," says
Thomas Wright, in his *Sorcery and Magic*.[120] It was during these days,
prolific in ecclesiastical murder and unrivaled for cruelty and ferocity,
that Jean Bodin wrote.[121]

While the orthodox clergy called forth whole legions of 'demons'
through magical incantations, unmolested by the authorities provided
they held fast to the established dogmas and taught no heresy, on the
other hand acts of unparalleled atrocity were perpetrated on poor, unfortunate fools. Gabriel Malagrida, an old man of seventy, was burnt by
these evangelical Jack Ketches in 1761. In the Amsterdam library there
is a copy of the report of his famous trial, reprinted from the Lisbon report. He was accused of sorcery and illicit intercourse with the Devil,
who had "disclosed to him *futurity*." (?) The prophecy imparted by the
Arch-Enemy to the poor visionary Jesuit is reported in the following
terms: "The culprit hath confessed that the demon, under the form of
the blessed Virgin, having commanded him to write the life of Antichrist [?], told him that he, Malagrida, was a second John, but more clear
than John the Evangelist; that there were to be three Antichrists, and
that the last should be born at Milan, of a monk and a nun, in the year
1920; that he would marry Proserpine, one of the infernal furies," etc.

The prophecy is to be verified forty-three years hence. Even were all
the children born of monks and nuns really to become antichrists if
allowed to grow up to maturity, the fact would seem far less deplorable
than the discoveries made in so many convents when the foundations
have been removed for some reason. If the assertion of Luther is to be
disbelieved on account of his hatred for popery, then we may name discoveries of the same character made quite recently in Austrian and
Russian Poland. Luther [122] speaks of a fish-pond at Rome, situated near
a convent of nuns, which, having been cleared out by order of Pope
Gregory, disclosed at the bottom over six thousand infant skulls; and a
nunnery at Neinburg in Austria, whose foundations when searched disclosed the same relics of celibacy and chastity!

---

120. Vol. I, p. 300.   121. *La démonomanie, ou traité des sorciers.*
                               122. *Tischreden*, p. 307.

Ecclesia non novit sanguinem! meekly repeated the scarlet-robed cardinals. And to avoid the spilling of blood which horrified them, they instituted the Holy Inquisition. If, as the occultists maintain, and science half confirms, our most trifling acts and thoughts are indelibly impressed upon the eternal mirror of the astral ether, there must be somewhere, in the boundless realm of the unseen universe, the imprint of a curious picture. It is that of a gorgeous standard waving in the heavenly breeze at the foot of the great 'white throne' of the Almighty — on its crimson damask face a cross, symbol of 'the Son of God who died for mankind,' with an *olive* branch on one side, and a sword, stained to the hilt with human gore, on the other; a legend selected from the *Psalms* emblazoned in golden letters, reading thus: *Exurge, Domine, et judica causam meam.* For such appears the standard of the Inquisition, on a photograph in our possession, from an original procured at the Escorial of Madrid.

Under this Christian standard, in the brief space of fourteen years, Tomas de Torquemada, the confessor of Queen Isabella, burned over ten thousand persons, and sentenced to the torture eighty thousand more. Orobio, the well-known writer, who was detained so long in prison, and who hardly escaped the flames of the Inquisition, immortalized this institution in his works when once at liberty in Holland. He found no better argument against the Holy Church than to embrace the Judaic faith and submit even to circumcision. "In the cathedral of Saragossa," says a writer on the Inquisition, "is the tomb of a famous inquisitor. Six pillars surround the tomb; *to each is chained a Moor*, as preparatory to being burned. On this St. Foix ingenuously observes: 'If ever the Jack Ketch of any country should be rich enough to have a splendid tomb, this might serve as an excellent model!'" [123] To make it complete, however, the builders of the tomb ought not to have omitted a bas-relief of the famous horse which was burnt for sorcery and witchcraft. Granger tells the story, describing it as having occurred in his time. The poor animal "had been taught to tell the spots upon cards, and the hour of the day by the watch. Horse and owner were both indicted by the sacred office for dealing with the Devil, and both were burned, with a great ceremony of *auto-da-fé* at Lisbon in 1601, as wizards!" [124]

This immortal institution of Christianity did not remain without its Dante to sing its praise. "Macedo, a Portuguese Jesuit," says the author of *Demonologia*, "has discovered the origin of the Inquisition in the terrestrial Paradise, and presumes to allege that God was the first who began the functions of an inquisitor over Cain and the workmen of Babel!" [124a]

Nowhere during the Middle Ages were the arts of magic and sorcery

123. *Demonologia*, p. 302.   124. Jas. Granger: *Biogr. Hist. of England*: 1769.
124a. *Op. cit.*, p. 306.

more practised by the clergy than in Spain and Portugal. The Moors were profoundly versed in the occult sciences, and at Toledo, Seville, and Salamanca there were, once upon a time, great schools of magic. The kabalists of the latter town were skilled in all the abstruse sciences; they knew the virtues of precious stones and other minerals, and had extracted from alchemy its most profound secrets.

The authentic documents pertaining to the great trial of the Maréchale d'Ancre, during the regency of Marie de Médicis, disclose that the unfortunate woman perished through the fault of the priests with whom, like a true Italian, she surrounded herself. She was accused by the people of Paris of sorcery, because it had been asserted that she had used, after the ceremony of exorcism, newly-killed white cocks. Believing herself constantly bewitched, and being in very delicate health, the Maréchale had the ceremony of exorcism publicly applied to herself in the Church of the Augustines; as to the birds, she used them as an application to the forehead on account of dreadful pains in the head, and had been advised to do so by Montalto, the Jew physician of the queen, and by the Italian priests.

In the sixteenth century the Cura de Bargota of the diocese of Callahora, Spain, became the world's wonder for his magical powers. His most extraordinary feat consisted, it was said, in transporting himself to any distant country, witnessing political and other events, and then returning home to predict them in his own country. He had a familiar demon, who served him faithfully for long years, says the *Chronicle*, but the *cura* turned ungrateful and cheated him. Having been apprised by his demon of a conspiracy against the Pope's life, in consequence of an intrigue of the latter with a fair lady, the *cura* transported himself to Rome (in his double, of course) and thus saved his Holiness' life. After which he repented, confessed his sins to the gallant Pope, and *got absolution*. "On his return he was delivered, as a matter of form, into the custody of the inquisitors of Logroño, but was acquitted and restored to his liberty very soon." [125]

Friar Pietro, a Dominican monk of the fourteenth century — the magician who presented the famous Dr. Eugenio Torralva, a physician attached to the house of the admiral of Castile, with a *demon* named Zequiel — won his fame through the subsequent trial of Torralva. The procedure and circumstances attendant upon the extraordinary trial are described in the original papers preserved in the Archives of the Inquisition. The Cardinal of Volterra, and the Cardinal of Santa Cruz, bot'₁ saw and communicated with Zequiel, who proved, during the whole ₁ Torralva's life, to be a pure, kind, elemental spirit, doing many benefice —

125. Thos. Wright: *Narratives of Sorcery and Magic*, II, xx, xviii.

actions and remaining faithful to the physician to the last hour of his life. Even the Inquisition acquitted Torralva on that account; and although an immortality of fame was insured to him by the satire of Cervantes, neither Torralva nor the monk Pietro are fictitious heroes, but historical personages, recorded in ecclesiastical documents of Rome and Cuenca, in which town the trial of the physician took place in the years 1528 to 1530.[126]

The book of Dr. W. G. Soldan, of Stuttgart, has become as famous in Germany as Bodin's book on *Demonomania* in France. It is the most complete German treatise on sixteenth century witchcraft. One interested in learning the secret machinery underlying these thousands of legal murders, perpetrated by a clergy who pretended to believe in the Devil, and succeeded in making others believe in him, will find it divulged in the above-mentioned work.[127] The true origin of the daily accusations and death-sentences for sorcery are cleverly traced to personal and political enmities, and above all to the hatred of the Catholics toward the Protestants. The crafty work of the Jesuits is seen at every page of the bloody tragedies; and it is in Bamberg and Würzburg, where these worthy sons of Loyola were most powerful at that time, that the cases of witchcraft were most numerous. On the next page we give a curious list of some victims, many of whom were children between the ages of seven and eight years, and Protestants. "Of the multitudes of persons who perished at the stake in Germany during the first half of the seventeenth century for sorcery, the crime of many was their attachment to the religion of Luther," says T. Wright, ". . . and the petty princes were not unwilling to seize upon any pretense to fill their coffers . . . the persons most persecuted being those whose property was a matter of consideration. . . . At Bamberg, as well as at Würzburg, the bishop was a sovereign prince in his dominions. The Prince-Bishop, John George II, who ruled Bamberg . . . after several unsuccessful attempts to root out Lutheranism, distinguished his reign by a series of sanguinary witch-trials, which disgrace the annals of that city. . . . We may form some notion of the proceedings of his worthy agent [128] from the statement of the most authentic historians of this city that between 1625 and 1630 not less than 900 trials took place in the two courts of Bamberg and Zeil; and a pamphlet published at Bamberg by authority in 1659 states the number of persons, whom Bishop John George had caused to be burned for sorcery, to have been 600." [129]

126. *Narratives of Sorcery and Magic*, II, xviii.
127. *Geschichte der Hexenprocesse, aus den Quellen dargestellt:* Stuttgart, 1843.
128. Frederick Forner, Suffragan of Bamberg, author of a treatise against heretics and sorcerers, under the title of *Panoplia armaturae Dei*.
129. *Sorcery and Magic*, by T. Wright, M. A., F. S. A., etc., Corresponding Member of the National Institute of France, II, pp. 183-5.

Regretting that space prevents our giving one of the most curious
lists in the world of burned witches, we will nevertheless make a few
extracts from the original record as printed in Hauber's *Bibliotheca
magica*. One glance at this horrible catalog of murders in Christ's
name is sufficient to show that out of 162 persons burned, more than
one-half of them are designated as *strangers* (*i. e.*, Protestants) in this
hospitable town; and of the other half we find *thirty-four children*, the
oldest of whom was fourteen, the youngest *an infant* child of Dr. Schütz.
To make the catalog shorter we will present of each of the twenty-nine
burnings, only the most remarkable.[130]

IN THE FIRST BURNING, FOUR PERSONS

Old Ancker's widow.
The wife of Liebler.
The wife of Gutbrodt.
The wife of Höcker.

IN THE SECOND BURNING, FOUR PERSONS

Two strange women (names unknown).
The old wife of Beutler.

IN THE THIRD BURNING, FIVE PERSONS

Tungersleber, a minstrel.
Four wives of citizens.

IN THE FOURTH BURNING, FIVE PERSONS

A strange man.

IN THE FIFTH BURNING, NINE PERSONS

Lutz, an eminent shop-keeper.
The wife of Baunach, a senator.

IN THE SIXTH BURNING, SIX PERSONS

The fat tailor's wife.
A strange man.
A strange woman.

---

130. Besides these burnings in Germany, which amount to many thousands, we find
some very interesting statements in Prof. Draper's *Conflict between Religion and Science*.
On page 146, he says: "The families of the convicted were plunged into irretrievable
ruin. Llorente, the historian of the Inquisition, computes that Torquemada and his
collaborators, in the course of eighteen years, burned at the stake 10,220 persons,
6,860 in effigy, and otherwise punished 97,321! . . . With unutterable disgust and
indignation, we learn that the papal government realised much money by selling to
the rich dispensations to secure them from the Inquisition."

IN THE SEVENTH BURNING, SEVEN PERSONS

A strange girl of twelve years old.
A strange man, a strange woman.
A strange bailiff (Schultheiss).
Three strange women.

IN THE EIGHTH BURNING, SEVEN PERSONS

Baunach, a senator, the fattest citizen in Würzburg.
A strange man.
Two strange women.

IN THE NINTH BURNING, FIVE PERSONS

A strange man.
A mother and daughter.

IN THE TENTH BURNING, THREE PERSONS

Steinacher, a very rich man.
A strange man, a strange woman.

IN THE ELEVENTH BURNING, FOUR PERSONS

Two women and two men.

IN THE TWELFTH BURNING, TWO PERSONS

Two strange women.

IN THE THIRTEENTH BURNING, FOUR PERSONS

A little girl nine or ten years old.
A younger girl, her little sister.

IN THE FOURTEENTH BURNING, TWO PERSONS

The mother of the two little girls before mentioned.
A girl twenty-four years old.

IN THE FIFTEENTH BURNING, TWO PERSONS

A boy twelve years of age, in the first school.
A woman.

IN THE SIXTEENTH BURNING, SIX PERSONS

A boy of ten years of age.

IN THE SEVENTEENTH BURNING, FOUR PERSONS

A boy eleven years old.
A mother and daughter.

IN THE EIGHTEENTH BURNING, SIX PERSONS

Two boys, twelve years old.
The daughter of Dr. Junge.
A girl of fifteen years of age.
A strange woman.

IN THE NINETEENTH BURNING, SIX PERSONS

A boy of ten years of age.
Another boy, twelve years old.

IN THE TWENTIETH BURNING, SIX PERSONS

Göbel's child, the most beautiful girl in Würzburg.
Two boys, each twelve years old.
Stepper's little daughter.

IN THE TWENTY-FIRST BURNING, SIX PERSONS

A boy fourteen years old.
The little son of Senator Stolzenberger.
Two alumni.

IN THE TWENTY-SECOND BURNING, SIX PERSONS

Stürman, a rich cooper.
A strange boy.

IN THE TWENTY-THIRD BURNING, NINE PERSONS

David Croten's boy, nine years old.
The two sons of the prince's cook, one fourteen, the other ten years old.

IN THE TWENTY-FOURTH BURNING, SEVEN PERSONS

Two boys in the hospital.
A rich cooper.

IN THE TWENTY-FIFTH BURNING, SIX PERSONS

A strange boy.

IN THE TWENTY-SIXTH BURNING, SEVEN PERSONS

Weydenbush, a senator.
The little daughter of Valkenberger.
The little son of the town council bailiff.

IN THE TWENTY-SEVENTH BURNING, SEVEN PERSONS

A strange boy.
A strange woman.
Another boy.

IN THE TWENTY-EIGHTH BURNING, SIX PERSONS

The infant daughter of Dr. Schütz.

A blind girl.

IN THE TWENTY-NINTH BURNING, SEVEN PERSONS

The fat noble lady (*Edelfrau*).

A doctor of divinity.

Item

	'Strange' men and women, *i. e., Protestants,*	28
Summary:	Citizens, apparently all WEALTHY people,	100
	Boys, girls, and little children,	34
	In nineteen months,	162 persons

"There were," says Wright, "little girls of from seven to ten years of age among the witches, and *seven and twenty* of them were convicted and burnt," at some of the other *brände*, or burnings. "The numbers brought to trial in these terrible proceedings were so great, and they were treated with so little consideration, that it was usual not even to take the trouble of setting down their names, but they were cited as the accused No. 1, No. 2, No. 3, and so on. The Jesuits took their confessions in private." [131]

What room is there in a theology which exacts such holocausts as these to appease the bloody appetites of its priests, for the following gentle words:

"Suffer the little children to come unto me, and forbid them not: for of such is the kingdom of heaven." "Even so it is not the will of your Father . . . that one of these little ones should perish." "But whoso shall offend one of these little ones which believe in me, it *were better for him that a millstone were hanged* about his neck and that he were drowned in the depth of the sea."

We sincerely hope that the above words have proved no vain threat to these child-burners.

Did this butchery in the name of their Moloch-god prevent these treasure-hunters from resorting to the black art themselves? Not in the least; for in no class were such consulters of 'familiar' spirits more numerous than among the clergy during the fifteenth, sixteenth, and seventeenth centuries. True, there were some Catholic priests among the victims, but though these were generally accused of having "been

---

131. *Sorcery and Magic;* 'The Burnings at Würzburg,' II, p. 186.

led into practices too dreadful to be described," it was not so. In the twenty-nine burnings above catalogued we find the names of *twelve vicars, four* canons, and two doctors of divinity *burnt alive.* But we have only to turn to such works as were published at the time to assure ourselves that each popish priest executed was accused of "damnable heresy," *i. e.,* a tendency to reformation — a crime more heinous far than sorcery.

We refer those who would learn how the Catholic clergy united duty with pleasure in the matter of exorcisms, revenge, and treasure-hunting, to volume II, chapter i, of Wm. Howitt's *History of the Supernatural.* "In what came to be called *pneumatologia occulta et vera,* all the forms of adjuration and conjuration were laid down," says this veteran writer. He then proceeds to give a long description of the favorite *modus operandi.* The *Dogme et rituel de la haute magie* of the late Éliphas Lévi, treated with so much abuse and contempt by Des Mousseaux, tells nothing of the weird ceremonies and practices but what was practised legally and with the tacit if not open consent of the Church, by the priests of the Middle Ages. The exorcist-priest entered a circle at midnight; he was clad in a new surplice, and had a consecrated band hanging from the neck, covered with sacred characters. He wore on the head a tall pointed cap, on the front of which was written in Hebrew the holy word, the Tetragrammaton — the ineffable name. It was written with a new pen dipped in the blood of a white dove. What the exorcists most yearned after, was to release miserable spirits *which haunt spots where hidden treasures lie.* The exorcist sprinkles the circle with the blood of a black lamb and a white pigeon. The priest had to adjure the evil spirits of hell — Acheront, Magoth, Asmodei, Beelzebub, Belial, and all the damned souls, in the mighty names of Jehovah, Adonai, Elohah, and Sabaoth, which latter was the God of Abraham, Isaac, and Jacob, who dwelt in the Urim and Thummim. When the damned souls flung in the face of the exorcist that he was a sinner, and could not get the treasure from them, the priest-sorcerer had to reply that "all his sins were washed out in the blood of Christ,[132] and he bid them depart as cursed ghosts and damned flies." When the exorcist dislodged them at last, the poor soul was "comforted in the name of the Savior, and *consigned to the care of good angels,*" who were less powerful, we must think, than the exorcizing Catholic worthies, "and the rescued treasure, of course, was secured for the Church."

"Certain days," adds Howitt, "are laid down in the calendar of

---

132. And retinted in the blood of the millions murdered in his name — in the no less innocent blood than his own, of the little child-*witches!*

the Church as most favorable for the practice of exorcism; and, if the devils are difficult to drive, a fume of sulphur, assafoetida, bear's gall, and rue is recommended, which, it was presumed, would outstench even devils." [133]

This is the Church, and this the priesthood, which in the nineteenth century pays 5000 priests to teach the people of the United States the infidelity of science and the infallibility of the Bishop of Rome!

We have already noticed the confession of an eminent prelate that the elimination of Satan from theology would be fatal to the perpetuity of the Church. But this is only partially true. The Prince of Sin would be gone, but sin itself would survive. If the Devil were annihilated, the *Articles of Faith* and the *Bible* would remain. In short there would still be a pretended divine revelation, and the necessity for self-assumed inspired interpreters. We must, therefore, consider the authenticity of the *Bible* itself. We must study its pages, and see if they indeed contain the commands of the Deity, or but a compendium of ancient traditions and hoary myths. We must try to interpret them for ourselves — if possible. As to its pretended interpreters, the only possible similitude we can find for them in the *Bible* is to compare them with the man described by the wise King Solomon in his *Proverbs* as the possessor of these "six things . . . yea *seven* . . . which the Lord doth hate," and which are an abomination unto Him, to wit: "A *proud* look, a *lying* tongue, and hands that shed *innocent blood;* a heart *that deviseth wicked imaginations*, feet that be swift in running to mischief; a *false witness* that speaketh lies, and *he that soweth discord among brethren*" (*Proverbs*, vi, 16-19).

Of which of these are the long line of men who have left the imprint of their feet in the Vatican guiltless?

"When the demons," says Augustine, "*insinuate* themselves in the creatures, they begin by conforming themselves *to the will of every one.* . . . In order to attract men, they begin by seducing them, by simulating obedience. . . . *How could one know, had he not been taught by the demons themselves*, what they like or what they hate; *the name which attracts, or that which forces them into obedience;* all this art, in short, of *magic*, the whole science of the magicians?" [134]

To this impressive dissertation of the 'saint,' we will add that no magician has ever denied that he had learned the *art* from 'spirits,' whether, being a medium, they acted independently on him, or he had

133. *Hist. of the Supernatural*, II, pp. 13-16.
134. Augustine: *The City of God*, XXI, vi;
Des Mousseaux: *Mœurs et pratiques des démons*, p. 181.

been initiated into the science of 'evocation' by his fathers who knew it before himself. But who was it then that taught the exorcist? The priest who clothes himself with an authority not only over the magician, but even over all these 'spirits,' whom he calls demons and *devils* as soon as he finds them obeying any one but himself? He must have learned somewhere from some one that power which he pretends to possess. For, ". . . *how could one know had he not been taught by the demons themselves . . . the name which attracts, or that which forces them into obedience?*" asks Augustine.

Useless to remark that we know the answer beforehand: "Revelation . . . *divine* gift . . . the Son of God; nay, God Himself, through His direct Spirit, who descended on the apostles as the Pentecostal fire," and who is now alleged to overshadow every priest who sees fit to exorcize for either glory or a gift. Are we then to believe that the recent scandal of public exorcism, performed about the 14th of October 1876, by the senior priest of the Church of the Holy Spirit, at Barcelona, Spain, was also done under the direct superintendence of the Holy Ghost? [135] It will be urged that the "bishop was not

---

135. A correspondent of the London *Times* describes the Catalonian exorcist in the following lines:

"About the 14th of October it was privately announced that a young woman of seventeen or eighteen years of age, of the lower class, having long been afflicted with 'a hatred of holy things,' the senior priest of the Church of the Holy Spirit would cure her of her disease. The exhibition was to be held in a church frequented by the best part of the community. The church was dark, but a sickly light was shed by wax lights on the sable forms of some eighty or a hundred persons who clustered round the *presbiterio*, or sanctuary, in front of the altar. Within the little enclosure or sanctuary, separated from the crowd by a light railing, lay on a common bench, with a little pillow for her head to recline upon, a poorly-clad girl, probably of the peasant or artisan class; her brother or husband stood at her feet to restrain her (at times) frantic kicking by holding her legs. The door of the vestry opened; the exhibitor — I mean the priest — came in. The poor girl, not without just reason, 'had an aversion to holy things,' or at least the 400 devils within her distorted body had such an aversion, and in the confusion of the moment, thinking that the father was 'a holy thing,' she doubled up her legs, screamed out with twitching mouth, her whole body writhing, and threw herself nearly off the bench. The male attendant seized her legs, the women supported her head and swept out her disheveled hair. The priest advanced and, mingling familiarly with the shuddering and horror-struck crowd, said, pointing at the suffering child, now sobbing and twitching on the bench, 'Promise me, my children, that you will be prudent (*prudentes*), and of a truth, sons and daughters mine, you shall see marvels.' The promise was given. The exhibitor went to procure stole and short surplice (*estola y roquete*), and returned in a moment, taking his stand at the side of the 'possessed with the devils,' with his face toward the group of students. The order of the day's proceedings was a lecture to the bystanders, and the operation of exorcising the devils. 'You know,' said the priest, 'that so great is this girl's aversion to holy things, myself included, that she goes into convulsions, kicks, screams and distorts her body the moment she arrives at the corner of this street, and her convulsive struggles reach their climax when she enters the sacred house of the Most High.' Turning to the prostrate, shuddering, most unhappy object of his attack, the priest commenced: 'In the name of

cognisant of this freak of the clergy"; but even if he were, how could he have protested against a rite considered since the days of the apostles one of the most holy prerogatives of the Church of Rome? So late as in 1852, only twenty-five years ago, these rites received a public and solemn sanction from the Vatican, and a new *Ritual of Exorcism* was published in Rome, Paris, and other Catholic capitals. Des Mousseaux, writing under the immediate patronage of Father Ventura, the General of the Theatines of Rome, even favors us with lengthy extracts from this famous ritual, and explains the reason *why* it was enforced again. It was in consequence of the revival of Magic under the name of Modern Spiritualism.[136] The bull of Pope Innocent VIII is exhumed and translated for the benefit of Des Mousseaux's readers. "We have heard," exclaims the Sovereign Pontiff, "that a great number of persons of both sexes have feared not to enter into relations with the spirits of hell; and that, by their practice of sorcery . . . they strike with sterility the conjugal bed, destroy the germs of humanity in the bosom of the mother, and throw spells on them, and set a barrier to the multiplication of animals . . . etc., etc."; then follow curses and anathemas against the practice.[137]

This belief of the Sovereign Pontiffs of an enlightened Christian country is a direct inheritance from the most ignorant multitudes of the southern Hindû rabble — the 'heathen.' The diabolical arts of certain *kangâlins* (witches) and *jâdûgars* (sorcerers) are firmly believed in by these people. The following are among their most dreaded powers: to inspire love and hatred at will; to send a devil to take possession of a person and torture him; to expel him; to cause sudden death

---

God, of the saints, of the blessed Host, of every holy sacrament of our Church, I adjure thee, Rusbel, come out of her.' (N. B. 'Rusbel' is the name of a devil, the devil having 257 names in Catalonia.) Thus adjured, the girl threw herself — in an agony of convulsion, till her distorted face, foam-bespattered lips and writhing limbs grew well-nigh stiff — at full length upon the floor, and in language semi-obscene, semi-violent, screamed out, 'I don't choose to come out, you thieves, scamps, robbers.' At last, from the quivering lips of the girl, came the words, 'I will'; but the devil added, with traditional perversity, 'I will cast the 100 out, but by the mouth of the girl.' The priest objected. The exit, he said, of 100 devils out of the small Spanish mouth of the woman would 'leave her suffocated.' Then the maddened girl said she must undress herself for the devils to escape. This petition the holy father refused. 'Then I will come out through the right foot, but first' — the girl had on a hempen sandal, she was obviously of the poorest class — 'you must take off her sandal.' The sandal was untied; the foot gave a convulsive plunge; the devil and his myrmidons (so the *cura* said, looking round triumphantly) had gone to their own place. And assured of this the wretched dupe of a girl lay quite still. The bishop was not cognisant of this freak of the clergy, and the moment it came to the ears of the civil authorities, the sharpest means were taken to prevent a repetition of the scandal."

136. *La magie au XIXme siècle*, p. 138, *sq.*
137. *Mœurs et pratiques des démons*, p. 175.

or an incurable disease; to either strike cattle with or protect them from
epidemics; to compose philters that will either strike with sterility or pro-
voke unbounded passions in men and women, etc., etc. The sight alone
of a man said to be such a sorcerer excites in a Hindû profound terror.

And now we will quote in this connexion the truthful remark of a
writer who passed years in India in the study of the origin of such superstitions: "Vulgar magic in India, like a degenerated infiltration, goes
hand-in-hand with the most ennobling beliefs of the sectarians of the
Pitris. It was the *work of the lowest clergy*, and designed to hold the
populace in a perpetual state of fear. It is thus that in all ages and
under every latitude, side by side with philosophical speculations of the
highest character, one always finds *the religion of the rabble*." [138]   In
India it was the work of the *lowest clergy;* in Rome, that of the *highest
Pontiffs*. But then, have they not as authority their greatest saint,
Augustine, who declares that "whoever believes not in the evil spirits,
refuses to believe in Holy Writ?" [139]

Therefore, in the second half of the nineteenth century we find the
counsel for the Sacred Congregation of Rites (exorcism of demons included), Father Ventura de Raulica, writing thus, in a letter published
by Des Mousseaux in 1865:

"We are in full magic! and, under false names, the Spirit of lies and impudicity
goes on perpetrating his horrible depredations. . . . The most grievous feature in this
is that even among the most serious persons they do not attach the importance to the
strange phenomena which they deserve, these manifestations that we witness, and which
become with every day more weird, striking, as well as most fatal.

"I cannot sufficiently admire and praise, from this standpoint, the zeal and courage
displayed by you in your work. The facts which you have collected are calculated to
throw light and conviction into the most skeptical minds; and after reading this remarkable work, written with so much learnedness and conscientiousness, blindness is
no longer possible.

"If anything could surprise us, it would be the indifference with which these phenomena have been treated by *false* Science, endeavoring, as she has, to turn into ridicule
so grave a subject; the childish simplicity exhibited by her in the desire to explain the
facts by absurd and contradictory hypotheses. . . . [140]

[Signed]   "*Father Ventura de Raulica*, etc., etc."

Thus encouraged by the greatest authorities of the Church of Rome,
ancient and modern, the Chevalier argues the necessity and the efficacy
of exorcism by the priests. He tries to demonstrate — *on faith*, as usual
— that the power of the spirits of hell is closely related to certain rites,

---

138. L. Jacolliot: *Le spiritisme, etc.*, p. 162.
139. Augustine: *The City of God*, XXI, vi.
140. *Mœurs, etc.*, p. ii (ed. 1865); also *La magie au XIXme siècle*, p. 115.

words and formal signs. "In the diabolical Catholicism," he says, "as well as in the *divine* Catholicism, potential grace is *bound* (*liée*) to certain signs." While the power of the Catholic priest proceeds from God, that of the Pagan priest proceeds from the Devil. The Devil, he adds, "is forced to submission" before the holy minister of God — "*he dares not* LIE." [141]

We beg the reader to note well the underlined sentence, as we mean to test its truth impartially. We are prepared to adduce proofs, undeniable and undenied even by the Popish Church — forced, as she was, into the confession — proofs of hundreds of cases in relation to the most solemn of her dogmas, wherein the 'spirits' lied from beginning to end. How about certain holy relics authenticated by visions of the blessed Virgin, and a host of saints? We have at hand a treatise by a pious Catholic, Guibert de Nogent, on the relics of saints. With honest despair he acknowledges the "great number of false relics, as well as false legends," and severely censures the inventors of these lying miracles. "It was on the occasion *of one of our Savior's teeth*," writes the author of *Demonologia*, "that de Nogent took up his pen on this subject, by which the monks of St. Médard de Soissons pretended to work miracles; a pretension which he asserted to be as chimerical as that of several persons who believed they possessed the navel, and other parts less comely, of the body of Christ." [142]

"A monk of St. Antony," says Stephens,[143] "having been at Jerusalem, saw there several relics, among which was a bit of *the finger of the Holy Ghost*, as sound and entire as it had ever been; the snout of the seraph that appeared to St. Francis; one of the nails of a cherub; one of the ribs of the *Verbum caro factum* (the Word made flesh); some rays of the star that appeared to the three kings of the East; a phial of St. Michael's sweat, that exuded when he was fighting against the Devil, etc. 'All which things,' observes the monkish treasurer of relics, 'I have brought home with me very devoutly.' "

And if the foregoing is set aside as the invention of a Protestant enemy, may we not be allowed to refer the reader to the history of England and authentic documents which state the existence of a relic not less extraordinary than the best of the others? Henry III received from the Grand Master of the Templars a phial containing a small portion of the sacred blood of Christ which he had shed upon the cross. It was attested to be genuine by the seals of the Patriarch of Jerusalem and others. The procession bearing the sacred phial from St. Paul's to

---

141. Des Mousseaux: *Mœurs, etc.*, p. 431; also ch. xv, etc.
142. *Demonologia*, p. 432: London, 1831.
143. 'Apologia pro Herodotum,' in H. Stephens' edit. of Herodotus, c. 39.

Westminster Abbey is described by the historian: "Two monks received
the phial, and deposited it in the Abbey . . . which made all England
shine with glory, dedicating it to God and St. Edward." [144]

The story of the Prince Radzivill is well known. It was the undeniable deception of the monks and nuns surrounding him and his own
confessor which made the Polish nobleman become a Lutheran. He felt
at first so indignant at the 'heresy' of the Reformation spreading in
Lithuania, that he traveled all the way to Rome to pay his homage of
sympathy and veneration to the Pope. The latter presented him with a
precious box of relics. On his return home his confessor saw the Virgin,
who descended from her glorious abode for the sole purpose of blessing
these relics and authenticating them. The superior of the neighboring
convent and the mother-abbess of a nunnery both saw the same vision,
with a re-enforcement of several saints and martyrs; they prophesied
and "felt the Holy Ghost" ascending from the box of relics and overshadowing the prince. A demoniac provided for the purpose by the
clergy was exorcized in full ceremony, and upon being touched by the box
immediately recovered, and rendered thanks on the spot to the Pope and
the Holy Ghost. After the ceremony was over the guardian of the
treasury in which the relics were kept, threw himself at the feet of the
prince, and confessed that on their way back from Rome he had lost the
box of relics. Dreading the wrath of his master, he had procured a similar
box, "which he had filled with the small bones of dogs and cats"; but
seeing how the prince was deceived, he preferred confessing his guilt to
such blasphemous tricks. The prince said nothing, but continued for
some time testing — not the relics, but his confessor and the vision-seers.
Their mock raptures made him discover so thoroughly the gross imposi-
tions of the monks and nuns that he joined the Reformed Church.

This is history. Bayle [145] shows that when the Roman Church is no
longer able to deny that there have been false relics, she resorts to sophistry, and replies that if false relics have wrought miracles it is "because of
the good intentions of the believers, who thus obtained from God a reward
of their good faith!" The same Bayle shows, by numerous instances,
that whenever it was proved that several bodies of the same saint, or
three heads of him, or three arms (as in the case of Augustine) were said
to exist in different places, and that they could not well be all authentic,
the cool and invariable answer of the Church was that they were all
genuine; for "God had multiplied and miraculously reproduced them
for the greater glory of His Holy Church!" In other words they would
have the faithful believe that the body of a deceased saint may, through
divine miracle, acquire the physiological peculiarities of a crawfish!

---

144. *Demonologia*, p. 436.   145. *Dict. hist. et crit.*

We fancy that it would be hard to demonstrate to satisfaction that the visions of Catholic saints are, in any one particular instance, better or more trustworthy than the average visions and prophecies of our modern 'mediums.' The visions of Andrew Jackson Davis — however our critics may sneer at them — are by long odds more philosophical and more compatible with modern science than the Augustinian speculations. Whenever the visions of Swedenborg, the greatest among the modern seers, run astray from philosophy and scientific truth, it is when they most nearly run parallel with theology. Nor are these visions any more useless to either science or humanity than those of the great orthodox saints. In the life of St. Bernard it is narrated that as he was once in church, upon a Christmas eve, he prayed that the very hour in which Christ was born might be revealed to him; and when the "true and correct hour came, he saw the divine babe appear in his manger." What a pity that the divine babe did not embrace so favorable an opportunity to fix the correct day and year of his death, and thereby reconcile the controversies of his putative historians. The Tischendorfs, Lardners, and Colensos, as well as many a Catholic divine, who have vainly squeezed the marrow out of historical records and their own brains, in the useless search, would at least have had something for which to thank the saint.

As it is, we are hopelessly left to infer that most of the beatific and divine visions of *The Golden Legend,* and those to be found in the more complete biographies of the most important 'saints,' as well as most of the visions of our own persecuted seers and seeresses, were produced by ignorant and undeveloped 'spirits' passionately fond of personating great historical characters. We are quite ready to agree with the Chevalier Des Mousseaux, and other unrelenting persecutors of magic and spiritualism in the name of the Church, that modern spirits are often 'lying spirits'; that they are ever on hand to humor the respective hobbies of the persons who communicate with them at 'circles'; that they *deceive* them and, therefore, are not *always* good 'spirits.'

But having conceded so much we will now ask of any impartial person: is it possible to believe at the same time that the *power* given to the exorcist-priest, that supreme and *divine* power of which he boasts, has been given to him by God for the purpose of deceiving people? and that the prayer pronounced by him *in the name of Christ,* and which, forcing the *demon* into submission, makes him reveal himself, is calculated at the same time to make the devil confess *not the truth,* but that only which it is the *interest of the church to which the exorcist belongs,* should *pass for truth?* And this is what invariably happens. Compare for instance the responses given by the demon to Luther, with those obtained from the devils by St. Dominic. The one argues against the

private mass, and upbraids Luther with placing the Virgin Mary and
saints before Christ, and thus dishonoring the Son of God; [146] while the
demons exorcized by St. Dominic, upon seeing the Virgin whom the
holy father had also evoked to help him, roar out: "Oh! our enemy!
oh! our damner! . . . why didst thou descend from heaven to torment us?
Why art thou so powerful an intercessor for sinners! Oh! *thou most
certain and secure way to heaven* . . . thou commandest us *and we are
forced to confess* that nobody is damned who only perseveres in thy holy
worship, etc., etc." [147] Luther's "Saint Satan" assures him that while
believing in the transubstantiation of Christ's body and blood he had
been worshiping merely bread and wine; and the *devils* of all the Catholic
saints promise *eternal damnation* to whomsoever disbelieves or even so
much as doubts the dogma!

Before leaving the subject, let us give one or two more instances from
Alban Butler's *The Lives of the Fathers, Martyrs and other principal Saints*,
selected from such narratives as are fully accepted by the Church. We
might fill volumes with proofs of undeniable confederacy between the
exorcizers and the demons. Their very nature betrays them. Instead of
being independent, crafty entities bent on the destruction of men's souls
and spirits, the majority of them are simply the elementals of the kabalists; creatures with no intellect of their own, but faithful mirrors of the
WILL which evokes, controls, and guides them. We will not waste our
time in drawing the reader's attention to doubtful or obscure thaumaturgists and exorcizers, but take as our standard one of the greatest
saints of Catholicism, and select a bouquet from that same prolific conservatory of pious lies, *The Golden Legend*, of James de Voragine. [148]

St. Dominic, the founder of the famous order of that name, is one of
the mightiest saints on the calendar. His order was the first that received
a solemn confirmation from the Pope, [149] and he is well known in history
as the associate and counsellor of the infamous Simon de Montfort, the
papal general, whom he helped to butcher the unfortunate Albigenses in
and near Toulouse. The story goes that this saint and the Church after
him claim that he received from the Virgin, *in propriâ personâ*, a rosary
whose virtues produced such stupendous miracles that they threw entirely into the shade those of the apostles, and even of Jesus himself. A man,
says the biographer, an abandoned sinner, was bold enough to doubt the

---

146. Told by Luther in *De missâ privatâ et unctione sacerdotum.*
147. See the *Life of St. Dominic,* and the story about the miraculous rosary; *The Golden
Legend;* also J. Bollandus, S. J.: *Acta sanctorum,* Augusti, tom. XXXV, pp. 409, 410: Paris.
148. James de Varasse, known by the Latin name of Jacobus de Voragine, was Vicar
General of the Dominicans and Bishop of Genoa in 1290.
149. Thirteenth century.

virtue of the Dominican rosary; and for this unparalleled blasphemy was punished on the spot by having 15,000 devils take possession of him. Seeing the great suffering of the tortured demoniac, St. Dominic forgot the insult and called the devils to account.[149a]

Following is the colloquy between the 'blessed exorcist' and the demons:

Question — How did you take possession of this man, and how many are you?

Answer of the Devils — We came into him for having spoken disrespectfully of the rosary. We are 15,000.

Question — Why did so many as 15,000 enter him?

Answer — Because there are fifteen decades in the rosary which he derided, etc.

Dominic — Is not all true I have said of the virtues of the rosary?

Devils — Yes! Yes! (*they emit flames through the nostrils of the demoniac*). Know all ye Christians that Dominic never said one word concerning the rosary that is not most true; and know ye further that if you do not believe him, great calamities will befall you.

Dominic — Who is the man in the world the Devil hates the most?

Devils — (*In chorus*.) Thou art the very man (*here follow verbose compliments*).

Dominic — Of which state of men among Christians are there the most damned?

Devils — In hell we have merchants, pawnbrokers, fraudulent bakers, grocers, Jews, apothecaries, etc., etc.

Dominic — Are there any priests or monks in hell?

Devils — There are a great number of priests, but *no monks*, with the exception of such as have transgressed the rule of their order.

Dominic — Have you any Dominicans?

Devils — Alas! alas! we have not one yet, but we expect a great number of them after their devotion is a little cooled.

We do not pretend to give the questions and answers literally, for they occupy twenty-three pages; but the substance is here, as may be seen by any one who cares to read *The Golden Legend*. The full description of the hideous bellowings of the demons, their enforced glorification of the saint, and so on, is too long for this chapter. Suffice it to say that as we read the numerous questions offered by Dominic and the answers of the demons, we become fully convinced that they corroborate in every detail the unwarranted assertions and support the interests of the Church. The narrative is suggestive. The legend graphically describes the battle of the exorcist with the legion from the bottomless pit. The sulphurous flames which burst forth from the nose, mouth, eyes, and ears, of the demoniac; the sudden appearance of over a hundred angels, clad in golden armor; and, finally, the descent of the blessed Virgin herself, in person, bearing a golden rod, with which she adminis-

---

149a. Cf. Jean Martin: *La légende de m. st. Dominique:* Paris, 1510.

ters a sound thrashing to the demoniac, to force the devils to confess that
of herself which we scarcely need repeat. The whole catalog of theological truths uttered by Dominic's devils was embodied in so many
articles of faith by his Holiness the present Pope in 1870, at the last
Oecumenical Council.

From the foregoing it is easy to see that the only substantial difference between infidel 'mediums' and orthodox saints lies in the relative
usefulness of the *demons*, if demons we must call them. While the Devil
faithfully supports the Christian exorcist in his *orthodox* (?) views, the
modern spook generally leaves his medium in the lurch. For, by lying,
he acts *against* his or her interests rather than otherwise, and thereby
too often casts foul suspicion on the genuineness of the mediumship.
Were modern 'spirits' *devils*, they would evidently display a little more
discrimination and cunning than they do. They would act as the *demons*
of the saint which, compelled by the ecclesiastical magician and by the
power of "the name . . . which forces them into submission," *lie in
accordance with the direct interest* of the exorcist and his church. The
moral of the parallel we leave to the sagacity of the reader.

"Observe well," exclaims Des Mousseaux, "that there are *demons*
which will sometimes speak the truth." "The exorcist," he adds, quoting
the *Ritual*, "must command the demon to tell him whether he is detained in the body of the demoniac through some magic art, or by
signs, or any objects which usually serve for this evil practice. In case
the exorcized person has swallowed the latter, he must vomit them
back; and if they are not in his body, the demon must indicate the
proper place where they are to be found; and having found them, they
must be burned." [150] Thus some "demons reveal the existence of the
bewitchment, tell who is its author, and indicate the means to destroy
the *malefice*. But beware ever to resort, in such a case, to magicians,
sorcerers, or mediums. You must call to help you but the minister of
your Church! The Church believes in magic, as you well see," he adds,
"since she expresses it so formally. And those who *disbelieve in magic*,
can they still hope to share the faith of their own Church? And who can
teach them better? To whom did Christ say: 'Go ye therefore, and
teach all nations . . . and lo, I am with you always, even to the end of
the world'?" [151]

Are we to believe that he said this but to those who wear these black
or scarlet liveries of Rome? Must we then credit the story that this
power was given by Christ to Simon Stylites, the saint who sanctified
himself by perching on a pillar (*stylos*) sixty feet high, for thirty-six years

150. *Rituale Romanum*, p. 478: Paris, 1851-2.
151. *Mœurs et pratiques des démons*, p. 177.

of his life, without ever descending from it, in order that, among other miracles related in *The Golden Legend*, he might cure a *dragon* of a sore eye? "Near Simon's pillar was the dwelling of a dragon, so very venomous that the stench was spread for miles round his cave." This reptile-hermit met with an accident; he got a thorn in his eye, and, becoming blind, crept to the saint's pillar, and pressed his eye against it for three days, without touching any one. Then the blessed saint, from his aërial seat, *"three feet in diameter,"* ordered earth and water to be placed on the dragon's eye, out of which suddenly emerged a thorn (or stake), a cubit in length; when the people saw the 'miracle' they glorified the Creator. As to the grateful dragon, he arose and, "having adored God for two hours, returned to his cave" [152] — a half-converted saurian, we must suppose.

And what are we to think of that other narrative, to disbelieve in which is *"to risk one's salvation,"* as we were informed by a Pope's missionary, of the Order of the Franciscans? When St. Francis preached a sermon in the wilderness, the birds assembled from the four cardinal points of the world. They warbled and applauded every sentence; they sang a holy mass in chorus; finally they dispersed to carry the glad tidings all over the universe. A grasshopper, profiting by the absence of the Holy Virgin, who generally kept company with the saint, remained perched on the head of the "blessed one" for a whole week. Attacked by a ferocious wolf, the saint, who had no other weapon but the sign of the cross which he made upon himself, instead of running away from his rabid assailant, began arguing with the beast. Having imparted to him the benefit to be derived from the holy religion, St. Francis never ceased talking until the wolf became as meek as a lamb, and even shed tears of repentance over his past sins. Finally, he "stretched his paws in the hands of the saint, followed him like a dog through all the towns in which he preached, and became half a Christian!" [153] Wonders of zoölogy! a horse turned sorcerer, a wolf and a dragon turned Christians!

These two anecdotes, chosen at random from among hundreds, if rivaled are not surpassed by the wildest romances of the Pagan thaumaturgists, magicians, and spiritualists! And yet, when Pythagoras is said to have subdued animals, even wild beasts, merely through a powerful mesmeric influence, he is pronounced by one-half of the Catholics a

---

152 See the narrative selected from the 'Golden Legend' by Alban Butler; also J. Bollandus, S. J.: *Acta sanctorum*, Januarii, tom. I, p. 271: Paris.

153. See *The Golden Legend; Life of St. Francis;* P. Sabatier: *Actus beati Francisci et soc. ejus,* xvi, xxiii: Paris, 1902; *Annales minorum,* II, year 1221, §§ 34, 19, ed. of L. Wadding, 1732; Luca Vadingo: *Alcuna miracoli di Francesco d'Assisi,* Roma, 1711; J. Bollandus: *Acta sanct.,* Octubri (Analecta de S. Francisco confessore); and *Demonologia,* pp. 398, 428.

bare-faced impostor, and by the rest a sorcerer, who worked magic in
confederacy with the Devil! Neither the she-bear, nor the eagle, nor
yet the bull that Pythagoras is said to have persuaded to give up eating
beans, were alleged to have answered with human voices; while St.
Benedict's "black raven," whom he called "brother," argues with him,
and croaks his answers like a born casuist. When the saint offers him
one-half of a poisoned loaf, the raven grows indignant and reproaches
him in Latin as though he had just graduated at the Propaganda!

If it be objected that *The Golden Legend* is now but half-supported
by the Church; and that it is known to have been compiled by the writer
from a collection of the lives of the saints, for the most part unauthenti-
cated, we can show that, at least in one instance, the biography is no
legendary compilation, but the history of one man, by another one who
was his contemporary. Archdeacon Jortin and Gibbon [154] demonstrated
years ago that the early Fathers used to select narratives, wherewith to
ornament the lives of their apocryphal saints, from Ovid, Homer, Livy,
and even from the unwritten popular legends of Pagan nations. But such
is not the case in the above instances. St. Bernard lived in the twelfth
century, and St. Dominic was nearly contemporaneous with the author of
The Golden Legend. De Voragine died in 1298, and Dominic, whose exorcisms and life he describes so minutely, instituted his order in the first
quarter of the thirteenth century. Moreover de Voragine was Vicar-
General of the Dominicans himself, in the middle of the same century,
and therefore described the miracles wrought by his hero and patron but
a few years after they were alleged to have happened. He wrote them in
the same convent; and while narrating these wonders he had probably
fifty persons at hand who had been eye-witnesses to the saint's mode of
living. What must we think, in such a case, of a biographer who seriously
describes the following: One day, as the blessed saint was occupied in his
study, the Devil began pestering him in the shape of a flea. He frisked
and jumped about the pages of his book until the harassed saint, unwilling as he was to act unkindly, even toward a devil, felt compelled to
punish him by fixing the troublesome devil on the very sentence on which
he stopped, by clasping the book. At another time the same devil appeared under the shape of a monkey. He grinned so horribly that
Dominic, in order to get rid of him, ordered the devil-monkey to take the
candle and hold it for him until he had done reading. The poor imp did
so, and held it until it was consumed to the very end of the wick; and
notwithstanding his pitiful cries for mercy the saint compelled him to
hold it till his fingers were burned to the bones!

Enough! The approbation with which this book was received by the

---

154. See *The Decline and Fall, etc.*, ch. xxviii.

Church, and the peculiar sanctity attributed to it, is sufficient to show the estimation in which veracity was held by its patrons. We may add, in conclusion, that the finest quintessence of Boccaccio's *Decameron* appears prudery itself by comparison with the filthy realism of *The Golden Legend*.

We cannot regard with too much astonishment the pretensions of the Catholic Church in seeking to convert Hindûs and Buddhists to Christianity. While the 'heathen' keeps to the faith of his fathers, he has at least the one redeeming quality — that of not having apostasized for the mere pleasure of exchanging one set of idols for another. There may be for him some novelty in his embracing Protestantism; for in that he gains the advantage, at least, of limiting his religious views to their simplest expression. But when a Buddhist has been enticed into exchanging his Shoe Dagoon for the Slipper of the Vatican, or the eight hairs from the head of Gautama and Buddha's tooth, which work miracles, for the locks of a Christian saint, and a tooth of Jesus, which work far less clever miracles, he has no cause to boast of his choice. In his address to the Literary Society of Java, Sir T. S. Raffles is said to have narrated the following characteristic anecdote: "On visiting the great temple on the hills of Nagasaki, the English commissioner was received with marked regard and respect by the venerable patriarch of the northern provinces, a man eighty years of age, who entertained him most sumptuously. On showing him round the courts of the temple, one of the English officers present heedlessly exclaimed, in surprise, 'Jasus Christus!' The patriarch turning half round, with a placid smile, bowed significantly, expressive of, 'we know your Jasus Christus!' and said, 'Well, don't obtrude him upon us in our temples, and we remain friends.' And so, with a hearty shake of the hands, these two opposites parted." [155]

There is scarcely a report sent by the missionaries from India, Tíbet, and China, but laments the diabolical 'obscenity' of the heathen rites, their lamentable impudicity; all of which "are so strongly suggestive of devil-worship," as Des Mousseaux tells us. We can scarcely be assured that the morality of the Pagans would be in the least improved were they allowed a free inquiry into the life of, say, the psalmist-king, the author of those sweet *Psalms* which are so rapturously repeated by Christians. The difference between David performing a phallic dance before the holy ark — emblem of the female principle — and a Hindû Vishnavite bearing the same emblem on his forehead, favors the former only in the eyes of those who have studied neither the ancient faith nor their own. When a religion which compelled David to cut off and deliver two hundred foreskins of his enemies before he could become the king's son-in-law (*1 Sam.,*

---

155. Chas. Coleman: *The Mythology of the Hindus*, p. 331.

xviii, 25-27) is accepted as a standard by Christians, they would do well
not to cast into the teeth of heathen the impudicities of their faiths.
Remembering the suggestive parable of Jesus, they ought to cast the
beam out of their own eye before plucking at the mote in their neighbor's.
The sexual element is as marked in Christianity as in any one of the
'heathen religions.' Certainly, nowhere in the *Vedas* can be found the
coarseness and downright immodesty of language, that Hebraists now
discover throughout the Mosaic *Bible.*

It would profit little were we to dwell much upon subjects which have
been disposed of in such a masterly way by an anonymous author whose
work electrified England and Germany last year; [156] while as regards the
particular topic under notice, we cannot do better than recommend the
scholarly writings of Dr. Inman. Albeit one-sided, and in many instances unjust to the ancient heathen, Pagan, and Jewish religions, the
facts treated in *Ancient Pagan and Modern Christian Symbolism* are unimpeachable. Nor can we agree with some English critics who charge
him with an intent to destroy Christianity. If by *Christianity* is meant
the external religious forms of worship, then he certainly seeks to destroy
it, for in his eyes, as well as in those of every truly religious man who has
studied ancient exoteric faiths and their symbology, Christianity is pure
heathenism, and Catholicism, with its fetish-worshiping, is far worse
and more pernicious than Hindûism in its most idolatrous aspect. But
while denouncing the exoteric forms and unmasking the symbols, it is
not the religion of Christ that the author attacks, but the artificial system
of theology. We will allow him to illustrate the position in his own
language, and quote from his preface:

"When vampires were discovered by the acumen of any observer,"
he says, "they were, we are told, ignominiously killed by a stake being
driven through the body; but experience showed them to have such
tenacity of life that they rose again and again, notwithstanding renewed
impalement, and were not ultimately laid to rest till wholly burned. In
like manner, the regenerated Heathendom, which dominates over the
followers of Jesus of Nazareth, has risen again and again, after being
transfixed. Still cherished by the many, it is denounced by the few.
Amongst other accusers, I raise my voice against the Paganism which
exists so extensively in ecclesiastical Christianity, and will do my utmost
to expose the imposture.

"In a vampire story, told in *Thalaba* by Southey, the resuscitated
being takes the form of a dearly beloved maiden, and the hero is obliged
to kill her with his own hand. He does so; but whilst he strikes the

---

156. *Supernatural Religion: An Inquiry into the Reality of Divine Revelation.*

form of the loved one he feels sure that he slays only a demon. In like manner, when I endeavor to destroy the current Heathenism, which has assumed the garb of Christianity, *I do not attack real religion.*[157] Few would accuse a workman of malignancy who cleanses from filth the surface of a noble statue. There may be some who are too nice to touch a nasty subject, yet even they will rejoice when some one else removes the dirt. Such a scavenger is much wanted." [158]

But is it merely Pagans and heathen that the Catholics persecute, and about whom, like Augustine, they cry to the Deity, "Oh, my God! *so do I wish Thy enemies to be slain*"? Oh, no! their aspirations are more Mosaic and Cain-like than that. It is against their next of kin in faith, against their schismatic brothers that they are now intriguing within the walls which sheltered the murderous Borgias. The *larvae* of the infanticidal, parricidal and fratricidal Popes have proved themselves fit counsellors for the Cains of Castelfidardo and Mentana. It is now the turn of the Slavonian Christians, the Oriental Schismatics — the Philistines of the Greek Church!

His Holiness the Pope, after exhausting in a metaphor of self-laudation every point of resemblance between the great biblical prophets and himself, has finally and truly compared himself with the Patriarch Jacob "wrestling against his God." He now crowns the edifice of Catholic piety by openly sympathizing with the Turks! The vicegerent of God inaugurates his infallibility by encouraging, in a true Christian spirit, the acts of that Moslem David, the modern Bashi-Bazuk; and it seems as if nothing would more please his Holiness than to be presented by the latter with several thousands of the Bulgarian or Servian "foreskins." True to her policy to be all things to all men to promote her own interests, the Romish Church is, at this writing (1876), benevolently viewing the Bulgarian and Servian atrocities, and, probably, maneuvering with Turkey against Russia. Better Islam and the hitherto-hated Crescent over the sepulcher of the Christian god, than the Greek Church established at Constantinople and Jerusalem as the state-religion. Like a decrepit and toothless ex-tyrant in exile, the Vatican is eager for any alliance that promises, if not a restoration of its own power, at least the weakening of its rival. The axe its inquisitors once swung, it now toys

---

157. Neither do we, if by *true religion* the world shall at last understand the adoration of one Supreme, Invisible and Unknown Deity by works and acts, not by the profession of vain human dogmas. But our intention is to go farther. We desire to demonstrate that if we exclude ceremonial and fetish worship from being regarded as essential parts of religion, then the true Christ-like principles have been exemplified, and true Christianity practised since the days of the apostles, exclusively among Buddhists and 'heathen.'

158. *Ancient Pagan and Modern Christian Symbolism*, p. xvi.

with in secret, feeling its edge, and waiting and hoping against hope. In
her time the Popish Church has lain with strange bedfellows, but never
before now has sunk to the degradation of giving her moral support to
those who for over 1200 years spat in her face, called her adherents "infidel dogs," repudiated her teachings and denied godhood to her God!

The press of even Catholic France is fairly aroused at this indignity,
and openly accuses the Ultramontane portion of the Catholic Church
and the Vatican of siding, during the present Eastern struggle, with the
Mohammedan against the Christian. "When the Minister of Foreign
Affairs in the French Legislature spoke some mild words in favor of the
Greek Christians, he was only applauded by the liberal Catholics, and
received coldly by the Ultramontane party," says the French correspondent of a New York paper.

"So pronounced was this, that M. Lemoinne, the well-known editor
of the great liberal Catholic journal, the *Débats*, was moved to say that
the Roman Church felt more sympathy for the Moslem than the schismatic, just as they preferred an infidel to the Protestant. 'There is at
bottom,' says this writer, 'a great affinity between the *Syllabus* and the
Koran, and between the two heads of the faithful. The two systems are
of the same nature, and are united on the common ground of a one and
unchangeable theory.' In Italy, in like manner, the King and Liberal
Catholics are in warm sympathy with the unfortunate Christians, while
the Pope and Ultramontane faction are believed to be inclining to the
Mohammedans."

The civilized world may yet expect the apparition of the materialized
Virgin Mary within the walls of the Vatican. The so often-repeated
'miracle' of the Immaculate Visitor in the medieval ages has recently
been enacted at Lourdes, and why not once more, as a *coup de grâce* to
all heretics, schismatics and infidels? The miraculous wax taper is yet
seen at Arras, the chief city of Artois; and at every new calamity threatening her beloved Church the 'Blessed Lady' appears personally and
lights it with her own fair hands, in view of a whole 'biologized' congregation. This sort of 'miracle,' says E. Worsley, wrought by the
Roman Catholic Church, "being most certain and never doubted of by
any." [159] Neither has the private correspondence with which the most
'Gracious Lady' honors her friends been doubted. There are two
precious missives from her in the archives of the Church. The first pur-
ports to be a letter in answer to one addressed to her by Ignatius. She
confirms all things learned by her correspondent from "her friend" —

159. *Discourse of Miracles wrought in the Roman Catholick Church, or a full Refutation of
Dr. Stillingfleet's unjust Exceptions against Miracles*, p. 64: Oxford, 1676.

meaning the Apostle John. She bids him hold fast to his vows, and adds as an inducement: "*I and John will come together and pay you a visit.*" [160]

Nothing was known of this unblushing fraud till the letters were published at Paris in 1495. By a curious accident it appeared at a time when threatening inquiries began to be made as to the genuineness of the fourth Synoptic. Who could doubt, after such a confirmation from headquarters! But the climax of effrontery was capped in 1534, when another letter was received from the 'Mediatrix,' which sounds more like the report of a lobby-agent to a brother-politician. It was written in excellent Latin, and was found in the Cathedral of Messina, together with the image to which it alludes. Its contents run as follows:

"Mary Virgin, Mother of the Redeemer of the world, to the Bishop, Clergy, and the other faithful of Messina sendeth health and benediction from *herself* and son: [161]

"Whereas ye have been mindful of establishing the worship of me; now this is to let you know that by so doing ye have found great favor in my sight. I have a long time reflected with pain upon your city, which is exposed to much danger from its contiguity to the fire of Etna, and I have often had words about it with my son, for he was vexed with you because of your guilty neglect of my worship, so that he would not care a pin about my intercession. Now, however, that you have come to your senses, and have happily begun to worship me, he has conferred upon me the right to become your everlasting protectress; but, at the same time, I warn you to mind what you are about, and give me no cause of repenting of my kindness to you. The prayers and festivals instituted in my honor please me tremendously (*vehementer*), and if you faithfully persevere in these things, and provided you oppose to the utmost of your power the heretics which now-a-days are spreading through the world, by which both my worship and that of the other saints, male and female, are so endangered, you shall enjoy my perpetual protection.

"In sign of this compact, I send you down from Heaven the image of myself, cast by celestial hands, and if ye hold it in the honor to which it is entitled, it will be an evidence to me of your obedience and your faith. Farewell. Dated in Heaven, whilst sitting near the throne of my son, in the month of December, of the 1534th year from his incarnation.

"MARY VIRGIN"

The reader should understand that this document is no anti-Catholic forgery. The author from whom it is taken,[162] says that the authenticity of the missive "is attested by the Bishop himself, his Vicar-General,

---

160. After this, why should the Roman Catholics object to the claims of the Spiritualists? If, without proof, they believe in the 'materialization' of Mary and John, for Ignatius, how can they logically deny the materialization of Katie and John (King), when it is attested by the careful experiments of Mr. Crookes, the English chemist, and the cumulative testimony of a large number of witnesses?

161. The 'Mother of God' takes precedence therefore of God?

162. See the *New Era* for July, 1875; N. Y.

Secretary, and six Canons of the Cathedral Church of Messina, all of whom have signed that attestation with their names, and confirmed it upon oath.

"Both the epistle and image were found upon the high altar, where they had been placed by angels from heaven."

A Church must have reached the last stages of degradation, when such sacrilegious trickery as this could be resorted to by its clergy, and accepted with or without question by the people.

No! far be such a religion from the man who feels the workings of an immortal spirit within him! There never was nor ever will be a truly philosophical mind, whether of Pagan, heathen, Jew, or Christian, but has followed the same path of thought. Gautama-Buddha is mirrored in the precepts of Christ; Paul and Philo Judaeus are faithful echoes of Plato; and Ammonius Saccas and Plotinus won their immortal fame by combining the teachings of all these grand masters of true philosophy. "Prove all things; hold fast that which is good," ought to be the motto of all brothers on earth. Not so is it with the interpreters of the *Bible*. The seed of the Reformation was sown on the day that the second chapter of *The Catholic Epistle of James* jostled the eleventh chapter of the *Epistle to the Hebrews* in the same *New Testament*. One who believes in Paul cannot believe in James, Peter, and John. The Paulists, to remain Christians with their apostle, must withstand Peter "to the face"; and if Peter "was to be blamed" and *was wrong*, then he was not infallible. How then can his successor (?) boast of his infallibility? Every kingdom divided against itself is brought to desolation; and every house divided against itself must fall. A plurality of masters has proved as fatal in religions as in politics. What Paul preached, was preached by every other mystic philosopher. "Stand *fast therefore in the liberty* wherewith Christ hath made us free, and *be not entangled again with the yoke of bondage!*" exclaims the honest apostle-philosopher; and adds, as if prophetically inspired: "But if ye bite and devour one another, take heed that ye be not consumed one of another."

That the Neo-Platonists were not always despised or accused of demonolatry is evidenced in the adoption by the Roman Church of their very rites and theurgy. The identical evocations and incantations of the Pagan and Jewish Kabalist are now repeated by the Christian exorcist, and the theurgy of Iamblichus was adopted word for word. "Distinct as were the Platonists and Pauline Christians of the earlier centuries," writes Professor A. Wilder, "many of the more distinguished teachers of the new faith were deeply tinctured with the philosophical leaven. Synesius, the Bishop of Cyrene, was the disciple of Hypatia. *St. Anthony reiterated the theurgy of Iamblichus.* The *Logos*, or word of the *Gospel according to John*, was a Gnostic personification. Clement of Alexandria, Origen, and others of the Fathers drank deeply from the fountains of philosophy. The ascetic idea which carried away the Church was like that which was practised by Plotinus . . . all through the Middle Ages there rose up men who accepted the interior doctrines which were promulgated by the renowned teacher of the Academy." [163]

To substantiate our accusation that the Latin Church first despoiled the Kabalists and theurgists of their magical rites and ceremonies, before hurling anathemas upon their devoted heads, we will now translate for the reader fragments from the forms of *exorcism* employed by Kabalists and Christians. The identity in phraseology may perhaps disclose one of the reasons why the Romish Church has always desired to keep the faithful in ignorance of the meaning of her Latin prayers and ritual. Only those directly interested in the deception have had the opportunity to compare the rituals of the Church and of the magicians. The best Latin scholars were, until a comparatively recent date, either churchmen or dependent upon the Church. Common people could not read Latin, and even if they could, the reading of the books on magic was prohibited under the penalty of anathema and excommunication. The cunning device of the confessional made it almost impossible to consult, even surreptitiously, what the priests call a *grimoire* (a devil's scrawl) or *Ritual of Magic*. To make assurance doubly sure, the Church began destroying or concealing everything of the kind she could lay her hands upon.

The following are translated from the *Kabalistic Ritual*, and that generally known as the *Roman Ritual*. The latter was promulgated in 1851 and 1852, under the sanction of Cardinal Engelbert, Archbishop of Malines, and of the Archbishop of Paris. Speaking of it, the demonologist Des Mousseaux says: "It is the ritual of Paul V, revised by the most learned of modern Popes, by the contemporary of Voltaire, Benedict XIV." [164]

KABALISTIC (Jewish and Pagan)	ROMAN CATHOLIC
Exorcism of Salt	*Exorcism of Salt* [166]
The Priest-Magician blesses the Salt, and says: "*Creature of Salt*,[165] in thee may remain the WISDOM [of God]; and may it preserve from all corruption *our minds and*	The Priest blesses the *Salt* and says: "*Creature of Salt*, I exorcise thee in the name of the living God . . . *become the health of the soul and of the body!* Every-

163. 'Paul and Plato.'
164. See *La magie au XIXme siècle*, p. 139.
165. *Creature* of salt, air, water, or of any object to be *enchanted* or *blessed*, is a technical expression in magic, adopted by the Christian clergy.
166. *Roman Ritual*, pp. 291-296, etc., etc.: Paris, 1851-2.

bodies. Through 'Hokhmael [חכמאל, God of wisdom], and the power of *Rua'h* 'Hokhmael [Spirit of the Holy Ghost] may the spirits of matter [bad spirits] recede before it. . . . *Amen.*"

where where thou art thrown *may the unclean spirit be put to flight. . . . Amen.*"

Exorcism of Water (and Ashes)

"Creature of the Water, I exorcise thee . . . by *the three names* which are Netsa'h, Hod, and Yesod [kabalistic trinity], in the beginning and in the end, by Alpha and Omega, which are in the Spirit Azoth [Holy Ghost, or the '*Universal Soul*'], I exorcise and adjure thee. . . . Wandering eagle, may the Lord command thee by the *wings of the bull and his flaming sword.*" (The cherub placed at the east gate of Eden.)

Exorcism of Water

"Creature of the water, in the name of the Almighty God, the Father, the Son, and the Holy Ghost . . . *be exorcized.* . . . I adjure thee in the name of the Lamb [the magician says *bull* or ox — *per alas Tauri*], of the Lamb that trod upon the basilisk and the aspic, and who crushes under his foot the lion and the dragon."

Exorcism of an Elemental Spirit

"Serpent, in the name of the Tetragrammaton, the Lord; He commands thee, by the angel and the lion.

"Angel of darkness, obey, and run away with this holy [exorcised] water. Eagle in chains, obey this sign, and retreat before the breath. Moving serpent, crawl at my feet, or be tortured by *this sacred fire*, and evaporate before this holy incense. Let water return to water [the elemental spirit of water]; let the fire burn, and the air circulate; let the earth return to earth by the virtue of the Pentagram, which is the Morning Star, and in the name of the tetragrammaton which is traced in the center of *the Cross of Light. Amen.*"

Exorcism of the Devil

.   .   .   .
"O Lord, let him who carries along with him the terror, flee, struck in his turn by terror and defeated. O thou, who art the Ancient Serpent . . . tremble before the hand of him who, having triumphed of the tortures of hell [?] *devictis gemitibus inferni*, recalled the souls to light. . . . The more whilst thou decay, the more terrible will be thy torture . . . by Him who reigns over the living and the dead .   .   . and who will judge the century by fire, *saeculum per ignem*, etc. In the name of the Father, Son, and the Holy Ghost. *Amen.*" [167]

It is unnecessary to try the patience of the reader any longer, although we might multiply examples. It must not be forgotten that we have quoted from the latest revision of the *Ritual*, that of 1851-2. If we were to go back to the former one we should find a far more striking identity, not merely of phraseology but of ceremonial form. For the purpose of comparison we have not even availed ourselves of the ritual of ceremonial magic of the *Christian* kabalists of the Middle Ages, wherein the

---

167. *Roman Ritual*, pp. 421-435.

language modeled upon a belief in the divinity of Christ is, with the exception of a stray expression here and there, identical with the Catholic Ritual. [168] The latter however makes one improvement, for the originality of which the Church should be allowed all credit. Certainly nothing so fantastical could be found in a ritual of magic. "Give place," it says, apostrophizing the 'Demon,' "give place to Jesus Christ . . . thou *filthy, stinking, and ferocious beast* . . . dost thou rebel? Listen and tremble, Satan; enemy of the faith, enemy of the human race, introducer of death . . . root of all evil, promoter of vice, soul of envy, origin of avarice, cause of discord, prince of homicide, whom God curses; author of incest and sacrilege, inventor of all obscenity, *professor* of the most detestable actions, *and Grand Master of Heretics* [!!] [*Doctor haereticorum!*] What! . . . dost thou still stand? Dost dare to resist, and thou knowest that Christ our Lord is coming? . . . Give place to Jesus Christ, give place to the Holy Ghost, which by His blessed Apostle Peter has flung thee down before the public, in the person of Simon the Magician" (*te manifeste stravit in Simone mago*).[169]

After such a shower of abuse no devil having the slightest feeling of self-respect could remain in such company; unless indeed he should chance to be an Italian Liberal, or King Victor Emmanuel himself; both of whom, thanks to Pius IX, have become anathema-proof.

It really seems too bad to strip Rome of all her symbols at once; but justice must be done to the despoiled hierophants. Long before the sign of the Cross was adopted as a Christian symbol, it was employed as a secret sign of recognition among neophytes and adepts. Says Lévi: "The sign of the Cross adopted by the Christians does not belong exclusively to them. It is kabalistic, and represents the oppositions and quaternary equilibrium of the elements. We see by the occult verse of the *Pater*, to which we have called attention in another work, that there were originally two ways of making it, or at least two very different formulae to express its meaning — one reserved for priests and initiates; the other given to neophytes and the profane. Thus for example the *initiate*, carrying his hand to his forehead, said: *To thee;* then he added, *belong;* and continued while carrying his hand to the breast — *the kingdom;* then, to the left shoulder — *justice;* to the right shoulder — *and mercy.* Then he joined the two hands, adding: *throughout the generating cycles:* '*Tibi sunt Malkhuth, et Geburah et 'Hesed per Aeonas*' — a sign of the Cross, *absolutely* and magnificently kabalistic, which the profanations of Gnosticism made the militant and official Church completely *lose.*" [170]

---

168. See *Art Magic*, art. on Peter d'Abano.
169. *Roman Ritual*, pp. 429-433; see *La magie au XIXme siècle*, pp. 142-3.
170. *Dogme et rituel de la haute magie*, Rituel, ch. iv.

How fantastical therefore is the assertion of Father Ventura that while Augustine was a Manichaean, a philosopher, ignorant of and refusing to humble himself before the sublimity of the "grand Christian revelation," he knew nothing, understood naught of God, man, or universe; "he remained poor, small, obscure, sterile, and wrote nothing, did nothing really grand or useful. But, hardly had he become a Christian when his reasoning powers and intellect, enlightened at the *luminary of faith*, elevated him to the most sublime heights of philosophy and theology." And his other proposition that Augustine's genius, as a consequence, "developed itself in all its grandeur and prodigious fecundity . . . his intellect radiated with that immense splendor which, reflecting itself in his immortal writings, has never ceased for one moment during fourteen centuries to illuminate the Church and the world!" [171]

Whatever Augustine was as a Manichaean, we leave Father Ventura to discover; but that his accession to Christianity established an everlasting enmity between theology and science is beyond doubt. While forced to confess that "the Gentiles had possibly something *divine* and true in their doctrines," [172] he nevertheless declared that for their superstition, idolatry and pride they had "to be detested, and, unless they improved, to be punished by divine judgment." This furnishes the clew to the subsequent policy of the Christian Church, even to our day. If the Gentiles did not choose to come into the Church, all that was divine in their philosophy should go for naught, and the divine wrath of God should be visited upon their heads. What effect this produced is succinctly stated by Draper: "No one did more than this Father to bring science and religion into antagonism; it was mainly he who diverted the *Bible* from its true office — a guide to purity of life — and placed it in the perilous position of being the arbiter of human knowledge, an audacious tyranny over the mind of man. The example once set, there was no want of followers; the works of the Greek philosophers were stigmatized as profane; the transcendently glorious achievements of the Museum of Alexandria were hidden from sight by a cloud of ignorance, mysticism, and unintelligible jargon, out of which there too often flashed the destroying lightnings of ecclesiastical vengeance." [173]

Augustine [174] and Cyprian [175] admit that Hermes and Osthán believed in one true God; the first two maintaining, as well as the two Pagans, that he is invisible and incomprehensible, except spiritually. Moreover we invite any man of intelligence — provided he be not a religious fanatic

---

171. Ventura de Raulica: *Conférences*, II, part I, p. lvi, preface.
172. Cf. *The City of God*, VIII, ix; X, ii; etc.   173. *Conflict betw. Rel. and Science*, p. 62.
174. *De baptismo contra Donatistas*, lib. VI, c. xliv.
175. *Sancti C. Cypriani opera*, s. v. 'De idolorum vanitate,' p. 14: Oxonii, 1682.

— after reading fragments chosen at random from the works of Hermes and Augustine on the Deity, to decide which of the two gives a more philosophical definition of the 'unseen Father.' We have at least one writer of fame who is of our opinion. Draper calls the Augustinian productions a "rhapsodical conversation" with God, an "incoherent dream." [176]

Father Ventura depicts the saint as attitudinizing before an astonished world upon "the most sublime heights of philosophy." But here steps in again the same unprejudiced critic, who makes the following remarks on this colossus of Patristic philosophy. "Was it for this preposterous scheme —" he asks, "this product of ignorance and audacity — that the works of the Greek philosophers were to be given up? It was none too soon that the great critics who appeared at the Reformation, by comparing the works of these writers with one another, brought them to their proper level, and taught us to look upon them all with contempt." [177]

For such men as Plotinus, Porphyry, Iamblichus, Apollonius, and even Simon Magus, to be accused of having formed a pact with the Devil, whether the latter personage exist or not, is so absurd as to need but little refutation. If Simon Magus — the most problematical of all in a historical sense — ever existed otherwise than in the overheated fancy of Peter and the other apostles, he was evidently no worse than any of his adversaries. A difference in religious views, however great, is insufficient *per se* to send one person to heaven and the other to hell. Such uncharitable and peremptory doctrines might have been taught in the Middle Ages; but it is too late now for even the Church to put forward this traditional scarecrow. Research begins to suggest that which, if ever verified, will bring eternal disgrace on the Church of the Apostle Peter, whose very imposition of herself upon that disciple must be regarded as the most unverified and unverifiable of the assumptions of the Catholic clergy.

The erudite author of *Supernatural Religion* [178] assiduously endeavors to prove that by *Simon Magus* we must understand the apostle Paul, whose Epistles were secretly as well as openly calumniated by Peter, and charged with containing "*dysnoëtic* learning." The Apostle of the Gentiles was brave, outspoken, sincere, and very learned; the Apostle of Circumcision, cowardly, cautious, *insincere*, and very ignorant. That Paul had been partially at least, if not completely, initiated into the theurgic mysteries, admits of little doubt. His language, the phraseology so peculiar to the Greek philosophers, certain expressions used but by the initiates, are so many sure ear-marks to that supposition. Our suspicion

---

176. *Conflict, etc.,* p. 60.　　　177. *Ibid.,* p. 66.　　　178. Part II, ch. v.

has been strengthened by an able article, entitled 'Paul and Plato,' in one of the New York periodicals,[179] in which the author puts forward one remarkable and, for us, very precious observation. He shows Paul, in his *Epistles to the Corinthians*, abounding with "expressions suggested by the initiations of Sabazius and Eleusis, and the lectures of the [Greek] philosophers. He [Paul] designates himself an *idiotēs* — a person unskilful in the world, but not in the *gnosis* or philosophical learning. 'We speak wisdom among the perfect or initiated,' he writes; 'not the wisdom of this world, nor of the archons of this world, but divine wisdom in a mystery, secret — which *none of the Archons of this world knoweth.*' "

What else can the apostle mean by these unequivocal words, but that he himself, as belonging to the *mystae* (initiated), spoke of things shown and explained only in the Mysteries? The "divine wisdom in a mystery which none of the *archons of this world knoweth*," has evidently some direct reference to the *basileus* of the Eleusinian initiation, who *did know*. The *basileus* belonged to the staff of the great hierophant, and was an *archon* of Athens; and as such was one of the chief *mystae* belonging to the *interior* Mysteries, to which a very select and small number obtained an entrance.[180] The magistrates supervising the Eleusinians were called archons.

Another proof that Paul belonged to the circle of the 'Initiates' lies in the following fact. The apostle had his head shorn at Cenchrea (where Lucius, *Apuleius*, was initiated) because "he had a vow." The *nazars* — or set apart — as we see in the Jewish Scriptures, had to cut their hair which they wore long, and which "no razor touched" at any other time, and sacrifice it on the altar of initiation. And the nazars were a class of Chaldaean theurgists. We will show further that Jesus belonged to this class.

Paul declares that: "According to the grace of God which is given unto me, as a wise *masterbuilder*, I have laid the foundation." [181]

This expression, masterbuilder, used only *once* in the whole *Bible*, and by Paul, may be considered as a whole revelation. In the Mysteries the third part of the sacred rites was called *Epopteia*, or revelation, reception into the secrets. In substance it means that stage of divine clairvoyance when everything pertaining to this earth disappears, and earthly sight is paralysed, and the soul is united free and pure with its Spirit, or God. But the real significance of the word is 'overseeing,' from ὄπτομαι — *I see myself*. In Sanskrit the word *avâpta* has the same meaning,

179. By A. Wilder, editor of *The Eleusinian and Bacchic Mysteries*, of Thomas Taylor.
180. T. Taylor: *The Eleus. and Bacch. Myst.*, p. 14, ed. A. Wilder: 4th edit.,
    New York, 1891.   181. *1 Cor.*, iii, 10.

as well as *to obtain*.[182]   The word *epopteia* is a compound one, from
ἐπί — upon, and ὄπτομαι — to look, or an overseer, an inspector —
also used for a masterbuilder. The title of master-mason, in Freemasonry, is derived from this, in the sense used in the Mysteries.
Therefore, when Paul entitles himself a "masterbuilder," he is using
a word pre-eminently kabalistic, theurgic, and masonic, and one which
no other apostle uses. He thus declares himself an *adept*, having the
right to *initiate* others.

If we search in this direction with those sure guides, the Grecian
Mysteries and the Kabala, before us, it will be easy to find the secret
reason why Paul was so persecuted and hated by Peter, John and James.
The author of the *Revelation* was a Jewish kabalist *pur sang*, with all the
hatred inherited by him from his forefathers toward the Mysteries.[183]
His jealousy during the life of Jesus extended even to Peter; and it
is only after the death of their common master that we see the two
apostles — the former of whom wore the Miter and the Petaloon of
the Jewish Rabbis — preach so zealously the rite of circumcision. In
the eyes of Peter, Paul, who had humiliated him, and whom he felt so
much his superior in 'Greek learning' and philosophy, must have
naturally appeared as a magician, a man polluted with the '*Gnosis*,'
with the 'wisdom' of the Greek Mysteries — hence, perhaps, "Simon [184]
the Magician."

As to Peter, biblical criticism has shown before now that he had
probably no more to do with the foundation of the Latin Church at
Rome, than to furnish the pretext so readily seized upon by the cunning
Irenaeus to benefit this Church with the new name of the apostle —
Petra or *Kiffa*, a name which allowed itself so readily, by an easy play
upon words, to be connected with *Petroma*, the double set of stone

---

182. In its most extensive meaning, the Sanskrit word has the same literal sense as the
Greek term; both imply 'revelation,' by no human agent, but through the 'receiving
of the sacred drink.' In India the initiated received the 'Soma,' sacred drink, which
helped to liberate his soul from the body; and in the Eleusinian Mysteries it was the
sacred drink offered at the Epopteia. The Grecian Mysteries are wholly derived from
the Brâhmanical Vedic rites, and the latter from the ante-Vedic religious Mysteries —
primitive Buddhist philosophy.

183. It is needless to state that *the Gospel according to John* was not written by John,
but by a Platonist or a Gnostic belonging to the Neo-Platonic school.

184. The fact that Peter persecuted the 'Apostle to the Gentiles,' under that name,
does not necessarily imply that there was no Simon Magus individually distinct from
Paul. It may have become a generic name of abuse. Theodoret and Chrysostom, the
earliest and most prolific commentators on the Gnosticism of those days, seem actually
to make of Simon a rival of Paul, and to state that between them passed frequent mes-
sages. The former, as a diligent propagandist of what Paul terms the "antitheses of
the Gnosis" (1st Epistle to Timothy), must have been a sore thorn in the side of the
apostle. There are sufficient proofs of the actual existence of Simon Magus.

tablets used by the hierophant at the initiations, during the final Mystery. In this, perhaps, lies concealed the whole secret of the claims of the Vatican. As Professor Wilder happily suggests: "In the Oriental countries the designation פתר, Peter [in Phoenician and Chaldaic, an interpreter] appears to have been the title of this personage [the hierophant]. . . . There is in these facts some reminder of the peculiar circumstances of the Mosaic Law . . . and also of the claim of the Pope to be the successor of Peter, the hierophant or interpreter of the Christian religion." [185]

As such we must concede to him, to some extent, the right to be such an interpreter. The Latin Church has faithfully preserved in symbols, rites, ceremonies, architecture, and even in the very dress of her clergy, the tradition of the Pagan worship — of the public or exoteric ceremonies, we should add; otherwise her dogmas would embody more sense and contain less blasphemy against the majesty of the Supreme and Invisible God.

An inscription found on the coffin of Queen *Menthu-ḥetep,* of the eleventh dynasty (2782 B. C.), now proved to have been transcribed from the seventeenth chapter of the *Book of the Dead* (dating not later than "4500 B. C."), is more than suggestive. This monumental text contains a group of hieroglyphics, which, when interpreted, read thus:

PTR. RF. SU.

Peter- ref- su.

Baron Bunsen shows this sacred formulary mixed up with a whole series of glosses and various interpretations forty centuries old. "This is identical with saying that the record [the true interpretation] was at that time no longer intelligible. . . . We beg our readers to understand," he adds, "that a sacred text, a hymn, containing the words of a departed spirit, existed in such a state about 4000 years ago . . . as to be all but unintelligible to royal scribes." [186]

That it was unintelligible to the uninitiated among the latter is as well proved by the confused and contradictory glosses, as that it was a 'mystery'-word, known to the hierophants of the sanctuaries, and moreover a word chosen by Jesus to designate the office assigned by him to one of his apostles. This word PTR was partially interpreted, owing to another word similarly written in another group of hieroglyphics on a

185. Taylor: *Eleus. and Bacchic Mysteries,* ed. A. Wilder, pp. 17-18 (4th ed.). Had we not trustworthy kabalistic tradition to rely upon, we might be perhaps forced to question whether the authorship of the *Revelation* is to be ascribed to the apostle of that name. He seems to be termed John the Theologist.

186. Bunsen: *Egypt's Place in Universal History,* V, pp. 89-90.

stele, the sign [187] used for it being an opened eye. Bunsen mentions as
another explanation of PTR — 'to show.' "It appears to me," he remarks, "that our PTR is literally the old Aramaic and Hebrew 'Patar,'
which occurs in the history of Joseph as the specific word for *interpret-
ing;* whence also *Pitrun* is the term for interpretation of a text, a
dream." [188] In a manuscript of the first century, a combination of the
Demotic and Greek texts, [189] and most probably one of the few which
miraculously escaped the Christian vandalism of the second and third
centuries, when all such precious manuscripts were burned as magical,
we find occurring in several places a phrase which perhaps may throw
some light upon this question. One of the principal heroes of the manuscript, who is constantly referred to as "the Judaean Illuminator" or
Initiate, Τελωτής, is made to communicate but with his *Patar;* the
latter being written in Chaldaic characters. Once the latter word is
coupled with the name *Shimeon.* Several times the 'Illuminator,' who
rarely breaks his contemplative solitude, is shown inhabiting a Κρύπτη
(cave) and teaching the multitudes of eager scholars standing outside, not
orally, but through this *Patar.* The latter receives the words of wisdom
by applying his ear to a circular hole in a partition which conceals the
teacher from the listeners, and then conveys them, with explanations and
glosses, to the crowd. This with a slight change was the method used
by Pythagoras, who, as we know, never allowed his neophytes to see
him during the years of probation, but instructed them from behind
a curtain in his cave.

But whether the 'Illuminator' of the Graeco-Demotic manuscript
is identical with Jesus or not, the fact remains that we find the latter
selecting a 'mystery'-appellation for one who is made to appear later by
the Catholic Church as the janitor of the Kingdom of Heaven and the
interpreter of Christ's will. The word Patar or Peter locates both master
and disciple in the circle of initiation, and connects them with the 'Secret
Doctrine.' The great hierophant of the ancient Mysteries never allowed
the candidates to see or hear him personally. He was the *deus ex machinâ,* the presiding but invisible Deity, uttering his will and instructions
through a second party; and 2000 years later we discover that the
Dalai-Lamas of Tibet had been following for centuries the same traditional program during the most important religious mysteries of lamaism.

---

187. Or principal determinative. See E. de Rougé: *Stele,* pp. 44, 473; Ptar (videns)
is interpreted on it 'to appear,' with a sign of interrogation after it — the usual mark of
scientific perplexity. In Bunsen's fifth volume of *Egypt's Place, etc.,* the interpretation
following is "Illuminator," which is more correct.

188. Bunsen: *Egypt's Place in Universal History,* V, p. 90.

189. It is the property of a mystic whom we met in Syria.

If Jesus knew the secret meaning of the title bestowed by him on Simon, then he must have been initiated, otherwise he could not have learned it; and if he was an initiate of either the Pythagorean Essenes, the Chaldaean Magi, or the Egyptian Priests, then the doctrine taught by him was but a portion of the 'Secret Doctrine' taught by the Pagan hierophants to the few select adepts admitted within the sacred adyta.

But we will discuss this question farther on. For the present we will endeavor briefly to indicate the extraordinary similarity — or rather identity — of rites and ceremonial dress of the Christian clergy with those of the old Babylonians, Assyrians, Phoenicians, Egyptians, and other Pagans of hoary antiquity.

If we would find the model of the Papal tiara, we must search the records of the ancient Assyrian tablets. We invite the reader to give his attention to Dr. Inman's illustrated work, *Ancient Pagan and Modern Christian Symbolism*. On page sixty-four he will readily recognise the head-gear of the successor of St. Peter in the coiffure worn by gods or angels in ancient Assyria, "where it appears crowned by an emblem of the [*male*] trinity" (the Christian Cross). "We may mention in passing," adds Dr. Inman, "that as the Romanists adopted the miter and the tiara from 'the cursed brood of Ham,' so they adopted the episcopalian crook from the augurs of Etruria, and the artistic form with which they clothe their angels from the painters and urn-makers of Magna Graecia and Central Italy."

Would we push our inquiries farther, and seek to ascertain as much in relation to the nimbus and the tonsure of the Catholic priest and monk? [190] We shall find undeniable proofs that they are solar emblems. Chas. Knight, in his *Old England Pictorially Illustrated*, gives a drawing by St. Augustine representing an ancient Christian bishop in a dress probably identical with that worn by the great 'saint' himself. The *pallium*, or the ancient stole of the bishop, is the feminine sign when worn by a priest in worship. On St. Augustine's picture it is bedecked with Buddhistic crosses, and in its whole appearance it is a representation of the Egyptian T (tau), assuming slightly the figure of the letter Y. "Its lower end is the mark of the masculine triad," says Inman; "the right hand (of the figure) has the forefinger extended, like the Assyrian priests while doing homage *to the grove*. . . . When a male dons the pallium in worship, he becomes the representative of the trinity in the unity, the *arba*, or mystic four." [191]

"Immaculate is our Lady Isis," is the legend around an engraving

---

190. The Priests of Isis were tonsured.
191. *Ancient Pagan and Modern Christian Symbolism*, pp. 51, 52; see also his *Ancient Faiths Embodied in Ancient Names*, II, pp. 915-918.

of Serapis and Isis, described by King, in *The Gnostics and their Remains,*
H KYPIA EICIC AΓNH ". . . the very terms applied afterwards to
that personage (the Virgin Mary) who succeeded to her form, titles, symbols, rites, and ceremonies. . . . Thus, her devotees carried into the new
priesthood the former badges of their profession, the obligation to celibacy, the tonsure, and the surplice, omitting, unfortunately, the frequent
ablutions prescribed by the ancient creed." "The 'Black Virgins,' so
highly reverenced in certain French cathedrals . . . proved, when at last
critically examined, to be basalt figures of Isis!" [192]

Before the shrine of Jupiter Ammon were suspended tinkling bells,
from the sound of whose chiming the priests deduced their auguries;
"A golden bell and a pomegranate . . . round about the hem of the
robe," was the result with the Mosaic Jews.[193] But in the Buddhistic
system, during the religious services, the gods of the Deva-Loka are
always invoked and invited to descend upon the altars, by the ringing of
bells suspended in the pagodas. The bell of the sacred table of Siva at
Kuhama is described in *Kailåsa,* and every Buddhist *vihåra* and lamasery
has its bells.

We thus see that the bells used by Christians come to them directly
from the Buddhist Tîbetans and Chinese. The beads and rosaries have
the same origin, and have been used by Buddhist monks for over 2300
years. The *lingams* in the Hindû temples are ornamented upon certain
days with large berries, from a tree sacred to *Mahådeva,* which are strung
into rosaries. The title of 'nun' is an Egyptian word, and had with them
the accepted meaning; the Christians did not even take the trouble to
translate the word *Nonna.* The aureole of the saints was used by the
antediluvian artists of Babylonia whenever they desired to honor or deify
a mortal's head. In a celebrated picture in Moor's *Hindoo Pantheon,* entitled, "Krishna nursed by *Devaki,* from a highly-finished picture," the
Hindû Virgin is represented as seated on a lounge and nursing Krishna.
The hair brushed back, the long veil, and the golden aureole around the
Virgin's head, as well as around that of the Hindû Savior, are striking.
No Catholic, well versed as he might be in the mysterious symbolism
of iconology, would hesitate for a moment to worship at that shrine the
Virgin Mary, the mother of his God! [194] In Indur Subba, the south
entrance of the Caves of Ellora, may be seen to this day the figure of
Indra's wife, *Indråni,* sitting with her infant son-god, pointing the finger
to heaven with the same gesture as the Italian Madonna and child.[195]

192. *The Gnostics and their Remains,* p. 71; 2nd ed., p. 173.   193. *Exod.,* xxxix, 25, 26.
194. E. Moor: *The Hindoo Pantheon,* plate 59, pp. 197-8; see also Lundy: *Monumental Christianity,* p. 217; and Inman: *Anct. Pagan and Mod. Chr. Symbolism,* p. 27.
195. Inman: *op. cit.,* p. 29.

In *Anct. Pagan and Mod. Christian Symbolism* the author gives a figure
from a medieval woodcut — the like of which we have seen by dozens in
old psalters — in which the Virgin Mary, with her infant, is represented
as the Queen of Heaven on the "crescent moon, the emblem of virginity.
Being before the sun, she almost eclipses its light. Than this, nothing
could more completely identify the Christian mother and child with Isis
and Horus, Ishtar, Venus, Juno, and a host of other Pagan goddesses,
who have been called 'Queen of Heaven,' 'Queen of the Universe,'
'Mother of God,' 'Spouse of God,' the 'Celestial Virgin,' the 'Heavenly
Peace-Maker,' etc." [196]

Such pictures are not purely astronomical. They represent the male
god and the female goddess, as the sun and moon in conjunction, "the
union of the triad with the unit." The horns of the cow on the head of
Isis have the same significance.

And so above, below, outside, and inside the Christian Church, in
the priestly garments, and the religious rites, we recognise the stamp of
exoteric heathenism. On no subject within the wide range of human
knowledge has the world been more blinded or deceived with such per-
sistent misrepresentation as on that of antiquity. Its hoary past and its
religious faiths have been misrepresented and trampled under the feet of
its successors; its hierophants and prophets, *mystae* and *epoptae* [197] of the
once sacred adyta of the temple shown as demoniacs and devil-worshipers. Decked in the despoiled garments of the victim, the Christian priest
now anathematizes the latter with rites and ceremonies which he has
learned from the theurgists themselves. The Mosaic *Bible* is used as a
weapon against the people who furnished it. The heathen philosopher is
cursed under the very roof which has witnessed his initiation; and the
"monkey of God" (*i. e.*, the devil of Tertullian), "the originator and
founder of magical theurgy, the science of illusions and lies, whose father
and author is the demon," is exorcized with holy water by the hand which
holds the identical *lituus* [198] with which the ancient augur, after a solemn
prayer, used to determine the regions of heaven, and evoke, in the name
of the HIGHEST, the minor god (now termed the Devil), who unveiled to
his eyes futurity, and enabled him to prophesy! On the part of the
Christians and the clergy it is nothing but shameful ignorance, prejudice,
and that contemptible pride so boldly denounced by one of their own
reverend ministers, J. B. Gross,[199] which rails against all investigation
"as a useless or a criminal labor, whenever it is to be feared that it will
result in the overthrow of pre-established systems of faith." On the part
of the scholars it is the same apprehension of the possible necessity of

---

196. *Ibid.*, p. 76.   197. Initiates and seers.
198. The augur's, and now bishop's, pastoral crook.   199. *The Heathen Religion.*

having to modify some of their erroneously-established theories of science. "Nothing but such pitiable prejudice," says Gross, "can have thus misrepresented the theology of heathenism, and distorted — nay, caricatured — its forms of religious worship. It is time that posterity should raise its voice in vindication of violated truth, and that the present age should learn a little of that common sense of which it boasts with as much self-complacency as if the prerogative of reason was the birthright only of modern times."

All this gives a sure clew to the real cause of the hatred felt by the early and medieval Christian toward his Pagan brother and dangerous rival. We hate only what we fear. The Christian thaumaturgist once having broken all association with the Mysteries of the temples and with "these schools so renowned for magic," described by St. Hilarion,[200] could certainly little expect to rival the Pagan wonder-workers. No apostle, with the exception perhaps of healing by mesmeric power, has ever equaled Apollonius of Tyana; and the scandal created among the apostles by the miracle-doing Simon Magus is too notorious to be repeated here. "How is it," asks Justin Martyr, in evident dismay, "how is it that the talismans of Apollonius the [τελέσματα] have power in certain members of creation, for they prevent, as we see, the fury of the waves, and the violence of the winds, and the attacks of wild beasts; and whilst our Lord's miracles are preserved by tradition alone, those of Apollonius are most numerous, and actually manifested in present facts, so as to lead astray all beholders?"[201] This perplexed martyr solves the problem by attributing very correctly the efficacy and potency of the charms used by Apollonius to his profound knowledge of the sympathies and antipathies (or repugnances) of nature.

Unable to deny the evident superiority of their enemies' powers, the Fathers had recourse to the old but ever-successful method — that of slander. They honored the theurgists with the same insinuating calumny that had been resorted to by the Pharisees against Jesus. "Thou hast a daemon," the elders of the Jewish Synagog had said to him. "Thou hast the Devil," repeated the cunning Fathers with equal truth, addressing the Pagan thaumaturgist; and the widely-bruited charge, erected later into an article of faith, won the day.

But the modern heirs of these ecclesiastical falsifiers, who denounce magic, spiritualism, and even magnetism as being produced by a demon, forget or perhaps never read the classics. None of our bigots has ever looked with more scorn on the *abuses* of magic than did the true initiate

---

200. *Pères du désert d'Orient,* II, p. 283.
201. Justin Martyr: *Quaestiones,* xxiv.

of old. No modern or even medieval law could be more severe than
that of the hierophant. True, he had more discrimination, charity, and
justice than the Christian clergy; for while banishing the 'unconscious'
sorcerer, the person troubled with a demon, from within the sacred precincts of the adyta, the priests, instead of mercilessly burning him, took
care of the unfortunate 'possessed one.' Having hospitals expressly
for that purpose in the neighborhood of temples, the ancient 'medium,'
if obsessed, was taken care of and restored to health. But with one who
had, by conscious *witchcraft*, acquired powers dangerous to his fellow-
creatures, the priests of old were as severe as justice herself. "Any person *accidentally* guilty of homicide, or of any crime, or convicted of
witchcraft, was excluded from the Eleusinian Mysteries."[202] And so were
they from all others. This law, mentioned by all writers on the ancient
initiation, speaks for itself. The claim of Augustine,[203] that all the explanations given by the Neo-Platonists were invented by themselves, is absurd. For nearly all the ceremonies in their true and successive order are
given by Plato himself, in a more or less covered way. The Mysteries are
as old as the world, and one well versed in the esoteric mythologies of
various nations can trace them back to the days of the ante-Vedic period
in India. A condition of the strictest virtue and purity is required from
the *Vatu*, or candidate, in India before he can become an initiate, whether
he aims to be a simple fakir, a *Purohita* (public priest) or a *Sannyâsî*,
a saint of the second degree of initiation, the most holy as the most
revered of them all. After having conquered, in the terrible trials preliminary to admittance to the inner temple in the subterranean crypts of
his pagoda, the *sannyâsî* passes the rest of his life in the temple, practising the eighty-four rules and ten virtues prescribed to the *Yogis*.

"No one who has not practised, during his whole life, the ten virtues
which the divine Manu makes incumbent as a duty, can be initiated into
the Mysteries of the council," say the Hindû books of initiation.

These virtues are: "Resignation; the act of rendering good for evil;
temperance; probity; purity; chastity, and repression of the physical
senses; the knowledge of the Holy Scriptures; that of the *Superior*
soul [spirit]; worship of truth; abstinence from anger."[203a] These virtues must alone direct the life of a true *Yogi*. "No unworthy adept ought
to defile the ranks of the holy initiates by his presence for twenty-four
hours." The adept becomes guilty after having once broken any one
of these vows. Surely the exercise of such virtues is inconsistent with
the idea one has of *devil*-worship and lasciviousness of purpose!

And now we will try to give a clear insight into one of the chief ob-

---

202. Taylor: *Eleus. and Bacchic Myst.*, ed. A. Wilder, p. 18 (4th edit.); also Porphyry
and others.   203. *The City of God*, X.   203a. *Manu*, VI, *slokas* 92-3.

jects of this work. What we desire to prove is that underlying every
ancient popular religion was the same ancient wisdom-doctrine, one and
identical, professed and practised by the initiates of every country, who
alone were aware of its existence and importance. To ascertain its origin,
and the precise age in which it was matured, is now beyond human
possibility. A single glance, however, is enough to assure one that it
could not have attained the marvelous perfection in which we find it
pictured to us in the relics of the various esoteric systems, except after a
succession of ages. A philosophy so profound, a moral code so ennobling,
and practical results so conclusive and so uniformly demonstrable, is not
the growth of a generation, or even a single epoch. Fact must have been
piled upon fact, deduction upon deduction, science have begotten science,
and myriads of the brightest human intellects have reflected upon the
laws of nature, before this ancient doctrine could have taken concrete
shape. The proofs of this identity of fundamental doctrine in the old
religions are found in the prevalence of a system of initiation; in the
secret sacerdotal castes who had the guardianship of mystical words of
power; and in the public display of a phenomenal control over natural
forces, indicating association with preterhuman beings. Every approach
to the Mysteries of all these nations was guarded with the same jealous
care, and in all the penalty of death was inflicted upon initiates of any
degree who divulged the secrets entrusted to them. We have seen that
such was the case in the Eleusinian and Bacchic Mysteries, among the
Chaldaean Magi, and the Egyptian hierophants; while with the Hindûs,
from whom they were all derived, the same rule has prevailed from time
immemorial. We are left in no doubt upon this point; for the *Agrushada
Parikshai* says explicitly, "Every initiate, to whatever degree he may
belong, who reveals the great sacred formula, must be put to death."

Naturally enough this same extreme penalty was prescribed in all the
multifarious sects and brotherhoods which at different periods have
sprung from the ancient stock. We find it with the early Essenes, Gnostics, theurgic Neo-Platonists, and medieval philosophers; and in our day
even the Masons perpetuate the memory of the old obligations in the
penalties of throat-cutting, dismemberment, and disemboweling, with
which the candidate is threatened. As the Masonic 'master's word' is
communicated only at 'low breath,' so the selfsame precaution is prescribed in the Chaldaean *Book of Numbers* and the Jewish *Merkabah.*
When initiated, the neophyte was led by an *ancient* to a secluded spot,
and there the latter whispered *in his ear* the great secret.[204] The Mason
swears, under the most frightful penalties, that he will not communicate

---

204. A. Franck: *La Kabbale,* ch. i.

the secrets of any degree "to a brother of an *inferior degree*"; and the *Agrushada Parikshai* says: "Any initiate of the third degree who before the prescribed time reveals the superior truths to the initiates of the second degree, must be put to death." Again, the Masonic apprentice consents to have his "tongue torn out by the roots" if he divulge anything to the profane; and in the Hindû books of initiation, the same *Agrushada Parikshai*, we find that any initiate of the first degree (the lowest) who betrays the secrets of his initiation to members of other castes, for whom the science should be a closed book, must have "his *tongue cut out*" and suffer other mutilations.

As we proceed, we will point out the evidences of this identity of vows, formulas, rites and doctrines between the ancient faiths. We will also show that not only is their memory still preserved in India, but also that the Secret Association is still alive and as active as ever. After reading what we have to say, it may be inferred that the chief pontiff and hierophant, the *Brahmâtma*, is still accessible to those 'who know,' though perhaps recognised by another name; and that the ramifications of his influence extend throughout the world. But we will now return to the early Christian period.

As though he were not aware that there was any esoteric significance in the exoteric symbols, and that the Mysteries themselves were composed of two parts, the lesser at Agrae, and the higher ones at Eleusinia, Clemens Alexandrinus, with a rancorous bigotry that one might expect from a renegade Neo-Platonist but is astonished to find in this generally honest and learned Father, stigmatized the Mysteries as indecent and diabolical. Whatever were the rites enacted among the neophytes before they passed to a higher form of instruction; however misunderstood were the trials of *Katharsis* or purification, during which they were submitted to every kind of probation; and however much the material or physical aspect might have led to calumny, it is but wicked prejudice which can induce anyone to say that under this external meaning there was not a far deeper and spiritual significance.

It is positively absurd to judge the ancients from our own standpoint of propriety and virtue. And most assuredly it is not for the Church — which now stands accused by all the modern symbologists of having adopted precisely these same emblems in their coarsest aspect, and feels herself powerless to refute the accusations — to throw the stone at those who were her models. When men like Pythagoras, Plato and Iamblichus, renowned for their severe morality, took part in the Mysteries, and spoke of them with veneration, it ill behooves our modern critics to judge them so rashly upon their merely external aspect. Iamblichus explains the worst; and his explanation, for an unprejudiced mind, ought to be perfectly satisfactory. "Exhibitions of this kind," he says, "in the Mysteries were designed to free us from licentious passions, by gratifying the sight, and at the same time vanquishing all evil thought, through *the awful sanctity* with which these rites were invested." [205] "The wisest and best men in the Pagan world," adds Dr. Warburton, "are unanimous in this, that the Mysteries were instituted pure, and proposed the noblest ends by the worthiest means." [206]

In these celebrated rites, although persons of both sexes and all classes were allowed to take a part, and a participation in them was even obligatory, very few indeed attained the higher and final initiation. The gradation of the Mysteries is given us by Proclus in the fourth book of his *Theology of Plato.*[207] "The perfective rite τελετή, precedes in order the initiation *muesis*, and the initiation *epopteia*, or the final apocalypse (revelation)." Theon of Smyrna, in *Mathematica*, also divides the mystic rites into five parts: "the first of which is the previous purification; for *neither are the Mysteries communicated to all* who are willing to receive them; but there are certain persons who are prevented by the voice of the crier (κῆρυξ), . . . since it is necessary that such as are not expelled from the Mysteries should first be refined by certain purifications, which the reception of the sacred rites succeeds. The third part is denominated *epopteia* or reception. And the fourth, which is the end and design of the revelation, is *the binding of the head and fixing of the crowns* [208] . . . whether after this he [the initiated person] becomes . . . a hierophant or sustains some other part of the sacerdotal office. But the fifth, which is produced from all these, *is friendship and interior communion with God.*" And this was the last and most awful of all the Mysteries.

There are writers who have often wondered at the meaning of this claim to a "friendship and interior communion with God." Christian authors have denied the pretensions of the 'Pagans' to such 'communion,' affirming that only Christian saints were and are capable of enjoying it; materialistic skeptics have altogether scoffed at the ideas of both. After long ages of religious materialism and spiritual stagnation, it has most certainly become difficult if not altogether impossible to substantiate the claims of either party. The old Greeks, who had

---

205. *Mysteries of the Egyptians, Chaldaeans, and Assyrians,* ch. xi.
206. *Divine Legation of Moses demonstrated, etc.,* II, p. 172.
207. *On the Theol. of Plato,* p. 200 (Taylor's edit.): London, 1816.
208. This expression must not be understood literally; for in the initiation of certain Brotherhoods it has a secret meaning, hinted at by Pythagoras, when he describes his feelings after the initiation and tells that he was crowned by the gods in whose presence he had drunk 'the waters of life' — in Hindustani, *âb-i-hayât,* fount of life. Cf. Taylor: *Eleusinian and Bacchic Mysteries,* ed. A. Wilder, pp. 82-3; 4th edit.

once crowded around the Agora of Athens with its altar to the 'Unknown God,' are no more; and their descendants firmly believe that they have found the 'Unknown' in the Jewish Jehovah. The divine ecstasies of the early Christians have made room for visions of a more modern character, in perfect keeping with progress and civilization. The 'Son of man' appearing to the rapt vision of the ancient Christian as coming from the seventh heaven, in a cloud of glory, and surrounded with angels and winged seraphim, has made room for a more prosaic and at the same time more business-like Jesus. The latter is now shown as making morning calls upon Mary and Martha in Bethany; as seating himself on "the *ottoman*" with the younger sister, a lover of "ethics," while Martha goes off to the kitchen to cook. Anon the heated fancy of a blasphemous Brooklyn preacher and harlequin, the Reverend Dr. Talmage, makes us see her rushing back "with besweated brow, a pitcher in one hand and the tongs in the other . . . into the presence of Christ," and blowing him up for not caring that her sister hath left her "to serve alone." [209]

From the birth of the solemn and majestic conception of the un-revealed Deity of the ancient adepts, down to such caricatured descriptions of him who died on the Cross for his philanthropic devotion to humanity, long centuries have intervened, and their heavy tread seems to have almost entirely obliterated all sense of a spiritual religion from the hearts of his professed followers. No wonder then that the sentence of Proclus is no longer understood by the Christians, and is rejected as a 'vagary' by the materialists, who in their negation are less blasphemous and atheistical than many of the reverends and members of the churches. But although the Greek *epoptai* are no more, we have now in our own age a people, far more ancient than the oldest Hellenes, who practise the so-called 'preterhuman' gifts to the same extent as did their ancestors far earlier than the days of Troy. It is to this people that we draw the attention of the psychologist and philosopher.

One need not go very deep into the literature of the Orientalists to become convinced that in most cases they do not even suspect that in

---

209. This original and very long sermon was preached in a church at Brooklyn, N. Y., on the 15th day of April, 1877. On the following morning the reverend orator was called in the *Sun* a gibbering charlatan; but this deserved epithet will not prevent other reverend buffoons doing the same and even worse. And this is the religion of Christ! Far better disbelieve in him altogether than caricature one's God in such a manner. We heartily applaud the *Sun* for the following views: "And then when Talmage makes Christ say to Martha in the tantrums: 'Don't worry, but sit down on this ottoman,' he adds the climax to a scene that the inspired writers had nothing to say about. Talmage's buffoonery is going too far. If he were the worst heretic in the land, instead of being straight in his orthodoxy, he would not do so much evil to religion as he does by his familiar blasphemies."

the arcane philosophy of India there are depths which they have not sounded, and *cannot* sound, for they pass on without perceiving them. There is a pervading tone of conscious superiority, a ring of contempt in the treatment of Hindû metaphysics, as though the European mind is alone enlightened enough to polish the rough diamond of the old Sanskrit writers, and separate right from wrong for the benefit of their descendants. We see them disputing over the external forms of expression without a conception of the great vital truths these hide from the profane view.

"As a rule the Brâhmanas," says Jacolliot, "rarely go beyond the class of *grihasta* [priests of the vulgar castes] and *purohita* [exorcizers, divines, prophets, and evocators of spirits]. And yet we shall see . . . once that we have touched upon the question and study of manifestations and phenomena, that these initiates of the *first* degree [the lowest] attribute to themselves, and in appearance possess faculties developed to a degree which has never been equaled in Europe. As to the initiates of the second and especially of the third category, they pretend to be enabled to ignore time, space, and to command life and death." [210]

Such initiates as these M. Jacolliot *did not meet;* for, as he says himself, they only appear on the most solemn occasions, and when the faith of the multitudes has to be strengthened by phenomena of a superior order. "They are never seen, either in the neighborhood of, or even inside the temples, except at the grand quinquennial festival of the fire. On that occasion they appear about the middle of the night, on a platform erected in the center of the sacred lake, like so many phantoms, and by their conjurations they illumine the space. A fiery column of light ascends from around them, rushing from earth to heaven. Unfamiliar sounds vibrate through the air, and five or six hundred thousand Hindûs, gathered from every part of India to contemplate these demi-gods, throw themselves with their faces buried in the dust, invoking the souls of their ancestors." [211]

Let any impartial person read *Le spiritisme dans le monde,* and he cannot believe that this "implacable rationalist," as Jacolliot takes pride in terming himself, said one word more than is warranted by what he had seen. His statements support and are corroborated by those of other skeptics. As a rule, the missionaries, even after passing half a lifetime in the country of "devil-worship," as they call India, either disingenuously *deny* altogether what they cannot help knowing to be true, or ridiculously attribute phenomena to this power of the Devil, that outrival the 'miracles' of the apostolic ages. And what do we see this French

---

210. *Le spiritisme dans le monde,* p. 68.   211. *Ibid.,* pp. 78, 79.

author, notwithstanding his incorrigible rationalism, forced to admit after having narrated the greatest wonders? Watch the fakirs as he would, he is compelled to bear the strongest testimony to their perfect honesty in the matter of their miraculous phenomena. "Never," he says, "have we succeeded in detecting a single one in the act of deceit." One fact should be noted by all who, without having been in India, still fancy they are clever enough to expose the fraud of *pretended* magicians. This skilled and cool observer, this redoubtable materialist, after his long sojourn in India, affirms, "We unhesitatingly avow that we have not met either in India or in Ceylon a single European, even among the oldest residents, who has been able to indicate the means employed by these devotees for the production of these phenomena!"

And how should they? Does not this zealous Orientalist confess to us that even he, who had every available means at hand to learn many of their rites and doctrines at first hand, failed in his attempts to make the Brâhmanas explain to him their secrets? "All that our most diligent inquiries of the *Purohitas* could elicit from them respecting the acts of their superiors (the invisible initiates of the temples) amounts to very little." And again, speaking of one of the books, he confesses that while purporting to reveal all that is desirable to know it "falls back into mysterious formulas, in combinations of magical and occult letters, the secret of which it has been impossible for us to penetrate," etc.

The fakirs, although they can never reach beyond the first degree of initiation, are nevertheless the only agents between the living world and the 'silent brothers,' or those initiates who never cross the thresholds of their sacred dwellings. The *Fukarâ-Yogis* belong to the temples, and who knows but these cenobites of the sanctuary have far more to do with the psychological phenomena which attend the fakirs, and have been so graphically described by Jacolliot, than the *Pitris* themselves? Who can tell but that the fluidic specter of the ancient Brâhmana seen by Jacolliot was the *Scin-lecca*, the spiritual *double*, of one of these mysterious *sannyâsis?*

Although the story has been translated and commented upon by Professor Perty of Geneva, still we will venture to give it in Jacolliot's own words: "A moment after the disappearance of the hands, the fakir continuing his evocations (*mantras*) more earnestly than ever, a cloud like the first, but more opalescent and more opaque, began to hover near the small brasier, which, by request of the Hindû, I had constantly fed with live coals. Little by little it assumed a form entirely human, and I distinguished the specter — for I cannot call it otherwise — of an old Brâhmana sacrificator, kneeling near the little brasier.

"He bore on his forehead the signs sacred to Vishnu, and around his body the triple cord, sign of the initiates of the priestly caste. He joined his hands above his head, as during the sacrifices, and his lips moved as if they were reciting prayers. At a given moment he took a pinch of perfumed powder and threw it upon the coals; it must have been a strong compound, for a thick smoke arose on the instant and filled the two chambers.

"When it was dissipated I perceived the specter, which, two steps from me, was extending to me its fleshless hand; I took it in mine, making a salutation, and I was astonished to find it, although bony and hard, warm and living.

" 'Art thou, indeed,' said I at this moment in a loud voice, 'an ancient inhabitant of the earth?'

"I had not finished the question, when the word AM (yes) appeared and then disappeared in letters of fire on the breast of the old Brâhmana, with an effect much like that which the word would produce if written in the dark with a stick of phosphorus.

" 'Will you leave me nothing in token of your visit?' I continued.

"The spirit broke the triple cord, composed of three strands of cotton, which begirt his loins, gave it to me, and vanished at my feet."

"Oh Brahmâ! what is this mystery which takes place every night? . . . When lying on the matting, with eyes closed, the body is lost sight of, and the soul escapes to enter into conversation with the Pitris. . . . Watch over it, O Brahmâ, when, forsaking the resting body, it goes away to hover over the waters, to wander in the immensity of heaven, and penetrate into the dark and mysterious nooks of the valleys and grand forests of the Himavat!" (*Agrushada Parikshai*) [212]

The fakirs, when belonging to some particular temple, never act but under orders. Not one of them, unless he has reached a degree of extraordinary sanctity, is freed from the influence and guidance of his *guru*, his teacher, who first initiated and instructed him in the mysteries of the *occult* sciences. Like the *subject* of the European mesmerizer, the average fakir can never rid himself entirely of the psychological influence exercised on him by his *guru*. Having passed two or three hours in the silence and solitude of the inner temple in prayer and meditation, the fakir, when he emerges thence, is mesmerically strengthened and prepared; he produces wonders far more varied and powerful than before he entered. The 'master' has *laid his hands upon him*, and the fakir feels strong.

It may be shown, on the authority of many Brâhmanical and Buddhist sacred books, that there has ever existed a great difference between adepts of the higher order, and purely psychological subjects — like many

---

212. Louis Jacolliot: *La spiritisme dans le monde*, pp. 319-320, 65.

of these fakirs, who are mediums in a certain qualified sense. True, the fakir is ever talking of Pitris, and this is natural; for they are his protecting deities. But are the Pitris *disembodied human beings of our race?* This is the question, and we will discuss it in a moment.

We say that the fakir may be regarded in a degree as a medium; for he is — what is not generally known — under the direct mesmeric influence of a living adept, his *sannyâsî* or *guru.* When the latter dies, the power of the former, unless he has received the last transfer of spiritual forces, wanes and often even disappears. Why, if it were otherwise, should the fakirs have been excluded from the right of advancing to the second and third degree? The lives of many of them exemplify a degree of self-sacrifice and sanctity unknown and utterly incomprehensible to Europeans, who shudder at the bare thought of such self-inflicted tortures. But however shielded from control by vulgar and earth-bound spirits, however wide the chasm between a debasing influence and their self-controlled souls, and however well protected by the seven-knotted magical bamboo rod which he receives from the guru, still the fakir lives in the outer world of sin and matter, and it is possible that his soul may be tainted, perchance by the magnetic emanations from profane objects and persons, and thereby give access to strange spirits and *gods.* To admit one so situated, one not under any and all circumstances sure of the mastery over himself, to a knowledge of the awful mysteries and priceless secrets of initiation, would be impracticable. It would not only imperil the security of that which must, at all hazards, be guarded from profanation, but it would be consenting to admit behind the veil a fellow being, whose mediumistic irresponsibility might at any moment cause him to lose his life through an involuntary indiscretion. The same law which prevailed in the Eleusinian Mysteries before our era holds good now in India.

Not only must the adept have mastery over himself, but he must be able to control the inferior grades of spiritual beings, nature-spirits, and earthbound souls, in short the very ones by whom, if by any, the fakir is liable to be affected.

For the objector to affirm that the Brâhmana-adepts and the fakirs admit that of themselves they are powerless, and can only act with the help of disembodied human spirits, is to state that these Hindûs are unacquainted with the laws of their sacred books and even the meaning of the word *Pitris.* The *Laws of Manu,* the *Atharva-Veda,* and other books, prove what we now say. "All that exists," says the *Atharva-Veda,* "is in the power of the gods. The gods are under the power of magical conjurations. The magical conjurations are under the control of the Brâhmanas. Hence the gods are in the power of the Brâhmanas." This is logical, albeit seemingly paradoxical, and it is the fact. And this fact will explain to those who have not hitherto had the clew (among whom Jacolliot must be numbered, as will appear on reading his works), why the fakir should be confined to the first or lowest degree of that course of initiation whose highest adepts, or hierophants, are the *sannyásis*, or members of the ancient Supreme Council of Seventy.

Moreover, in Book I of the Hindû *Genesis*, or *Book of Creation* of *Manu*, the *Pitris* are called the *lunar* ancestors of the human race. They belong to a race of beings different from ourselves, and cannot properly be called 'human spirits' in the sense in which the spiritualists use this term. This is what is said of them:

"Then they [the gods] created the *Yakshas*, the *Râkshasas*, the *Pisâchas*,[213] the *Gandharvas*[214] the *Apsarases*, the *Asuras*, the *Nâgas*,[215] the *Sarpas*, the *Supurnas*, and the *Pitris*" — *lunar ancestors of the human race* (see *Institutes of Manu*, I, *sloka* 37, and also where the *Pitris* are termed "progenitors of mankind," III, 201).

The Pitris are a distinct race of spirits belonging to the mythological hierarchy (or rather to the kabalistical nomenclature) and must be included with the good genii, the daemons of the Greeks, or the inferior gods of the invisible world; and when a fakir attributes his phenomena to the Pitris he means only what the ancient philosophers and theurgists meant when they maintained that all the 'miracles' were obtained through the intervention of the gods, or the good and bad daemons who control the powers of nature, the *elementals* who are subordinate to the power of him 'who knows.' A ghost or human phantom would be termed by a fakir *palit*, or *bhûtnâ*, as that of a female human spirit *pichhalpâ'î*, not *pitri*. True, *pitaras* (plural) means fathers, ancestors; and *pitrâ'î* is a kinsman; but these words are used in quite a different sense from that of the Pitris invoked in the mantras.

To maintain before a devout Brâhmana or a fakir that any one can converse with the spirits of the dead, would be to shock him with what would appear to him blasphemy. Does not the following verse of the *Bhâgavata-Purâna* state that this supreme felicity is alone reserved to the holy *sannyásis*, the *gurus* and *yogis?*

"Long before they finally rid themselves of their mortal envelopes, the souls who have practised only good, such as those of the *sannyásis* and the *vânaprasthas*, acquire the faculty of conversing with the souls which preceded them to the *svarga*." [216]

---

213. *Pisâchas*, daemons of the race, of the gnomes, the giants, and the vampires.
214. *Gandharvas*, good daemons, celestial seraphs, singers.
215. *Asuras* and *Nâgas* are the Titanic spirits and the dragon or serpent-headed spirits.
   216. Cited in the proem of the *Agrushada Parikshai*.

In this case the Pitris instead of genii are the spirits, or rather souls, of the departed ones. But they will freely communicate only with those whose atmosphere is as pure as their own, and to whose prayerful *kalassa* (invocation) they can respond without the risk of defiling their own celestial purity. When the soul of the invocator has reached the *Sayadyam*, or perfect identity of essence with the Universal Soul, when matter is utterly conquered, then the adept can freely enter into daily and hourly communion with those who, though unburdened with their corporeal forms, are still themselves progressing through the endless series of transformations included in the gradual approach to the *Paramâtman*, or the grand Universal Soul.

Bearing in mind that the Christian Fathers have always claimed for themselves and their saints the name of 'friends of God,' and knowing that they borrowed this expression, with many others, from the technology of the Pagan temples, it is but natural to expect them to show an evil temper whenever alluding to these rites. Ignorant, as a rule, and having had biographers as ignorant as themselves, we could not well expect to find in the accounts of their beatific visions a descriptive beauty such as we find in the Pagan classics. Whether the visions and objective phenomena claimed by both the fathers of the desert and the hierophants of the sanctuary are to be discredited, or accepted as facts, the splendid imagery employed by Proclus and Apuleius in narrating the small portion of the final initiation that they dared reveal, throws completely into the shade the plagiarized tales of the Christian ascetics, faithful *copies* though they were intended to be. The story of the temptation of St. Anthony in the desert by the female dæmon is a parody upon the preliminary trials of the neophyte during the *Mikra*, or minor Mysteries of Agrae — those rites at the thought of which Clement railed so bitterly, and which represented the bereaved Demeter in search of her child, and her good-natured hostess Baubo.[217]

Without entering again into a demonstration that in Christian, and especially Irish Roman Catholic, churches [218] the same apparently indecent customs as the above prevailed until the end of the last century, we will recur to the untiring labors and works of that honest and brave defender of the ancient faith, Thomas Taylor. However much dogmatic Greek scholarship may have found to say against his "mistranslations," his memory must be dear to every true Platonist, who seeks rather to learn the inner thought of the great philosopher than enjoy the mere external mechanism of his writings. Better classical translators may

217. Arnob.: *Adv. gent.* V, 25; Clem. Alex.: *Hortatory Address to the Greeks*, c. ii.
218. See Inman: *Ancient Pagan and Modern Christian Symbolism*, p. 66.

have rendered us, in more correct phraseology, Plato's *words*, but
Taylor shows us Plato's *meaning*, and this is more than can be said of
Zeller, Jowett, and their predecessors. Therefore as Professor A. Wilder
writes, "Taylor's works have met with favor at the hands of men
capable of profound and recondite thinking; and it must be conceded
that he was endowed with a superior qualification — that of an in-
tuitive perception of the interior meaning of the subjects which he
considered. Others may have known more Greek, but he knew more
Plato." [219]

Taylor devoted his whole useful life to the search after such old
manuscripts as would enable him to have his own speculations concerning
several obscure rites in the Mysteries corroborated by writers who had
been initiated themselves. It is with full confidence in the assertions of
various classical writers that we say that ridiculous, perhaps licentious in
some cases, as may appear ancient worship to the modern critic, it ought
not to have so appeared to the Christians. During the medieval ages,
and even later, they accepted pretty nearly the same without understanding the secret import of its rites, and were quite satisfied with the
obscure and rather fantastic interpretations of their clergy, who accepted
the exterior form and distorted the inner meaning. We are ready to
concede, in full justice, that centuries have passed since the great
majority of the Christian clergy, who *are not allowed to pry into God's
mysteries nor seek to explain* that which the Church has once accepted
and established, have had the remotest idea of their symbolism, whether
in its exoteric or esoteric meaning. Not so with the head of the Church
and its highest dignitaries. And if we fully agree with Inman that it is
"difficult to believe that the ecclesiastics who sanctioned the publication
of such a print [220] could have been as ignorant as modern ritualists," we
are not at all prepared to believe with the same author "that the latter,
if they knew the real meaning of the symbols commonly used by the
Roman Church, would *not* have adopted them."

To eliminate what is plainly derived from the sex and nature worship of the ancient heathens, would be equivalent to pulling down the

219. Thos. Taylor: *Eleusinian and Bacchic Mysteries*, p. 27: 4th ed.

220. Illustrated figures "from an ancient Rosary of the blessed Virgin Mary, printed
at Venice, 1524, with a license from the Inquisition." In the illustrations given by Dr.
Inman the Virgin is represented in an Assyrian 'grove,' the *abomination in the eyes
of the Lord*, according to the Bible prophets. "The book in question," says the author,
"contains numerous figures, all resembling closely the Mesopotamian emblem of *Ishtar*.
The presence of the woman *therein* identifies the two as symbolic of Isis, or *la nature;*
and a man bowing down in adoration thereof shows the same idea as is depicted in
Assyrian sculptures, where males offer to the goddess *symbols of themselves*." See *Ancient
Pagan and Modern Christian Symbolism*, p. 91: 2nd ed., New York.

whole Roman Catholic image-worship — the *Madonna* element — and reforming the faith to Protestantism. The enforcement of the late dogma of the Immaculation was prompted by this very secret reason. The science of symbology was making too rapid progress. Blind faith in the Pope's infallibility and in the immaculate nature of the Virgin and *of her ancestral female lineage to a certain remove* could alone save the Church from the indiscreet revelations of science. It was a clever stroke of policy on the part of the vicegerent of God. What matters it if, by "conferring upon her such an honor," [221] as Don Pasquale di Franciscis naïvely expresses it, he has made a goddess of the Virgin Mary, an Olympian Deity who, having been by her very nature placed in the impossibility of sinning, can claim no virtue, no personal merit for her purity, precisely for which, as we were taught to believe in our younger days, she was chosen among all other women. If his Holiness has deprived her of this, perhaps on the other hand he thinks that he has endowed her with at least one physical attribute not shared by the other virgin-goddesses. But even this new dogma which, in company with the new claim to *infallibility*, has quasi-revolutionized the Christian world, is not original with the Church of Rome. It is but a return to a hardly-remembered *heresy* of the early Christian ages, that of the Collyridians, so called from their *sacrificing cakes* to the Virgin, whom they claimed to be *Virgin-born.* [222] The new sentence, "O Virgin Mary, *conceived without sin*," is simply a tardy acceptance of that which was at first deemed a "*blasphemous heresy*" by the orthodox Fathers.

To think for one moment that any of the popes, cardinals or other high dignitaries "were not aware" from the first to the last of the external meanings of their symbols, is to do injustice to their great learning and their spirit of Machiavellism. It is to forget that the emissaries of Rome will never be stopped by any difficulty which can be skirted by the employment of Jesuitical artifice. The policy of complaisant conformity was never carried to greater lengths than by the missionaries in Ceylon who, according to the Abbé Dubois — certainly a learned and competent authority—"conducted the images of the Virgin and Savior on triumphal cars, imitated from the orgies of Jaggernath, and introduced the dancers from the Brahmanical rites into the ceremonial of the church." [223] Let us at least thank these black-frocked politicians for their consistency in employing the car of Jagannâtha, upon which the 'wicked he

221. *Speeches of Pope Pius IX*, II, 26; cf. W. E. Gladstone: *Rome, etc.*, p. 1
222. Cf. C. W. King: *The Gnostics, etc.*, p. 231, 2nd ed.; *The Genealogy of the Bl. Virgin Mary*, by Faustus, bishop of Ries.
223. *Edinburgh Review*, April, 1851, p. 411; cited in Pococke: *India in Greece*, pp. 318-9. London, 1852.

convey the *lingam* of Śiva. To have used *this* car to carry in its turn the Romish representative of the female principle in nature, is to show discrimination and a thorough knowledge of the oldest mythological conceptions. They have blended the two deities, and thus represented, in a Christian procession, the 'heathen' *Brahmâ*, or *Nara* (the father), *Nârî* (the mother), and *Virâj* (the son).

Says *Manu:* "The Sovereign Master who exists through himself, divides his body into two halves, male and female, and from the union of these two principles is born *Virâj*, the Son." [224]

There was not a Christian Father who could have been ignorant of these symbols in their physical meaning; for it is in this latter aspect that they were abandoned to the ignorant rabble. Moreover they all had as good reasons to suspect the occult symbolism contained in these images; although as none of them — Paul excepted, perhaps — had been initiated, they could know nothing whatever about the nature of the final rites. Any person revealing these mysteries was put to death, regardless of sex, nationality or creed. A Christian Father would no more be proof against *an accident* than a Pagan *Mysta* or the Μύστης.

If during the *Aporrheta* or preliminary arcanes, there were some practices which might have shocked the pudicity of a Christian convert — though we doubt the sincerity of such statements — their mystical symbolism was all sufficient to relieve the performance of any charge of licentiousness. Even the episode of the Matron Baubo — whose rather eccentric method of consolation was immortalized in the minor Mysteries — is explained by impartial mystagogues quite naturally. Ceres-Demeter and her earthly wanderings in search of her daughter are the allegorized descriptions of one of the most metaphysico-psychological subjects ever treated of by human mind. It is a mask for the transcendent narrative of the initiated seers; the celestial vision of the freed soul of the initiate of the last hour describing the process by which the soul that has not yet been incarnated descends for the first time into matter, "Blessed is he who, having seen those *common concerns* of the underworld, knows both the end of life and its divine origin from Jupiter," says Pindar.[225] Taylor shows, on the authority of more than one initiate, that the "dramatic performances of the Lesser Mysteries were designed by their founders to signify *occultly* the condition of the unpurified soul invested with an earthly body, and enveloped in a material and physical

224. *Manu*, I, *śloka* 32: Sir W. Jones, translating from the Northern 'Manu,' renders this *śloka* as follows: "Having divided his own substance, the mighty Power became half male, half female, or *nature active and passive;* and from that female he produced VIRÂJ."

225. In Clem. Alex.: *Strom.*, III, iii.

nature . . . that the soul, indeed, till purified by philosophy, suffers death through its union with the body." [226]

The body is the sepulcher, the prison of the soul, and many Christian Fathers held with Plato that the soul is *punished* through its union with the body. Such is the fundamental doctrine of the Buddhists and of many Brâhmanists too. When Plotinus remarks that "when the soul has descended into generation [from its *half*-divine condition] she partakes of evil, and is carried a great way into a state the opposite of her first purity and integrity, to be entirely merged in which is nothing more than to fall into dark mire," [227] he only repeats the teachings of Gautama-Buddha. If we have to believe the ancient initiates at all, we must accept their interpretation of the symbols. And if moreover we find them perfectly coinciding with the teachings of the greatest philosophers and that which we know symbolizes the same meaning in the modern Mysteries in the East, we must believe them to be right.

If Demeter was considered the intellectual soul — or rather the *Astral* soul, half emanation from the spirit and half tainted with matter through a succession of spiritual evolutions — we may readily understand what is meant by the Matron Baubo, the Enchantress who, before she succeeds in reconciling the soul, Demeter, to its new position finds herself obliged to assume the sexual forms of an infant. Baubo is *matter*, the physical body; and the intellectual, as yet pure astral soul can be ensnared into its new terrestrial prison but by the display of innocent babyhood. Until then, doomed to her fate, Demeter (or *Magna-mater*, the Soul) wonders and hesitates and suffers; but once having partaken of the magic potion prepared by Baubo she forgets her sorrows; for a certain time she parts with that consciousness of higher intellect that she was possessed of before entering the body of a child. Thenceforth she must seek to rejoin it again; and when the age of reason arrives for the child, the struggle — forgotten for a few years of infancy — begins again. The astral soul is placed between matter (body) and the highest intellect (its immortal spirit or *nous*). Which of those two will conquer? The result of the battle of life lies between the triad. It is a question of a few years of physical enjoyment on earth and — if it has begotten abuse — of the dissolution of the earthly body being followed by death of the astral body, which thus is prevented from being united with the highest spirit of the triad which alone confers on us individual immortality; or on the other hand of becoming immortal *mystae;* initiated before the death of the body into the divine truths of the after-life. Demi-gods below, and GODS above.

---

226. Taylor: *Eleus. and Bacch. Myst.*, pp. 34, 35: 4th edit.
227. *Ennead* I, bk. viii.

Such was the chief object of the Mysteries represented as diabolical
by theology, and ridiculed by modern symbologists. To disbelieve that
there exist in man certain arcane powers which by psychological study
he can develop in himself to the highest degree, become a hierophant
and then impart to others under the same conditions of earthly discipline,
is to cast an imputation of falsehood and lunacy upon a number of the
best, purest and most learned men of antiquity and of the Middle Ages.
What the hierophant was allowed to see at the last hour is hardly hinted
at by them. And yet Pythagoras, Plato, Plotinus, Iamblichus, Proclus
and many others knew and affirmed their reality [*i. e.*, of these arcane
powers].

Whether in the 'inner temple,' or through the study of theurgy carried
on privately, or by the sole exertion of a whole life of spiritual labor, they
[the aspirants] all obtained the practical proof of such divine possibilities
for man, fighting his battle with life on earth to win a life in the eternity.
What the last *epopteia* was is alluded to by Plato in *Phaedrus* (§ 64);
". . . being initiated in those *Mysteries*, which it is lawful to call the most
blessed of all mysteries . . . we were freed from the molestations of evils
which otherwise await us in a future period of time. Likewise, in consequence of this divine *initiation*, we became *spectators* of entire, simple,
immovable, and *blessed visions*, resident in a pure light." This sentence
shows that they saw *visions*, gods, spirits. As Taylor correctly observes,
from all such passages in the works of the initiates it may be inferred
"that the most sublime part of the *epopteia* . . . consisted in beholding
the gods themselves invested with a resplendent light," [228] or the highest
planetary spirits. The statement of Proclus upon this subject is unequivocal: "In all the initiations and Mysteries, the gods exhibit many
forms of themselves, and appear in *a variety of shapes*, and sometimes
indeed a formless light of themselves is held forth to the view; sometimes
this light is according *to a human form*, and sometimes it proceeds into
a different shape." [229]

"Whatever is *on earth is the resemblance and* SHADOW *of something
that is in the sphere*, while that resplendent thing [the prototype of the
soul-spirit] remaineth in *unchangeable* condition, it is well also with its
shadow. But when the *resplendent one* removeth far from its shadow life
removeth from the latter to a distance. And yet that very light is the
shadow of something still more resplendent than itself." Thus speaks
Desâtir, the Persian *Book of Shet the Prophet Zirtusht*,[230] thereby showing
its identity of esoteric doctrines with those of the Greek philosophers.

The second statement of Plato confirms our belief that the Mysteries

228. *Eleus. and Bacch. Myst.*, p. 107: 4th ed.   229. Proclus: *On Plato's Republic;*
cf. T. Taylor: *The Works of Plato*, II, p. 328: London, 1804.   230. Verses 35-38.

of the ancients were identical with the Initiations, as practised now
among the Buddhists and the Hindû adepts. The highest visions, the
most *truthful*, are produced, not through *natural* ecstatics or 'mediums,'
as it is sometimes erroneously asserted, but through a regular discipline
of gradual initiations and development of psychical powers. The Mystae
were brought into close union with those whom Proclus calls "mystical
natures," "resplendent gods," because, as Plato says, "we were ourselves pure and immaculate, being liberated from this *surrounding vest-
ment*, which we denominate body, and to which we are now bound like
an oyster to its shell" (*Phaedr., loc. cit.*).

So the doctrine of planetary and terrestrial Pitris was revealed
entirely, in ancient India as well as now, only at the last moment of
initiation, and to the adepts of superior degrees. Many are the fakirs
who, though pure, honest and self-devoted, have yet never seen the
astral form of a purely *human pitar* (an ancestor or father) otherwise
than at the solemn moment of their first and last initiation. It is in
the presence of his instructor, the *guru*, and just before the *vatu*-fakir
is dispatched into the world of the living, with his seven-knotted bamboo
wand for all protection, that he is suddenly placed face to face with
the unknown PRESENCE. He sees it, and falls prostrate at the feet
of the evanescent form, but is not entrusted with the great secret
of its evocation; for it is the supreme mystery of the holy syllable.
The AUM contains the evocation of the Vedic triad, the *Trimûrti* Brahmâ,
Vishnu, Siva, say the Orientalists; [231] it contains the evocation of
something more real and objective than this triune abstraction — we say,
respectfully contradicting the eminent scientists. It is the trinity of
man himself, on his way to become immortal through the solemn
union of his inner triune SELF — the exterior, gross body, the husk,
not even being taken in consideration in this human trinity.[232] It is

---

231. The Supreme Buddha is invoked with two of his acolytes of the theistic triad,
Dharma and *Sangha.* This triad is addressed in Sanskrit in the following terms:

> *Namo Buddhâya,*
> *Namo Dharmâya,*
> *Namo Sanghâya,*
> *Aum!*

while the Tibetan Buddhists pronounce their invocations as follows:

> *Nan-won Fo-tho-ye,*
> *Nan-won Tho-ma-ye,*
> *Nan-won Seng-kia-ye,*
> *Aan!*

See also *Journal Asiatique,* tome VII, p. 286.

232. The body of man — his coat of skin — is an inert mass of matter, *per se;* it is
but the *sentient* living body within the man that is considered as the man's body proper,
and it is that which, together with the fontal soul or purely astral body, directly connected with the immortal spirit, constitutes the trinity of man.

when this trinity, in anticipation of the final triumphant reunion beyond the gates of corporeal death becomes for a few seconds a UNITY, that the candidate is allowed, at the moment of the initiation, to behold his future self. Thus we read in the Persian *Desdtîr*, of the 'Resplendent one'; in the Greek philosopher-initiates, of the *Augoeides* — the self-shining "blessed vision resident in the pure light"; in Porphyry,[233] that Plotinus was united to his 'god' four times during his lifetime; and so on.

"In ancient India, the mystery of the triad, known only to the initiates, could not, under the penalty of death, be revealed to the vulgar," says Vrihaspati.

Neither could it in the ancient Grecian and Samothracian Mysteries. *Nor can it be now.* It is in the hands of the adepts, and must remain a mystery to the world so long as the materialistic savant regards it as an undemonstrated fallacy, an insane hallucination; and the dogmatic theologian, a snare of the Evil One.

Subjective communication with the human, god-like spirits of those who have preceded us to the silent land of bliss, is in India divided into three categories. Under the spiritual training of a *guru* or *sannyâsî*, the *vatu* (disciple or neophyte) begins *to feel* them. Were he not under the immediate guidance of an adept, he would be controlled by the invisibles and utterly at their mercy, for among these subjective influences he is unable to discern the good from the bad. Happy the sensitive who is sure of the purity of his spiritual atmosphere!

To this subjective consciousness, which is the *first* degree, is after a time added that of clairaudience. This is the *second* degree or stage of development. The sensitive — when not naturally made so by psychological training — now audibly hears, but is still unable to discern and is incapable of verifying his impressions; and one who is unprotected, the tricky powers of the air but too often delude with semblances of voice and speech. But the *guru's* influence is there; it is the most powerful shield against the intrusion of the *bhûtnâ* into the atmosphere of the *vatu*, consecrated to the pure, human, and celestial Pitris.

The *third* degree is that in which the fakir or any other candidate both feels, hears, and sees; and wherein he can at will produce the *reflexions* of the Pitris on the mirror of astral light. All depends upon his psychological and mesmeric powers, which are always proportionate to the intensity of his *will*. But the fakir will never control the *Âkâśa*, the spiritual life-principle, the omnipotent agent of every phenomenon, in the same degree as an adept of the third and highest initiation. And the

233. Porphyry: *Plotini vita* (ap. Ficin.), cap. xxiii.

phenomena produced by the will of the latter do not generally appear in market-places for the satisfaction of open-mouthed investigators.

The unity of God, the immortality of the spirit, belief in salvation only through our works, merit and demerit; such are the principal articles of faith of the Wisdom-religion, and the ground-work of Vedaism, Buddhism, Pârstism; and such we find to have been even that of the ancient Osirism when we, after abandoning the popular sun-god to the materialism of the rabble, confine our attention to the *Books of Hermes*, the thrice-great.

"The THOUGHT concealed as yet the world in silence and darkness. . . . Then the Lord who exists through Himself, and *who is not to be divulged to the external senses of man*, dissipated darkness and manifested the perceptible world."

"He that can be perceived only by the spirit, that escapes the organs of sense, who is without visible parts, eternal, the soul of all beings, that none can comprehend, displayed His own splendor" (*Manu*, I, *slokas* 5-7).

Such is the ideal of the Supreme in the mind of every Hindû philosopher.

"Of all the duties, the principal one is to acquire the knowledge of the supreme soul [the spirit]; it is the first of all sciences, *for it alone confers on man immortality*" (*Manu*, XII, *sloka* 85).

And our scientists talk of the Nirvâna of Buddha and the Moksha of Brahmâ as of complete annihilation! It is thus that the following verse is interpreted by some materialists:

"The man who recognises the *Supreme Soul* in his own soul, as well as in that of all creatures, and who is equally just to all [whether man or animal] obtains the happiest of all fates, that to be finally *absorbed* in the bosom of Brahmâ" (*Manu*, XII, *sloka* 125).

The doctrine of the Moksha and the Nirvâna, as understood by the school of Max Müller, can never bear confronting with numerous texts that can be found, if required, as a final refutation. There are sculptures in many pagodas which contradict, point-blank, the imputation. Ask a Brâhmana to explain Moksha, address yourself to an educated Buddhist and pray him to define for you the meaning of Nirvâna. Both will answer you that in every one of these religions Nirvâna represents the dogma of the spirit's immortality. That to reach the Nirvâna means absorption into the great universal soul, the latter representing a *state*, not an individual being or an anthropomorphic god, as some understand the great EXISTENCE. That a spirit reaching such a state becomes a *part* of the integral *whole*, but never loses its individuality for all that. Henceforth the spirit lives spiritually without any fear of further modifications of form; for form pertains to matter, and the state of *Nirvâna* implies a complete purification or a final riddance from even the most sublimated particle of matter.

The word *absorption*, when it is proved that the Hindûs and Buddhists believe in the *immortality* of the spirit, must necessarily mean intimate union, not annihilation. Let Christians call them idolaters, if they still dare do so, in the face of science and the latest translations of the sacred Sanskrit books; they have no right to present the speculative philosophy of ancient sages as an inconsistency and the philosophers themselves as illogical fools. With far better reason we can accuse the ancient Jews of utter *nihilism*. There is not a word contained in the Books of Moses — or the prophets either — which taken literally implies the spirit's immortality. Yet every devout Jew hopes likewise to be "gathered into the bosom of A-Braham."

The hierophants and some Brâhmanas are accused of having administered to their *epoptai* strong drinks or anaesthetics to produce visions which were to be taken by the latter as realities. They did and do use sacred beverages which, like the Soma-drink, possess the faculty of freeing the astral form from the bonds of matter; but in those visions there is as little to be attributed to hallucination as in the glimpses which the scientist, by the help of his optical instrument, gets into the microscopic world. A man cannot perceive, touch and converse with pure spirit through any of his bodily senses. Only spirit alone can talk to and see spirit; and even our astral soul, the *Doppelgänger*, is too gross, too much tainted yet with earthly matter, to trust entirely to its perceptions and intimations.

How dangerous *untrained* mediumship may often become, and how thoroughly this danger was understood and provided against by the ancient sages, is perfectly exemplified in the case of Socrates. The old Grecian philosopher was a 'medium'; hence he had never been initiated into the Mysteries; for such was the rigorous law. But he had his 'familiar spirit' as they call it, his *daimonion;* and this invisible counsellor became the cause of his death. It is generally believed that if he was not initiated into the Mysteries it was because he himself neglected to become so. But the *Secret Records* teach us that it was because he could not be admitted to participate in the sacred rites, and precisely as we state on account of his mediumship. There was a law against the admission not only of such as were convicted of deliberate *witchcraft*,[234]

---

234. We really think that the word 'witchcraft' ought once for all to be understood in the sense which properly belongs to it. Witchcraft may be either conscious or unconscious. Certain wicked and dangerous results may be obtained through the mesmeric powers of a so-called sorcerer, who misuses the potent fluid; or again they may be achieved through

but even of those who were known to have 'a familiar spirit.' The law was just and logical, because a genuine medium is more or less irresponsible; and the eccentricities of Socrates are thus accounted for in some degree. A medium must be *passive;* and if a firm believer in his 'spirit-guide' he will allow himself to be ruled by the latter, not by the rules of the sanctuary. A *medium* of olden times, like the modern 'medium,' was subject to be *entranced* at the will and pleasure of the 'power' which *controlled* him; therefore, he could not well have been entrusted with the awful secrets of the final initiation, "never to be revealed under the penalty of death." The old sage, in unguarded moments of 'spiritual inspiration,' revealed that which he had never learned; and was therefore put to death as an atheist.

How then, with such an instance as that of Socrates in relation to the visions and spiritual wonders at the *epoptai* of the Inner Temple, can any one assert that these seers, theurgists, and thaumaturgists were all 'spirit-mediums'? Neither Pythagoras, Plato, nor any of the later more important Neo-Platonists; neither Iamblichus, Longinus, Proclus, nor Apollonius of Tyana, were ever mediums; for in such case they would not have been admitted to the Mysteries at all. As Taylor proves —"This assertion of divine visions in the Mysteries is clearly confirmed by Plotinus.[235] And in short, that magical evocation formed a part of the sacerdotal office in them, and that this was universally believed by all antiquity long before the era of the later Platonists," [236] shows that apart from natural 'mediumship' there has existed from the beginning of time a mysterious science, discussed by many but known only to a few.

The use of it is a longing toward our only true and real home — the after-life, and a desire to cling more closely to our parent spirit; abuse of it is sorcery, witchcraft, *black* magic. Between the two is placed natural 'mediumship'; a soul clothed with imperfect matter, a ready agent for either the one or the other, and utterly dependent on its surroundings of life, constitutional heredity — physical as well as mental — and on the nature of the 'spirits' it attracts around itself. A blessing or a curse, as fate will have it, unless the medium is purified of earthly dross.

The reason why in every age so little has been generally known of the mysteries of initiation is twofold. The first has already been explained by more than one author, and lies in the terrible penalty following the least indiscretion. The second is due to the superhuman difficulties and even dangers which the daring candidate of old had to encounter, and either conquer or die in the attempt unless, what is still worse, he lost his

---

an easy access of malicious tricky 'spirits' (so much the worse if human) to the atmosphere surrounding a medium. How many thousands of such irresponsible innocent victims have met infamous deaths through the tricks of those Elementaries!

235. Plotinus: *Enneads* I, vi; VI, ix.   236. *Eleus. and Bac. Myst.*, pp. 110-11: 4th ed.

reason. There was no real danger to him whose mind had become thoroughly spiritualized, and so prepared for every terrific sight. He who fully recognised the power of his immortal spirit, and never doubted for one moment its omnipotent protection, had naught to fear. But woe to the candidate in whom the slightest physical fear — sickly child of matter — made him lose sight of, and faith in, his own invulnerability. He who was not wholly confident of his moral fitness to accept the burden of these tremendous secrets was doomed.

The *Talmud* [237] gives the story of the four Tanaim who are made, in allegorical terms, to enter into *the garden of delights; i. e.,* to be initiated into the occult and final science.

"According to the teaching of our holy masters the names of the four who entered the garden of delight, are: Ben Azai, Ben Zoma, A'her, and Rabbi A'qîbah.

"Ben Azai looked and — lost his sight. . . .

"Ben Zoma looked and — lost his reason. . . .

"A'her made depredations in the plantation [mixed up the whole and failed]. But A'qîbah, who had entered in peace, came out of it in peace, for the saint, whose name be blessed, had said, 'This old man is worthy of serving us with glory.' "

"The learned commentators of the *Talmud*, the Rabbis of the synagog, explain that the *garden of delight*, in which those four personages are made to enter, is but that mysterious science, the most terrible of sciences *for weak intellects, which it leads directly to insanity*," says Ad. Franck, in his *La Kabbale*.[238] It is not the pure at heart, and he who studies but with a view to perfecting himself and so more easily acquiring the promised immortality, who need have any fear; but rather he who makes of the science of sciences a sinful pretext for worldly motives, who should tremble. *The latter will never withstand the kabalistic evocations of the supreme initiation.*

The licentious performances of the thousand and one early Christian sects may be criticized by partial commentators as well as the ancient Eleusinian and other rites. But why should they [the latter] incur the censure of the theologians, the Christians, when their own 'Mysteries' of "the divine incarnation with Joseph, Mary, and the angel" in a sacred trilogy used to be enacted in more than one country, and were famous at one time in Spain and Southern France? Later they fell, like many other once secret rites, into the hands of the populace. It is but a few years since, that during every Christmas week Punch-and-Judy-boxes, containing the above-named personages, with an additional display of the

---

237. *Mishnah 'Hagiga,* 14b.   238. Part I, ch. i.

infant Jesus in his manger, were carried about the country in Poland and
Southern Russia. They were called *Kaliadovki*, a word the correct
etymology of which we are unable to give unless it is from the verb
Kaliadovât, a word that we as willingly abandon to learned philologists.
We have seen this show in our days of childhood. We remember the
three king-Magi represented by three dolls in powdered wigs and colored
tights; and it is from recollecting the simple, profound veneration depicted on the faces of the pious audience, that we can the more readily
appreciate the honest and just remark by the editor, in the introduction
to the *Eleusinian and Bacchic Mysteries,* who says: "It is ignorance
which leads to profanation. Men ridicule what they do not properly
understand. . . . The undercurrent of this world is set toward one goal;
and inside of human credulity — call it human weakness, if you please —
is a power almost infinite, a holy faith capable of apprehending the
supremest truths of all existence."

If that abstract sentiment called *Christian charity* prevailed in the
Church, we should be well content to leave all this unsaid. We have no
quarrel with Christians whose faith is sincere and whose practice coin-
cides with their profession. But with an arrogant, dogmatic, and dis-
honest clergy we have nothing to do except to see the ancient philosophy
— antagonized by modern theology in its puny offspring, Spiritualism —
defended and righted so far as we are able, so that its grandeur and suffi-
ciency may be thoroughly displayed. It is not alone for the esoteric
philosophy that we fight; nor for any modern system of moral philosophy, but for the inalienable right of private judgment, and especially
for the ennobling idea of a future life of activity and accountability.

We eagerly applaud such commentators as Godfrey Higgins, Inman,
Payne Knight, King, Dunlap, and Dr. Newton, however much they dis-
agree with our own mystical views, for their diligence is constantly being
rewarded by fresh discoveries of the Pagan paternity of Christian symbols. But otherwise all these learned works are useless. Their researches only cover half the ground. Lacking the true key of interpretation, they see the symbols only in a physical aspect. They have no pass-
word to cause the gates of mystery to swing open; and ancient spiritual
philosophy is to them a closed book. Diametrically opposed though
they be to the clergy in their ideas respecting it, in the way of interpretation they do little more than their opponents for a questioning public.
Their labors tend to strengthen materialism; as those of the clergy,
especially the Romish clergy, do to cultivate belief in diabolism.

If the study of Hermetic philosophy held out no other hope of reward,
it would be more than enough to know that by it we may learn with what
perfection of justice the world is governed. A sermon upon this text is

preached by every page of history. Among all there is not one that conveys a deeper moral than the case of the Roman Church. The divine law of compensation [Karma] was never more strikingly exemplified than in the fact that by her own act she has deprived herself of the only possible key to her own religious mysteries. The assumption of Godfrey Higgins that there are two doctrines maintained in the Roman Church, one for the masses and the other — the esoteric — for the 'perfect,' or the initiates, as in the ancient Mysteries, appears to us unwarranted and rather fantastic. She has lost the key, we repeat; otherwise no terrestrial power could have prostrated her, and except as having a superficial knowledge of the means of producing 'miracles' her clergy can in no way be compared in their wisdom with the hierophants of old.

In burning the works of the theurgists; in proscribing those who affect their study; in affixing the stigma of demonolatry to magic in general, Rome has left her exoteric worship and *Bible* to be helplessly riddled by every free-thinker, her sexual emblems to be identified with coarseness, and her priests unwittingly to turn magicians and even sorcerers in their exorcisms, which are but necromantic evocations. Thus retribution, by the exquisite adjustment of divine law, is made to overtake this scheme of cruelty, injustice, and bigotry, through her own suicidal acts.

True philosophy and divine truth are convertible terms. A religion which dreads the light cannot be a religion based on either truth or philosophy — hence it must be false. The ancient Mysteries were mysteries to the profane only, whom the hierophant never sought nor would accept as proselytes; to the initiates the Mysteries became explained as soon as the final veil was withdrawn. No mind like that of Pythagoras or Plato would have contented itself with an unfathomable and incomprehensible mystery, like that of the Christian dogma. There can be but one truth, for two small truths on the same subject can only constitute one great error. Among thousands of exoteric or popular conflicting religions which have been propagated since the days when the first men were enabled to interchange their ideas, not a nation, not a people, nor the most abject tribe, but after its own fashion has believed in an Unseen God, the First Cause of unerring and immutable laws, and in the immortality of our spirit. No creed, no false philosophy, no religious exaggerations, could ever destroy that feeling. It must therefore be based upon an absolute truth. On the other hand every one of the numberless religions and religious sects views the Deity after its own fashion; and, fathering on the unknown its own speculations, forces these purely human outgrowths of overheated imagination on the ignorant masses, and calls them 'revelation.' As the dogmas of every religion and sect often differ radically, they cannot be *true*. And if untrue, what are they?

"The greatest curse to a nation," remarks Dr. Inman, "is not *a bad religion*, but a form of faith which prevents manly inquiry. I know of no nation of old that was priest-ridden which did not fall under the swords of those who did not care for hierarchs.

"The greatest danger is to be feared from those ecclesiastics who wink at vice, and encourage it as a means whereby they can gain power over their votaries. So long as every man does to other men as he would that they should do to him, and *allows no one to interfere between him and his Maker*, all will go well with the world." [239]

---

239. *Ancient Pagan and Modern Christian Symbolism*, preface, p. xxxiv.

CHAPTER III

"KING — Let us from point to point this story know."
— *All's Well That Ends Well*, V, iii

"He is the One, self-proceeding; and from Him all things proceed.
And in them He Himself exerts His activity; no mortal
BEHOLDS HIM, but HE beholds all!"— *Orphic Hymn* [240]

"And Athens, O Athena, is thy own!
Great Goddess, hear! and on my darkened mind
Pour thy pure light in measure unconfined;
That sacred light, O all-protecting Queen,
Which beams eternal from thy face serene.
My soul, while wandering on the earth, inspire
With thy own blesséd and impulsive fire!"
— PROCLUS: *To Minerva* (Taylor's translation)

"Now *faith* is the substance of things. . . . By faith the harlot Rahab perished not with them that believed not, when she had *received the spies with peace.*"—*Hebrews*, xi, 1, 31
"What doth it profit, my brethren, though a man say he hath faith, and have not works? *Can* FAITH *save him?* . . . Likewise also was not Rahab the harlot *justified by works,* when she had received the messengers, and had sent them out another way?"
— *James*, ii, 14, 25

CLEMENT describes Basilides, the Gnostic, as "a philosopher devoted to the contemplation of divine things." [241] This very appropriate expression may be applied to many of the founders of the more important sects which later were all engulfed in one — that stupendous compound of unintelligible dogmas enforced by Irenaeus, Tertullian and others, which is now termed Christianity. *If these must be called heresies, then early Christianity itself must be included in the number.* Basilides and Valentinus preceded Irenaeus and Tertullian; and the two latter Fathers had less facts than the two former Gnostics to show that their *heresy* was plausible. Neither divine right nor truth brought about the triumph of their [Irenaeo-Tertullianic] Christianity; fate alone was propitious. We can assert, with entire plausibility, that there is not one of all these sects — Kabalism, Judaism, and our present Christianity included — but sprang from the two main branches of that one mother-trunk, the once universal religion, which antedated the Vedic ages — we speak of that prehistoric Buddhism which merged later into Brâhmanism.

---

240. Cf. Justin: *Hortatory Address to the Greeks*, xv; Gesnerus: ΟΡΦΕΩΣ ΑΠΑΝΤΑ.
241. Wrongly ascribed to Clement, who however describes the Basilidean *doctrine* as in part occupied with "divine teaching." Cf. *Strom.* VIII, xi, "he the Gnostic conceives truly and grandly in virtue of his reception of divine teaching"; cf. King: *The Gnostics etc.*, p. 258 (edit. 1887).

The religion which the primitive teaching of the early few apostles most resembled — a religion preached by Jesus himself — is the elder of these two, Buddhism. The latter as taught in its primitive purity, and carried to perfection by the last of the Buddhas, Gautama, based its moral ethics on three fundamental principles. It alleged, 1, that every thing existing exists from natural causes; 2, that virtue brings its own reward, and vice and sin their own punishment; and, 3, that the state of man in this world is probationary. We might add that on these three principles rested the universal foundation of every religious creed; God and individual immortality for every man — if he could but win it. However puzzling the subsequent theological tenets; however seemingly incomprehensible the metaphysical abstractions which have convulsed the theology of every one of the great religions of mankind as soon as it was placed on a sure footing, the above is found to be the essence of every religious philosophy, with the exception of later Christianity. It was that of Zoroaster, of Pythagoras, of Plato, of Jesus, and even of Moses, albeit the teachings of the Jewish law-giver have been so piously tampered with.

We will devote the present chapter mainly to a brief survey of the numerous sects which have claimed to be Christian; that is to say, have believed in a *Christos*, or an ANOINTED ONE. We will also endeavor to explain the latter appellation from the kabalistic standpoint, and show it reappearing in every religious system. It might be profitable, at the same time, to see how far the earliest apostles — Paul and Peter — agreed in their preaching of the new Dispensation. We will begin with Peter.

We must once more return to that greatest of all the Patristic frauds; the one which has undeniably helped the Roman Catholic Church to its unmerited supremacy, viz.: the barefaced assertion in the teeth of historical evidence that Peter suffered martyrdom at Rome. It is only too natural that the Latin clergy should cling to it, for with the exposure of the fraudulent nature of this allegation the dogma of apostolic succession must fall to the ground.

There have been many able works of late in refutation of this preposterous claim. Among others we note Mr. G. Reber's *The Christ of Paul*, which overthrows it quite ingeniously. The author proves, 1, that there was no church established at Rome until the reign of Antoninus Pius; 2, that as Eusebius and Irenaeus both agree that Linus was the second Bishop of Rome, into whose hands 'the blessed apostles' Peter and Paul committed the church after building it,[242] this could not have been at any other time than between A. D. 64 and 68; 3, that this interval of years happens during the reign of Nero, for Eusebius states that Linus held this office twelve years (*Ecclesiastical History*, III, xiii), entering

---

242. Irenaeus: *Against Heresies*, III, iii, 2, 3.

upon it A. D. 69, one year after the death of Nero, and dying himself in 81. After this the author maintains on very solid grounds that Peter could not have been in Rome A. D. 64, for he was then in Babylon, where he wrote his first Epistle, the date of which is fixed by Dr. Lardner and other critics at precisely this year. But we believe that his best argument is in proving that it was not in the character of the cowardly Peter to risk himself in such close neighborhood with Nero, who "was feeding the wild beasts of the Amphitheater with the flesh and bones of Christians" [243] at that time.

Perhaps the Church of Rome was quite consistent in choosing as her titular founder the apostle who thrice denied his master at the moment of danger; and the only one moreover, except Judas, who provoked Christ in such a way as to be addressed as the 'Enemy.' "Get thee behind me, SATAN!" exclaims Jesus, rebuking the tempting apostle.[244]

There is a tradition in the Greek Church which has never found favor at the Vatican. The former traces its origin to one of the Gnostic leaders — Basilides, perhaps, who lived under Trajan and Adrian, at the end of the first and the beginning of the second century. With regard to this particular tradition, if the Gnostic is Basilides, then he must be accepted as a sufficient authority, having claimed to have been a disciple of the apostle Matthew, and to have had for master Glaucias, a disciple of St. Peter himself. Were the narrative attributed to him authenticated, the London Committee for the Revision of the Bible would have to add a new verse to *Matthew*, *Mark*, and *John*, which tell the story of Peter's denial of Christ.

This tradition, then, of which we have been speaking, affirms that when, frightened at the accusation of the servant of the high priest, the apostle had thrice denied his master and the cock had crowed, Jesus, who was then passing through the hall in custody of the soldiers, turned and looking at Peter said: "Verily I say unto thee, Peter, thou shalt deny me throughout the coming ages, and never stop until thou shalt be old, and shalt stretch forth thy hands, and another shall gird thee and carry thee whither thou wouldst not." The latter part of this sentence, say the Greeks, relates to the Church of Rome, and prophesies her constant apostasy from Christ under the mask of false religion. Later it was inserted in the twenty-first chapter of *John*, but the whole of this chapter had been pronounced a forgery even before it was found that this *Gospel* was never written by John the apostle at all.

The anonymous author of *Supernatural Religion*,[244a] a work which in

---

243. *The Christ of Paul*, p. 123.   244. *Mark*, viii, 33.
244a. "The authorship has now been acknowledged by Mr. Walter R. Cassells" — Prof. J. Estlin Carpenter: *The Bible in the Nineteenth Century*, p. 298, note 2: 1903.

two years passed through several editions, and is alleged to have been written by an eminent theologian, proves conclusively the spuriousness of the four gospels, or at least their complete transformation in the hands of the too-zealous Irenaeus and his champions. The fourth gospel is completely upset by this able author; the extraordinary forgeries of the Fathers of the early centuries are plainly demonstrated, and the relative value of the synoptics is discussed with an unprecedented power of logic. The work carries conviction in its every line. From it we quote the following:

"We gain infinitely more than we lose in abandoning belief in the reality of Divine Revelation. Whilst we retain pure and unimpaired the light of Christian Morality, we relinquish nothing but the debasing elements added to it by human superstition. We are no longer bound to believe a theology which outrages Reason and moral sense. We are freed from base anthropomorphic views of God and his government of the universe; and from Jewish mythology we rise to higher conceptions of an infinitely wise and beneficent Being, hidden from our finite minds, it is true, in the impenetrable glory of Divinity, but whose Laws of wondrous comprehensiveness and perfection we ever perceive in operation around us. . . . The argument so often employed by theologians, that Divine Revelation is necessary for man, and that certain views contained in that Revelation are required by our moral consciousness, is purely imaginary and derived from the Revelation which it seeks to maintain. The only thing absolutely necessary for man is TRUTH; and to that, and that alone, must our moral consciousness adapt itself." [245]

We will consider further in what light was regarded the Divine revelation of the Jewish *Bible* by the Gnostics, who yet believed in Christ in their own way — a far better and less blasphemous one than the Roman Catholic. The Fathers have forced on the believers in Christ a *Bible*, the laws prescribed in which he was the first to break; the teachings of which he utterly rejected; and for which crimes he was finally crucified. Of whatever else the Christian world can boast, it can hardly claim logic and consistency as its chief virtues.

The fact alone that Peter remained to the last an 'apostle of the circumcision,' speaks for itself. *Whosoever else might have built the Church of Rome, it was not Peter.* If such were the case, the successors of this apostle would have to submit themselves to circumcision, were it but for the sake of consistency. To show that the claims of the popes are not utterly groundless, Dr. Inman asserts that report says that "in our Christian times, Popes have to be privately perfect," [246] but we do not know whether this is carried to the extent of the Levitical Jewish law.

---

245. *Supernatural Religion*, part III, ch. iii.
246. *Ancient Pagan and Modern Christian Symbolism*, p. xxviii.

The first fifteen Christian bishops of Jerusalem, commencing with James and including Judas, were all circumcised Jews.[247]

In the *Sepher Toledoth Yeshu*,[248] a Hebrew manuscript of great antiquity, the account of Peter is different. Simon Peter, it says, was one of their own brethren, though he had somewhat departed from the laws, and the Jewish hatred and persecution of the apostle seems to have existed but in the fecund imagination of the Fathers. The author speaks of him with great respect and fairness, calling him "a faithful servant of the living God," who passed his life in austerity and meditation, "living in Babylon at the summit of a tower," composing hymns, and preaching charity. He adds that Peter always recommended the Christians not to molest the Jews, but as soon as he was dead, behold another preacher went to Rome and pretended that Simon Peter had altered the teachings of his master. He invented a burning hell and threatened every one with it; promised miracles, but worked none.

How much there is in the above of fiction and how much of truth, it is for others to 'decide; but it certainly bears more the evidence of sincerity and fact on its face, than the fables concocted by the Fathers to answer their end.

We may the more readily credit this friendship between Peter and his late co-religionists, as we find in Theodoret the following assertion: "The Nazarenes are Jews, honoring the ANOINTED [Jesus] as a *just man* and using the *Evangel* according to Peter." [249] Peter was a Nazarene, according to the *Talmud*. He belonged to the sect of the later Nazarenes, which dissented from the followers of John the Baptist and became a rival sect; and which — as tradition goes — was instituted by Jesus himself.

History finds the first Christian sects to have been either Nazarenes like John the Baptist; or Ebionites, among whom were many of the relatives of Jesus; or Essenes (Iessaens), of which the *Therapeutae* healers, of which the Nazaria were a branch. All these sects, which only in the days of Irenaeus began to be considered heretical, were more or less kabalistic. They believed in the expulsion of daemons by magical incantations, and practised this method; Jervis terms the Nabatheans and other such sects

247. Euseb.: *Eccl. Hist.*, IV, v; Sulpicius Severus: *Chronica*, II, 31.

248. It appears that the Jews attribute a high antiquity to *Sepher Toledoth Yeshu*. It was mentioned for the first time by Martin, about the beginning of the thirteenth century, for the Talmudists took great care to conceal it from the Christians. Lévi says that Porchetus Salvaticus [Paris, 1520] published some portions of it, which were used by Luther (see VIII, Jena edit. [see also Wittemberg edit., 1556, V, pp. 509-535]). The Hebrew text, which was missing, was at last found by Münster and Buxtorf, and published in 1681 by Christopher Wagenseil, in a collection entitled *Tela Ignea Satanae*, or The Burning Darts of Satan [Altdorf, 2 vols., and by Jacob Huldrich, as *Historia Jeschuae Nazareni*, Leyden, 1705] (see also É. Lévi: *La science des esprits*).

249. Theodoret: *Haeret. fabul.*, II, ii.

"wandering Jewish exorcists," [250] the Arabic word *Nabaa* meaning to wander, and the Hebrew נבא, *naba*, to prophesy. The *Talmud* indiscriminately calls all the Christians *Nozari*.[251] All the Gnostic sects alike believed in magic. Irenaeus, in describing the followers of Basilides, says, "They use images, invocations, incantations, and all other things pertaining unto magic." [252] Dunlap, on the authority of Lightfoot, shows that Jesus was called *Nazaraios*, in reference to his humble and mean external condition; "for *Nazaraios* means separation, alienation from other men." [253]

The real meaning of the word *nazar*, נזר, signifies to vow or consecrate one's self to the service of God. As a noun it is a *diadem* or emblem of such consecration, a head so consecrated.[254] Joseph was styled a *nazar*.[255] "The head of Joseph, the vertex of the nazar among his brethren." Samson and Samuel (שמשון שמראל), Semes-on and Semva-el) are described alike as *nazars*. Porphyry, treating of Pythagoras, says that he was purified and initiated at Babylon by Zar-adas, the head of the sacred college. May it not be surmised, therefore, that the Zoro-Aster was the *nazar* of Ishtar, Zar-adas or Na-Zar-Ad,[256] being the same with change of idiom? Ezra, or עזרא, was a priest and scribe, a hierophant; and the first Hebrew colonizer of Judaea was זרובבל, Zoru-Babel, or the Zoro or *nazar* of Babylon.

The Jewish Scriptures indicate two distinct worships and religions among the Israelites; that of Bacchus-worship under the mask of Jehovah, and that of the Chaldaean initiates to whom belonged some of the *nazars*, the theurgists, and a few of the prophets. The headquarters of these were always at Babylon and Chaldaea, where two rival schools of Magians can be distinctly shown. Those who would doubt the statement will have in such a case to account for the discrepancy between history and Plato, who of all men of his day was certainly one of the best informed. Speaking of the Magians, he shows them as instructing the Persian kings of [*i. e.*, in the worship according to] Zoroaster, as the son or priest of Oromazdes; [257] and yet Darius, in the inscription at Behistun, boasts of having restored the cult of Ormazd and put down the Magian rites! Evidently there were two distinct and antagonistic Magian schools, the oldest and the most esoteric of the two being that which, satisfied with its unassailable knowledge and secret power, was content apparently to relinquish her exoteric popularity and yield her supremacy into the hands of the reforming Darius. The later Gnostics showed the same prudent

250. Jervis W. Jervis: *On Genesis*, p. 324: London, 1852.
251. J. Lightfoot: *Hor. Hebr. et Talm.*, p. 501. 252. *Against Heresies*, I, xxiv, 5.
253. Dunlap: *Sôd, the Son of the Man*, p. x. 254. *Jer.*, vii, 29: "Cut off thine hair, O Jerusalem, and cast it away, and take up a lamentation on high places."
255. *Gen.*, xlix, 26. 256. Nazareth? [See also Clem. Alex.: *Strom.*, I, xv; Apuleius: *Floridora*, II.] 257. *I Alcib.*, § 37; cf. Cicero: *On Divination*, § 1.

policy by accommodating themselves in every country to the prevailing religious forms, still secretly adhering to their own essential doctrines.

There is another hypothesis possible, which is that Zero-Ishtar was the high priest of the Chaldaean worship, or a Magian hierophant. When the Aryans of Persia, under Darius Hystaspes, overthrew the Magian Gomates, and *restored* the Mazdean worship, there ensued an amalgamation by which the Magian Zoro-astar became the Zara-thustra of the *Vendîdâd*. This was not acceptable to the other Aryans, who adopted the Vedic religion as distinguished from that of the *Avesta*. But this is only a hypothesis.

And whatever Moses is now believed to have been, we will demonstrate that he was an initiate. The Mosaic religion was at best a sun-and-serpent worship, diluted perhaps with some slight monotheistic notions before the latter were forcibly crammed into the so-called 'inspired Scriptures' by Ezra, at the time he was alleged to have rewritten the Mosaic books. At all events the *Book of Numbers* was a later book; and there the sun-and-serpent worship is as plainly traceable as in any Pagan story. The tale of the fiery serpents is an allegory in more than one sense. The 'serpents' were the *Levites* or *Ophites*, who were Moses' bodyguard (see *Exodus*, xxxii, 26); and the command of the 'Lord' to Moses to hang the heads of the people "before the Lord against the sun," which is the emblem of this Lord, is unequivocal.

The *nazars* or prophets, as well as the Nazarenes, were an anti-Bacchus caste, in so far that in common with all the initiated prophets they held to the spirit of the symbolical religions, and offered a strong opposition to the idolatrous and exoteric practices of the dead letter. Hence the frequent stoning of the prophets by the populace under the leadership of those priests who made a profitable living out of the popular superstitions. Ottfried Müller shows how much the Orphic Mysteries differed from the *popular* rites of Bacchus,[258] although the *Orphikoi* are known to have followed the worship of Bacchus. The system of the purest morality and of a severe asceticism promulgated in the teachings of Orpheus, and so strictly adhered to by his votaries, is incompatible with the lasciviousness and gross immorality of the popular rites. The fable of Aristaeus pursuing Eurydice into the woods where a serpent occasions her death,[259] is a very plain allegory which was in part explained in the earliest times. Aristaeus is *brutal power*, pursuing Eurydice, the esoteric doctrine, into the woods where the serpent (emblem of every sun-god, and worshiped under its grosser aspect even by the Jews) kills her; *i. e.*, forces truth to become still more esoteric, and seek shelter in

---

258. K. O. Müller: *A History of the Literature of Ancient Greece*, pp. 230-240.
259. Vergil: *Georgica*, IV, 282, *sq.*

the Underworld, which is not the hell of our theologians. Moreover the fate of Orpheus, torn to pieces by the Bacchantes, is another allegory to show that the gross and popular rites are always more welcome than divine but simple truth, and proves the great difference that must have existed between the esoteric and the popular worship. As the poems of both Orpheus and Musaeus were said to have been lost since the earliest ages, so that neither Plato nor Aristotle recognised anything authentic in the poems extant in their time, it is difficult to say with precision what constituted their peculiar rites. Still we have the oral tradition, and every inference to draw therefrom; and this tradition points to Orpheus as having brought his doctrines from India, and as one whose religion was that of the oldest Magians — hence that to which belonged the initiates of all countries, beginning with Moses, the 'sons of the Prophets,' and the ascetic *nazars* (who must not be confounded with those against whom thundered Hosea and other prophets) to [and including] the Essenes.[259a] This latter sect were Pythagoreans before they became degenerated rather than perfected in their system through the Buddhist missionaries who, Pliny tells us, established themselves on the shores of the Dead Sea ages before his time, "*per saeculorum millia.*" [260] But if on the one hand these Buddhist monks were the first to establish monastic communities and inculcate the strict observance of dogmatic conventual rule, on the other they were also the first to enforce and popularize those stern virtues exemplified by *Sâkya-muni*, previously exercised only in isolated cases of well-known philosophers and their followers; virtues preached two or three centuries later by Jesus, practised by a few Christian ascetics, and gradually abandoned and even entirely forgotten by the Christian Church.

The *initiated* nazars had ever held to this rule, which had to be followed before their time by the adepts of every age; and the disciples of John were but a dissenting branch of the Essenes. Therefore we cannot well confound them with all the *nazars* spoken of in the *Old Testament*, and who are accused by Hosea with having separated or consecrated themselves to *Bosheth*, בשת (see Hebrew text) [261]; which word implied the greatest possible abomination. To infer, as some critics and theologians do, that it means to separate one's self to *chastity* or continence, is either advisedly to pervert the true meaning, or to be totally ignorant of the Hebrew language. The eleventh verse of the first chapter of Micah half explains the word in its veiled translation: "Pass ye away, thou inhabitant of Saphir, etc.," and in the original text the word is *Bosheth*. Certainly neither Baal, nor Iahoh Kadosh, with his *Kadeshim*, was a god of ascetic virtue, albeit the *Septuagint* terms them, as well as the *galli*

259a. Cf. p. 132, following.   260. Pliny: *Nat. Hist.*, V, 15.   261. *Hosea*, ix, 10.

— the perfected priests — τετελεσμένοι, the *initiated* and the *consecrated*.[262] The great *Sôd* of the *Kadeshim*, translated in *Psalms*, lxxxix, 7, by "assembly of the saints," was anything but a mystery of the *'sanctified'* in the sense given to the latter word by Webster.

The Nazireate sect existed long before the laws of Moses,[263] and originated among people most inimical to the 'chosen' ones of Israel, viz., the people of Galilee, the ancient *olla-podrida* of idolatrous nations, where was built Nazara, the present Nasra. It was in Nazara that the ancient Nazoria or Nazireates held their 'Mysteries of Life' or 'assemblies' (as the word now stands in the translation) [264] which ['*conciones*'] were the secret mysteries of initiation,[265] utterly distinct in their practical form from the popular Mysteries which were held at Byblus in honor of Adonis. While the true *initiates* of the ostracised Galilee were worshiping the true God and enjoying transcendent visions, what were the 'chosen' ones about? Ezekiel tells us this (ch. viii) when in describing what he saw he says that the *form* of a hand took him by a lock of his head and transported him from Chaldaea unto Jerusalem. "And there stood seventy men of the senators of the house of Israel. . . . 'Son of man, hast thou seen what the ancients . . . do in the dark?'" inquires the 'Lord.' "At the door of the house of the Lord . . . behold there sat women weeping for Tammuz" (Adonis). We really cannot suppose that the Pagans have ever surpassed the 'chosen' people in certain shameful *abominations* of which their own prophets accuse them so profusely. To admit this truth, one need hardly be a Hebrew scholar; let him read the *Bible* in English and meditate over the language of the 'holy' prophets.

This accounts for the hatred of the later Nazarenes for the orthodox Jews — followers of the *exoteric* Mosaic Law — who are ever taunted by this sect with being the worshipers of Iurbo-Adunai, or Lord Bacchus. Passing under the disguise of *Adoni-Iahoh* (original text, *Isaiah*, lxi, 1), Iahoh and Lord Sabaoth, the Baal-Adonis, or Bacchus, worshiped in the groves and *public sôds* or Mysteries, under the polishing hand of Ezra becomes finally the later-voweled Adonai of the Massorah — the One and Supreme God of the Christians!

"Thou shalt not worship the Sun who is named Adunai," says the *Codex* of the Nazarenes; "whose name is also *Kadush* [266] and El-El. This Adunai will elect to himself a nation and congregate *in crowds* [his worship will be exoteric]. Jerusalem will become the refuge and city of

262. Movers: *Die Phönix.*, I, p. 683. 263. Cf. *Numb.*, vi, 2; Munk: *Palestine*, p. 169.
264. Norberg: *Codex Nazaraeus*, II, p. 305. 265. See Lucian: *De Syria Dea.*
266. Cf. *Psalms*, lxxxix, 18.

the *Abortive*, who shall perfect themselves [circumcise] with a sword
. . . and shall adore Adunai." [267]

The oldest Nazarenes, who were the descendants of the Scripture
nazars, and whose last prominent leader was John the Baptist, although
never very orthodox in the sight of the scribes and Pharisees of Jerusalem, were nevertheless respected and left unmolested. Even Herod
"feared the multitude" because they regarded John as a prophet
(*Matthew*, xiv, 5). But the followers of Jesus evidently adhered to a
sect which became a still more exasperating thorn in their side [*i. e.*, of the
scribes and Pharisees]. It appeared as a heresy *within* another heresy;
for while the *nazars* of the olden times, the 'Sons of the Prophets,' were
Chaldaean kabalists, the adepts of the new dissenting sect showed themselves reformers and innovators from the first. The great similitude
traced by some critics between the rites and observances of the earliest
Christians and those of the Essenes may be accounted for without the
slightest difficulty. The Essenes, as we remarked just now, were the
converts of Buddhist missionaries who had overrun Egypt, Greece, and
even Judaea at one time, since the reign of Aśoka the zealous propagandist; and while it is evidently to the Essenes that belongs the honor of
having had the Nazarene reformer Jesus as a pupil, still the latter is
found disagreeing with his early teachers on several questions of formal
observance. He cannot strictly be called an Essene, for reasons which
we will indicate farther on, neither was he a *nazar*, or Nazaria of the
older sect. What Jesus *was*, may be found in the *Codex Nazaraeus*,
from the unjust accusations of the Bardesanian Gnostics.

"Jesu is *Nebu*, the false Messiah, the destroyer of the old orthodox
religion," says the *Codex*. [268] He is the founder of the sect of the new
nazars, and, as the words clearly imply, a follower of the Buddhist
doctrine. In Hebrew the word *naba*, נבא, means to speak by inspiration; and נבו is *nebo*, a god of wisdom. But Nebo is also *Mercury*,
and *Mercury is Buddha* in the Hindû monogram [iconography] of planets.
Moreover we find the Talmudists holding that Jesus was inspired by the
genius of Mercury. [269]

The Nazarene reformer had undoubtedly belonged to one of these
sects; though perhaps it would be next to impossible to decide absolutely which. But what is self-evident is that he preached the philosophy of *Buddha-Śâkyamuni*. Denounced by the later prophets, cursed
by the Sanhedrim, the *nazars* — they were confounded with others of
that name "who separated themselves unto that shame," [270] — were
secretly, if not openly, persecuted by the orthodox synagog. It be-

---

267. *Cod. Naz.*, I, p. 47.   268. I, p. 55; Norberg: *Onomasticon*, p. 74.
269. Alphonsus de Spina: *Fortalitium fidei*, ii, 2.   270. *Hosea*, ix, 10.

comes clear why Jesus was treated with such contempt from the first, and deprecatingly called "the Galilean." Nathaniel inquires, at the very beginning of his career — "Can there any good thing come out of Nazareth?" (John, i, 46) and merely because he knows him to be a *nazar*. Does not this clearly hint that even the older *nazars* were not really Hebrew religionists, but rather a class of Chaldaean theurgists? Besides, as the *New Testament* is noted for its mistranslations and transparent falsifications of texts, we may justly suspect that the word Nazareth was substituted for that of *nasaria*, or *nozari;* and that it [the text] originally read "Can any good thing come from a *nozari*, or Nazarene?" a follower of St. John the Baptist, with whom we see him [Jesus] associating from his first appearance on the stage of action, after having been lost sight of for a period of nearly twenty years. The blunders of the *Old Testament* are as nothing to those of the *gospels*. Nothing shows better than these self-evident contradictions the system of pious fraud upon which the superstructure of the Messiahship rests. "This *is Elias* which was for to come," says Matthew of John the Baptist, thus forcing an ancient kabalistic tradition into the frame of evidence (xi, 14). But when addressing the Baptist himself, they ask him (John, i, 21), "Art thou Elias?" "And he saith, *I am not!*" Which knew best — John or his biographer? And which is divine revelation?

The motive of Jesus was evidently like that of Gautama-Buddha, to benefit humanity at large by producing a religious reform which should give it a religion of pure ethics, the true knowledge of God and nature having remained until then solely in the hands of the esoteric sects and of their adepts. As Jesus used *oil* and the Essenes never used aught but pure water,[271] he cannot be called a strict Essene. On the other hand, the Essenes were also 'set apart'; they were healers (*asaya*) and dwelt in the desert as all ascetics did.

But although he did not abstain from wine, he could have remained a Nazarene all the same. For in chapter vi of *Numbers*, we see that after the priest has waved a part of the hair of a Nazarite "for a wave-offering before the Lord," "after that the Nazarite may drink wine" (verse 20). The bitter denunciation by the reformer of the people who would be satisfied with nothing, is worded in the following exclamation: "John came neither eating bread nor drinking wine; and ye say, He hath a devil. The Son of man is come eating and drinking; and ye say, Behold a gluttonous man, and a winebibber." And yet he was an Essene and Nazarene, for we not only find him sending a message to Herod, to say that he was one of those who cast out devils, and who performed

---

271. "The Essenes considered oil as a defilement," says Josephus: *The Jewish War*, II, viii, 3.

cures, but actually calling himself a prophet and declaring himself equal to the other prophets.[272]

The author of *Sôd* shows Matthew trying to connect the appellation of Nazarene with a prophecy,[273] and inquires "Why then does Matthew state that the prophet said he should be called *Nazaria?*" Simply "because he belonged to that sect, and a prophecy would confirm his claims to the Messiahship. . . . Now it does not appear that the prophets anywhere state that the Messiah will be called a *Nazarene.*"[274] The fact alone that Matthew tries in the last verse of chapter ii to strengthen his claim that Jesus dwelt in Nazareth *merely to fulfil a prophecy*, does more than weaken the argument, it upsets it entirely; for the first two chapters have sufficiently been proved to be later forgeries.

Baptism is one of the oldest rites and was practised by all the nations in their Mysteries, as sacred ablutions. Dunlap seems to derive the name of the *nazars* from *nazah*, sprinkling;[275] Bahak-Zivo is the genius who called the world into existence[276] out of the 'dark water,' say the Nazarenes; and Richardson's *Persian, Arabic, and English Lexicon* asserts that the word *Bahâk* means 'raining.'[277] But the *Bahak-Zivo* of the Nazarenes cannot be traced so easily to Bacchus, who "was the rain-god," for the *nazars* were the greatest opponents of Bacchus-worship. "Bacchus is brought up by the Hyades, the rain-nymphs," says Preller,[278] and Dunlap shows furthermore[279] that at the conclusion of the religious Mysteries the priests baptized (washed) their monuments and anointed them with oil. All this is but a very indirect proof. The Jordan baptism need not be shown a substitution for the *exoteric* Bacchic rites and the libations in honor of Adonis or Adoni — whom the Nazarenes abhorred — in order to prove them [the Nazarenes] to have been a sect sprung from the 'Mysteries' of the 'Secret Doctrine'; and their rites can by no means be confounded with those of the Pagan populace, who had simply fallen into the idolatrous and unreasoning faith of all plebeian multitudes. John was the prophet of these Nazarenes, and in Galilee he was termed 'the Savior,' but he was not the founder of that sect which derived its tradition from the remotest Chaldaeo-Akkadian theurgy.

"The early plebeian Israelites were Canaanites and Phoenicians, with

272. *Luke,* xiii, 32-3.

273. *Matt.,* ii, 23. We must bear in mind that the Gospel according to Matthew in the New Testament is not the original Gospel of the apostle of that name. The authentic Evangel was for centuries in the possession of the Nazarenes and the Ebionites, as we show further on the admission of St. Jerome himself, who confesses that he had to *ask permission* of the Nazarenes to translate it. [*De viris illust.*, cap. iii; *Comm. in Matt.*, xii, 13.]

274. *Sôd, the Son of the Man,* p. x.   275. *Ibid.*, p. viii (insert) note.
276. *Codex Nazaraeus,* II, p. 233.   277. *Sôd, Myst. Adoni,* p. 79.
278. L. Preller: *Griechische Mythologie,* I, p. 415.   279. *Sôd, Myst. Adoni,* p. 46, *sq.*

the same worship of the Phallic gods — Bacchus, Baal or Adon, Iacchos — Iao or Jehovah"; but even among them there had always been a class of *initiated* adepts. Later the character of this *plebs* was modified by Assyrian conquests; and finally the Persian colonizations superimposed the Pharisean and Eastern ideas and usages, from which the *Old Testament* and the Mosaic institutes were derived. The Asmonean priest-kings promulgated the canon of the *Old Testament* in contradistinction to the *Apocrypha* or Secret Books of the Alexandrian Jews — kabalists.[280] Till John Hyrcanus they were Asideans (Chasidim) and Pharisees (Pârsîs), but then they became Sadducees or Zadokites — asserters of sacerdotal rule as contradistinguished from rabbinical. The Pharisees were lenient and intellectual; the Sadducees, bigoted and cruel.

Says the *Codex:* "John, son of the Aba-Saba-Zacharia, conceived by his mother *Aneshbet* in her hundredth year, had baptized for *forty-two years*[281] when Jesu Messias came to the Jordan to be baptized with John's baptism. . . . But he will *pervert John's doctrine*, changing the baptism of the Jordan, and perverting the sayings of justice."[282]

The baptism was changed from *water* to that of the Holy Ghost, undoubtedly in consequence of the ever-dominant idea of the Fathers to institute a reform, and make the Christians distinct from St. John's Nazarenes, the Nabatheans and Ebionites, in order to make room for new dogmas. Not only do the Synoptics tell us that Jesus was baptizing the same as John, but John's own disciples complained of it, though surely Jesus cannot be accused of following a purely Bacchic rite. The parenthesis in verse 2nd of *John*, iv, "Though Jesus himself baptized not," is so clumsy as to show upon its face that it is an interpolation. Matthew makes John say that he that should come after him would not baptize them with water, but "with *the Holy Ghost and with fire.*" *Mark, Luke,* and *John* corroborate these words. [Such rites in which] water, fire, and spirit, or Holy Ghost [are used] had all their origin in India, as we will show.

---

280. The word Apocrypha was very erroneously adopted in the sense of doubtful and spurious. The word means *hidden* and *secret;* and that which is secret may be often more true than that which is revealed.

281. The statement, if reliable, would show that Jesus was between fifty and sixty years old when baptized; for the Gospels make him but a few months younger than John. The kabalists say that Jesus was over forty years old when first appearing at the gates of Jerusalem. The present copy of the *Codex Nazaraeus* is dated 1042, but Dunlap finds in Irenaeus (2nd century) quotations from and ample references to this book. "The basis of the material common to Irenaeus and the *Codex Nazaraeus* must be at least as early as the first century," says the author in his preface to *Sôd, the Son of the Man*, p. i.

282. *Codex Nazaraeus*, I, p. 109; Dunlap: *Op. cit.*, p. 48.

Now there is one very strange peculiarity about this sentence of John. It is flatly denied in *Acts*, xix, 2-5. Apollos, a Jew of Alexandria, belonged to the sect of St. John's disciples; he had been baptized, and had instructed others in the doctrines of the Baptist. And yet when Paul, cleverly profiting by his [Apollos'] absence at Corinth, finds certain disciples of Apollos at Ephesus, and asks them whether they received *the Holy Ghost*, he is naïvely answered, "We have not so much as heard whether there be any Holy Ghost!" "Unto what then were ye baptized?" he inquires. "*Unto John's baptism*," they say. Then Paul is made to repeat the words attributed to John by the Synoptics; and these men "were baptized in the name of the Lord Jesus," exhibiting moreover at the same instant the usual polyglot gift which accompanies the descent of the Holy Ghost.

How then? St. John the Baptist, who is called the "precursor," that "the prophecy might be fulfilled," the great prophet and martyr, whose words ought to have had such an importance in the eyes of his disciples, announces the "Holy Ghost" to his listeners; causes crowds to assemble on the shores of the Jordan, where, at the great ceremony of Christ's baptism, the promised "Holy Ghost" appears within the opened heavens, and the multitude hears the voice, and yet there are disciples of St. John who have "never so much as *heard* whether there be any Holy Ghost"!

Verily the disciples who wrote the *Codex Nazaraeus* were right. Only it is not Jesus himself, but those who came after him, and who concocted the *Bible* to suit themselves, that "*perverted* John's doctrine, *changed* the baptism of the Jordan, and perverted the sayings of justice."

It is useless to object that the present *Codex* was written centuries after the direct apostles of John preached. So were our *Gospels*. When this astounding interview of Paul with the 'Baptists' took place, Bardesanes had not yet appeared among them, and the sect was not considered a 'heresy.' Moreover we are enabled to judge how little St. John's promise of the "Holy Ghost," and the appearance of the "Ghost" himself, had affected his disciples, by the displeasure shown by them toward the disciples of Jesus, and the kind of rivalry manifested from the first. Nay, so little is John himself sure of the identity of Jesus with the expected Messiah, that after the famous scene of the baptism at the Jordan, and the oral assurance by the *Holy Ghost* Himself that "*This is my beloved Son*" (*Matthew*, iii, 17), we find 'the Precursor,' in *Matthew*, xi, 3, sending two of his disciples from his prison to inquire of Jesus: "Art thou *he* that should come, or do we look *for another?*"!!

This flagrant contradiction alone ought to have long ago satisfied reasonable minds as to the putative divine inspiration of the *New Testa-*

ment. But we may offer another question: If baptism is the sign of regeneration and an ordinance instituted by Jesus, why do not Christians now baptize as Jesus is here represented as doing, "with the Holy Ghost and with fire," instead of following the custom of the Nazarenes? In making these palpable interpolations, what possible motive could Irenaeus have had except to cause people to believe that the appellation of Nazarene, which Jesus bore, came only from his father's residence at Nazareth, and not from his affiliation with the sect of *Nazaria,* the healers?

This expedient of Irenaeus was a most unfortunate one, for from time immemorial the prophets of old had been thundering against the baptism of fire as practised by their neighbors, which imparted the 'spirit of prophecy' or the Holy Ghost. But the case was desperate; the Christians were universally called Nazoraens and Iessaeans (according to Epiphanius), and Christ simply ranked as a Jewish prophet and healer — so self-styled, so accepted by his own disciples, and so regarded by their followers. In such a state of things there was no room for either a new hierarchy or a new God-head; and since Irenaeus had undertaken the business of manufacturing both, he had to put together such materials as were available, and fill the gaps with his own fertile inventions.

To assure ourselves that Jesus was a true Nazarene — albeit with ideas of a new reform — we must not search for the proof in the translated *Gospels,* but in such original versions as are accessible. Tischendorf, in his translation from the Greek of *Luke,* iv, 34, has it "Iēsou Nazarēne"; and in the Syriac it reads "Iasua, thou *Nazaria.*" Thus, if we take into account all that is puzzling and incomprehensible in the four *Gospels,* revised and corrected as they now stand, we shall easily see for ourselves that the true, original Christianity, such as was preached by Jesus, is to be found only in the so-called Syrian heresies. Only from them can we extract any clear notions about what was primitive Christianity. Such was the faith of Paul when Tertullus, the orator, accused the apostle before the governor Felix. What he complained of was that "we have found this man . . . a mover of sedition . . . a ringleader of *the sect of the Nazarenes";* [283] and, while Paul denies every other accusation, he confesses that "after the way which they call heresy, *so worship I the God of my fathers.*" [284] This confession is a whole revelation. It shows: 1, that Paul admitted belonging to the sect of the Nazarenes; 2, that he worshiped the *God of his fathers,* not the trinitarian Christian God of whom he knows nothing, and who was not invented until after his death; and, 3, that this unlucky confession satisfactorily explains why the treatise, *Acts of the Apostles,* together with John's *Revelation,* which at one

---

283. *Acts,* xxiv, 5.   284. *Ibid.,* 14.

period was utterly rejected, were kept out of the canon of the *New Testament* for such a length of time.

At Byblos, the neophytes as well as the hierophants were, after participating in the Mysteries, obliged to fast and remain in solitude for some time. There was strict fasting and preparation before as well as after the Bacchic, Adonian, and Eleusinian orgies; and Herodotus hints, with fear and veneration, about the LAKE of Bacchus, in which "they [the priests] made at night exhibitions of his life and sufferings." [285] In the Mithraic sacrifices, during the initiation, a preliminary scene of death was simulated by the neophyte, and it preceded the scene showing him himself "being born again by the rite *of baptism*." A portion of this ceremony is still enacted at the present day by the Masons, when the neophyte, as the Grand Master Hiram Abiff, lies dead, and is raised by the strong grip of the lion's paw.

The priests were circumcised. The neophyte could not be initiated without having been present at the solemn Mysteries of the LAKE. The Nazarenes were baptized in the Jordan; and could not be baptized elsewhere; they were also circumcised, and had to fast before as well as after the purification by baptism. Jesus is said to have fasted in the wilderness for forty days, immediately after his baptism. To the present day, there is outside every temple in India a lake, stream, or a reservoir full of holy water, in which the Brâhmanas and the Hindû devotees bathe daily. Such places of consecrated water are necessary to every temple. The bathing festivals, or *baptismal* rites, occur twice every year; in October and April. Each lasts ten days; and, as in ancient Egypt and Greece, the statues of their gods, goddesses, and idols are immersed in water by the priests; the object of the ceremony being to wash away from them the sins of their worshipers which they have taken upon themselves, and which pollute them, until washed off by holy water. During the *Arûtî*, the bathing ceremony, the principal god of every temple is carried in solemn procession to be baptized in the sea. The Brâhmana priests, carrying the sacred images, are followed generally by the Mahârâja — barefoot and nearly naked. *Three times* the priests enter the sea; the third time they carry with them all the images. Holding them up with prayers repeated by the whole congregation, the Chief Priest plunges the statues of the gods *thrice*, in the name of the *mystic trinity*, into the water; after which they are purified.[286]

---

285. Herodotus, II, §§ 170, 171.

286. The Hindû High Pontiff — the Chief of the Namburis, who lives in the Cochin Land, is generally present during these festivals of 'Holy Water' immersions. He travels sometimes to very great distances to preside over the ceremony.

The Orphic hymn calls *water* the greatest purifier of men and gods.

Our Nazarene sect is known to have existed some 150 years B. C., and to have lived on the banks of the Jordan, and on the eastern shore of the Dead Sea, according to Pliny and Josephus.[287] But in King's *Gnostics* we find quoted another statement which says that the Essenes had been established on the shores of the Dead Sea "for thousands of ages" before Pliny's time.[288]

According to Munk the term 'Galilean' is nearly synonymous with that of 'Nazarene'; furthermore, he shows the relations of the former with the Gentiles as very intimate. The populace had probably gradually adopted in their constant intercourse certain rites and modes of worship of the Pagans; and the scorn with which the Galileans were regarded by the orthodox Jews is attributed by him to the same cause. Their friendly relations had certainly led them, at a later period, to adopt the 'Adonia,' or the sacred rites over the body of the lamented Adonis, as we find Jerome plainly lamenting this circumstance. "Over Bethlehem," he says, "the grove of Thammuz, that is of Adonis, was casting its shadow! And in the GROTTO where formerly the infant Jesus cried, the lover of Venus was being mourned." [289]

It was after the rebellion of Bar Cochba that the Roman Emperor established the Mysteries of Adonis at the Sacred Cave in Bethlehem; and who knows but this was the *petra* or rock-temple on which the church was built? The Boar of Adonis was placed above the gate of Jerusalem which looked toward Bethlehem.

Munk says that the "Nazireate was an institution established before the laws of Moses." [290] This is evident, as we find this sect not only mentioned but minutely described in *Numbers* (ch. vi). In the commandment given in this chapter to Moses by the 'Lord,' it is easy to recognise the rites and laws of the Priests of Adonis.[291] The abstinence and purity strictly prescribed by both are identical. Both allowed

---

287. Pliny: *Nat. Hist.*, V, xv; Joseph.: *Antiq.*, XIII, v, 9; XV, x, 4, 5; XVIII, i, 5.

288. King thinks it a great exaggeration and is inclined to believe that these Essenes, who were most undoubtedly Buddhist monks, were "merely a continuation of the associations known as Schools of the Prophets." — *The Gnostics etc.*, p. 52 (2nd ed.).

289. Jerome: *Epistles*, 49, *ad Paulinum.*

290. Munk: *Palestine*, p. 169.

291. Bacchus and Ceres — or the mystical *Wine* and *Bread*, used during the Mysteries — become, in the 'Adonia,' Adonis and Venus. Movers shows that "*Iao* is Bacchus" (*Die Phön.*, I, p. 550); and his authority is Lydus, *De mens.*, IV, 38, 74, with others; see also Dunlap: *Spirit-History, etc.*, p. 195. *Iao* is a Sun-god and the Jewish Jehovah; the intellectual or Central Sun of the kabalists. See Julian: *Oratio in solem*, p. 136; Proclus: *On I Alcib.*, IV, p. 96. But this 'Iao' is not the Mystery-god.

their hair *to grow long* [292] as the Hindû coenobites and fakirs do to this day, while other castes shave their hair and abstain on certain days from wine. The prophet Elijah, a Nazarene, is described in *2 Kings* and by Josephus as "a hairy man girt with a girdle of leather." [293] And John the Baptist and Jesus are both represented as wearing very long hair. [294] John is "clothed with camel's hair" and wearing a girdle of hide, and Jesus in a long garment "without any seams" . . . "and very white, like snow," says Mark; the very dress worn by the Nazarene priests and the Pythagorean and Buddhist Essenes, as described by Josephus.

If we carefully trace the terms *nazar* and *nazaret* throughout the best known works of ancient writers, we shall meet them in connexion with 'Pagan' as well as Jewish adepts.   Thus Alexander Polyhistor says of Pythagoras that he was a disciple of the Assyrian *Nazaratus,* whom some suppose to be Ezekiel. [295] Diogenes Laertius [296] states most positively that Pythagoras, after being initiated into all the Mysteries of the Greeks and barbarians, "went into Egypt and afterward visited the Chaldaeans and Magi"; and Apuleius [297] maintains that it was Zoroaster who instructed Pythagoras.

Were we to suggest that the Hebrew *nazars,* the railing prophets of the 'Lord,' had been initiated into the so-called Pagan mysteries, and belonged (or at least a majority of them) to the same Lodge or circle of adepts as those who were considered idolaters — that their 'circle of prophets' was but a collateral branch of a secret association, which we may well term 'international' — what a visitation of Christian wrath should we not incur! And still, the case looks strangely suspicious.

Let us first recall to our mind that which Ammianus Marcellinus [298] and other historians relate of Darius Hystaspes. The latter, penetrating into Upper India (Bactriana), learned pure rites and stellar and cosmical sciences from 'Brachmans,' and communicated them to the Magi. Now Hystaspes is shown in history to have crushed the Magi, and introduced — or rather forced upon them — the pure religion of Zoroaster, that of Ormazd. How is it, then, that an inscription is found on the tomb of Darius, stating that he was "teacher and hierophant of magic, or

---

292. Josephus: *Antiq.*, IV, iv, 4.   293. *Ibid.*, IX, ii, 1; *2 Kings*, i, 8.

294. In relation to the well-known fact of Jesus wearing his hair long, and being always so represented, it becomes quite startling to find how little the unknown Editor of the *Acts* knew about the Apostle Paul, since he makes him say in *1 Corinthians*, xi, 14, "Doth not Nature itself teach you, that if a *man have long hair, it is a shame unto him?*" Certainly Paul could never have said such a thing! Therefore, if the passage is genuine, Paul knew nothing of the prophet whose doctrines he had embraced and for which he died; and if false — how much is reliable in what remains?

295. Clem. Alex.: *Strom.*, I, xv.   296. *Vita Pythag.*, iii.

297. *Florid.*, II, xv; cf. Hyde: *Hist. rel. vet. Persarum,* p. 309: Oxonii, 1700.

298. *Roman Hist.*, XXIII, vi, 33.

magianism"? Evidently there must be some historical mistake, and history confesses it. In this imbroglio of names, Zoroaster, the teacher and instructor of Pythagoras, can be neither the Zoroaster nor Zarathustra who instituted sun-worship among the Pârsis; nor he who appeared at the court of Gushtasp (Hystaspes) the alleged father of Darius; nor, again, the Zoroaster who placed his magi above the kings themselves. The oldest Zoroastrian scripture — the *Avesta* — does not betray the slightest traces of the reformer having ever been acquainted with any of the nations that subsequently adopted his mode of worship. He seems utterly ignorant of the neighbors of Western Iran, the Medes, the Assyrians, the Persians, and others. If we had no other evidences of the great antiquity of the Zoroastrian religion than the discovery of the blunder committed by some scholars in our own century, who regarded King Vistaspa (Gushtasp) as identical with the father of Darius, whereas the Persian tradition points directly to Vistaspa as the last of the line of Kaianian princes who ruled in Bactriana, it ought to be enough, for the Assyrian conquest of Bactriana took place 1200 years B. C.[299]

Therefore it is but natural that we should see in the appellation of Zoroaster not a name but a generic term, whose significance must be left to philologists to agree upon. *Guru*, in Sanskrit, is a spiritual teacher; and as Zuruastara means in the same language he who worships the sun, why is it impossible that, by some natural change of language due to the great number of different nations which were converted to the sun-worship, the word *guru-astara*, the spiritual teacher of sun-worship, so closely resembling the name of the founder of this religion, became gradually transformed from its primal form to *Zuryastara* or Zoroaster? The opinion of the Kabalists is that there was but one Zarathustra and many *guruastaras* or spiritual teachers, and that one such *guru*, or rather *huru-aster*, as he is called in the old manuscripts, was the instructor of Pythagoras. To philology and our readers we leave the explanation for what it is worth. Personally we believe in it, as we credit on this subject Kabalistic tradition far more than the explanation of scientists, no two of whom have been able to agree up to the present year.

Aristotle states that Zoroaster lived 6000 years before Plato; [300] Hermippus of Alexandria, who is said to have read the genuine books of the Zoroastrians, although Alexander the Great is accused of having destroyed them, shows Zoroaster as the pupil of Agonaces (Agon-ach, or the Ahon-God) and as having lived 5000 years before the fall of Troy.[301]

---

299. Max Müller has sufficiently proved the case in his lecture on the 'Zend-Avesta' (*Chips, etc.*, I, p. 86). He calls Gushtasp "the mythical pupil of Zoroaster." Mythical, perhaps, only because the period in which he lived and learned with Zoroaster is too remote to allow our modern science to speculate upon it with any certainty.
300. Pliny: *Nat. Hist.*, XXX, 2.   301. *Ibid.*

Er or Eros, whose vision is related by Plato in the *Republic*,[302] is declared by Clemens Alexandrinus to have been Zordusth.[303] While the Magus who dethroned Cambyses was a Mede, and Darius proclaims that he put down the Magian rites to establish those of Ormazd, Xanthus of Lydia declares Zoroaster to have been the chief of the Magi![304]

Which of them is wrong? or are they all right, and is it only the modern interpreters who fail to explain the difference between the Reformer and his apostles and followers? This blundering of our commentators reminds us of that of Suetonius, who mistook the Christians for one Christos, or *Crestos*, as he spells it, and assured his readers that Claudius banished him for the disturbance he made among the Jews.[305]

Finally, and to return again to the *nazars*, Zaratus [306] is mentioned by Pliny in the following words: "He was Zoroaster and *Nazaret*." As Zoroaster is called *princeps* of the Magi, and *nazar* signifies separated or consecrated, is *nazar* not a Hebrew rendering of *mag?* Volney believes so. The Persian word *Na-zaruan* means millions of years, and refers to the Chaldaean 'Ancient of Days.' Hence the name of the *Nazars* or Nazarenes, who were consecrated to the service of the Supreme one God, the kabalistic Ain-Soph, or the Ancient of Days, the 'Aged of the aged.'

But the word *nazar* may also be found in India. In Hindustani *nazar* is sight, internal or *supernatural* vision; *nazar band-i* means fascination, a mesmeric or magical spell; and *nazarān* is the word for sight-seeing or vision.

Professor Wilder thinks that as the word *Zeruana* is nowhere to be found in the *Avesta* but only in the later Pârsî books, it came from the Magians, who composed the Persian sacred caste in the Sassan period, but were originally Assyrians. "Turan, of the poets," he says, "I consider to be Aturia, or Assyria; and that Zohak (Az-dahaka, Dei-okes, or Astyages), the Serpent-king, was Assyrian, Median, and Babylonian — when those countries were united."

This opinion does not, however, in the least affect our statement that the secret doctrines of the Magi, of the pre-Vedic Buddhists, of the hierophants of the Egyptian Thoth or Hermes, and of the adepts of whatever age and nationality, including the Chaldaean Kabalists and the Jewish *nazars*, were *identical* from the beginning. When we use the term *Buddhists*, we do not mean to imply by it either the exoteric Buddhism instituted by the followers of Gautama-Buddha, or the modern Buddhistic religion, but the secret philosophy of *Śākyamuni*, which in its essence is

302. Plato: *Repub.*, X, xiii.   303. *Strom.*, V, xiv.
304. Diog. Laert.: *Lives of the Philosophers*, Introd., § 2.   305. *Life of Claudius*, § 25.
306. Pliny: *Nat. Hist.*, XXX, ii; cf. Cl. Alex.: *Strom.*, I, xv (p. 397, Ante-Nic. Chr. Libr.), "Pythagoras was a pupil of Nazaratus," a footnote adding, "Otherwise *Zaratus . . . who*, Huet says, was Zoroaster."

certainly identical with the ancient wisdom-religion of the sanctuary, the pre-Vedic Brâhmanism. The 'schism' of Zoroaster, as it is called, is a direct proof of it. For it was no *schism*, strictly speaking, but merely a partially-public exposition of strictly monotheistic religious truths hitherto taught only in the sanctuaries, and that he had learned from the Brâhmanas. Zoroaster, the primeval institutor of sun-worship, cannot be called the founder of the dualistic system; neither was he the first to teach the unity of God, for he taught only what he himself had learned with the Brâhmanas. And that Zarathustra and his followers, the Zoroastrians, "had been settled in India before they immigrated into Persia," is also proved by Max Müller. "That the Zoroastrians and their ancestors started from India," he says, "during the Vedic period, can be proved as distinctly as that the inhabitants of Massilia started from Greece. . . . Many of the gods of the Zoroastrians come out . . . as mere reflexions and deflexions of the primitive and authentic gods of the *Veda*." [307]

If now we can prove — and we can do so on the evidence of the Kabala and the oldest traditions of the wisdom-religion, the philosophy of the old sanctuaries — that all these gods, whether of the Zoroastrians or of the *Veda*, are but so many personated *occult powers* of nature, the faithful servants of the adepts of secret wisdom — Magic — we are on secure ground.

Thus whether we say that Kabalism and Gnosticism proceeded from Mazdeanism or from Zoroastrianism, it is all the same, unless we meant the *exoteric* worship — which we do not. Likewise, and in this sense, we may echo King, the author of *The Gnostics*,[308] and several other archaeologists, and maintain that both the former proceeded from *Buddhism*, at once the simplest and most satisfying of philosophies, and which resulted in one of the purest religions of the world. It is only a matter of chronology to decide which of these religions, differing but in external form, is the oldest, therefore the least adulterated. But even this bears but very indirectly, if at all, on the subject we treat of. Already, some time before our era, the adepts, except in India, had ceased to congregate in large communities; but—whether among the Essenes, or the Neo-Platonists, or again among the innumerable struggling sects born but to die— the same doctrines, identical in substance and spirit, if not always in form, are encountered. By *Buddhism*, therefore, we mean that religion signifying literally the doctrine of wisdom, and which by many ages antedates the metaphysical philosophy of *Siddhârtha-Sâkyamuni*.

After nineteen centuries of enforced eliminations from the canonical books of every sentence which might put the investigator on the true

---

307. Max Müller: 'The Zend *Avesta*,' in *Chips, etc.*, I, pp. 82, 83.   308. 2nd ed., p. 55.

path, it has become very difficult to show, to the satisfaction of exact science, that the 'Pagan' worshipers of Adonis, their neighbors, the Nazarenes, and the Pythagorean Essenes, the healing Therapeutes,[309] the Ebionites, and other sects, were all, with very slight differences, followers of the ancient theurgic Mysteries. And yet by analogy and a close study of the *hidden* sense of their rites and customs, we can trace their kinship.

It was given to a contemporary of Jesus to become the means of pointing out to posterity, by his interpretation of the oldest literature of Israel, how deeply the kabalistic philosophy agreed in its esoterism with that of the profoundest Greek thinkers. This contemporary, an ardent disciple of Plato and Aristotle, was Philo Judaeus. While explaining the Mosaic books according to a purely kabalistic method, he is the famous Hebrew writer whom Kingsley calls the Father of New Platonism.

It is evident that Philo's Therapeutes are a branch of the Essenes. Their name indicates it — 'Εσσαῖοι, *Asaya*, physicians. Hence the contradictions, forgeries, and other desperate expedients to reconcile the prophecies of the Jewish canon with the Galilean nativity and godship.

Luke, who was a physician, is designated in the Syriac texts as *Asaia*, the Essaian or Essene. Josephus and Philo Judaeus have sufficiently described this sect to leave no doubt in our mind that the Nazarene Reformer, after having received his education in their dwellings in the desert, and been duly initiated in the Mysteries, preferred the free and independent life of a wandering *Nazaria*, and so separated or *inazarenized* himself from them, thus becoming a traveling Therapeute, a Nazaria, a healer. Every Therapeute, before quitting his community, had to do the same. Both Jesus and St. John the Baptist preached the end of the Age;[310] which proves their knowledge of the secret computation of the priests and kabalists, who with the chiefs of the Essene communities alone had the secret of the duration of the cycles. The latter were kabalists and theurgists; "they had their *mystic* books, and predicted future events," says Munk.[311]

Dunlap, whose personal researches seem to have been quite successful in that direction, traces the Essenes, Nazarenes, Dositheans, and some other sects as having all existed before Christ: "They rejected pleasures, *despised riches, loved one another*, and more than other sects neglected

---

309. Philo Judaeus: *De vita contemplativa.*
310. The real meaning of the division into *ages* is esoteric and Buddhistic. So little did the uninitiated Christians understand it that they accepted the words of Jesus *literally* and firmly believed that he meant the end of the world. There had been many prophecies about the forthcoming age. Vergil, in the fourth *Eclogue*, mentions the Metatron — a new offspring, with whom the *iron age* shall end, and a *golden one* arise.
311. *Palestine*, pp. 517, *sq.*

wedlock, deeming the conquest of the passions to be virtuous," [312] he says.

These are all virtues preached by Jesus; and if we are to take the gospels as a standard of truth, Christ was a metempsychosist or "*reincarnationist*" — again like these same Essenes, whom we see to have been Pythagoreans in all their doctrines and habits. Iamblichus asserts that the Samian philosopher spent a certain time at Carmel with them.[313] In his discourses and sermons Jesus always spoke in parables and used metaphors with his audience. This habit was again that of the Esseneans and the Nazarenes; the Galileans who dwelt in cities and villages were never known to use such allegorical language. Indeed, some of his disciples being Galileans as well as himself, felt even surprised to find him using with the people such a form of expression. "Why speakest thou unto them in parables?"[314] they often inquired. "Because, it is given unto you to know the Mysteries of the kingdom of heaven, but to them it is not given," was the reply, which was that of an initiate. "Therefore speak I to them in parables; because they seeing see not, and hearing they hear not, neither do they understand." Moreover, we find Jesus expressing his thoughts still more clearly — and in sentences which are purely Pythagorean — when, during the *Sermon on the Mount,* he says:

> "Give ye not that which is sacred to the dogs,
> Neither cast ye your pearls before swine;
> For the swine will tread them under their feet,
> And the dogs will turn and rend you."

Professor A. Wilder, the editor of Taylor's *Eleusinian and Bacchic Mysteries,* observes "a like disposition on the part of Jesus and Paul to classify their doctrines as esoteric and exoteric, 'the Mysteries of the Kingdom of God' for the apostles, and 'parables' for the multitude. 'We speak wisdom,' says Paul, 'among them that *are perfect*' [or initiated]." [315]

In the Eleusinian and other Mysteries the participants were always divided into two classes, the *neophytes* and the *perfect.* The former were sometimes admitted to the preliminary initiation: the dramatic performance of Ceres, or the soul, descending to Hades.[316] But it was

---

312. *Sôd, the Son of the Man,* p. xi.

313. *Life of Pythag.,* iii (T. Taylor). Munk derives the name of the *Iessaeans* or Essenes from the Syriac *Asaya* — the healers, or physicians, thus showing their identity with the Egyptian Therapeutae.— *Palestine,* p. 515.

314. *Matt.,* xiii, 10-13.   315. P. 47 (4th ed.).

316. This descent to Hades signified the inevitable fate of each soul to be united for a time with a terrestrial body. This union, or dark prospect for the soul to find itself

given only to the '*perfect*' to enjoy and learn the Mysteries of the divine *Elysium*, the celestial abode of the blessed; this Elysium being unquestionably the same as the 'Kingdom of Heaven.' To contradict or reject the above, would be merely to shut one's eyes to the truth.

The narrative of the Apostle Paul, in his second *Epistle to the Corinthians* (xii, 3, 4), has struck several scholars, well versed in the descriptions of the mystical rites of the initiation given by some classics, as alluding most undoubtedly to the final *Epopteia*.[317] "I knew a certain man — *whether in body or outside of body*, I know not: God knoweth — who was rapt into Paradise, and heard things ineffable ἄῤῥητα ῤήματα, *which it is not lawful for a man to repeat*." These words have rarely, so far as we know, been regarded by commentators as an allusion to the beatific visions of an '*initiated*' seer. But the phraseology is unequivocal. These things "*which it is not lawful to repeat*," are hinted at in the same words, and the reason for it assigned is the same as that which we find repeatedly expressed by Plato, Proclus, Iamblichus, Herodotus and other classics. "We speak WISDOM [only] among them that are PERFECT," says Paul; the plain and undeniable translation of the sentence being: "We speak of the profounder (or final) esoteric doctrines of the Mysteries (which were denominated *wisdom*) only among them that are *initiated*."[318] So in relation to the "man who was rapt into Paradise" — and who was evidently Paul himself[319] — the Christian word Paradise having replaced that of Elysium. To complete the proof, we might recall the words of Plato, given elsewhere, which show that before an initiate could see the gods in their purest light, he had to become *liberated* from his body; *i. e.*, to separate his astral soul from it.[320] Apuleius also describes his initiation into the Mysteries in the same way: "I approached the confines of death; and having trodden on the threshold of Proserpina returned, having been carried through all the elements. In the depths of midnight I saw the sun glittering with a splendid light, together with *the infernal and supernal gods*, and to these divinities approaching, I paid the tribute of devout adoration."[321]

---

imprisoned within the dark tenement of a body, was considered by all the ancient philosophers, and is even by the modern Buddhists, as a punishment.

317. Taylor: *Eleus. and Bacch. Myst.*, ed. A. Wilder, p. 87 (4th edit.).

318. "The profounder esoteric doctrines of the ancients were denominated *wisdom*, and afterward *philosophy*, and also the *gnosis*, or knowledge. They related to the human soul, its divine parentage, its supposed degradation from its high estate by becoming connected with 'generation' or the physical world, its onward progress and restoration to God by regenerations, . . . transmigrations." *Ibid.*, pp. 31, 32.

319. Cyril of Jerusalem asserts it. See *Catech.*, VI, x.

320. *Phaedrus*, § 64.　　　　　321. *The Golden Ass*, xi (Taylor's ed., p. 283).

Thus in common with Pythagoras and other hierophant reformers, Jesus divided his teachings into exoteric and esoteric. Following faithfully the Pythagoreo-Essenean ways, he never sat at a meal without saying 'grace.' "The priest prays before his meal," says Josephus, describing the Essenes. Jesus also divided his followers into 'neophytes,' 'brethren,' and the 'perfect,' if we may judge by the difference he made between them. But his career, at least as a public Rabbi, was of a too short duration to allow him to establish a regular school of his own; and, with the exception, perhaps, of John, it does not seem that he had initiated any other apostle. The Gnostic amulets and talismans are mostly the emblems of the apocalyptic allegories. The 'seven vowels' are closely related to the 'seven seals'; and the mystic title Abraxas partakes as much of the composition of *Shem ham-mephorash,* 'the holy word' or ineffable name, as the name called: The word of God, that *"no man knew but he himself,"* [322] as John expresses it.

It would be difficult to escape from the well-adduced proofs that the *Apocalypse* is the production of an initiated Kabalist, when this *Revelation* presents whole passages taken from the books of *Enoch* and *Daniel,* which latter is in itself an abridged imitation of the former; and when furthermore we ascertain that the Ophite Gnostics who rejected the *Old Testament* entirely, as "emanating from an inferior being" (Jehovah), accepted the most ancient prophets, such as Enoch, and deduced the strongest support from his book for their religious tenets, the demonstration becomes evident. We will show further how closely related are all these doctrines. Besides there is the history of Domitian's persecutions of magicians and philosophers, which affords as good a proof as any that John was generally considered a kabalist. As the apostle was included among the number, and moreover conspicuous, the imperial edict banished him not only from Rome, but even from the continent. It was not the Christians whom — confounding them with the Jews, as some historians will have it — the emperor persecuted, but the astrologers and kabalists.[323]

The accusations against Jesus of practising the magic of Egypt were numerous and at one time universal, in the towns where he was

---

322. *Rev.,* xix, 12.

323. See Suetonius in *Vita Domitiani,* §§ 3, 12, 14. It is neither cruelty, nor an insane indulgence in it, which shows this emperor in history as passing his time in catching flies and transfixing them with a golden bodkin, but religious superstition. The Jewish astrologers had predicted to him that he had provoked the wrath of Beelzebub, the 'Lord of the flies,' and would perish miserably through the revenge of the dark god of Ekron and die like King Ahaziah, because he persecuted the Jews.

known. The Pharisees, as claimed in the *Bible*, had been the first
to fling this charge in his face, although Rabbi Wise considers Jesus
himself a Pharisee. The *Talmud* certainly points to James the Just
as one of that sect.[324] But these partisans are known to have always
stoned every prophet who denounced their evil ways, and it is not
on this fact that we base our assertion. These accused him of sorcery,
and of driving out devils by Beelzebub, their prince, with as much
justice as later the Catholic clergy had in accusing of the same more
than one innocent martyr. But Justin Martyr states on better authority
that the men of his time *who were not Jews* asserted that the miracles
of Jesus were performed by magical art — μαγικὴ φαντασία — the very
expression used by the skeptics of those days to designate the feats
of thaumaturgy accomplished in the Pagan temples. "They even
ventured to call him a magician and a deceiver of the people," complains the martyr.[325] In the *Gospel of Nicodemus* (the *Acta Pilati*),
the Jews bring the same accusation before Pilate. "Did we not tell
thee he was a magician?"[326] Celsus speaks of the same charge, and
as a Neo-Platonist believes in it.[327] The Talmudic literature is full
of the most minute [alleged] particulars, and their greatest accusation is
that "Jesus could fly as easily in the air as others could walk."[328]
St. Augustine asserted that it was generally believed that he had been
initiated in Egypt, and that he wrote books concerning magic, which he
delivered to John. There was a work called *Magia Jesu Christi*, which
was attributed to Jesus[329] himself. In the *Clementine Recognitions* the
charge is [recognised as having been] brought against Jesus that he did
not perform his miracles as a Jewish prophet, but as a magician, *i. e.*, an
initiate of the 'heathen' temples.[330]

It was usual then, as it is now, among the intolerant clergy of op-
posing religions, as well as among the lower classes of society, and even
among those patricians who, for various reasons had been excluded
from any participation of the Mysteries, to accuse sometimes the highest

---

324. We believe that it was the Sadducees and not the Pharisees who crucified
Jesus. They were Zadokites — partisans of the house of Zadok, or the sacerdotal family.
In the *Acts* the apostles were said to be persecuted by the Sadducees, but never by
the Pharisees. In fact, the latter never persecuted any one. They had the scribes,
rabbis, and learned men in their numbers, and were not, like the Sadducees, jealous
of their order.

325. Justin Martyr: *Dial. with Trypho*, lix, 7.

326. *Gosp. of Nicodemus*, ii, 3 (Hone, and Grynaeus).

327. Origen: *Cont. Cels.*, I, lxviii; II, xlviii, *sq.*   328. Johanan: *Meg.* 51.

329. Augustine: *De consensu evang.*, i, 9; Fabricius: *Cod. apocr. N. T.*, I, p. 305, *sq.*
330. I, lviii.

hierophants and adepts of sorcery and black magic. So Apuleius, who had been initiated, was likewise accused of witchcraft, and of carrying about him the figure of a skeleton — a potent agent, as it is asserted, in the operations of the black art. But one of the best and most unquestionable proofs of our assertion may be found in the so-called Museo Gregoriano. On the sarcophagus, which is paneled with bas-reliefs representing the miracles of Christ,[331] may be seen the full figure of Jesus who, in the resurrection of Lazarus, appears beardless "and equipped with a wand in the received guise of a *necromancer* [?] whilst the corpse of Lazarus is swathed in bandages exactly as an Egyptian mummy."

Had posterity possessed several such representations executed during the first century when the figure, dress, and every-day habits of the Reformer were still fresh in the memory of his contemporaries, perhaps the Christian world would be more Christ-like; the dozens of contradictory, groundless and utterly meaningless speculations about the 'Son of Man' would have been impossible; and humanity would now have but one religion and one God. It is this absence of all proof, the lack of the least positive clew about him whom Christianity has deified, that has caused the present state of perplexity. No pictures of Christ were possible until after the days of Constantine, when the Jewish element was nearly eliminated among the followers of the new religion. The Jews, apostles, and disciples, whom the Zoroastrians and the Pârsis had inoculated with a holy horror of any form of images, would have considered it sacrilegious to represent in any way or shape their master. The only authorized image of Jesus, even in the days of Tertullian, was an allegorical representation of the 'Good Shepherd,' [332] which was no portrait, but the figure of a man with a jackal-head, like Anubis.[333] On this gem, as seen in the collection of Gnostic amulets, the Good Shepherd bears upon his shoulders the lost lamb. He seems to have a human head upon his neck; but, as King correctly observes, "it only *seems so* to the uninitiated eye." On closer inspection, he becomes the double-headed Anubis, having one head human, the other a jackal's, while his girdle assumes the form of a serpent rearing aloft its crested head. "This figure," adds the author of *The Gnostics etc.*, "had two meanings — one obvious for the vulgar; the other mystical, and recognisable by the *initiated alone*. It was perhaps the signet of some chief

---

331. King: *The Gnostics, etc.*, p. 145 (1st ed.); the author places this sarcophagus among the earliest productions of that art which later inundated the world with mosaics and engravings, representing the events and personages of the 'New Testament.'

332. Tertullian: *De pudicitia*, vii, 1. See *The Gnostics and their Remains*, p. 144 (1st ed.).

333. *The Gnostics, etc.* pl. i, p. 200 (1st ed.).

teacher or apostle." [334] This affords a fresh proof that the Gnostics and early *orthodox* (?) Christians were not so wide apart in their *secret doctrine*. King deduces from a quotation from Epiphanius, that even as late as 400 A. D. it was considered an atrocious sin to attempt to represent the bodily appearance of Christ. Epiphanius [335] brings it as an idolatrous charge against the Carpocratians that "they kept painted portraits, and *even gold and silver images*, and *in other materials*, which they pretended to be portraits of Jesus, and made by Pilate after the likeness of Christ. . . . These they keep in secret, along with Pythagoras, Plato, and Aristotle, and setting them all up together, they worship and offer sacrifices unto them *after the Gentiles' fashion*."

What would the pious Epiphanius say were he to be resuscitated and to step into St. Peter's Cathedral at Rome! Ambrosius seems very much shocked at the idea that some persons fully credited the statement of Lampridius that Alexander Severus had in his private chapel an image of Christ among other great philosophers. [336] "That the Pagans should have preserved the likeness of Christ," he exclaims, "but the disciples have neglected to do so, is a notion the mind shudders to entertain, much less to believe."

All this points undeniably to the fact, that except a handful of self-styled Christians who subsequently won the day, all the civilized portion of the Pagans who knew of Jesus honored him as a philosopher, an *adept* whom they placed on the same level with Pythagoras and Apollonius. Whence such a veneration on their part for a man, were he simply, as represented by the Synoptics, a poor, unknown Jewish carpenter from Nazareth? As an incarnated God there is no single record of him on this earth capable of withstanding the critical examination of science; as one of the greatest reformers, an inveterate enemy of every theological dogmatism, an opponent of bigotry, a teacher of one of the most sublime codes of ethics, Jesus is one of the grandest and most clearly-defined figures on the panorama of human history. His age may, with every day, be receding farther and farther back into the gloomy and hazy mists of the past; and [the Christian] theology — based on human fancy and supported by untenable dogmas — may, nay, must with every day lose more of its unmerited prestige; alone the grand figure of the philosopher and moral reformer instead of growing paler will become with every century more pronounced and more clearly defined. It will reign supreme and universal only on that day when the whole of humanity recognises but one father — the UNKNOWN ONE above — and one brother — the whole of mankind below. '

334. This gem is in the collection of the author of *The Gnostics, etc* See p. 201 (1st ed.).
335. *Panaria*, lib. I, tom. II, Haer. XXVII, vi.   336. *The Gnostics, etc.*, p. 227 (1887).

In a pretended letter of Lentulus, a senator and a distinguished historian, to the Roman senate, there is a description of the personal appearance of Jesus. The letter itself,[337] written in horrid Latin, is pronounced a bare-faced forgery; but we find therein an expression which suggests many thoughts. Albeit a forgery it is evident that whosoever invented it has nevertheless tried to follow tradition as closely as possible. The hair of Jesus is represented in it as "wavy and curling . . . flowing down upon his shoulders," and as "*having a parting in the middle of the head after the fashion of the Nazarenes.*" This last sentence shows: 1. That there was such a tradition, based on the biblical description of John the Baptist, the *Nazaria*, and the custom of this sect. 2. Had Lentulus been the author of this letter, it is difficult to believe that Paul should never have heard of it; and had he known its contents, he would never have pronounced it a *shame* for men to wear their hair long,[338] thus shaming his Lord and Christ-God. 3. If Jesus did wear his hair long and "parted in the middle of the forehead, after the fashion of the Nazarenes" (as well as of John, the only one of his apostles who followed it), then we have one good reason more to say that Jesus must have belonged to the sect of the Nazarenes, and been called NASARIA for this reason and not because he was an inhabitant of Nazareth, for they never wore their hair long. The Nazarite, who *separated* himself unto the Lord, allowed "no razor to come upon his head." "He shall be holy, and shall let the locks of the hair of his head grow," says *Numbers* (vi, 5). Samson was a Nazarite, *i. e.*, vowed to the service of God, and in his hair was his strength. "No razor shall come upon his head; the child shall be a Nazarite unto God from the womb" (*Judges*, xiii, 5). But the final and most reasonable conclusion to be inferred from this is that Jesus, who was so opposed to all the orthodox Jewish practices, would *not* have allowed his hair to grow had he not belonged to this sect, which in the days of John the Baptist had already become a heresy in the eyes of the Sanhedrim. The *Talmud*, speaking of the Nazaria, or the Nazarenes (who had abandoned the world like Hindû yogis or hermits) calls them a sect of physicians, of wandering exorcists; as also does Jervis. "They went about the country, living on alms and performing cures."[339] Epiphanius says that the Nazarenes come next in heresy to the Cerinthians whether having existed "before them or after them, nevertheless *synchronous,*" and then adds that "all Christians at that time were equally called *Nazarenes*"![340]

---

337. Grynaeus: *Orthodoxographa,* Latin part, I, 2:⸗Basileae, 1569.
338. *1 Corinthians,* xi, 14.
339. I. M. Yost: *The Israelite Indeed,* II, p. 238; *Talmud, Mishnah Nazir.*
340. *Panaria,* lib. I, tom. II, Haer. XXIX, i; XXX, i.

In the very first remark made by Jesus about John the Baptist, we find him stating that he is "Elias, which was for to come." This assertion, if it is not a later interpolation for the sake of having a prophecy fulfilled, means again that Jesus was a kabalist; unless indeed we have to adopt the doctrine of the French spiritists and suspect him of believing in [personal] reincarnation. Except the kabalistic sects of the Essenes, the Nazarenes, the disciples of Shimon ben Yo'hai, and Hillel, neither the orthodox Jews, nor the Galileans, believed or knew anything about the doctrine of permutation. And the Sadducees rejected even that of the resurrection.

"But the author of this restitutio was Mosah, our master, upon whom be peace! Who was the revolutio [transmigration] of Seth and Hebel, that he might cover the nudity of his Father Adam — Primus," says the Kabala.[341] Thus the hint of Jesus that John was the revolutio, or transmigration, of Elias, seems to prove beyond any doubt the school to which he belonged.

Until the present day uninitiated Kabalists and Masons believe permutation to be synonymous with transmigration and metempsychosis. But they are as much mistaken in regard to the doctrine of the true Kabalists as to that of the Buddhists. True, the Zohar says in one place, "All souls are subject to transmigration, and men do not know the ways of the Holy One, blessed be He; they do not know that they are brought before the tribunal, both before they enter this world and after they quit it,"[342] and the Pharisees also held this doctrine, as Josephus shows (Antiquities, XVIII, i, 3). Also the doctrine of Gilgul held the strange theory of the 'Whirling of the Soul,' which taught that the bodies of Jews buried far away from the Holy Land, still preserve a particle of soul which can neither rest nor quit them until it reaches the soil of the 'Promised Land.' And this 'whirling' process was thought to be accomplished by the soul being conveyed back through an actual evolution of species; transmigrating from the minutest insect up to the largest animal. But this was an exoteric doctrine. We refer the reader to the Kabbala denudata of Knorr von Rosenroth; his language, however obscure, may yet throw some light upon the subject.

But this doctrine of permutation, or revolutio, must not be understood as a belief in reincarnation. That Moses was considered the transmigration of Abel and Seth, does not imply that the kabalists — those who were initiated at least — believed that the identical spirit of either of Adam's sons reappeared under the corporeal form of Moses. It only shows what was the mode of expression they used when hinting at one of

---

341. Kabbala denudata, II, p. 155; also Vallis Regia: Paris.
342. Zohar, II, p. 99 b (Amst. ed.).

the profoundest mysteries of the Oriental Gnosis, one of the most majestic articles of faith of the Secret Wisdom. It was purposely veiled so as to half conceal and half reveal the truth. It implied that Moses, like certain other god-like men, was believed to have reached the highest of all states on earth — the rarest of all psychological phenomena — the perfect union of the immortal spirit with the terrestrial *duad* had occurred. The trinity was complete. A *god* was incarnate. But how rare such incarnations!

That expression, 'Ye are gods,' which, to our biblical students, is a mere abstraction, has for the kabalists a vital significance. Each immortal spirit that sheds its radiance upon a human being is a god — the Microcosmos of the Macrocosmos, part and parcel of the Unknown God, the First Cause, of which it is a direct emanation. It is possessed of all the attributes of its parent source. Among these attributes are omniscience and omnipotence. Endowed with these, but yet unable fully to manifest them while in the body, during which time they are obscured, veiled, limited by the capabilities of physical nature, the thus divinely-inhabited man may tower far above his kind, evince a god-like wisdom, and display deific powers; for while the rest of mortals around him are but *overshadowed* by their divine SELF, with every chance given to them to become immortal hereafter, but with no other security than their personal efforts to win the kingdom of heaven, the man so chosen has already become an immortal while yet on earth. His prize is secured. Henceforth he will live forever in eternal life. Not only he may have "dominion" [343] over all the works of creation by employing the "excellence" of the NAME (the ineffable one) but be higher in this life, not, as Paul is made to say, "a little lower than the angels." [344]

The ancients never entertained the sacrilegious thought that such perfected entities were incarnations of the One Supreme and for ever invisible God. No such profanation of the awful Majesty entered into their conceptions. Moses and his antitypes and types were to them but complete men, gods on earth, for their *gods* (divine spirits) had entered unto their hallowed tabernacles, the purified physical bodies. The disembodied spirits of the heroes and sages were termed gods by the ancients. Hence the accusation of polytheism and idolatry on the part of those who were the first to anthropomorphize the holiest and purest abstractions of their forefathers.

---

343. *Psalms*, viii, 6.

344. This contradiction, which is attributed to Paul in *Hebrews*, by making him say of Jesus in chapter i, 4: "Being made *so much better* than the angels," and then immediately stating in chapter ii, 9, "But we see Jesus, who was made *a little lower* than the angels," shows how unscrupulously the writings of the apostles, if they ever wrote any, were tampered with.

The real and hidden sense of this doctrine was known to all the initiates. The Tanaim imparted it to their elect ones, the Isarim, in the solemn solitudes of crypts and deserted places. It was one of the most esoteric and jealously guarded teachings, for human nature was the same then as it is now, and the sacerdotal caste as confident as now in the supremacy of its knowledge, and as ambitious of ascendency over the weaker masses; with the difference perhaps that its hierophants could prove the legitimacy of their claims and the verity of their doctrines, whereas now, *believers* must be content with blind faith.

While the kabalists called this mysterious and rare occurrence of the union of spirit with the mortal charge entrusted to its care, the 'descent of the Angel Gabriel' (the latter being a kind of generic name for it), the *Messenger of Life*, and the angel Metatron; and while the Nazarenes termed the same Abel-Zivo,[345] the *Delegatus* sent by the Lord of Celsitude, it was universally known as the 'Anointed Spirit.'

Thus it is the acceptation of this doctrine which caused the Gnostics to maintain that Jesus was a man overshadowed by the Christos or Messenger of Life, and that his despairing cry from the cross *Eloi, Eloi, Lama Sabachthani*, was wrung from him at the instant when he felt that this inspiring Presence had finally abandoned him, for — as some affirmed — his faith *had* abandoned him when on the cross.

The early Nazarenes, who must be numbered among the Gnostic sects, believing that Jesus was a prophet, held nevertheless in relation to him the same doctrine of the divine 'overshadowing' of certain 'men of God,' sent for the salvation of nations, and to recall them to the path of righteousness. "The Divine mind is eternal, and it is pure light, and poured out through splendid *and immense space* (pleroma). It is Genetrix of the Aeons. But one of them [the Demiurge] went to matter (chaos) stirring up confused (*turbulentos*) movements; and by a certain portion of *heavenly* light fashioned it, properly constituted for use and appearance, but the beginning of every evil. The Demiurge (of matter) claimed divine honor.[346] Therefore Christus ('the anointed'), the prince of the Aeons (powers), was sent (*expeditus*), who *taking on the person* of a most devout Jew, Iesu, *was to conquer him;* but who having *laid it* (the body) *aside*, departed on high." [347] We will explain farther on the full significance of the name Christos and its mystic meaning.

And now, in order to make such passages as the above more intelligible, we will endeavor to define, as briefly as possible, the dogmas in

345. *Codex Nazaraeus*, I, p. 23.

346. *Ibid.*, Norberg's preface, pp. iv, v.

347. "According to the Nazarenes and Gnostics, the Demiurge, the creator of the material world, is not the highest God." (Dunlap: *Sôd, the Son of the Man, passim.*)

which, with very trifling differences, nearly all the Gnostic sects believed. It was in Ephesus where flourished in those days the greatest college, wherein the abstruse Oriental speculations and the Platonic philosophy were taught in conjunction. It was a focus of the universal 'secret' doctrines; the weird laboratory whence, fashioned in elegant Grecian phraseology, sprang the quintessence of Buddhistic, Zoroastrian, and Chaldaean philosophy. Artemis, the gigantic concrete symbol of theosophico-pantheistic abstractions, the great mother Multimamma, androgyne and patroness of the 'Ephesian writings,' was conquered by Paul; but although the zealous converts of the apostles pretended to burn all their books on "curious arts," τὰ περίεργα, enough of these remained for them to study when their first zeal had cooled off. It was from Ephesus that spread nearly all the *Gnosis* which antagonized so fiercely the Irenaean dogmas; and still it was Ephesus, with her numerous collateral branches of the great college of the Essenes, which proved to be the hotbed of all the kabalistic speculations brought by the Tanaim from the captivity. "In Ephesus," says J. Matter, "the notions of the Jewish-Egyptian school, and the semi-Persian speculations of the kabalists had then recently come to swell the vast conflux of Grecian and Asiatic doctrines; so there is no wonder that teachers should have sprung up there who strove to combine the religion newly preached by the apostle with the ideas there so long established." [348]

Had not the Christians burdened themselves with the *Revelations* of a little nation, and accepted the Jehovah of Moses, the Gnostic ideas would never have been termed *heresies;* once relieved of their dogmatic exaggerations the world would have had a religious system based on pure Platonic philosophy, and surely something would then have been gained.

Now let us see what are the greatest *heresies* of the Gnostics. We will select Basilides as the standard for our comparisons, for all the founders of other Gnostic sects group round him, like a cluster of planets borrowing light from their sun.

Basilides maintained that he had had all his doctrines from the apostle Matthew, and from Peter through Glaucias, the disciple of the latter. [349] According to Eusebius, [350] he published twenty-four volumes of *Commentaries upon the Gospel,* [351] all of which were burned,

---

348. C. W. King: *The Gnostics, etc.*, p. 7 (2nd ed., 1887).

349. Clem. Alex.: *Strom.,* VII, xvii; Hippol.: *Refut. of all Heresies,* VII, viii.

350. *Ecclesiastical History,* IV, vii.

351. The gospel interpreted by Basilides was not our present 'gospels,' which, as is proved by the greatest authorities, were not in his days in existence. See *Supernatural Religion,* part II, ch. vi, 'Basilides.'

a fact which makes us suppose that they contained more truthful matter than the school of Irenaeus was prepared to deny. He asserted that the unknown, eternal, and uncreated Father having first brought forth *Nous*, or Mind, the latter emanated from itself — the *Logos*. The Logos (the 'Word' of John) emanated in its turn *Phronesis*, or the Intelligences (Divine-human spirits). From Phronesis sprang *Sophia*, or feminine wisdom, and *Dynamis* — strength. [352] These were the personified attributes of the Mysterious godhead, the Gnostic quinternion, typifying the five spiritual, but intelligible substances, personal virtues or beings external to the unknown godhead. This is pre-eminently a kabalistic idea. It is still more Buddhistic. The earliest system of the Buddhistic philosophy — which preceded by far Gautama-Buddha — is based upon the uncreated substance of the 'Unknown,' the *Ādi-Buddha*. [353] This eternal, infinite Monad possesses, as proper to its own essence, five acts of wisdom. From these, by five separate acts of *Dhyâna*, emanated five *Dhyâni-Buddhas*; these, like *Ādi-Buddha*, are quiescent in their system (passive). Neither *Ādi*, nor any of the five *Dhyâni-Buddhas*, were ever incarnated, but seven of their emanations became Avatars, *i. e.*, were incarnated on this earth.

---

352. Irenaeus: *Against Heresies*, I, xxiv, 3.

353. The five make mystically ten. They are androgynes. "Having divided his body in two parts, the Supreme Wisdom became male and female" (*Manu*, I, *śloka* 32). There are many early Buddhistic ideas to be found in Brâhmanism.

The prevalent idea that the last of the Buddhas, Gautama, is the ninth incarnation of Vishnu, or the *ninth* Avatar, is disclaimed partially by the Brâhmanas, and wholly rejected by the learned Buddhist theologians. The latter insist that the worship of Buddha possesses a far higher claim to antiquity than that of any of the Brâhmanical deities of the *Vedas*, which they call secular literature. The Brâhmanas, they show, came from other countries, and established their heresy on [the worship of] the already accepted popular *deities*. They conquered the land by the sword, and succeeded in burying truth, by building a theology of their own on the ruins of the more ancient one of Buddha, which had prevailed for ages. They admit the divinity and spiritual existence of some of the Vedántic gods; but as in the case of the Christian angel-hierarchy they believe that all these deities are greatly subordinate, even to the incarnated Buddhas. They do not even acknowledge the creation of the physical universe. Spiritually and *invisibly* it has existed from all eternity, and thus it was made merely visible to the human senses. When it first appeared it was called forth from the realm of the invisible into the visible by the impulse of *Ādi-Buddha* — the 'Essence.' They reckon twenty-two such visible appearances of the universe governed by Buddhas, and as many destructions of it, by fire and water in regular successions. After the last destruction by the flood, at the end of the precedent cycle — the exact calculation, embracing several millions of years, is a secret cycle — the world, during the present age of the *Kali-Yuga* — *Mahâ-Bhadra-Kalpa* — has been ruled successively by four Buddhas, the last of whom was Gautama, the 'Holy One.' The fifth, *Maitreya-Buddha*, is yet to come. This latter is the expected kabalistic King Messiah, the Messenger of Light, and Sosiosh, the Persian Savior, who will come on a *white* horse. It is also the 'Lord' of the Christian Second Advent. See *Apocalypse* of St. John.

Describing the Basilidean system, Irenaeus, quoting the Gnostics, declares as follows:

"When the uncreated, *unnamed* Father saw the corruption of mankind, he sent his first-born *Nous*, into the world, in the form of Christ, for the redemption of all who believe in him, out of the power of those who fabricated the world [the Demiurge and his six sons, the planetary genii]. He appeared amongst men as the man Jesus, and wrought miracles. This Christ did *not die* in person, but Simon the Cyrenian suffered in his stead, *to whom he lent his bodily form;* . . . for the Divine Power, the Nous of the Eternal Father, *is not corporeal*, and *cannot die.* . . . Whoso, therefore, maintains that Christ has died, is still the bondsman of ignorance; whoso denies the same, he is free, and hath understood the purpose of the Father." [354]

So far, and taken in its abstract sense, we do not see anything blasphemous in this system. It may be a *heresy* against the theology of Irenaeus and Tertullian,[355] but there is certainly nothing sacrilegious against the religious idea itself, and it will seem to every impartial thinker far more consistent with divine reverence than the anthropomorphism of actual Christianity. The Gnostics were called by the orthodox Christians, *Docetae*, or Illusionists, for believing that Christ did not, nor could, suffer death actually — in the physical body. The later Bráhmanical books contain likewise much that is repugnant to the reverential feeling and idea of the Divinity; and as well as the Gnostics, the Bráhmanas explain such legends as may shock the divine dignity of the Spiritual beings called gods by attributing them to *Máyá* or illusion.

A people brought up and nurtured for countless ages among all the psychological phenomena of which the civilized (!) nations read, but reject as incredible and worthless, cannot well expect to have its religious system even understood — let alone appreciated. The profoundest and most transcendental speculations of the ancient metaphysicians of India and other countries are all based on that great Buddhistic and Bráhmanical principle underlying the whole of their religious metaphysics — *illusion* of the senses. Everything that is finite is illusion, all that which is eternal and infinite is reality. Form, color, that which we hear and feel, or see with our mortal eyes, exists only so far as it can be conveyed to each of us through our senses. The universe for a man born blind does not exist in either form or color, but it exists in its *privation* (in the Aristotelean sense), and is a reality for the spiritual senses

---

354. Irenaeus: *Against Heresies*, I, xxiv, 4.
355. Tertullian turned the tables on himself by rejecting, later in life, the doctrines for which he fought with such an acerbity, and by becoming a Montanist.

of the blind man. We all live under the powerful dominion of phantasy. Only the highest and invisible *originals* emanated from the thought of the Unknown, are real and permanent beings, forms, and ideas; on earth we see but their reflexions,— more or less correct, and ever dependent on the physical and mental organization of the person who beholds them.

Ages untold before our era the Hindû Mystic, Kapila, who is considered by many scientists as a skeptic, because they judge him with their habitual superficiality, magnificently expressed this idea in the following terms:

"Man [physical man] counts for so little that hardly anything can demonstrate to him his proper existence and that of nature. Perhaps that which we regard as the universe, and the divers beings which seem to compose it, have nothing real, and are but the product of continued illusion —.*mâyâ* — of our senses."

And the modern Schopenhauer, repeating this philosophical idea, 10,000 years old now, says: "Nature is non-existent, *per se*. . . . Nature is the infinite illusion of our senses." Kant, Schelling, and other metaphysicians have said the same, and their school maintains the idea. The objects of sense being ever delusive and fluctuating, cannot be a reality. Spirit alone is unchangeable, hence — it alone is no illusion. This is pure Buddhist doctrine. The religion of the *Gnosis* (knowledge), the most evident offshoot of Buddhism, was entirely based on this metaphysical tenet. Christos suffered *spiritually* for us, and far more acutely than did the illusionary Jesus while his body was being tortured on the Cross.

In the ideas of the Christians, Christ is but another name for Jesus. The philosophy of the Gnostics, the initiates, and hierophants understood it otherwise. The word Christos, Χριστός, like all Greek words, must be sought in its philological origin — the Sanskrit. In this latter language *Kris* means sacred,[356] and the Hindû deity was named Kris-na (the pure or the sacred) from that. On the other hand, the Greek *Christos* bears several meanings, as anointed (pure oil, *chrism*) and others. In all languages, though the synonym of the word means pure or sacred essence, it is the first emanation of the invisible Godhead, manifesting

---

356. In his debate with Jacolliot upon the right spelling of the Hindû Krishna, Mr. Textor de Ravisi, an ultramontane Catholic, tries to prove that the name of Christna ought to be written Krishna, for as the latter means black [Benfey, *Sanskr. Dict.*, gives the usual translation of Krishna as "black, dark-blue," but says "the origin of the signification is dubious"], and the statues of this deity are generally black, the word is derived from the color. We refer the reader to Jacolliot's answer in his recent work, *Christna et le Christ*, pp. 357-8, etc., for the conclusive evidence that the name is not derived from the color.

itself tangibly in spirit. The Greek Logos, the Hebrew Messiah, the Latin Verbum, and the Hindû *Virâj* (the son) are identically the same; they express an idea of collective entities — of flames detached from the one eternal center of light.

"The man who accomplishes pious but interested acts [with the sole object of his salvation] may reach the ranks of the *devas* [saints]; [357] but he who accomplishes, disinterestedly, the same pious acts, finds himself forever rid of the five elements" (of matter). "Perceiving the Supreme Soul in all beings and all beings in the Supreme Soul, in offering his own soul in sacrifice, he identifies himself with the Being who shines in his own splendor" (*Manu*, XII, *slokas* 90, 91).

Thus Christos as a unity is but an abstraction: a general idea representing the collective aggregation of the numberless spirit-entities, which are the direct emanations of the infinite, invisible, incomprehensible FIRST CAUSE — the individual spirits of men, erroneously called souls. They are the divine sons of God, of which some only overshadow mortal men — but this in the majority of cases, — some remain forever planetary spirits, and some — the smaller and rare minority — unite themselves during life with certain men. Such God-like beings as Gautama-Buddha, Jesus, Lao-Tse, Krishna, and a few others had united themselves with their spirits permanently — hence, they became gods on earth. Others, such as Moses, Pythagoras, Apollonius, Plotinus, Confucius, Plato, Iamblichus, and some Christian saints, having at intervals been so united, have taken rank in history as demi-gods and leaders of mankind. When unburdened of their terrestrial tabernacles, their freed souls, henceforth united forever with their spirits, rejoin the whole shining host, which is bound together in one spiritual solidarity of thought and deed, and is called 'the anointed.' Hence the meaning of the Gnostics, who, by saying that 'Christos' suffered spiritually for humanity, implied that his Divine Spirit suffered mostly.

Such and far more elevating were the ideas of Marcion, the great 'Heresiarch' of the second century, as he was termed by his opponents. He came to Rome toward the latter part of the half-century, from A. D. 139—142, according to Tertullian, Irenaeus, Clement, and most of his modern commentators, such as Bunsen, Tischendorf, Westcott, and many others. Credner and Schleiermacher [358] agree as to his high and irreproachable personal character, his pure religious aspira-

357. There is no equivalent for the word 'miracle,' in the Christian sense, among the Brâhmanas or Buddhists. The only correct translation would be *meipo*, a wonder, something remarkable; but not a violation of natural law. The 'saints' only produce *meipo*.

358. Credner: *Beiträge*, I, p. 40; Schleiermacher: *Sämmtl. Werke*, VIII; *Einl. N. T.*, p. 64: 1845.

tions and elevated views. His influence must have been powerful, as we find Epiphanius writing more than two centuries later that in his time the followers of Marcion were to be found throughout the whole world.[359]

The danger must indeed have been pressing and great, if we are to judge it by the opprobrious epithets and vituperation heaped upon Marcion by the 'Great African,' that Patristic Cerberus, whom we find ever barking at the door of the Irenaean dogmas. We have but to open his celebrated refutation of Marcion's *Antitheses*, to acquaint ourselves with the *fine-fleur* of monkish abuse of the Christian school; an abuse so faithfully carried on through the Middle Ages, to be renewed in our present day — at the Vatican. "Now, then, ye hounds, yelping at the God of truth, whom the apostle casts out, to all your questions! These are the bones of contention which ye gnaw," etc.[360] "The poverty of the 'Great African's' arguments keeps pace with his abuse," remarks the author of *Supernatural Religion*. "Their [the Fathers'] religious controversy bristles with misstatements, and is turbid with pious abuse. Tertullian was a master of this style, and the vehement vituperation with which he opens and often interlards his work against 'the impious and sacrilegious Marcion,' offers anything but a guarantee of fair and legitimate criticism." [361]

How firm these two Fathers — Tertullian and Epiphanius — were on their theological ground, may be inferred from the curious fact that they both intemperately and vehemently reproach "the beast" (Marcion) "with erasing passages from the *Gospel of Luke* which never were in *Luke* at all." "The lightness and inaccuracy," adds the critic, "with which Tertullian proceeds, are all the better illustrated by the fact that not only does he accuse Marcion falsely, but *he actually defines the motives* for which he expunged a passage *which never existed;* in the same chapter he also similarly accuses Marcion of erasing (from *Luke*) the saying that Christ had not come to destroy the law and the prophets, but to fulfil them, and he actually repeats the charge on two other occasions.[362] Epiphanius also commits the mistake of reproaching Marcion with omitting from *Luke* what is only found in *Matthew*." [363]

Having so far shown the amount of reliance to be placed on the Patristic literature, and it being unanimously conceded by the great majority of biblical critics that what the Fathers fought for was not *truth*,

---

359. *Panar.*, lib. I, tom. III, Haer. XLII, i.
360. Tertullian: *Adv. Marc.*, II, v.
361. Part II, vii.
362. *Adv. Marc.*, IV, ix; XVII, xxxvi; *Matthew*, v, 17.
363. *Supernatural Religion, loc. cit.*

but their own interpretations and unwarranted assertions,[364] we will now
proceed to state what were the views of Marcion, whom Tertullian desired to annihilate as the most dangerous *heretic* of his day. If we are
to believe Hilgenfeld, one of the greatest German biblical critics, then
"From the critical standing-point one must . . . consider the statements of the Fathers of the Church only as expressions of their *subjective view*, which itself requires proof." [365]

We can do no better nor make a more correct statement of facts
concerning Marcion than by quoting what our space permits from
Supernatural Religion,[366] the author of which bases his assertions on the
evidence of the greatest critics, as well as on his own researches. He
shows as existing in the days of Marcion "two broad parties in the
primitive Church" — one considering Christianity "a mere continuation of the Law, and dwarfing it into an Israelitish institution, a narrow
sect of Judaism; the other representing the glad tidings as the introduction of a new system, applicable to all, and supplanting the Mosaic
dispensation of the Law by a universal dispensation of grace. These
two parties," he adds, "were popularly represented in the early Church
by the two apostles, Peter and Paul, and their antagonism is faintly
revealed in the *Epistle to the Galatians*." [367]

---

364. The author of *Supernatural Religion* (part II, vii) remarks with great justice of
the 'Heresiarch' Marcion, "whose high personal character exerted so powerful an influence
upon his own time," that "it was the misfortune of Marcion to live in an age when Christianity had passed out of the pure morality of its infancy, when, untroubled by complicated questions of dogma, simple faith and pious enthusiasm had been the one great
bond of Christian brotherhood, into a phase of ecclesiastical development in which religion was fast degenerating into theology, and complicated doctrines were rapidly assuming that rampant attitude which led to so much bitterness, persecution, and schism.
In later times Marcion might have been honored as a reformer, in his own he was denounced as a heretic. Austere and ascetic in his opinions, he aimed at superhuman
purity, and although his clerical adversaries might scoff at his impracticable doctrines
regarding marriage and the subjugation of the flesh, they have had their parallels amongst
those whom the Church has since most delighted to honor, and, at least, the whole tendency of his system was markedly towards the side of virtue." These statements are
based upon Credner's *Beiträge*, I, p. 40; *cf.* Neander: *Allg. K. G.*, II, pp. 792, 815, *sq.;*
Milman: *History of Christianity*, p. 77, *sq.*, edit. 1867; Schleiermacher, etc., etc.

365. *Die Evv. Justin's* (Hilgenfeld); *Supernatural Religion, loc. cit.*

366. Part II, vii.

367. But on the other hand this antagonism is very *strongly* marked in the *Clementine Homilies*, in which Peter unequivocally denies that Paul, whom he calls Simon the
Magician, has ever had a *vision* of Christ, and calls him "an enemy." Canon Westcott
says: "There can be no doubt that St. Paul is referred to as 'the enemy'" (*On the
Canon*, p. 252, note 2; *Supernatural Religion*, part II, v). But this antagonism, which
rages unto the present day, we find even in St. Paul's *Epistles*. What can be more
energetic than such like sentences: "Such are *false* apostles, deceitful workers, transform-
ing themselves into the apostles of Christ. . . . I suppose I was not a whit behind
the very chiefest apostles" (*2 Corinthians*, xi, 13, 5). "Paul, an apostle (*not of men,*

Marcion, who recognised no other *Gospels* than a few *Epistles of Paul*, who rejected totally the anthropomorphism of the *Old Testament*, and drew a distinct line of demarcation between the old Judaism and Christianity, viewed Jesus neither as a King, Messiah of the Jews, nor the son of David who was in any way connected with the law or prophets, "but a divine being sent to reveal to man a wholly new spiritual religion, and a hitherto unknown God of goodness and grace." [368] The 'Lord God' of the Jews in his eyes, the Creator (Demiurge), was totally different and distinct from the Deity who sent Jesus to reveal the divine truth and preach the glad tidings, to bring reconciliation and

---

neither by man, but by Jesus Christ *and* God the Father, who raised him from the dead:) . . . but there be some that trouble you, and *would pervert* the gospel of Christ . . . *false brethren* . . . When Peter was come to Antioch I withstood him to the face, because he was to be blamed. For before that certain came from James, *he did eat* with the Gentiles: but when they were come he withdrew . . . fearing them which were of the circumcision. And the other Jews dissembled . . . insomuch that Barnabas also was carried away with their *dissimulation*," etc., etc. (*Gal.*, i, and ii). On the other hand, we find Peter, in the *Homilies*, indulging in various complaints which, although alleged to be addressed to Simon Magus, are evidently all direct answers to the above-quoted sentences from the Pauline Epistles, and *cannot* have anything to do with Simon. So, for instance, Peter said: "For some among the Gentiles have rejected my lawful preaching, and accepted certain *lawless* and *foolish* teaching of the hostile man [enemy]" — *Epistle of Peter to James*, § 2. He says further: "Simon [Paul] . . . who came before me to the Gentiles . . . and I have followed him as light upon darkness, as knowledge upon ignorance, as health upon disease" (*Homil.*, II, xvii). Still further, he calls him *Death* and a *deceiver* (*Ibid.*, II, xviii). He warns the Gentiles that "our Lord and *Prophet* [?] [*Jesus*] declared to us that the Evil One . . . announced that he would send from among his followers, apostles to *deceive*. Therefore, above all, remember to avoid every apostle, or teacher, or prophet, who first does not accurately compare his teaching with that of James, called the brother of my Lord" (see the difference between Paul and James on *faith*, *Hebrews*, xi, xii, and *James*, ii) ". . . lest this Evil One should send a false preacher, as he has sent to us Simon [?] preaching a counterfeit of truth in the name of our Lord, and disseminating error" (*Homil.*, XI, xxxv; see above quotation from *Gal.*, i, ii). He then denies Paul's assertion in the following words: "If, therefore, our Jesus indeed appeared in a vision to you . . . it was only as an irritated adversary. . . . But can any one through visions become wise in teaching? And if you say, 'it is possible,' then I ask, wherefore did the Teacher remain for a whole year and discourse to us who were attentive? And how can *we believe your story that he appeared to you*? And in what manner did he appear to you, when you hold opinions contrary to his teaching? . . . For you have set yourself up against me, who am a *firm rock*, *the foundation of the Church*. If you were not an opponent, you would not calumniate me, you would not revile my teaching [circumcision?] in order that, in declaring what I have myself heard from the Lord, I may not be believed, as though *I were condemned*. . . . But if you say that I am condemned, you blame God who revealed Christ to me" (*Homil.*, XVII, xix). "This last phrase," observes the author of *Supernatural Religion*, " 'if you say that I am condemned,' is an evident allusion to *Gal.*, ii, 11, 'I withstood him to the face, because he was condemned' " (*Supernatural Religion*, part II, v). "There cannot be a doubt," says the just-quoted author, "that the apostle Paul is attacked in this religious romance, as the great enemy of the true faith, under the hated name of Simon the Magician, whom Peter follows everywhere for the purpose of unmasking and confuting him" (*loc. cit.*). And if so, then we must believe that it was St. Paul who broke both his legs in Rome when flying in the air.

368. *Supernatural Religion*, part II, vii.

salvation to all. The mission of Jesus — according to Marcion — was to abrogate the Jewish 'Lord,' who "was opposed to the God and Father of Jesus Christ as *matter is to spirit, impurity to purity.*" [369]

Was Marcion so far wrong? Was it blasphemy, or was it intuition, divine inspiration in him to express that which every honest heart yearning for truth more or less feels and acknowledges? If in his sincere desire to establish a purely spiritual religion, a universal faith based on unadulterated truth, he found it necessary to make of Christianity an entirely new and separate system from that of Judaism, did not Marcion have the very words of Christ for his authority? "No man putteth a piece of new cloth unto an old garment, for that which is put in to fill it up taketh from the garment, and the rent is made worse. Neither do men put new wine into old bottles: else the bottles break, and the wine runneth out, and the bottles perish: but *they put new wine into new bottles,* and both are preserved." In what particular does the jealous, wrathful, revengeful God of Israel resemble the unknown deity, the God of mercy preached by Jesus; — *his* Father who is in Heaven, and the Father of all humanity? This Father alone is the God of spirit and purity, and to compare Him with the subordinate and capricious Sinaitic Deity is an error. Did Jesus ever pronounce the name of Jehovah? Did he ever identify *his* Father with this severe and cruel Judge; his God of mercy, love, and justice, with the Jewish genius of retaliation? Never! From that memorable day when he preached his Sermon on the Mount, an immeasurable void opened between his God and that other deity who fulminated his commands from that other mount — Sinai. The language of Jesus is unequivocal; it implies not only rebellion but defiance of the Mosaic 'Lord God.' "Ye have heard," he tells us, "that it hath been said, An eye for an eye, and a tooth for a tooth: but *I say* unto you, That ye resist not evil: but whosoever shall smite thee on thy right cheek, turn to him the other also. . . . Ye have heard that it hath been said [by the same 'Lord God' on Sinai], Thou shalt love thy neighbor, and hate thine enemy. But *I say* unto you, Love your enemies, bless them that curse you, do good to them that hate you, and pray for them which despitefully use you, and persecute you" (*Matthew* v, 38-44).

And now, open *Manu* and read:

"Resignation, *the action of rendering good for evil,* temperance, probity, purity, repression of the senses, the knowledge of the *Sâstras* [the holy books], that of the supreme soul, truthfulness, abstinence from anger — such are the ten virtues in which duty consists. . . . Those who

---

369. *Supernatural Religion,* part II, vii.

study these ten precepts of duty, and after having studied them conform their lives thereto, will reach to the supreme condition" (*Manu*, VI, *ślokas* 92-3).

If *Manu* did not trace these words many thousands of years before the era of Christianity, at least no voice in the whole world will dare deny them a less antiquity than several centuries B. C. The same in the case of the precepts of Buddhism.

If we turn to the *Pratimoksha-Sûtra* and other religious tracts of the Buddhists, we read the ten following commandments:

1. Thou shalt not kill any living creature.
2. Thou shalt not steal.
3. Thou shalt not break thy vow of chastity.
4. Thou shalt not lie.
5. Thou shalt not betray the secrets of others.
6. Thou shalt not wish for the death of thy enemies.
7. Thou shalt not desire the wealth of others.
8. Thou shalt not pronounce injurious and foul words.
9. Thou shalt not indulge in luxury (sleep on soft beds or be lazy).
10. Thou shalt not accept gold or silver.[370]

"Good master, what shall I do that I may have eternal life?" asks a man of Jesus. "Keep the commandments." "Which?" "Thou shalt do no murder, Thou shalt not commit adultery, Thou shalt not steal, Thou shalt not bear false witness," [371] is the answer.

"What shall I do to obtain possession of Bhodi? [knowledge of eternal truth]" asks a disciple of his Buddhist master. "What way is there to become an *Upâsaka?*" "Keep the commandments." "What are they?" "Thou shalt abstain all thy life from murder, theft, adultery, and lying," answers the master.[372]

Identical injunctions are they not? Divine injunctions, the living up to which would purify and exalt humanity. But are they more divine when uttered through one mouth than another? If it is god-like to return good for evil, does the enunciation of the precept by a Nazarene give it any greater force than its enunciation by an Indian or Tibetan philosopher? We see that the Golden Rule did not originate with Jesus; that its birthplace was India. Do what we may, we cannot deny *Sâkya-Muni*-Buddha a less remote antiquity than several centuries before the birth of Jesus. In seeking a model for his system of ethics why should

370. *Pratimoksha-Sûtra*, Pâli-Burmese copy; see also
Le lotus de la bonne loi, translated by Burnouf, p. 444.
371. *Matthew*, xix, 16-18.   372. *Pitakattayan*, III, Pâli version.

Jesus have gone to the foot of the Himâlayas rather than to the foot of Sinai, but that the doctrines of Manu and Gautama harmonized exactly with his own philosophy, while those of Jehovah were to him abhorrent and terrifying? The Hindûs taught to return *good for evil*, but the Jehovistic command was: "An eye for an eye" and "a tooth for a tooth."

Would Christians still maintain the identity of the 'Father' of Jesus and Jehovah, if evidence sufficiently clear could be adduced that the 'Lord God' was no other than the Pagan Bacchus, Dionysos? Well, this identity of the Jehovah at Mount Sinai with the god Bacchus is hardly disputable. The name יהוה is Yava, or Iao according to Diodorus and Lydus, and Iao is the *secret* name of the Phoenician Mystery-god; [373] it was actually adopted from the Chaldaeans with whom it also was the secret name of the creator. Wherever Bacchus was worshiped there was a tradition of a place called Nysa, and a cave where he was reared. Beth-San or Scythopolis in Palestine once had that designation; so had a spot on Mount Parnassus. But Diodorus declares that Nysa was between Phoenicia and Egypt; Euripides states that Dionysos came to Greece from India; and Diodorus [374] adds his testimony: "Osiris was brought up in Nysa, in Arabia the Happy; he was the son of Zeus, and was named from his father [nominative Zeus, genitive *Dios*] and the place *Dio-Nysos*" — the Zeus or Jove of Nysa. This identity of name or title is very significant. In Greece Dionysos was second only to Zeus, and Pindar says:

"So Father Zeus governs all things, and Bacchus he governs also."

But outside of Greece Bacchus was the all-powerful "Zagreus, the highest of gods." Moses seems to have worshiped him personally and together with the populace at Mount Sinai; unless we admit that Moses was an *initiated* priest, an adept, who knew how to lift the veil which hangs behind all such exoteric worship, but kept the secret. "*And Moses built an altar, and called the name of it Jehovah-*Nissi!" or *Iao-Nisi.* What better evidence is required to show that the Sinaitic god was indifferently Bacchus, Osiris, and Jehovah? Mr. Sharpe appends his testimony that the place where Osiris was born "was Mount Sinai, called by the Egyptians Mount Nissa." [374a] The Brazen Serpent was a *nis*, נחש, and the month of the Jewish Passover *nisan.*

If the Mosaic 'Lord God' was the only living God, and Jesus His only Son, how account for the rebellious language of the latter? Without hesitation or qualification he sweeps away the Jewish *lex talionis* and substitutes for it the law of charity and self-denial. If the *Old*

373. See *Judges*, xiii, 18, "And the angel of the Lord said unto him: Why askest thou after my name, seeing it is secret?"
374. Diod. Sic.: *Bibl. hist.*, I, xv.   374a. *Egyptian Mythol.*: 1863.

Testament is a divine revelation, how can the *New Testament* be? Are we
required to believe and worship a Deity who contradicts himself every
few hundred years? Was Moses inspired, or was Jesus *not* the son of
God? This is a dilemma from which the theologians are bound to rescue
us. It is from this very dilemma that the Gnostics endeavored to
snatch the budding Christianity.

Justice has been waiting nineteen centuries for intelligent commentators to appreciate this difference between the orthodox Tertullian and
the Gnostic Marcion. The brutal violence, unfairness, and bigotry of the
"great African" repel all who accept his Christianity. "How can a
god," inquired Marcion, "break his own commandments? How could
he consistently prohibit idolatry and image-worship and still cause Moses
to set up the brazen serpent? How command: Thou shalt not steal,
and then order the Israelites to *spoil* the Egyptians of their gold and
silver?" "Anticipating the results of modern criticism, Marcion denies
the applicability to Jesus of the so-called Messianic prophecies," writes
the author of *Supernatural Religion;* [375] "The Emmanuel of Isaiah is not
Christ; the 'Virgin,' his mother, is simply a 'young woman' [an *almah*
of the temple], and the sufferings of the servant of God (*Isaiah*, lii,
13-liii, 3) are not predictions of the death of Jesus." [376]

---

375. Part II, vii; *cf.* Tertullian: *Adv. Marc.*, III, xii, xiii.

376. Emmanuel was doubtless the son of the prophet himself, as described in the sixth
chapter; what was predicted can only be interpreted on that hypothesis. The prophet
had also announced to Ahaz the extinction of his line. "If ye will not believe, surely
ye shall not be established." Next comes the prediction of the placing of a new prince
on the throne — Hezekiah of Bethlehem — said to have been Isaiah's son-in-law, under
whom the captives should return from the uttermost parts of the earth. Assyria should
be humbled, and peace overspread the Israelitish country. (Cf. *Isaiah*, vii, 14-16; viii, 3,
4; ix, 6, 7; x, 12, 20, 21; xi; *Micah*, v, 2-7.) The popular party, the party of the prophets,
always opposed to the Zadokite priesthood, had resolved to set aside Ahaz and his time-
serving policy, which had let in Assyria upon Palestine, and to set up Hezekiah, a man
of their own, who should rebel against Assyria and overthrow the Assur-worship and
Baalim (*2 Kings*, xv, xvi). Though only the prophets hint this, it being cut out from the
historical books, it is noticeable that Ahaz offered his own child to Moloch, also that he
died at the age of thirty-six, and Hezekiah took the throne at twenty-five, in full adult age.

CHAPTER IV

"Nothing better than those MYSTERIES, by which, from a rough and fierce life, we are polished to gentleness (humanity, kindness), and softened."— CICERO: *On the Laws*, II, xiv

"Descend, O Soma, with that stream with which thou lightest up the Sun. . . . Soma, a Life Ocean spread through All, thou fillest creative the Sun with beams."
— *Rig-Veda*, II, 143

". . . the beautiful Virgin ascends, with long hair, and she holds two ears in her hand, and sits on a seat and feeds a BOY as yet little, and suckles him and gives him food."
— AVENARE [376a]

IT is alleged that the *Pentateuch* was written by Moses, and yet it contains the account of his own death (*Deuteronomy*, xxxiv, 6); and in *Genesis* (xiv, 14) the name Dan is given to a city, which *Judges* (xviii, 29) tells us was only called by that name at that late day, it having previously been known as Laish. Well might Josiah have rent his clothes when he had heard the words of the Book of the Law; for there was no more of Moses in it than there is of Jesus in the *Gospel according to John.*

We have one fair alternative to offer our theologians, leaving them to choose for themselves, and promising to abide by their decision. Only they will have to admit, either that Moses was an impostor, or that his books are forgeries, written at different times and by different persons; or, again, that they are full of fraudulent interpolations. In either case the work loses all claims to be considered divine *Revelation.* Here is the problem, which we quote from the *Bible* — the word of the God of Truth:

"And I appeared unto Abraham, unto Isaac, and unto Jacob, by the name of God Almighty, but by my name JEHOVAH was I not known to them" (*Exodus*, vi, 3), spake God unto Moses.

A very startling bit of information that, when, before arriving at the book of *Exodus*, we are told in *Genesis* (xxii, 14) that "Abraham called the name of that place" — where the patriarch had been preparing to cut the throat of his beloved son — "JEHOVAH-jireh!" (Jehovah sees). Which is the inspired text? — both cannot be — which the spurious one?

376a. Kircher: *Oedip. aegypt.*, III, v, p. 203.

Now if both Abraham and Moses had not belonged to the same holy group, we might perhaps help theologians by suggesting to them a convenient means of escape from this dilemma. They ought to call the reverend Jesuit Fathers — especially those who have been missionaries in India — to their rescue. The latter would not be for a moment disconcerted. They would coolly tell us that beyond doubt Abraham had heard the name of Jehovah and *borrowed* it from Moses. Do they not maintain that it was they who invented the *Sanskrit*, edited *Manu*, and composed the greater portion of the *Vedas?*

Marcion maintained, with the other Gnostics, the fallaciousness of the idea of an incarnate God, and therefore denied the corporeal reality of the living body of Christ. His entity was a mere *illusion;* it was not made of human flesh and blood, neither was it born of a human mother, for his divine nature could not be polluted with any contact with sinful flesh.[377] He accepted Paul as the only apostle preaching the pure gospel of truth, and accused the others of "depraving the pure form of the gospel doctrines delivered to them by Jesus, mixing up matters of the Law with the words of the Savior." [378]

Finally we may add that modern biblical criticism, which unfortunately became really active and serious only toward the end of the last century, now generally admits that Marcion's text of the only gospel he knew anything about — that of Luke — is far superior and by far more correct than that of our present Synoptics. We find in *Supernatural Religion* the following sentence, startling for every Christian: "We are, therefore, *indebted to Marcion* for *the correct version even* of '*the Lord's Prayer.*' " [379]

If leaving for the present the prominent founders of Christian sects, we now turn to the sect of the Ophites, which assumed a definite form about the time of Marcion and the Basilideans, we may find in it the reason for the *heresies* of all others. Like all other Gnostics they rejected the Mosaic *Bible* entirely. Nevertheless their philosophy, apart from some deductions original with several of the most important founders of the various branches of Gnosticism, was not new. Passing through the Chaldaean kabalistic tradition, it gathered its materials in the Hermetic books, and pursuing its flight still farther back for its metaphysical speculations, we find it floundering among the tenets of *Manu*, and the earliest Hindû ante-sacerdotal genesis. Many of our eminent antiquarians trace the Gnostic philosophies right back to Buddhism, which does not impair

---

377. Tertullian: *Adv. Marc.*, III, viii, *sq.*
378. *Sup. Rel.*, part II, vii; Iren.: *Against Heresies*, III, ii, 2; cf. III, xii, 12.
379. *Sup. Rel.*, *loc. cit.*

in the least either their or our arguments. We repeat, *Buddhism is simply the primitive source of Brâhmanism.* It is not against the primitive *Vedas* that Gautama protests. It is against the sacerdotal and official state religion of his country; and the Brâhmanas, who in order to make room for and give authority to the castes, at a later period crammed the ancient manuscripts with interpolated *slokas*, intended to prove that the castes were predetermined by the Creator by the very fact that each class of men was issued from a more or less noble limb of Brahmâ. Gautama-Buddha's philosophy was that taught from the beginning of time in the impenetrable secresy of the inner sanctuaries of the pagodas. We need not be surprised therefore to find again, in all the fundamental dogmas of the Gnostics, the metaphysical tenets of both Brâhmanism and Buddhism. They held that the *Old Testament* was the revelation of an inferior being, a subordinate divinity, and did not contain a single sentence of their *Sophia*, the Divine Wisdom. As to the *New Testament*, it had lost its purity when the compilers became guilty of interpolations. The revelation of divine truth was sacrificed by them to promote selfish ends and maintain quarrels. The accusation does not seem so very improbable to one who is well aware of the constant strife between the champions of circumcision and the 'Law,' and the apostles who had given up Judaism.

The Gnostic Ophites taught the doctrine of Emanations, so hateful to the defenders of the unity in the trinity, and *vice versa.* The Unknown Deity with them had *no name;* but his first female emanation was called Bythos or Depth.[380] It answered to the Shekhinah of the kabalists, the 'Veil' which conceals the 'Wisdom' in the *cranium* of the highest of the *three* heads. As the Pythagorean Monad, this *nameless* Wisdom was the *Source* of Light, and *Ennoia* or Mind is Light itself. The latter was also called the 'Primitive Man,' like the Adam Kadmon, or ancient Adam of the Kabala. Indeed, if man was created after his likeness and in the image of God, then this God was like his creature in shape and figure — hence he is the 'Primitive man.' The first Manu, the one evolved from *Svayambhû,* "he who exists unrevealed in his own glory," is also in one sense the primitive man, with the Hindûs.

Thus the 'nameless and the unrevealed' Bythos, his female reflexion, and Ennoia, the revealed Mind proceeding from both, or their Son, are the counterparts of the Chaldaean first triad as well as of the Brâhmanical *Trimûrti.* We shall compare: in all the three systems we see:

---

380. We give the systems according to an old diagram preserved among some Copts and the 'Hamsa-ites ('Druses') of Mount Lebanon. Irenaeus had perhaps some good reasons for disfiguring their doctrines.

THE GREAT FIRST CAUSE as the ONE, the primordial germ, the unrevealed and grand ALL, existing through himself. In the

INDIAN PANTHEON	THE CHALDAEAN	IN THE OPHITE
Brâhma-Dyaus	Ilu, Kabalistic Ain-Soph	The Nameless, or Secret Name

Whenever the Eternal awakes from its slumber and desires to manifest itself, it divides itself into male and female. It then becomes in every system

THE DOUBLE-SEXED DEITY, The universal Father and Mother

IN INDIA	IN CHALDAEA	IN THE OPHITE SYSTEM
Brahmâ	Eikon or Ain-Soph	Nameless Spirit
Nara (male), Nâri (female)	Anu (male), Anata (female)	Abrasax (male), Bythos (female)

From the union of the two emanates a third, or creative Principle — the SON, or the manifested Logos, the product of the Divine Mind.

IN INDIA	IN CHALDAEA	OPHITE SYSTEM
Virâj, the Son	Bel, the Son	Ophis (another name for Ennoia), the Son

Moreover each of these systems has a triple male trinity, each proceeding separately through itself from one female Deity. So, for instance:

IN INDIA	IN CHALDAEA	IN THE OPHITE SYSTEM
The Trinity — Brahmâ, Vishnu, Śiva, are blended into ONE, who is *Brahma* (neuter gender), creating and being created through the Virgin Nâri (the mother of perpetual fecundity)	The trinity — Anu, Bel, Hoa (or Sin, Samas, Bin), blend into ONE who is Anu (double-sexed) through the Virgin Mylitta	The trinity consisted of the Mystery named Sigē, Bythos, Ennoia. These become ONE who is *Abrasax*, from the Virgin *Sophia* (or *Pneuma*), who herself is an emanation of Bythos and the Mystery-god and emanates through them, Christos

To put the matter still more clearly, the Babylonian System recognises first — the ONE (*Ad*, or *Ad-ad*) who is never named but only acknowledged in thought as the Hindû *Svayambhû*. From this he becomes manifest as *Anu* or *Ana* — the one above all — *Monas*. Next comes the Demiurge called *Bel* or *El*, who is the active power of the Godhead. The third is the principle of Wisdom, *Hea* or *Hoa*, who also rules the sea and the underworld. Each of these has his divine consort, giving us *Anata*,

Belita, and *Davkina*. These, however, are only like the *Saktis*, and not especially remarked by theologists. But the female principle is denoted · by Mylitta, the Great Mother, called also Ishtar. So with the three male gods, we have the Triad or *Trimûrti*, and with Mylitta added, the *Arba* or Four (*Tetraktys* of Pythagoras), which perfects and potentializes all. Hence, the above-given modes of expression. The following Chaldaean scheme may serve as an illustration for all others:

$$\text{Triad} \begin{cases} \text{Anu,} \\ \text{Bel,} \\ \text{Hoa,} \end{cases} \begin{array}{l} \text{Mylitta — Arba-il,} \\ \quad \text{or} \\ \text{Four-fold God,} \end{array}$$

become, with the Christians,

$$\text{Trinity} \begin{cases} \text{God the Father,} \\ \text{God the Son,} \\ \text{God the Holy Ghost,} \end{cases} \begin{array}{l} \text{Mary, or mother of these three Gods} \\ \quad \text{since they are one,} \\ \text{or, the Christian Heavenly Tetraktys.} \end{array}$$

Hence Hebron, the city of the Kabiri, was called *Kirjath-Arba*, city of the Four. The Kabiri were *Axieros*, the noble Eros; *Axiokersos*, the worthy horned one; *Axiokersa*, Demeter and Kadmiel, Hoa, etc.

The Pythagorean ten denoted the *Arba-Il* or Divine Four, emblematized by the Hindû *lingam:* Anu, 1; Bel, 2; Hoa, 3, which makes 6. The triad and Mylitta as 4 make the ten.

Though he is termed the 'Primitive Man,' Ennoia, who is like the Egyptian Pymander, the 'Power of the Thought Divine,' the first intelligible manifestation of the Divine Spirit in material form, he is like the 'Only-Begotten' Son of the 'Unknown Father' of all other nations. He is the emblem of the first appearance of the divine Presence in his own works of creation, tangible and visible, and therefore comprehensible. The mystery-God, or the ever-unrevealed Deity, fecundates through His will Bythos, the unfathomable and infinite depth that exists in silence (*Sigê*) and (for our intellect) darkness, and that represents the abstract idea of all nature, the ever-producing Kosmos. As neither the male nor female principle, blended into the idea of a double-sexed Deity in ancient conceptions, could be comprehended by an ordinary human intellect, the theology of every people had to create for its religion a Logos or manifested word, in some shape or other. With the Ophites and other Gnostics who took their models direct from more ancient originals, the unrevealed Bythos and her male counterpart produce Ennoia, and the three in their turn produce Sophia,[381] thus completing the Tetraktys, which will emanate Christos, the very essence of the Father

381. Sophia is the highest prototype of woman — the first *spiritual* Eve. In the Bible the system is reversed and the intervening emanation being omitted, Eve is degraded to simple humanity.

Spirit. As the unrevealed One, or concealed Logos in its latent state, he has existed from all eternity in the *Arba-Il*, the metaphysical abstraction; therefore, he is ONE with all others as a unity, the latter (including all) being indifferently termed Ennoia, Sigē (silence), Bythos, etc. As the revealed one, he is Androgyne, Christos, and Sophia (Divine Wisdom), who descend into the man Jesus. Both Father and Son are shown by Irenaeus to have loved the beauty (*formam*) of the primitive woman,[382] who is Bythos — Depth — as well as Sophia, and as having produced conjointly Ophis and Sophia (double-sexed unity again), male and female wisdom, one being considered as the unrevealed Holy Spirit or elder Sophia — the *Pneuma* — the intellectual 'Mother of all things'; the other the revealed one or *Ophis*, typifying divine wisdom fallen into matter, or God-man — Jesus, whom the Gnostic Ophites represented by the serpent (Ophis).

Fecundated by the Divine Light of the Father and Son, the highest spirit and Ennoia, Sophia produces in her turn two other emanations — one perfect Christos, the second imperfect Sophia-Achamoth,[383] from חכמה, *'hokhamoth* (simple wisdom), who becomes the mediatrix between the intellectual and material worlds.

Christos was the mediator and guide between God (the Higher), and everything spiritual in man; Achamoth — the younger Sophia — performed the same function between the 'Primitive man,' Ennoia and matter. What was mysteriously meant by the general term, *Christos*, we have just explained.

Delivering a sermon on the 'Month of Mary,' we find the Rev. Dr. Preston, of New York City, expressing the Christian idea of the female principle of the trinity better and more clearly than we could, and substantially in the spirit of an ancient 'heathen' philosopher. He says that the "plan of the redemption made it necessary that a mother should be found, and Mary stands pre-eminently alone as the only instance when a creature was necessary to the consummation of God's work." We beg the right to contradict the reverend gentleman. As shown above, thousands of years before our era it was found necessary by all the 'heathen' theogonies to find a female principle, a 'mother' for the triune male principle. Hence Christianity does not present the 'only instance' of such a consummation of God's work — albeit, as this work shows, there was more philosophy and less materialism, or rather anthropomorphism, in it. But hear the reverend Doctor express 'heathen' thought in

---

382. *Against Heresies*, I, xxx.

383. In King's *Gnostics* we find the system a little incorrect. The author tells us that he followed Bellermann's *Drei Programmen über die Abraxas-gemmen*.

Christian ideas. "He" (God), he says, "prepared her (Mary's) virginal and celestial purity, for a mother defiled could not become the mother of the Most High. The holy virgin, even in her childhood, was more pleasing than all the Cherubim and Seraphim, and from infancy to the maturing maidenhood and womanhood she grew more and more pure. By her very sanctity she reigned over the heart of God. *When the hour came, the whole court of heaven was hushed, and the trinity listened for the answer of Mary, for without her consent the world could not have been redeemed.*"

Does it not seem as if we were reading Irenaeus explaining the Gnostic "*Heresy*, which taught that the Father and Son loved the beauty (*formam*) of the celestial Virgin"? or the Egyptian system of Isis being both wife, sister, and mother of Osiris-Horus? With the Gnostic philosophy there were but *two*, but the Christians have improved and perfected the system by making it completely 'heathen,' for it is the Chaldaean Anu-Bel-Hoa, merging into Mylitta. "Then while this month [of Mary]," adds Dr. Preston, "begins in the paschal season — the month when nature decks herself with fruits and flowers, the harbingers of a bright harvest — let us, too, begin for a golden harvest. In this month the dead come up out of the earth, figuring the resurrection; so when we are kneeling before the altar of the holy and immaculate Mary, let us remember that there should come forth from us the bud of promise, the flower of hope, and the imperishable fruit of sanctity."

This is precisely the substratum of the Pagan thought, which, among other meanings, by the rites of the resurrection of Osiris, Adonis, Bacchus, and other slaughtered sun-gods, symbolized the resurrection of all nature in spring, the germination of seeds that had been dead and sleeping during winter, and so were allegorically said to be kept in the underworld (Hades). They are typified by the three days passed in hell before their resurrection by Hercules, Christos and others.

This derivation, or rather *heresy*, as it is called in Christianity, is simply the Brâhmanic doctrine in all its archaic purity. Vishnu, the second personage of the Hindû trinity, is also the Logos, for he is made subsequently to incarnate himself in Krishna. And *Lakhmi* (or *Lakshmî*) — who, as in the case of Osiris and Isis, of Ain-Soph and Sephira, and of Bythos and Ennoia, is wife, sister, and daughter of Vishnu, through this endless correlation of male and female creative powers in the abstruse metaphysics of the ancient philosophies — is Sophia-Achamoth. Krishna is the mediator promised by Brahmâ to mankind, and represents the same idea as the Gnostic *Christos*. And *Lakshmî*, Vishnu's spiritual half, is the emblem of physical nature, the universal mother of all the material and revealed forms; the mediatrix and protector of nature, like Sophia-Achamoth, who is made by the Gnostics the mediatrix between the Great

Cause and Matter, as Christos is the mediator between him [the Great Cause] and spiritual humanity.

This Brâhmano-Gnostic tenet is more logical, and more consistent with the allegory of *Genesis* and the fall of man. When God curses the first couple, He is made to curse also the earth and everything that is on it. The *New Testament* gives us a Redeemer for the first sin of mankind, which was punished for having sinned; but there is not a word said about a Savior who would take away the unmerited curse from the earth and the animals, which had never sinned at all. Thus the Gnostic allegory shows a greater sense of both justice and logic than the Christian.

In the Ophite system, Sophia, the Androgyne Wisdom, is also the female spirit, or the Hindû female *Nârî* (*Nârâyana*), moving on the face of the waters — chaos, or future matter. She vivifies it from afar, but not touching the abyss of darkness. She is unable to do so, for Wisdom is purely intellectual, and cannot act directly on matter. Therefore Sophia is obliged to address herself to her Supreme Parent; but although life proceeds primally from the Unseen Cause, and its Ennoia, neither of them can, any more than herself, have anything to do with the lower chaos in which matter assumes its definite shape. Thus, Sophia is obliged to employ on the task her *imperfect* emanation, Sophia-Achamoth, the latter being of a mixed nature, half spiritual and half material.

The only difference between the Ophite cosmogony and that of the St. John Nazarenes is a change of names. We find an identical system in the Kabala, the *Book of Mystery* (*Liber Mysterii*).[384] All the three systems, especially that of the Kabalists and the Nazarenes, which were the *models* for the Ophite Cosmogony, belong to the pure Oriental Gnosticism. The *Codex Nazaraeus* opens with: "The Supreme King of Light (Mano), the great first one,"[385] etc., the latter being the emanation of Ferho — the unknown, formless LIFE. He is the chief of the Aeons, from whom proceed (or shoot forth) five refulgent rays of Divine light. Mano is *Rex Lucis*, the Bythos-Ennoia of the Ophites. "*Unus est Rex Lucis in suo regno, nec ullus qui eo altior, . . . nullus qui ejus similitudinem retulerit, nullus qui, sublatis oculis, viderit Coronam quae in ejus capite est.*"[386] He is the Manifested Light around the highest of the three kabalistic heads, the concealed wisdom; from him emanate the three *Lives*. Aebel-Zivo is the revealed Logos, Christos, the 'Apostle Gabriel,' and the first Legate or messenger of light. If Bythos and Ennoia are the Nazarene Mano, then the dual-natured, the semi-spiritual, semi-material Achamoth must be Fetahil when viewed from her spiritual aspect; and if regarded in her grosser nature, she is the Nazarene 'Spiritus.'

---

384. See *Siphra Dtzeniuthah*.
385. *Codex Nazaraeus*, I, p. 1, *sq.*   386. *Ibid.*, p. 11.

Fetahil,[387] who is the reflexion of his father, Lord Abatur, the *third life* — as the elder Sophia is also the third emanation — is the 'newest-man.' Perceiving his fruitless attempts to create a perfect material world, the 'Spiritus' calls to one of her progeny, the *Karabtanos* — Ilda-Baoth — who is without sense or judgment ('blind matter'), to unite himself with her in order to create something definite out of this confused (*turbulentos*) matter, which task she is enabled to achieve only after having produced from this union with *Karabtanos* the 'seven stellars.' Like the six sons or genii of the Gnostic Ilda-Baoth, they then frame the material world. The same story is repeated in Sophia-Achamoth. Delegated by her purely spiritual parent, the elder Sophia, to create the world of *visible forms*, she descended into chaos, and, overpowered by the emanation of matter, lost her way. Still ambitious to create a world of matter of her own, she busied herself hovering to and fro about the dark abyss, and imparted life and motion to the inert elements, until she became so hopelessly entangled in matter that, like Fetahil, she is represented sitting immersed in mud, and unable to extricate herself from it; until by the contact of matter itself she produces the *Creator* of the material world. He is the Demiurge, called by the Ophites Ilda-Baoth, and, as we shall directly show, the parent of the Jewish God in the opinion of some sects, and held by others to be the 'Lord God' Himself. It is at this point of the kabalistic-gnostic cosmogony that the Mosaic *Bible* begins. Having accepted the Jewish *Old Testament* as their standard, no wonder that the Christians were forced by the exceptional position in which they were placed through their own ignorance, to make the best of it.

The first groups of Christians, whom Renan shows numbering but from seven to twelve men in *each church*, belonged unquestionably to the poorest and most ignorant classes. They had and could have no idea of the highly philosophical doctrines of the Platonists and Gnostics, and evidently knew as little about their own newly-made-up religion. To these men — who if Jews, had been crushed under the tyrannical dominion of the 'law' as enforced by the elders of the synagogs; and if Pagans, had been always excluded, as the lower castes are until now in India, from the religious mysteries — the God of the Jews and the 'Father' preached by Jesus were all one. The contentions which reigned from the first years following the death of Jesus, between the two parties, the Pauline and the Petrine, were deplorable. What one did, the other deemed it a sacred duty to undo. If the *Homilies*

---

387. See *Codex Nazaraeus*, I, pp. 177, *sq.* Fetahil, sent to frame the world, finds himself immersed in the abyss of mud, and soliloquizes in dismay until the *Spiritus* (Sophia-Achamoth) unites herself completely with matter, and so creates the material world.

are considered apocryphal, and cannot very well be accepted as an infallible standard by which to measure the animosity which raged between the two apostles, we have the *Bible*, and the proofs afforded therein are plentiful.

So hopelessly entangled, to all outward appearance at least, seems Irenaeus in his fruitless endeavors to describe the true doctrines of the many Gnostic sects of which he treats, and to present them at the same time as abominable 'heresies,' that he either deliberately, or through ignorance, confounds all of them in such a way that few metaphysicians would be able to disentangle them without the Kabala and the *Codex* as the true keys. Thus for instance he cannot even tell the difference between the Sethianites and the Ophites, and tells us that both called the 'God of all,' '*Hominem,*' a MAN, and his mind the SECOND man, or the '*Son of man.*' So does Theodoret, who lived more than two centuries after Irenaeus, and who makes a sad mess of the chronological order in which the various sects succeeded each other.[388] Neither the Sethianites (a branch of the Jewish Nazarenes), nor the Ophites, a purely Greek sect, have ever held anything of the kind. Irenaeus contradicts his own words by describing in another place the doctrines of Cerinthus, the direct disciple of Simon Magus. He says that Cerinthus taught that the world was not created by the FIRST GOD, but by a virtue (*virtus*) or power, an Aeon so distant from the First Cause that he was even ignorant of HIM who *is above all things*. This Aeon subjected Jesus, he begot him physically through Joseph from one who was not a virgin, but simply the wife of that Joseph, and Jesus was born like all other men. Viewed from this physical aspect of his nature, Jesus was called the 'son of man.' It was only after his *baptism*, that *Christos*, the anointed, descended from the Princeliness of above in the figure of a dove, and then announced the UNKNOWN Father through Jesus.[389]

If therefore Jesus was physically considered as a son of man, and spiritually as the Christos who overshadowed him, how then could the 'GOD OF ALL,' the '*Unknown* Father,' be called by the Gnostics *Homo*, a MAN, and his Mind, Ennoia, the SECOND man, or *Son of man?* Neither in the Oriental Kabala, nor in Gnosticism, was the 'God of all' ever anthropomorphized. It is but the first, or rather the second emanations, for Shekhinah, Sephira, Depth, and other first-manifested female virtues are also emanations, that are termed 'primitive men.' Thus Adam Kadmon, Ennoia (or *Sigē*), the *logoi* in short, are the 'only-begotten' ones but not the *Sons* of man, which appellation properly belongs

388. Irenaeus: *Against Heresies*, I, xxx, 1; Theodoret: *Haereticarum fabularum.*
           389. Irenaeus: *op. cit.*, I, xxvi, 1.

to Christos the son of Sophia (the elder) and of the primitive man who produces him through his own vivifying light, which emanates from the source or *cause* of all (hence the *cause* of his light also), the 'Unknown Father.' There is a great difference made in the Gnostic metaphysics between the first unrevealed Logos and the 'anointed,' who is Christos. Ennoia may be termed, as Philo understands it, the *Second* God, but he alone is the 'Primitive and First man,' and by no means the Second one, as Theodoret and Irenaeus express it. It was only the inveterate desire of the latter, even in his *Against Heresies*, to connect Jesus in every possible way with the *Highest* God, that led him into so many falsifications.

Such an identification with the *Unknown* God, even of Christos the anointed — the Aeon who overshadowed him — let alone of the man Jesus, never entered the heads of the Gnostics, or even of the direct apostles and of Paul, whatever later forgeries [or interpolations] may have added [to the texts].

How daring and desperate were many such deliberate falsifications, was shown in the first attempts to compare the original manuscripts with later ones. In Bishop Horsley's edition of Sir Isaac Newton's works,[390] several manuscripts on theological subjects were cautiously withheld from publication. The article known as *Christ's Descent into Hell*, which is found in the later Apostles' Creed, is not to be found in the manuscripts of either the fourth or sixth centuries. It was an evident interpolation copied from the fables of Bacchus and Hercules, and forced upon Christendom as an article of faith. Concerning it the author of the preface to the *Catalogue of the Manuscripts of the King's Library* (preface, p. xxiv) remarks: "I wish that the insertion of the article of *Christ's Descent into Hell* into the Apostles' Creed could be as well accounted for as the *insertion* of the *said* verse," viz., *1 John, v, 7*.[391]

Now this verse reads: "For there are three that bear record in heaven, the Father, the Word, and the Holy Ghost: and these three are one." This verse, which has been "appointed to be read in churches," is now known to be spurious. It is not to be found "in any Greek manuscript, save one at Berlin," which was transcribed from some interpolated paraphrase between the lines. In the first and second editions of Erasmus' *The New Testament*, printed in 1516 and 1519, this allusion to these three heavenly witnesses is *omitted;* and the text is "not contained in any Greek manuscript which was written earlier than the fifteenth century."[392]

---

390. London, 1779-85, 4 vols.   391. See preface to the *Apocryphal New Testament:* London, printed for W. Hone, Ludgate Hill, 1820.

392. "It is first cited by Vigilius Tapsensis [Thapsensis], a Latin writer of no credit, in the latter end of the fifth century, and by him it is suspected to have been forged."—*Loc. cit.*

It was not mentioned by any of the Greek ecclesiastical writers nor by the early Latin fathers, so anxious to get at every proof in support of their trinity; and it was omitted by Luther in his German version. Edward Gibbon [393] was early in pointing out its spurious character. Archbishop Newcome rejected it, and the Bishop of Lincoln expressed his conviction that it is spurious.[394] There are twenty-six Greek authors — Irenaeus, Clement, and Athanasius included — who neither quote nor mention it; and seventeen Latin writers, numbering among them Augustine, Jerome, Ambrosius, Cyprian, and Pope Eusebius, who appear utterly ignorant of it. "It is evident that if the text of the heavenly witnesses had been known from the beginning of Christianity the ancients would have eagerly seized it, inserted it in their creeds, quoted it repeatedly against the heretics, and selected it for the brightest ornament of every book that they wrote upon the subject of the Trinity." [395]

Thus falls to the ground the strongest trinitarian pillar. Another not less obvious forgery is quoted from Sir Isaac Newton's words by the editor of the *Apocryphal New Testament*. Newton observes "that what the Latins have done to this text (*1 John*, v, 7), the Greeks have done to the words of St. Paul (*1 Tim.*, iii, 16). For, by changing OΣ into ΘΣ, the abbreviation of Θεος (God), in the Alexandrian manuscript, from which their subsequent copies were made, they now read, "*Great is the mystery of godliness*, GOD *manifested in the flesh*"; whereas all the churches, for the first four or five centuries, and the authors of all the ancient versions, Jerome as well as the rest, read: "Great is the mystery of godliness WHICH WAS *manifested in the flesh*." [396] Newton adds, that now that the disputes over this forgery are over, they that read GOD made manifest in the flesh, instead of the *godliness which was* manifested in the flesh, think this passage "one of the most obvious and pertinent texts for the business."

And now we again ask the question: Who were the first Christians? Those who were readily converted by the eloquent simplicity of Paul, who promised them, in the name of Jesus, *freedom* from the narrow bonds of ecclesiasticism. They understood but one thing; they were the "children of promise" (*Gal.*, iv, 28). The 'allegory' of the Mosaic *Bible* was unveiled to them; the covenant "from the Mount Sinai, which gendereth *to bondage*" was Agar (*ibid.*, 24), the old Jewish synagog, and she was "in bondage with her children" to Jerusalem, the new and

---

393. *Decline and Fall, etc.*, ch. xxxviii (III, pp. 703-4).

394. Chr. Wordsworth: *Elements of Theology*, II, p. 90, note.

395. See Porson's *Letters to Mr. Archdeacon Travis, in Answer to his Defence of the three Heavenly Witnesses*, pp. 363, 402, etc.: London, 1790.

396. Practically conceded in the *Revised Version N. T.* of 1881.

the free, "the mother of us all." On the one hand the synagog and the law which persecuted every one who dared to step across the narrow path of bigotry and dogmatism; on the other Paganism,[397] with its grand philosophical truths concealed from sight; unveiling itself but to the few, and leaving the masses hopelessly seeking to discover who was *the* god, among this overcrowded pantheon of deities and sub-deities. To others, the apostle of circumcision, supported by all his followers, was promising, if they obeyed the 'law,' a life hereafter, and a resurrection of which they had no previous idea. At the same time he never lost an occasion to contradict Paul, without naming him, but indicating him so clearly that it is next to impossible to doubt whom Peter meant. While he may have converted some men, who — whether they had believed in the Mosaic resurrection promised by the Pharisees, or had fallen into the nihilistic doctrines of the Sadducees, or had belonged to the polytheistic heathenism of the Pagan rabble — had no future after death, nothing but a mournful blank, we do not think that the work of contradiction, carried on so systematically by the two apostles, had greatly helped their work of proselytism. With the educated thinking classes they succeeded very little, as ecclesiastical history clearly shows. Where was the truth? where the inspired word of God? On the one hand, as we have seen, they heard the apostle Paul explaining that of the two covenants, "which things are an allegory," the old one from Mount Sinai, "which gendereth unto bondage," was *Agar* the bondwoman; Mount Sinai itself answered to 'Jerusalem,' which now is "in bondage" with her circumcised children; and the new covenant meant Jesus Christ — the "Jerusalem which is above and free"; and on the other Peter, who was contradicting and even abusing him. Paul vehemently exclaims, "Cast out the bondwoman and her son" (the old *law* and the synagog). "The son of the bondwoman shall not be heir with the son of the freewoman." "Stand

---

397. The term 'Paganism' is properly used by many modern writers with hesitation. Professor Alexander Wilder, in his edition of Payne Knight's *Symbolical Language of Ancient Art and Mythology*, p. xvi, note, says: "It ['Paganism'] has degenerated into slang, and is generally employed with more or less of an opprobrious meaning. The correcter expression would have been 'the ancient ethnical worships,' but it would be hardly understood in its true sense, and we accordingly have adopted the term in popular use, but not disrespectfully. A religion which can develop a Plato, an Epictetus, and an Anaxagoras, is not gross, superficial, or totally unworthy of candid attention. Besides, many of the rites and doctrines included in the Christian as well as in the Jewish Institute, appeared first in the other systems. Zoroastrianism anticipated far more than has been imagined. The cross, the priestly robes and symbols, the sacraments, the sabbath, the festivals and anniversaries, are all anterior to the Christian era by thousands of years. The ancient worship, after it had been excluded from its former shrines, and from the metropolitan towns, was maintained for a long time by the inhabitants of humble localities. To this fact it owes its later designation. From being kept up in the *pagi*, or rural districts, its votaries were denominated *pagans*, or provincials."

fast therefore in the liberty wherewith Christ hath made us free, and be not entangled again with the yoke of bondage. Behold, I Paul say unto you, that if ye be circumcised, Christ shall profit you nothing!" (*Gal.*, iv, 30; v, 2). What do we find Peter writing? Whom does he mean by saying, "They speak great swelling words of vanity. . . . While they promise them *liberty*, they themselves are the servants of corruption: for of whom a man is overcome, of the same he is brought in bondage. For if after *they have escaped* the pollutions of the world through the knowledge of the Lord and Savior Jesus Christ, they are again entangled therein, and overcome . . . it had *been better for them not to have known the way of righteousness*, than, after they have known it, to turn from the holy *commandment delivered unto them*" (*2 Peter*, ii, 18-21).

Peter certainly cannot have meant the Gnostics, for they had never seen "the holy commandment delivered unto them"; Paul had. They never promised any one "liberty" from bondage, but Paul had done so repeatedly. Moreover, the latter rejects the "old covenant," Agar the bondwoman, and Peter holds fast to it. Paul warns the people against the *powers* and *dignities* (the lower angels of the kabalists); and Peter, as will be shown further, respects them and *denounces those who do not.* Peter preaches circumcision, and Paul forbids it.

Later, when all these extraordinary blunders, contradictions, dissensions and inventions were forcibly crammed into a frame elaborately executed by the episcopal caste of the new religion, and called Christianity; and the chaotic picture itself was cunningly preserved from too close scrutiny by a whole array of formidable Church penances and anathemas, which kept the curious back under the false pretense of sacrilege and profanation of divine mysteries; and when millions of people had been butchered in the name of the God of mercy — then came the Reformation. It certainly deserves its name in the fullest parodoxical sense. It abandoned Peter and alleges to have chosen Paul for its only leader. And the apostle who thundered against the old law of bondage; who left full liberty to Christians to either observe the Sabbath or set it aside; who rejects everything anterior to John the Baptist, is now the professed standard-bearer of Protestantism, which holds to the *old* law more than did the Jews, imprisons those who view the Sabbath as Jesus and Paul did, and outvies the synagog of the first century in dogmatic intolerance!

But who then *were* the first Christians, may still be asked? Doubtless the Ebionites; and in this we follow the authority of the best critics. "There can be little doubt that the author [of the *Clementine Homilies*] was a representative of Ebionitic Gnosticism, which *had once been the purest form of primitive Christianity.* . . ." [398] And who were the Ebionites? The pupils and followers of the early Nazarenes, the kabalistic Gnostics. In the preface to the *Codex Nazaraeus*, the translator says: "That also the Nazarenes did not reject . . . the Aeons is natural. For of the Ebionites who acknowledged them [the Aeons], these were the instructors." [399]

We find, moreover, Epiphanius, the Christian Homer of *The Heresies*, telling us that "Ebion had the opinion of the Nazarenes, the form of the Cerinthians (who fable that the world was put together by angels), and the appellation of Christians." [400] An appellation certainly more correctly applied to them than to the orthodox (so-called) Christians of the school of Irenaeus and of the later Vatican. Renan shows the Ebionites numbering among their sect all the surviving relatives of Jesus. John the Baptist, his cousin and *precursor*, was the accepted Savior of the Nazarenes, and their prophet. His disciples dwelt on the other side of the Jordan, and the scene of the baptism of the Jordan is clearly and beyond any question proved by the author of *Sôd, the Son of the Man* to have been the site of the Adonis-worship. [401] "Over the Jordan and beyond the lake dwelt the Nasarenes, a sect said to have existed already at the birth of Iesus, and to have counted him among its number. They must have extended along the east of the Jordan, and southeasterly among the Arabians (*Gal.*, i, 17, 21; ii, 11) and Sabaeans in the direction of Basra; and again, they must have gone far north over the Lebanon to Antioch, also to the northeast to the Nasarian settlement in Beroea, where St. Jerome found them. In the desert the Mysteries of Adonis may have still prevailed; in the mountains Aiai Adonin was still a cry!" [402]

"Having been united (*conjunctus*) to the Nazarenes, each (Ebionite) imparted to the other out of his own wickedness, and decided that Christ *was of the seed of a man*," writes Epiphanius. [403]

And if they did, we must suppose they knew more about their contemporary prophet than Epiphanius 400 years later. Theodoret, as shown elsewhere, describes the Nazarenes as Jews who "honor the Anointed as a just man," and use the *evangel* called "*According to Peter.*" [404] Jerome finds the authentic and original *evangel*, written in Hebrew by Matthew the apostle-publican, in the library collected at Caesarea by the martyr Pamphilus. "*I received permission from the Nazaraeans*, who at Beroea of Syria use this [gospel], to transcribe it," he

---

398. *Supern. Rel.*, part II, v.   399. Norberg: *Cod. Naz.*, pref., p. v.
400. *Panar.*, lib. I, tom. II, Indic., § 8; Haer. XXVIII, i, XXX, i.
401. Preface, pp. v-xxiv.   402. *Ibid.*, p. vii.
403. *Panar.*, lib. I, tom. II, Haer. XXX, ii, iii.   404. *Haer. fabul.*, ii, 2.

writes toward the end of the fourth century.[405] "In the *evangel* which the *Nazarenes* and *Ebionites* use," adds Jerome, "which recently I translated from Hebrew into Greek, and which is called by most persons the *genuine Gospel of Matthew*," etc.[406]

That the apostles had received a 'secret doctrine' from Jesus, and that he himself taught one, is evident from the following words of Jerome, who confessed it in an unguarded moment. Writing to the Bishops Chromatius and Heliodorus, he complains that "a difficult work is enjoined, since this translation has been commanded me by your Felicities, which *Matthew himself, the Apostle and Evangelist*, DID NOT WISH TO BE OPENLY WRITTEN. For if it had not been SECRET, he [Matthew] would have added to the *evangel* that what he gave forth was his; but he made this book sealed up in the Hebrew characters, which he put forth *even in such a way* that the book, written in Hebrew letters and *by the hand of himself*, might be possessed *by the men most religious;* who also, in the course of time, received it from those who preceded them. But this very book they never gave to any one to be transcribed, and its *text* they related some one way and some another."[407] And he adds further on the same page: "And it happened that this book, having been published by a disciple of Manichaeus, named Seleucus, who also wrote falsely *The Acts of the Apostles*, exhibited matter not for edification, but for destruction; and that this book was approved in a synod which the ears of the Church properly refused to listen to."[408]

He admits himself that the book which he authenticates as being written "*by the hand of Matthew*" was nearly unintelligible to him,

405. Jerome: *De vir. illust.*, iii. "It is remarkable that, while all church fathers say that Matthew wrote in *Hebrew*, the whole of them use the Greek text as the genuine apostolic writing, without mentioning what relation the *Hebrew* Matthew has to our Greek one! It had many *peculiar additions* which are wanting in our evangel." (Olshausen: *Nachweis der Echtheit der sämmtlichen Schriften des Neuen Test.*, p. 35; p. xlix, in Amer. ed. of his *Bibl. Comm. N. T.*, 1860.

406. Jerome: *Comm. to Matt.*, xii, 13. Jerome adds that it was written in the Chaldaic language, but with Hebrew letters (*Dial. contra Pelag.*, iii, 2).

407. *Comm. to Matt.*, v, 445; *Sôd, the Son of the Man*, p. 46.

408. This accounts also for the rejection of the works of Justin Martyr, who used only this 'Gospel according to the Hebrews,' as also did most probably Tatian, his disciple. At what late period was fully established the *divinity* of Christ, we can judge by the mere fact that even in the fourth century Eusebius (*Eccl. Hist.*, III, xxv) did not denounce this book as spurious, but only classed it with such as the Apocalypse of John; and Credner (*Zur Gesch. des Kanons*, p. 120) shows Nicephorus, at the end of the eighth century, inserting it, together with the *Revelation* of John, in his 'Stichometry' among the *Antilegomena.* The Ebionites, the *genuine* primitive Christians, rejecting the rest of the apostolic writings, made use only of this Gospel (Irenaeus: *Agst. Her.*, I, xxvi, 2; also Euseb.: *Eccl. Hist.*, III, xxvii), and the Ebionites, as Epiphanius declares, firmly believed with the Nazarenes that Jesus was but a man "of the seed of a man" (Haer. XXX, iii).

notwithstanding that he translated it twice, for it was arcane or *a secret*. Nevertheless Jerome coolly sets down every commentary upon it, except his own, as *heretical*. More than that, Jerome knew that this *original Gospel of Matthew* was the expounder of the only true doctrine of Christ; and that it was the work of an evangelist who had been the friend and companion of Jesus. He knew that if of the two *Gospels*, the Hebrew in question and the Greek belonging to our present Scripture, one was spurious, hence heretical, it was not that of the Nazarenes; and yet, knowing all this, Jerome becomes more zealous than ever in his persecutions of the 'Heretics.' Why? Because to accept it [*i. e.*, the original Gospel] was equivalent to reading the death-sentence of the established Church. The *Gospel according to the Hebrews* was but too well known to have been the only one accepted for four centuries by the Jewish Christians, the Nazarenes and the Ebionites. And neither of the latter accepted the *divinity* of Christ.

If the commentaries of Jerome on the Prophets, his famous *Vulgate*, and numerous polemical treatises, are all as trustworthy as this version of the *Gospel according to Matthew*, then we have a divine revelation indeed.

Why wonder at the unfathomable mysteries of the Christian religion, since it is perfectly *human?* Have we not a letter written by one of the most respected Fathers of the Church to this same Jerome, which shows better than whole volumes their traditionary policy? This is what *Saint* Gregory of Nazianzen wrote to his friend and confidant *Saint* Jerome: "Nothing can impose better on a people than *verbiage;* the less they understand the more they admire. Our fathers and doctors have often said, not what they thought, but what circumstances and necessity forced them to."

But to return to our Sophia-Achamoth and the belief of the genuine primitive Christians.

After having produced Ilda-Baoth — Ilda from יָלָד, a child, and Baoth from בִּיצָה, the egg, or בֹּהוּ, *Baoth*, a waste, a desolation — Sophia-Achamoth suffered so much from the contact with matter, that after extraordinary struggles she escaped at last out of the muddy chaos. Although unacquainted with the pleroma, the region of her mother, she reached the middle space and succeeded in shaking off the material parts which had stuck to her spiritual nature; after which she immediately built a strong barrier between the world of intelligences (spirits) and the world of matter. Ilda-Baoth is thus the 'son of darkness,' the creator of our sinful world (the physical portion of it). He follows the example of Bythos and produces from himself six stellar spirits (sons). They are all in his own image, and reflexions one of the other, which become darker as they successively recede from their father. With the latter, they all inhabit seven regions disposed like a ladder, beginning under the middle space, the region of their mother Sophia-Achamoth, and ending with our earth, the *seventh* region. Thus they are the genii of the seven planetary spheres of which the lowest is the region of our earth (the sphere which surrounds it, our aether). The respective names of these genii of the spheres are *Iove* (Jehovah), *Sabaoth, Adonai, Eloi, Ouraios, Astaphaios.*[409] The first four, as every one knows, are the mystic names of the Jewish 'Lord God,'[410] being, as C. W. King expresses it, "thus degraded by the Ophites into the appellations of the subordinates of the Creator; the two last names are those of the genii of fire and water."

Ilda-Baoth, whom several sects regarded as the God of Moses, was not a pure spirit; he was ambitious and proud, and rejecting the spiritual light of the middle space offered him by his mother Sophia-Achamoth, he set himself to create a world of his own. Aided by his sons, the six planetary genii, he fabricated man, but this one proved a failure. It was a monster; soulless, ignorant, and crawling on all fours on the ground like a material beast. Ilda-Baoth was forced to implore the help of his spiritual mother. She communicated to him a ray of her divine light, and so animated man and endowed him with a soul. And now began the animosity of Ilda-Baoth toward his own creature. Following the impulse of the divine light, man soared higher and higher in his aspirations; very soon he began presenting, not the image of his Creator Ilda-Baoth, but rather that of the Supreme Being, the 'primitive man,' Ennoia. Then the Demiurge was filled with rage and envy; and fixing his jealous eye on the abyss of matter, his looks envenomed with passion were suddenly reflected in it as in a mirror; the reflexion became animate, and there arose out of the abyss Satan, serpent, Ophiomorphos — "the embodiment of envy and of cunning. He is the union of all that is most base in matter, with the hate, envy, and craft of a spiritual intelligence."[411]

After that, always in spite at the perfection of man, Ilda-Baoth created the three kingdoms of nature, the mineral, vegetable, and animal, with all evil instincts and properties. Impotent to annihilate the Tree of Knowledge, which grows in his sphere as in every one of the planetary regions, but bent upon detaching 'man' from his spiritual protectress, Ilda-Baoth forbade him to eat of its fruit, for fear it should reveal to man-

---

409. C. W. King: *The Gnostics, etc.,* p. 97; 2nd edit.

410. This Iove, Iao, or Jehovah is quite distinct from the God of the Mysteries, Iao, held sacred by all the nations of antiquity. We will show the difference presently.

411. King: *The Gnostics, etc.,* p. 98.

kind the mysteries of the superior world. But Sophia-Achamoth, who loved and protected the man whom she had animated, sent her own genius Ophis, in the form of a serpent, to induce man to transgress the selfish and unjust command. And 'man' suddenly became capable of comprehending the mysteries of creation.

Ilda-Baoth revenged himself by punishing the first pair, for man, through his *knowledge*, had already provided for himself a companion out of his spiritual and material half. He imprisoned man and woman in a dungeon of matter, in the body so unworthy of his nature, wherein man is still enthralled. But Achamoth protected him still. She established between her celestial region and 'man' a current of divine light, and kept constantly supplying him with this *spiritual* illumination.

Then follow allegories embodying the idea of dualism, or the struggle between good and evil, spirit and matter, which is found in every cosmogony, and the source of which is again to be sought in India. The types and antitypes represent the heroes of this Gnostic Pantheon, borrowed from the most ancient mythopoeic ages. But in these personages, Ophis and Ophiomorphos, Sophia and Sophia-Achamoth, Adam-Kadmon and Adam, the planetary genii and the divine Aeons, we can also recognise very easily the models of our biblical copies — the euhemerized patriarchs. The archangels, angels, virtues and powers, are all found, under other names, in the *Vedas* and the Buddhistic system. The Avestic Supreme Being, Zero-ana, or 'Boundless Time,' is the type of all these Gnostic and kabalistic 'Depths,' 'Crowns,' and even of the Chaldaean Ain-Soph. The six Amshaspends, created through the 'Word' of Ormazd, the 'First-Born,' have their reflexions in Bythos and his emanations, and the antitypes of Ormazd-Ahriman and his *devs* also enter into the composition of Ilda-Baoth and his six *material*, though not wholly evil, planetary genii.

Achamoth, afflicted with the evils which befall humanity notwithstanding her protection, beseeches the celestial mother Sophia — her antitype — to prevail on the unknown DEPTH to send down Christos (the son and emanation of the 'Celestial Virgin') to the help of perishing humanity. Ilda-Baoth and his six sons of matter are shutting out the divine light from mankind. Man must be saved. Ilda-Baoth had already sent his own agent, John the Baptist, from the race of Seth, whom he protects — as a prophet to his people; but only a small portion listened to him — the Nazarenes, the opponents of the Jews, on account of their worshiping Iurbo-Adunai.[412] Achamoth had assured her son, Ilda-

<hr>

412. Iurbo and Adunai, according to the Ophites, are names of Iao-Jehovah, one of the emanations of Ilda-Baoth. "Iurbo is called by the Abortions [the Jews] Adunai" (*Codex Nazaraeus*, III, p. 73).

Baoth, that the reign of Christos would be only temporal, and thus she induced him to send the forerunner, or precursor. Besides that, she made *him cause* the birth of the *man* Jesus from the Virgin Mary, her own type on earth, "for the creation of a material personage could only be the work of the Demiurge, not falling within the province of a higher power. As soon as Jesus was born, Christos, the perfect, uniting himself with Sophia [wisdom and spirituality], descended through the seven planetary regions, assuming in each an analogous form, and concealing his true nature from their genii, while he attracted into himself the sparks of divine light which they retained in their essence. Thus Christos entered into the *man* Jesus at the moment of his baptism in the Jordan. From that time Jesus began to work miracles; before that, he had been completely ignorant of his mission." [413]

Ilda-Baoth, discovering that Christos was bringing to an end his own kingdom of matter, stirred up the Jews against him, and Jesus was put to death.[414] When on the Cross, Christos and Sophia left his body and returned to their own sphere. The material body of the man Jesus was abandoned to the earth, but he himself was given a body made up of *aether* (astral soul). "Thenceforward he consisted of merely *soul* and *spirit*, which was the reason why the disciples did not recognise him after the resurrection. In this spiritual state of a *simulacrum*, Jesus remained on earth for eighteen months after he had risen. During this last sojourn, he received from Sophia that perfect knowledge, that true Gnosis, *which he communicated to the very few among the apostles* who were capable of receiving the same.

"Thence, ascending into the middle space, he sits on the right hand of Ilda-Baoth, but unperceived by him, and there collects all the souls which shall have been purified by the knowledge of Christ. When he has collected all the spiritual light that exists in matter, out of Ilda-Baoth's empire, the redemption will be accomplished and the world will be destroyed. Such is the meaning of the re-absorption of all Light into the pleroma or fullness, whence it originally descended." [415]

---

413. King: *The Gnostics and their Remains*, p. 100; 2nd edit.

414. In the *Gospel of Nicodemus* Ilda-Baoth is called *Satan* by the pious and anonymous author; — evidently one of the final flings at the half-crushed enemy. "As for me," says Satan, excusing himself to the prince of hell, "I tempted him [Jesus], and stirred up my old people, the Jews, against him" (Hone: *Apocr. N. T., Nicod.*, xv, 9; and Grynaeus: *Orthodoxographa*, vol. I, tom. ii, pp. 643, *sq.*). Of all examples of Christian ingratitude, this seems almost the most conspicuous. The poor Jews are first robbed of their sacred books, and then, in a spurious 'Gospel,' are insulted by the representation of Satan claiming them as his "old people." If they were his people, and at the same time are 'God's chosen people,' then the name of this God must be written Satan and not Jehovah. This is logic, but we doubt if it can be regarded as complimentary to the 'Lord God of Israel.'

415. *The Gnostics*, *loc. cit.*

The foregoing is from the description given by Theodoret and adopted by King in his *Gnostics*, with additions from Epiphanius and Irenaeus. But the former gives a very imperfect version, concocted partly from the descriptions of Irenaeus, and partly from his own knowledge of the later Ophites, who, toward the end of the third century, had blended already with several other sects. Irenaeus also confounds these sects very frequently, and the real theogony of the Ophites is given by none of them correctly. With the exception of a change in names, the above-given theogony is that of all the Gnostics, and also of the Nazarenes. Ophis is but the successor of the Egyptian *Chnuphis* (*Khnemu*), the Good Serpent with a lion's radiating head, and was held from days of the highest antiquity as an emblem of wisdom, or Thoth, the instructor and Savior of humanity, the 'Son of God.' "Oh men, live soberly . . . win your immortality!" exclaims Hermes, the thrice-great Trismegistus. "Instructor and guide of humanity, I will lead you on to salvation." [416] Thus the oldest sectarians regarded Ophis, the Agathodaimon, as identical with Christos; the serpent being the emblem of celestial wisdom and eternity, and, in the present case, the antitype of the Egyptian Chnuphis-serpent. These Gnostics, the earliest of our Christian era, held: "That the supreme Aeon, having emitted other Aeons out of himself, one of them, a female, *Prunikos* (concupiscence), descended into the chaos, whence, unable to escape, she remained suspended in the mid-space, being too clogged by matter to return above, and not falling lower where there was nothing in affinity with her nature. She then produced her son Ilda-Baoth, the God of the Jews, who, in his turn, produced seven Aeons, or angels,[417] who created the seven heavens." [417a]

In this plurality of heavens the Christians believed from the first, for we find Paul teaching of their existence, and speaking of a man "caught up to the *third* heaven" (*2 Cor.*, xii, 2). "From these seven angels Ilda-Baoth shut up all that was above him, lest they should know of anything superior to himself.[418] They then created man in the image of their Father,[419] but prone and crawling on the earth like a worm. But the

---

416. Champollion-Figeac: *Égypte ancienne*, p. 143.

417. This is the Nazarene system; the Spiritus, after uniting herself with Karabtanos (*matter*, turbulent and senseless), brings forth *seven badly-disposed stellars*, in the Orcus; "Seven Figures," which she bore "witless" (*Codex Nazaraeus*, I, p. 179). Justin Martyr (*Hortatory Address to the Greeks*, xxxii) evidently adopts this idea, for he tells us of "the sacred prophets, who say that one and the same *spirit* is divided into *seven* spirits" (*pneumata*). In the Apocalypse the Holy Spirit is subdivided into "*seven* spirits before the throne," from the Persian Mithraic mode of classifying.

417a. *The Gnostics*, p. 102.

418. This certainly looks like the "*jealous* God" of the Jews.

419. It is the *Elohim* (plural) who create Adam, and do not wish man to become "as one of us."

heavenly mother, Prunikos, wishing to deprive Ilda-Baoth of the power with which she had unwittingly endowed him, infused into man a celestial spark — the spirit. Immediately man rose upon his feet, soared in mind beyond the limits of the seven spheres, and glorified the Supreme Father, *Him that is above Ilda-Baoth.* Hence the latter, full of jealousy, cast down his eyes upon the lowest stratum of matter, and begot a potency in the form of a serpent, whom they [Ophites] call his son. Eve, obeying him as the son of God, was persuaded to eat of the Tree of Knowledge." [420]

It is a self-evident fact that the serpent of the *Genesis*, who appears suddenly and without any preliminary introduction, must have been the antitype of the Persian Arch-Devs, whose head is *Ashmog*, the "two-footed serpent of lies." If the *Bible*-serpent had been deprived of his limbs before he had tempted woman unto sin, why should God specify as a punishment that he should go "upon his belly"? Nobody supposes that he walked upon the extremity of his tail.

This controversy about the supremacy of Jehovah, between the Presbyters and Fathers on the one hand, and the Gnostics, the Nazarenes, and all the sects declared (as a last resort) heterodox on the other, lasted till the days of Constantine and later. That the peculiar ideas of the Gnostics about the *genealogy* of Jehovah, or the proper place that had to be assigned, in the Christian-Gnostic Pantheon, to the God of the Jews, were at first deemed neither blasphemous nor heterodox, is evident in the difference of opinions held on this question by Clement of Alexandria, for instance, and Tertullian. The former, who seems to have known Basilides better than anybody else, saw nothing heterodox or blamable in the mystical and transcendental views of the new Reformer. "In his eyes," remarks the author of *The Gnostics*, speaking of Clement, "Basilides was not a heretic, *i. e.*, an innovator as regards the doctrines of the Christian Church, but a mere theosophic philosopher, who sought to express *ancient truths* under new forms, and perhaps to combine them with the new faith, the truth of which he could admit without necessarily renouncing the old, exactly as is the case with the learned Hindûs of our day." [421]

Not so with Irenaeus and Tertullian. [422] The principal works of the latter *against the Heretics* were written after his separation from the Catholic Church, when he had ranged himself among the zealous followers of Montanus; they teem with unfairness and bigoted prejudice. [423]

---

420. Theodoret: *Haer. fabul.;* King: *The Gnostics*, pp. 102-3; 2nd edit.

421. *The Gnostics and their Remains*, p. 258.

422. Some persons hold that he was Bishop of Rome; others, of Carthage.

423. His polemical work directed against the so-called orthodox Church — the Catholic — notwithstanding its bitterness and usual style of vituperation, is far more fair, con-

He has exaggerated every Gnostic opinion into a monstrous absurdity, and his arguments are not based on coercive reasoning but simply on the blind stubbornness of a partisan fanatic. Discussing Basilides, the "pious, god-like, theosophic philosopher," as Clement of Alexandria thought him, Tertullian exclaims: "After this Basilides, the *heretic*, broke loose.[424] He asserted that there is a Supreme God, by name Abraxas, by whom Mind was created, whom the Greeks call *Nous*. From her emanated the Word; from the Word, Providence; from Providence, Virtue and Wisdom; from these two again, *Principalities*,[425] *Powers and Angels* were made; thence infinite productions and emissions of angels. . . . Among the lowest angels, indeed, and those that made this world, he sets *last of all* the god of the Jews, whom he denies to be God himself, affirming that he is but one of the angels." [426]

It would be equally useless to refer to the direct apostles of Christ, and show them as holding in their controversies that Jesus never made any difference between his 'Father' and the 'Lord-God' of Moses. For the *Clementine Homilies*, in which occur the greatest argumentations upon the subject, as shown in the disputations alleged to have taken place between Peter and Simon the Magician, are now also proved to have been falsely attributed to Clement the Roman. This work, if written by an Ebionite — as the author of *Supernatural Religion* declares, in common with some other commentators [427] — must have been written either far later than the Pauline period generally assigned to it, or the dispute

---

sidering that the 'great African' is said to have been expelled from the Church of Rome. If we believe St. Jerome, it is but the envy and the unmerited calumnies of the early Roman clergy against Tertullian which forced him to renounce the Catholic Church and become a Montanist. However, were the unlimited admiration of St. Cyprian (who terms Tertullian "The Master") and his estimate of him merited, we should see less error and paganism in the Church of Rome. The expression of Vincent of Lerius, "that every word of Tertullian was a sentence, and every sentence a triumph *over error*," does not seem very happy when we think of the respect paid to Tertullian by the Church of Rome, notwithstanding his partial apostasy and the *errors* in which the latter still abides and which she has even forced upon the world as *infallible* dogmas.

424. Were not the views of the Phrygian Bishop Montanus also deemed a HERESY by the Church of Rome? It is quite extraordinary to see how easily the Vatican encourages the abuse by one *heretic* Tertullian, of another *heretic* Basilides, when the abuse happens to further her own object.

425. Does not Paul himself speak of "*Principalities* and *Powers* in heavenly places" (*Ephesians*, iii, 10; i, 21), and confess that there be *Gods* many and *Lords* many (*Kurioi*)? And Angels, Powers (*Dunameis*), and *Principalities*? (See *1 Corinthians*, viii, 5; and *Romans*, viii, 38.)

426. Tertullian: *Against all Heresies*, ch. i.

427. Baur, Credner, Hilgenfeld, Kirchhofer, Lechler, Nicolas, Reuss, Ritschl, Schwegler, Westcott and Zeller; see *Supernatural Religion*, part II, v; 6th ed.

about the identity of Jehovah with God, the 'Father of Jesus,' must
have been distorted by later interpolations. This disputation is in its
very essence antagonistic to the early doctrines of the Ebionites. The
latter, as demonstrated by Epiphanius and Theodoret, were the direct
followers of the Nazarene sect [428] (the Sabaeans), the 'Disciples of John.'
Epiphanius says unequivocally that the Ebionites believed in the
Aeons (emanations), that the Nazarenes were *their instructors*, and that
"each imparted to the other out of his own wickedness." Therefore,
holding the same beliefs as the Nazarenes did, an Ebionite would not
have given Peter so much scope in the *Homilies* to expound his doctrine.
The old Nazarenes, as well as the later ones, whose views are embodied
in the *Codex Nazaraeus*, never called Jehovah otherwise than *Adonai,
Iurbo*, the God of the *Abortive* [429] (the orthodox Jews). [430] They kept
their beliefs and religious tenets so *secret* that even Epiphanius, writing
as early as the end of the fourth century,[431] confesses his ignorance as to
their real doctrine. "Dropping the name of Jesus," says the Bishop of
Salamis, "they neither call themselves *Iessaeans*, nor continue to hold the
name of the Jews, nor name themselves Christians, but *Nazarenes*. . . .
The resurrection of the dead is confessed by them . . . but concerning
Christ, *I cannot say* whether they think him a *mere man*, or as the
truth is, confess that he was born through the *Holy Pneuma* from the
Virgin." [432]

While Simon Magus argues in the *Homilies* from the standpoint of
every Gnostic (Nazarenes and Ebionites included), Peter, as a true
apostle of circumcision, holds to the old Law and as a matter of course
seeks to blend his belief in the divinity of Christ with his old Faith in
the 'Lord God' and ex-protector of the 'chosen people.' As the author
of *Supernatural Religion* shows the *Epitome* [433] to be "a blending of the
other two [parts of the *Clementines*] probably intended to purge them
from heretical doctrine," [434] and, together with a great majority of critics,
assigns to the *Homilies* a date not earlier than the third century, we may
well infer that they must differ widely from their original, if there ever
was one. Simon the Magician proves throughout the whole work that

---

428. Epiphanius: *Panar.*, lib. I, tom. II, Haer. XXX, ii.

429. The Ophites, for instance, made of Adonai, the third son of Ilda-Baoth, a malignant genius, and, like his other five brothers, a constant enemy and adversary of man, whose divine and immortal spirit gave man the means of becoming the rival of these genii.

430. *Codex Nazaraeus*, III, p. 73.

431. The Bishop of Salamis died A. D. 403.

432. *Panar.*, lib. I, tom. II, Haer. XXIX, vii.

433. The *Clementines* are composed of three parts — to wit: the *Homilies*, the *Recognitions*, and an *Epitome.*

434. *Supernatural Religion, loc. cit. supra.*

the Demiurge, the Architect of the World, is not the highest Deity; and he bases his assertions upon the words of Jesus himself, who states repeatedly that no man knew the Father. Peter is made in the *Homilies* to repudiate, with a great show of indignation, the assertion that the Patriarchs were not deemed worthy to know the Father; to which Simon objects again by quoting the words of Jesus, who thanks the "Lord of Heaven and earth" that what was hidden "from the wise" he has "revealed unto babes," proving very logically that according to these very words the Patriarchs could not have known the 'Father.' Then Peter argues, in his turn, that the expression, "what is *concealed* from the wise," etc., referred to the concealed *mysteries* of the creation.[435]

This argumentation of Peter, therefore, had it even emanated from the apostle himself, instead of being a "religious romance," as the author of *Supernatural Religion* calls it, would prove nothing whatever in favor of the identity of the God of the Jews with the 'Father' of Jesus. At best it would only demonstrate that Peter had remained from first to last 'an apostle of circumcision,' a Jew faithful to his old law, and a defender of the *Old Testament*. This conversation proves, moreover, the weakness of the cause he defends, for we see in the apostle a man who, although in most intimate relations with Jesus, can furnish us nothing in the way of direct proof that he ever thought of teaching that the all-wise and all-good Paternity he preached was the morose and revengeful thunderer of Mount Sinai. But what the *Homilies* do prove, is our assertion that there was a secret doctrine preached by Jesus to the few who were deemed worthy to become its recipients and custodians. "And Peter said: 'We remember that our Lord and teacher, as commanding, said to us, guard the mysteries for me, and the sons of my house. Wherefore also he explained to his disciples, *privately*, the *mysteries of the kingdom of heaven.*' "[436]

If we now recall the fact that a portion of the Mysteries of the 'Pagans' consisted of the ἀπόρρητα, *aporrheta*, or secret discourses; that the secret *Logia* or discourses of Jesus contained in the original *Gospel according to Matthew*, the meaning and interpretation of which St. Jerome confessed to be "a difficult task" for him to achieve, were of the same nature; and if we remember, further, that to some of the interior or final Mysteries only a very select few were admitted; and that finally it was from the number of the latter that were taken all the ministers of the holy 'Pagan' rites, we shall then clearly understand this expression of Jesus quoted by Peter: "Guard *the Mysteries for me and the sons of my*

---

435. *Clementine Homilies*, XVIII, i-xv.
436. *Ibid.*, XIX, xx.

house," *i. e.,* of my doctrine. And, if we understand it rightly, we cannot avoid thinking that this 'secret' doctrine of Jesus, even the technical expressions of which are but so many duplications of the Gnostic and Neo-Platonic mystic phraseology — that this doctrine, we say, was based on the same transcendental philosophy of Oriental *Gnosis* as the rest of the religions of those and earliest days. That none of the later Christian sects, despite their boasting, were the inheritors of it, is evident from the contradictions, blunders, and clumsy repatching of the mistakes of every preceding century by the discoveries of the succeeding one. These mistakes, in a number of manuscripts claimed to be authentic, are sometimes so ridiculous as to bear on their face the evidence of being pious forgeries. Thus, for instance, the utter ignorance of some patristic champions of the very gospels they claimed to defend. We have mentioned the accusation against Marcion by Tertullian and Epiphanius of mutilating the *Gospel* ascribed to Luke, and erasing from it that which is now proved to have never been in that Gospel at all. Finally, the method adopted by Jesus of speaking in parables, in which he only followed the example of his sect, is attributed in the *Homilies* [437] to a prophecy of *Isaiah!* Peter is made to remark: "For Isaiah said: 'I will open my mouth in parables, and I will utter things that have been kept secret from the foundation of the world.'" This erroneous reference to Isaiah of a sentence given in *Psalms,* lxxviii, 2, is found not only in the apocryphal *Homilies,* but also in the Sinaitic *Codex.* Commenting on the fact in *Supernatural Religion,* the author states that "Porphyry, in the third century, twitted Christians with this erroneous ascription by their inspired evangelist to Isaiah of a passage from a *Psalm,* and reduced the Fathers to great straits." [438] Eusebius and Jerome tried to get out of the difficulty by ascribing the mistake to an "ignorant scribe"; and Jerome even went to the length of asserting that the name of Isaiah never stood before the above sentence in any of the old codices, but that the name of Asaph was found in its place, only "*ignorant* men had removed it." [439] To this the author again observes that "the fact is that the reading 'Asaph' for 'Isaiah' is not found in any manuscript extant; and, although 'Isaiah' has *disappeared* from all but a few obscure codices, it cannot be denied that the name anciently stood in the text. In the Sinaitic *Codex,* which is probably the earliest manuscript extant, and which is assigned to the fourth century, 'the prophet *Isaiah*' stands in the text by the first hand, *but is erased* by the second." [440]

It is a most suggestive fact that there is not a word in the so-called sacred *Scriptures* to show that Jesus was actually regarded as a God by

437. *Clem. Homil.,* XVIII, xv.   438. Part II, v.   439. Jerome: *Hieronymi opera,* vii, p. *sq.;* 270, *Supern. Rel., loc. cit.*   440. *Supern. Rel., loc. cit.*

his disciples. Neither before nor after his death did they pay him divine honors. Their relation to him was only that of disciples and 'master'; by which name [κύριε] they addressed him, as the followers of Pythagoras and Plato addressed their respective masters before him. Whatever words may have been put into the mouths of Peter, John, Paul and others, there is not a single act of adoration recorded on their part, nor did Jesus himself ever declare his identity with *his Father*. [441] He accused the Pharisees of stoning their *prophets*, not of deicide. He termed himself the son of God, but took care to assert repeatedly that they were all the children of God, who was the Heavenly Father of all. In preaching this he but repeated a doctrine taught ages earlier by Hermes, Plato, and other philosophers. Strange contradiction! Jesus, whom we are asked to worship as the one living God, is found, immediately after his resurrection, saying to Mary Magdalene: "I am not yet ascended *to my Father;* but go to my brethren, and say unto them, I ascend unto *my Father* and *your* Father, and to *my* God and *your* God!" (*John*, xx, 17).

Does this look like identifying himself with his Father? "*My* Father and *your* Father, *my* God and *your* God," implies, on his part, a desire to be considered on a perfect equality with his brethren — nothing more. Theodoret writes: "The heretics agree with us respecting the beginning of all things. . . . But they say there is not one Christ (God), but one above, and the other below. And this last *formerly dwelt in many;* but *the Jesus*, they at one time say is *from* God, at another they call him a SPIRIT." [442] This spirit is the Christos, the *messenger* of life, who is sometimes called the Angel *Gabriel* (in Hebrew, the mighty one of God), and who took with the Gnostics the place of the Logos, while the Holy Spirit was considered *Life*. [443] With the sect of the Nazarenes, though, their 'Spiritus,' or Holy Ghost, had less honor. While nearly every Gnostic sect considered it a Female Power, whether they called it *Binah*, בינה, or *Sophia*, the Divine Intellect; with the Nazarene sect it was the *Female Spiritus*, the astral light, the genetrix of all things of *matter*, the chaos in its evil aspect, made *turbid* by the Demiurge. At the creation of man, "it was light on the side of the FATHER, and it was light [material light] on the side of the MOTHER. And this is the '*two-fold* man,'" says the *Zohar*. [444] "That day [the last one] will perish the seven badly-disposed stellars; also the sons of man, who have confessed the *Spiritus*, the Messias [false], the Deus, and the MOTHER of the SPIRITUS, shall perish." [445]

---

441. Cf. *The Secret Doctrine*, II, p. 113, regarding the Gnostic expression used in *John*, x, 30.

442. Theod.: *Haer. fabul.*, II, vii.   443. See Irenaeus: *Against Heresies*, I, xii, 4.

444. *Auszüge aus dem Buche Sohar*, p. 15: Berlin, 1857.   445. *Cod. Naz.*, II, pp. 147-9.

Jesus enforced and illustrated his doctrines with signs and wonders; and if we lay aside the claims advanced on his behalf by his deifiers, he did but what other kabalists did; and *only they* at that epoch, when, for two centuries the sources of prophecy had been completely dried up, and from this stagnation of public 'miracles' had originated the skepticism of the unbelieving sect of the Sadducees. Describing the 'heresies' of those days, Theodoret, who has no idea of the hidden meaning of the word Christos, the *anointed* messenger, complains that they (the Gnostics) assert *that this Messenger or Delegatus changes his body from time to time,* "*and goes into other bodies, and at each time is differently manifested.* And these [the overshadowed prophets] use incantations and invocations of various demons and baptisms in the confession of their principles. . . . They embrace astrology and magic, and the mathematical error," (?) he says.[446]

This "mathematical error," of which the pious writer complains, led subsequently to the rediscovery of the heliocentric system, erroneous as it may still be, and forgotten since the days of another 'magician' who taught it — Pythagoras. Thus the wonders of healing and the *thaums* of Jesus, which he imparted to his followers, show that they were learning in their daily communication with him the theory and practice of the new ethics, day by day, and in the familiar intercourse of intimate friendship. Their faith was progressively developed, like that of all neophytes, simultaneously with the increase of knowledge. We must bear in mind that Josephus, who certainly must have been well-informed on the subject, calls the art of expelling demons "a science." This growth of faith is conspicuously shown in the case of·Peter who, from having lacked enough faith to support him while he could walk on the water from the boat to his Master, at last became so expert a thaumaturgist that Simon Magus is said to have offered him money to be taught the secret of healing, and other wonders. And Philip is shown to have become an Aethrobat as good as Abaris of Pythagorean memory, but less expert than Simon Magus.

Neither in the *Homilies* nor any other early work of the apostles is there anything to show that any of his friends and followers regarded Jesus as anything more than a prophet. The idea is as clearly established in the *Clementines.* Except that too much room is afforded to Peter to establish the identity of the Mosaic God with the Father of Jesus, the whole work is devoted to Monotheism. The author seems as bitter against Polytheism as against the claim to the divinity of Christ.[447] He

---

446. Theodoret: *Haeret. fab.*, II, vii.

447. *Homilies*, II, xii; III, lvii-lix; X, xix; XVI, xv, *sq.* A. Schliemann: *Die Clementinen*, pp. 130, 134, *sq.*, 144, *sq. Supernatural Religion*, part III, i (6th edition).

seems to be utterly ignorant of the Logos, and his speculation is confined to Sophia, the Gnostic wisdom. There is no trace in it of a hypostatic trinity, but the same overshadowing of the Gnostic wisdom (Christos and Sophia) is attributed in the case of Jesus as it is in those of Adam, Enoch, Noah, Abraham, Isaac, Jacob and Moses.[448] These personages are all placed on one level, and called 'true prophets,' and the seven pillars of the world. More than that, Peter vehemently denies the fall of Adam, and with him the doctrine of atonement, as taught by Christian theology, utterly falls to the ground, *for he combats it as a blasphemy.*[449] Peter's theory of sin is that of the Jewish Kabalists, and is even, in a certain way, Platonic. Adam not only never sinned, but, "as a true prophet, possessed of the Spirit of God, which afterwards was in Jesus, *could not* sin."[450] In short, the whole of the work exhibits the belief of the author in the Kabalistic doctrine of permutation. The Kabala teaches the doctrine of transmigration of the spirit.[451] "Mosah is the *revolutio* of Seth and Hebel."[452]

"Tell me who it is who brings about the *re-birth* (the *revolutio*)?" is asked of the wise Hermes. "God's Son, the *only man*, through the will of God," is the answer of the 'heathen.'[453]

"God's son" is the immortal spirit assigned to every human being. It is this divine entity which is the "*only man*," for the casket which contains our soul, and the soul itself, are but half-entities; and without its overshadowing both body and astral soul, the two are but an animal *duad*. It requires a trinity to form the complete 'man,' and allow him to remain immortal at every 'rebirth' or *revolutio*, throughout the subsequent and ascending spheres, every one of which brings him nearer to the refulgent realm of eternal and *absolute* light.

"God's FIRST-BORN, who is the 'holy Veil,' the 'Light of Lights,' it is he who sends the *revolutio* of the Delegatus, for he is the *First Power*," says the Kabalist.[454]

"The *pneuma* [spirit] and the *dunamis* [power], which is from God, it is right to consider nothing else than the *Logos*, who is *also* [?] First-begotten to God," argues a Christian.[455]

"Angels and powers are in heaven!" says Justin,[456] thus bringing forth a purely Kabalistic doctrine. The Christians adopted it from the

448. *Clem. Homil.*, II, xvi-xviii; III, xx, *sq.;* etc.   449. *Ibid.*, III, xx, xxi.
450. A. Schliemann: *Die Clementinen*, pp. 130, 176, *sq.;* cf. *Supern. Rel.*, part III, i.
451. We will speak of this doctrine farther on.
452. Rosenroth: *Kabbala denudata*, II, p. 155.
453. L. Ménard: *Hermès Trismégiste*, pp. 89, 90: Paris, 1910.
454. Kleuker: *Nat. u. Urspr. d. Emanationslehre b. d. Kabbalisten*, pp. 10, 11.
455. Justin Martyr: *First Apol.*, xxxiii.   456. *Dialogue with Trypho*, cxxviii.

Zohar and the 'heretical' sects, and if Jesus mentioned these things, it was not in the official synagogs that he learned the theory, but directly in the Kabalistic teachings. In the Mosaic books very little mention is made of them, and Moses, who holds direct communications with the 'Lord God,' troubles himself very little about them. The doctrine was a secret one, and deemed by the orthodox synagog heretical. Josephus calls the Essenes heretics, saying: "Those admitted among the Essenes must swear to communicate their doctrines to no one any otherwise *than as they received them*, and equally to preserve the books *belonging to their sect*, and the *names of the angels*." [457] The Sadducees did not believe in angels, neither did the uninitiated Gentiles, who limited their Olympus to gods and demi-gods, or 'spirits.' Alone the kabalists and theurgists held to that doctrine from time immemorial, and as a consequence so did Plato, and Philo Judaeus after him, followed first by the Gnostics, and then by the Christians.

Thus if Josephus never wrote the famous interpolation forged by Eusebius concerning Jesus, on the other hand he has described in the Essenes all the principal features that we find prominent in the Nazarenes. When praying, they sought solitude. [458] "When thou prayest, enter into thy closet . . . and pray to thy Father which is in secret" (*Matt.*, vi, 6). "Everything spoken by them [Essenes] is stronger than an oath. Swearing is shunned by them" (Josephus: *Jewish War*, II, viii, 6). "But I say unto you, Swear not at all . . . but let your communication be, Yea, yea; Nay, nay" (*Matt.*, v, 34-37).

The Nazarenes, as well as the Essenes and the Therapeutae, believed more in their own interpretations of the 'hidden sense' of the more ancient Scriptures, than in the later laws of Moses. Jesus, as we have shown before, felt but little veneration for the commandments of his predecessor, with whom Irenaeus is so anxious to connect him.

The Essenes "enter into the houses of *those whom they never saw previously*, as if they were their intimate friends" (Josephus: *Jewish War*, II, viii, 4). Such was undeniably the custom of Jesus and his disciples.

Epiphanius, who places the Ebionite 'heresy' on the same level with that of the Nazarenes, also remarks that the Nazaraioi come next to the Cerinthians, [459] so much vituperated by Irenaeus. [460]

---

457. Josephus: *Jewish War*, II, viii, 7.

458. *Ibid.*, II, viii; Philo Jud.: *De vita contempl.* and *Quod omn. prob. liber*, § 12; *Frag.* in Euseb.: *Praep ev.*, VIII, viii; Munk: *Palestine*, pp. 35, 525, etc. Eusebius mentions their *semneion*, where they perform the mysteries of a retired life (*Eccl. Hist.*, II, xvii).   459. *Panar.*, lib. I, tom. II, Haer. XXIX, i; XXX, i.

460. Cerinthus is the same Gnostic — a contemporary of John the Evangelist — of whom Irenaeus invented the following anecdote: "There are those who heard him [Polycarp] say that John, the disciple of the Lord, going to bathe at Ephesus, and perceiving

Munk, in his work *Palestine*, affirms that there were 4000 Essenes living in the desert; that they had their mystical books, and predicted the future.[461] The Nabathaeans, with very little difference indeed, adhered to the same belief as the Nazarenes and the Sabaeans, and all of them honored John the Baptist more than his successor Jesus. The Persian Yezîdi say that they originally came to Syria from Basrah. They use baptism, and believe in seven archangels, though paying at the same time reverence to Satan. Their prophet Yezîd, who flourished long prior to Mohammed,[462] taught that God will send a messenger, and that the latter would reveal to him a book which is already written in heaven from eternity.[463] The Nabathaeans inhabited the Lebanon, as their descendants do to the present day, and their religion was from its origin purely kabalistic. Maimonides speaks of them as if he identified them with the Sabaeans. "I will mention to thee the writings . . . respecting the belief and institutions of the *Sabaeans*," he says. "The most famous is the book *The Agriculture of the Nabathaeans*, which has been translated by Ibn Wahohîjah. . . . This book is full of heathenish foolishness. . . . It speaks of the preparations of TALISMANS, the drawing down of the powers of the SPIRITS, MAGIC, DEMONS, and ghouls, which make their abode in the desert." [464]

There are traditions among the tribes living scattered about *beyond the Jordan*, as there are many such also among the descendants of the Samaritans at Damascus, Gaza, and at Nablus (the ancient Shechem). Many of these tribes have, notwithstanding the persecutions of eighteen centuries, retained the faith of their fathers in its primitive simplicity. It is there that we have to go for traditions based on *historical* truths, however disfigured by exaggeration and inaccuracy, and compare them with the religious legends of the Fathers, which they call revelation. Eusebius states that before the siege of Jerusalem the small Christian community — comprising members of whom many, if not all, knew Jesus and his apostles personally — took refuge in the little town of Pella, on the opposite shore of the Jordan.[465] Surely these simple people, separated for centuries from the rest of the world, ought to have preserved their traditions purer than those of any other nation! It is in Palestine that we have to search for the *clearest* waters of Christianity, let alone its source. The first Christians, after the death of Jesus, all joined together for a

Cerinthus within, rushed forth from the bath-house . . . crying out, 'Let us fly, lest the bath-house fall down, Cerinthus the enemy of the truth, being within it' " (Irenaeus: *Against Heresies*, III, iii, 4).

461. Munk: *Palestine*, p. 515; Dunlap: *Sôd, the Son of the Man*, p. xv.
462. Haxthausen: *Transcaucasia, etc.*, p. 229: 1854.
463. Shahrastâni, quoted by Dr. D. Chwolsohn: *Die Ssabier u. d. Ssabismus*, II, p. 625.
464. Maimonides: *Moreh Nebûkhîm*, quoted *ibid.*, II, p. 458.   465. *Eccl. Hist.*, III, v.

time, whether they were Ebionites, Nazarenes, Gnostics, or others. They had no Christian dogmas in those days, and their Christianity consisted in believing Jesus to be a prophet, this belief varying from seeing in him simply a "just" man,[466] or a holy, inspired prophet, a vehicle used by *Christos* and *Sophia* to manifest themselves through. These all united together in opposition to the synagog and the tyrannical technicalities of the Pharisees, until the primitive group separated into two distinct branches — which we may correctly term the Christian Kabalists of the Jewish Tanaim school, and the Christian Kabalists of the Platonic Gnosis.[467] The former were represented by the party composed of the followers of Peter, and John the author of the *Apocalypse;* the latter ranged with the Pauline Christianity, blending itself, at the end of the second century, with the Platonic philosophy, and engulfing, still later, the Gnostic sects, whose symbols and misunderstood mysticism overflowed the Church of Rome.

Amid this jumble of contradictions, what Christian is secure in confessing himself such? In the old Syriac *Gospel according to Luke* (iii, 22), the Holy Spirit is said to have descended in the likeness of a dove. "Jesus, full of the sacred Spirit, returned from Jordan, and the Spirit led him into the desert" (old Syriac, *Luke*, iv, 1, Tremellius). "The difficulty," says Dunlap, "was that the Gospels declared that John, the Baptist, saw the Spirit (the Power of God) descend upon Jesus after he had reached manhood; and if the Spirit then first descended upon him, there was some ground for the opinion of the Ebionites and Nazarenes who denied his *preceding* existence, and refused him the attributes of the Logos. The Gnostics, on the other hand, objected to the flesh, but conceded the Logos." [468]

John's *Apocalypsis*, and the explanations of sincere Christian bishops, like Synesius, who, to the last, adhered to the Platonic doctrines, make us think that the wisest and safest way is to hold to that sincere primitive faith which seems to have actuated the above-named bishop. This best, sincerest, and most unfortunate of Christians, addressing the 'Unknown,' exclaims: "O Father of the Worlds . . . Father of the Aeons . . . *Artificer of the Gods*, it is holy to praise!" [469] But Synesius had Hypatia for instructor, and this is why we find him confessing in all

---

466. "Ye have condemned and killed the just," says James in his epistle to the twelve tribes (v, 6).

467. Porphyry makes a distinction between what he calls "the *Antique* or *Oriental philosophy*," and the properly Grecian system, that of the Neo-Platonists. King says that all these religions and systems are branches of one antique and common religion, the Asiatic or Buddhistic (*The Gnostics and their Remains*, pp. 1, 13, etc.; 2nd ed.).

468. *Sôd, the Son of the Man*, p. 23.

469. Hymn III; cf. H. Druon: *Œuvres de Synésius:* Paris, 1878.

sincerity his opinions and profession of faith.[470] "The rabble desires nothing better than to be deceived. . . . As regards myself, therefore, *I will always be a philosopher with myself*, but I *must be priest* with the people."

"Holy is God the Father of all being, holy is God, whose wisdom is carried out into execution by his own Powers! . . . Holy art Thou, who through the Word had created all! Therefore, I believe in Thee, and bear testimony, and go into the LIFE and LIGHT." [471]   Thus speaks Hermes Trismegistus, the heathen divine. What Christian bishop could have said better than that?

The apparent discrepancy of the four gospels as a whole does not prevent every narrative given in the *New Testament* — however much disfigured — having a ground-work of truth. To this are cunningly adapted details made to fit the later exigencies of the Church. So, propped up partially by indirect evidence, still more by blind faith, they have become, with time, articles of faith. Even the fictitious massacre of the 'Innocents' by King Herod has a certain foundation to it, in its allegorical sense. Apart from the now-discovered fact that the whole story of such a massacre of the Innocents is bodily taken from the Hindû *Bhâgavata-Purâna*, and Brâhmanical traditions, the legend refers moreover, allegorically, to a historical fact. King Herod is the copy of Kansa, the tyrant of Mathurâ, the maternal uncle of Krishna, to whom astrologers predicted that a son of his niece *Devaki* would deprive him of his throne. Therefore he gives orders to kill the male child that is born to her; but Krishna escapes his fury through the protection of *Mahâdeva* (the great God), who causes the child to be carried away to another city out of Kansa's reach. After that, in order to be sure and kill the right boy, on whom he failed to lay his murderous hands, Kansa has all the male new-born infants within his kingdom killed. Krishna is also worshiped by the *gopas* (the shepherds) of the land.

Though this ancient Indian legend bears a very suspicious resemblance to the more modern biblical romance, Gaffarel and others attribute the origin of the latter to the persecutions during the Herodian reign of the kabalists and the *Wise men*, who had not remained strictly orthodox. The latter, as well as the prophets, were nicknamed the 'Innocents,' and the 'Babes,' on account of their holiness. As in the case of certain degrees of modern Masonry, the adepts reckoned their grade of initiation by a *symbolic* age. Thus Saul who, when chosen king, was "a choice and goodly man," and "from his shoulders upward was higher than any of the people," is described in Catholic versions, as a

---

470. Letter to his brother, A. D. 409.
471. L. Ménard: *Hermès Trismégiste*, pp. 14, 15.

"child of *one year* when he began to reign," which, in its literal sense, is a palpable absurdity. But in *1 Samuel*, x, his anointing by Samuel and initiation are described; and at verse 6th, Samuel uses this significant language: ". . . the Spirit of the Lord will come upon thee and thou shalt prophesy with them, *and shalt be turned into another man.*" The phrase above quoted is thus made plain — he had received one degree of initiation and was symbolically described as "a child one year old." The Catholic *Bible*, from which the text is quoted, with charming candor says in a foot-note: "It is extremely difficult to explain" (meaning that Saul was a child of one year). But undaunted by any difficulty the Editor, nevertheless, does take upon himself to explain it, and adds: "*A child of one year. That is, he was good and like an innocent child.*" An interpretation as ingenious as it is pious; and which, if it does no good, can certainly do no harm.[472]

If the explanation of the Kabalists is rejected, then the whole subject falls into confusion; worse still — for it becomes a direct plagiarism from the Hindû legend. All the commentators have agreed that a literal massacre of young children is nowhere mentioned in history; and that moreover an occurrence like that would have made such a bloody page in Roman annals that the record of it would have been preserved for us by every author of the day. Herod himself was subject to the Roman law; and undoubtedly he would have paid the penalty of such a monstrous crime with his own life. But if on the one hand we have not the slightest trace of this fable in history, on the other we find in the

---

472. It is the correct interpretation of the Bible allegories that makes the Catholic clergy so wrathful with the Protestants who freely scrutinize the Bible. How bitter this feeling has become, we can judge by the following words of the Reverend Father Parker of Hyde Park, New York, who, lecturing in St. Teresa's Catholic Church, on the 10th of December, 1876, said: "To whom does the Protestant Church owe its possession of the Bible, *which they wish to place in the hands of every ignorant person and child?* To monkish hands, that laboriously transcribed it before the age of printing. Protestantism has produced dissension in Church, rebellions and outbreaks in State, unsoundness in social life, and will never be satisfied short of the downfall of the Bible! Protestants must admit that the Roman Church has done more to scatter Christianity and extirpate idolatry than all their sects. From one pulpit it is said that there is no hell, and from another that there is immediate and unmitigated damnation. One says that Jesus Christ was only a man; another that you must be plunged bodily into water to be baptized, and refuses the rites to infants. Most of them have no prescribed form of worship, no sacred vestments, and their doctrines are as undefined as their service is informal. The founder of Protestantism, Martin Luther, was the worst man in Europe. The advent of the Reformation was the signal for civil war, and from that time to this the world has been in a restless state, uneasy in regard to Governments, and every day becoming more skeptical. The ultimate tendency of Protestantism is clearly nothing less than the destruction of all respect for the Bible, and the disruption of government and society." Very plain talk this. The Protestants might easily return the compliment.

official complaints of the Synagog abundant evidence of the persecution of the initiates. The *Talmud* also corroborates it.

The Jewish version of the birth of Jesus is recorded in the *Sepher Toledoth Yeshu* in the following words:

"Mary having become the mother of a Son, named Jehosuah, and the boy growing up, she entrusted him to the care of the Rabbi El'hanan, and the child progressed in knowledge, for he was well gifted with spirit and understanding.

"Rabbi Jehosuah, son of Pera'hiah, continued the education of Jehosuah (Jesus) after El'hanan, and *initiated* him in the *secret* knowledge"; but the King, Jannaeus, having given orders to slay all the initiates, Jehosuah ben Pera'hiah fled to Alexandria in Egypt, taking the boy with him.

While in Alexandria, continues the story, they were received in the house of a rich and learned lady (personified Egypt). Young Jesus found her beautiful, notwithstanding "*a defect in her eyes,*" and declared so to his master. Upon hearing this, the latter became so angry that his pupil should find in the land of bondage anything good, that "he cursed him and drove the young man from his presence." Then follow a series of adventures told in allegorical language, which show that Jesus supplemented his initiation in the Jewish Kabala with an additional acquisition of the secret wisdom of Egypt. When the persecution ceased, they both returned to Judaea.[473]

The real grievances against Jesus are stated by the learned author of *Tela Ignea Satanae* (the fiery darts of Satan) to be two in number: 1st, that he had discovered the great Mysteries of their Temple, by having been initiated in Egypt; and 2nd, that he had profaned them by exposing them to the vulgar, who misunderstood and disfigured them. These grievances are stated in the *Toledoth Yeshu* as follows: [474]

"There exists, in the sanctuary of the living God, a cubical stone, on which are sculptured the holy characters, the combination of which gives the explanation of the attributes and powers of the incommunicable name. This explanation is the secret key of all the occult sciences and forces in nature. It is what the Hebrews call the *Shem ham-mephorash.* This stone is watched by two lions of gold, who roar as soon as it is approached.[475] The gates of the temple were never lost sight of, and the

473. Babylonian *Talmud, Mishnah Sanhedrin,* fol. 107, and *Mishnah Sota,* fol. 47; see also Éliphas Lévi: *La science des esprits.*

474. This fragment is translated from the original Hebrew by Éliphas Lévi in his *La science des esprits.*

475. Those who know anything of the rites of the Hebrews must recognise in these lions the gigantic figures of the Cherubim, whose symbolical monstrosity was well calculated to frighten and put to flight the profane.

door of the sanctuary opened but once a year to admit the High Priest
alone. But Jesus, who had learned in Egypt the 'great secrets' at the
initiation, forged for himself invisible keys, and thus was enabled to penetrate into the sanctuary unseen. . . . He copied the characters on the
cubical stone, and hid them in his thigh; [476] after which, emerging from
the temple, he went abroad and began astounding people with his miracles. The dead were raised at his command, the leprous and the obsessed
were healed. He forced the stones which lay buried for ages at the
bottom of the sea to rise to the surface until they formed a mountain,
from the top of which he preached." The *Sepher Toledoth* states further
that, *unable to displace* the cubical stone of the sanctuary, Jesus fabricated one of clay, which he showed to the nations and passed it off for the
true cubical stone of Israel.

This allegory, like many others in such books, is written '*inside
and outside*' — it has its secret meaning, and ought to be read in two
ways. The kabalistic books explain its mystical meaning. Further, the
same Talmudist says, in substance, the following: Jesus was thrown in
prison, [477] and kept there forty days; then flogged as a seditious rebel;
then stoned as a blasphemer in a place called Lud, and finally allowed to
expire upon a cross. "All this," explains Lévi, "because he revealed to
the people the truths which they [the Pharisees] wished to bury for their
own use. He had divined the occult theology of Israel, had compared it
with the wisdom of Egypt, and found thereby the reason for a universal
religious synthesis." [478]

However cautious one ought to be in accepting anything about Jesus
from Jewish sources, it must be confessed that in some things they seem
to be more correct in their statements (whenever their direct interest in
stating facts is not concerned) than our good but too jealous Fathers.
One thing is certain — James, the 'Brother of the Lord,' is silent about
the *resurrection*. He terms Jesus nowhere 'Son of God,' nor even
Christ-God. Once only, speaking of Jesus, he calls him the "Lord of
glory," but so do the Nazarenes when writing about their prophet
Iohanan bar Zacharia, or John, son of Zacharias (St. John the Baptist).
Their favorite expressions about their prophet are the same as those used
by James when speaking of Jesus. A man "of the seed of a man,"
"Messenger of Life," of light, "my Lord Apostle," "King sprung of
Light," and so on. "Have not the faith of our *Lord* JESUS Christ,

---

476. Arnobius tells the same story of Jesus, and narrates how he was accused of having
robbed the sanctuary of the secret names of the Holy One, by means of which knowledge he performed all the miracles.— *Adv. gentes,* I, § 43.

477. This is a translation of Éliphas Lévi.

478. *La science des esprits,* p. 37.

the Lord of glory," etc., says James in his epistle (ii, 1), presumably addressing Christ as GOD. "Peace to thee, my *Lord,* JOHN Abo Sabo, Lord of Glory!" says the *Codex Nazaraeus* (II, p. 19), in a passage known to be merely an address to a prophet. "Ye have condemned and killed the *Just,"* says James (v, 6). "Iohanan (John) is the *Just* one, he comes in' the way of *justice,"* says Matthew (xxi, 32, Syriac text).

James does not even call Jesus *Messiah,* in the sense given to the title by the Christians, but alludes to the kabalistic 'King Messiah,' who is Lord of Sabaoth [479] (v, 4), and repeats several times that the 'Lord' will come, but identifies the latter nowhere with Jesus. "Be patient, therefore, brethren, unto the coming of the Lord . . . be patient, for the coming of the Lord *draweth nigh"* (v, 7, 8). And he adds: "Take, my brethren, the prophet [Jesus] *who has spoken in the name of the Lord,* for an example of suffering, affliction, and of patience." Though in the present version the word "prophet" stands in the plural, yet this is a deliberate falsification of the original, the purpose of which is too evident. James, immediately after having cited the "prophets" as an example, adds: "Behold . . . ye have *heard* of the patience of Job, and *have seen the end* of the Lord" — thus combining the examples of these two admirable characters, and placing them on a perfect equality. But we have more to adduce in support of our argument. Did not Jesus himself glorify the prophet of the Jordan? "What went ye out for to see? A prophet? Yea, I say unto you, and more than a prophet. . . . Verily, I say unto you, among them that are born *of women* there hath not risen a greater than John the Baptist."

And of whom was he who spoke thus born? It is but the Roman Catholics who have changed Mary, the mother of Jesus, into a *goddess.* In the eyes of all other Christians she was a woman, whether his own birth was immaculate or otherwise. According to strict logic, then, Jesus confessed John *greater* than himself. Note how completely this matter is disposed of by the language employed by the Angel Gabriel when addressing Mary: "Blessed art thou among *women."* These words are unequivocal. He does not adore her as the Mother of God, nor does he call her *goddess;* 'he does not even address her as 'Virgin,' but he calls her *woman,* and only distinguishes her above other women as having had better fortune, through her purity.

The Nazarenes were known as Baptists, Sabaeans, and "John's Christians" [Mendaeans]. Their belief was that the Messiah was not the Son of God, but simply a prophet who would follow John. "Johanan, the Son of the Abo Sabo Zachariah, shall say to himself, 'Whoever will

---

479. I. M. Jost: *The Israelite Indeed,* III, p. 61.

believe in my *justice* and my BAPTISM, shall be joined to my association; he shall share with me the seat which is the abode of life, of the supreme Mano, and of living fire'" (*Codex Nazaraeus*, II, p. 115). Origen remarks, "there are some who said of John [the Baptist] that he was the *anointed*" (Christus).[480] The Angel Rasiel of the kabalists is the Angel *Gabriel* of the Nazarenes, and it is the latter who is chosen of all the celestial hierarchy by the Christians to become the messenger of the 'annunciation.' "The genius sent by the 'Lord of Celsitude' is Aebel-Zivo, whose name is also called GABRIEL Legatus."[481] Paul must have had the sect of the Nazarenes in mind when he said: "And last of all he [Jesus] was seen of me also, as *of one born out of due time*" (1 Cor., xv, 8), thus reminding his listeners of the expression usual to the Nazarenes, who termed the Jews "the abortions, or born out of time." Paul prides himself on belonging to a heresy.[482]

When the metaphysical conceptions of the Gnostics, who saw in Jesus the Logos and the anointed, began to gain ground, the earliest Christians separated from the Nazarenes, who accused Jesus of perverting the doctrines of John, and changing the baptism of the Jordan.[483] "Directly," says Milman, "as it [the Gospel] got *beyond* the borders of Palestine, and the name of 'Christ' had acquired sanctity and veneration in the Eastern cities, he became a kind of *metaphysical impersonation*, while the religion lost its purely moral cast and assumed the character of a *speculative theogony*."[484] The only half-original document that has reached us from the primitive apostolic days, is the *Logia* of Matthew. The real, genuine doctrine has remained in the hands of the Nazarenes, in this *Gospel of Matthew* containing the 'secret doctrine,' the "Sayings of Jesus," mentioned by Papias. These sayings were, no doubt, of the same nature as the small manuscripts placed in the hands of the neophytes who were candidates for the Initiations into the Mysteries, and which contained the *Aporrheta*, the revelations of some important rites and symbols. For why should Matthew take such precautions to make them '*secret*' were it otherwise?

Primitive Christianity had its grip, pass-words, and degrees of initiation. The innumerable Gnostic gems and amulets are weighty proofs of it. It is a whole symbolical science. The Kabalists were the first to embellish the universal Logos [485] with such terms as 'Light of Light,'

---

480. *Origenis Adamantii, in Lucam*, II, p. 150 (cap. iii, homil. xxiv): Paris, 1574.
481. *Codex Nazaraeus*, I, p. 23.
482. "After the way which they call heresy, so worship I the God of my fathers" (*Acts*, xxiv, 14). 483. *Codex Nazaraeus*, I, p. 109.
484. *History of Christianity*, p. 200; original edition, 1840. 485. Dunlap says, in *Sôd, the Son of the Man* (p. 39, footnote), "Mr. Hall, of India, informs us that he has seen Sanskrit philosophical treatises in which the 'Logos' continually occurs."

the Messenger of LIFE and LIGHT,[486] and we find these expressions adopted *in toto* by the Christians, with the addition of nearly all the Gnostic terms, such as Pleroma (fullness), Archons, Aeons, etc. As to the 'First-Born,' the First, and the 'Only-Begotten,' these are as old as the world. Hippolytus shows the word 'Logos' as existing among the Brachmanes. "The *Brachmanes* say that the God is *Light*, not such as one sees, nor such as the sun and fire; but they have the *God* Logos, not the articulate, but the Logos of the Gnosis, through whom the hidden MYSTERIES of the Gnosis are seen by the wise." [487] The *Acts* and the fourth *Gospel* teem with Gnostic expressions. The kabalistic phrases, "God's first-born emanated from the Most High," together with *that which is the "Spirit of the Anointing,"* and again, "they called him the anointed of the Highest," [488] are reproduced in spirit and substance by the author of the *Gospel according to John.* "That was *the true light*," and "the light shineth in darkness." "And the WORD *was made flesh.*" "And of his *fullness* [pleroma] have all we received," etc. (*John,* i, 5, *sq.*).

The 'Christ,' then, and the 'Logos' existed ages before Christianity; the Oriental Gnosis was studied long before the days of Moses, and we have to seek for the origin of all these in the archaic periods of the primeval Asiatic philosophy. Peter's second *Epistle* and Jude's fragment, preserved in the *New Testament,* show by their phraseology that such terms belong to the kabalistic Oriental Gnosis, for they use the same expressions as did the Christian Gnostics who built up a part of their system from the Oriental Kabala. "Presumptuous are they [the Ophites], self-willed, they are not afraid to speak evil of DIGNITIES," says Peter (2nd Epistle, ii, 10), the original model for the later abusive Tertullian and Irenaeus.[489] "Likewise (even as Sodom and Gomorrah) also these *filthy* dreamers defile the flesh, despise DOMINION, and speak evil of DIGNITIES," says Jude (7, 8), repeating the very words of Peter, and thereby using expressions consecrated in the Kabala. *Dominion* is the 'Empire,' the *tenth* of the Kabalistic Sephiroth.[490] The *Powers* and

---

486. See *John,* i.   487. Hippol.: *Refut. of all Heresies,* I, xxi.

488. Kleuker: *Natur und Ursprung der Emanationslehre bei den Kabbalisten,* pp. 10, 11; see *Siphra Dtseniuthah,* etc.

489. "These as natural *brute beasts.*" "The dog is turned to his own vomit again; and *the sow* that was washed to her wallowing in the mire" (*2 Peter,* ii, 12, 22).

490. The types of the creation, or the attributes of the Supreme Being, are through the emanations of Adam Kadmon; these are: "The *Crown, Wisdom, Prudence, Magnificence, Severity, Beauty, Victory, Glory, Foundation, Empire.* Wisdom is called *Yah;* Prudence, *Yehovah;* Severity, *Elohim;* Magnificence, *Eloah;* Beauty, *Tiphereth;* Victory, and Glory, TZE'BAOTH; Empire or Dominion, ADONAI." Thus when the Nazarenes and other Gnostics of the more Platonic tendency twitted the Jews as "abortions who

Dignities are the subordinate genii of the Archangels and Angels of the *Zohar*.[491] These emanations are the very life and soul of the Kabala and Zoroastrianism; and the *Talmud* itself in its present state is all borrowed from the Zend *Avesta*. Therefore, by adopting the views of Peter, Jude, and other Jewish apostles, the Christians have become but a dissenting sect of the Persians, for they do not even interpret the meaning of all such *Powers* as the true kabalists do. Paul's warning his converts against the worshiping of angels, shows how well he appreciated, even so early as his period, the dangers of borrowing from a metaphysical doctrine, the philosophy of which could be rightly interpreted only by its well-learned adherents, the Magi and the Jewish Tanaim. "Let no man beguile you of your reward in a voluntary humility and *worshiping of angels*, intruding into those things which he hath not seen, vainly puffed up by his fleshly mind," [492] is a sentence laid right at the door of Peter and his champions. In the *Talmud*, Michael is Prince of Water, who has *seven* inferior spirits subordinate to him. He is the patron, the guardian angel of the Jews, as Daniel informs us (x, 21); and the Greek Ophites — who identified him with their Ophiomorphos, the personified creation of the envy and malice of Ilda-Baoth, the Demiurge (Creator of the *material* world), and undertook to prove that he was also Samael, the Hebrew prince of the evil spirits, or Persian *devs* — were naturally regarded by the Jews as blasphemers. But did Jesus ever sanction this belief in angels except in so far as hinting that they were the messengers and subordinates of God? And here the origin of the later splits between Christian beliefs is directly traceable to these two early contradictory views.

Paul, believing in all such occult powers in the world "unseen," but ever "present," says: "Ye walked according to the AEON of this world, according to the *Archon* [Ilda-Baoth, the Demiurge] that has the domination of the air," and "We wrestle not against flesh and blood, but against the *dominations*, the *powers*, the lords of darkness, the mischievousness of spirits in the upper regions." [492a] This sentence, "Ye were dead in sin and error," for "ye walked according to the *Archon*," or Ilda-Baoth, the God and creator of matter of the Ophites, shows unequivocally that: 1st, Paul, notwithstanding some dissent from the more important doctrines of the Gnostics, shared more or less their cosmogonical views on the emanations; and 2nd, he was fully aware that this Demi-

worship their god Iurbo, *Adunai*," we need not wonder at the wrath of those who had accepted the old Mosaic system, but at that of Peter and Jude who claimed to be followers of Jesus and dissented from the views of him who was also a Nazarene.

491. According to the Kabala, *Empire* or *Dominion* is "the consuming fire, and his wife is the Temple or the Church."   492. *Coloss.*, ii, 18.
492a. Cf. this version of Paul's words with that given in *Ephes.*, ii, 2; vi, 12; ii, 1.

urge, whose Jewish name was Jehovah, was *not* the God preached by Jesus. And now, if we compare the doctrine of Paul with the religious views of Peter and Jude, we find that, not only did they worship Michael, the Archangel, but that also they *reverenced* SATAN, because the latter was also, before his fall, an angel! This they do quite openly, and abuse the Gnostics [493] for speaking "evil" of him. No one can deny the following: Peter, when denouncing those who are not afraid to speak evil of "*dignities*," adds immediately, "Whereas angels, which are greater in power and might, *bring not railing accusation* against them [the dignities] before the Lord" (*2 Peter*, ii, 11). Who are the dignities? Jude, in his general epistle, makes the word as clear as day. The *dignities* are the DEVILS!! Complaining of the disrespect shown by the Gnostics to the *powers* and *dominions*, Jude argues in the very words of Peter: "Yet Michael the Archangel, when contending *with the devil* he disputed about the body of Moses, *durst not bring against him a railing accusation*, but said, The Lord rebuke thee" (verse 9). Is this plain enough? If not, then we have the Kabala to prove who were the *dignities*.

Considering that *Deuteronomy* tells us that the '*Lord*' Himself buried Moses in a valley of Moab (xxxiv, 6), "and no man knoweth of his sepulcher unto this day," this biblical *lapsus linguae* of Jude gives a strong coloring to the assertions of some of the Gnostics. They only claimed what was secretly taught by the Jewish kabalists themselves; to wit: that the highest supreme God was unknown and invisible; "the King of Light is a closed eye"; that Ilda-Baoth, the Jewish second Adam, was the real Demiurge; and that Iao, Adonai, Sabaoth, and Eloi were the quaternary emanation which formed the unity of the God of the Hebrews — Jehovah. Moreover, the latter was also called Michael and Samael by them, and regarded but as an angel, several removes from the Godhead. In holding to such a belief, the Gnostics countenanced the teachings of the greatest of the Jewish doctors, Hillel, and other Babylonian divines. Josephus shows the great deference of the official Synagog in Jerusalem to the wisdom of the schools of Central Asia. The colleges of Sora, Pumbiditha, and Nahaidea were considered the headquarters of esoteric and theological learning by all the schools of Palestine. The Chaldaean version of the *Pentateuch*, made by the well-known Babylonian divine, Onkelos, was regarded as the most authoritative of all; and it is according to this learned Rabbi that Hillel and other Tanaim after him held that the Being who appeared to Moses in the burning bush on Mount Sinai, and who finally buried him, was the *angel* of the Lord,

---

493. It is more likely that both abused Paul, who preached against this belief; and that the Gnostics were only a pretext. (See Peter's second Epistle.)

Memro, and not the Lord Himself; and that he whom the Hebrews of the *Old Testament* mistook for *Iahoh* was but His messenger, one of His sons, or emanations. All this establishes but one logical conclusion — namely, that the Gnostics were by far the superiors of the disciples, in point of education and general information, and even in a knowledge of the religious tenets of the Jews themselves. While they were perfectly well-versed in the Chaldaean wisdom, the well-meaning, pious, but fanatical as well as ignorant disciples, unable fully to understand or grasp the religious spirit of their own system, were driven in their disputations to such convincing logic as the use of "brute beasts," "sows," "dogs," and other epithets so freely bestowed by Peter.

Since then the epidemic has reached the apex of the sacerdotal hierarchy. From the day when the founder of Christianity uttered the warning that he who shall say to his brother, "Thou fool, shall be in danger of hell-fire," all who have passed as its leaders, beginning with the ragged fishermen of Galilee, and ending with the jeweled pontiffs, have seemed to vie with each other in the invention of opprobrious epithets for their opponents. So we find Luther passing a final sentence on the Catholics, and exclaiming that "The Papists are all asses, put them in whatever form you like; whether they are boiled, roasted, baked, fried, skinned, hashed, they will be always the same asses." Calvin called the victims he persecuted, and occasionally burned, "malicious barking dogs, full of bestiality and insolence, base corrupters of the sacred writings," etc. Dr. Warburton terms the Popish religion "an impious farce," and Monseigneur Dupanloup asserts that the Protestant Sabbath service is the "Devil's mass," and all clergymen are "thieves and ministers of the Devil."

The same spirit of incomplete inquiry and ignorance has led the Christian Church to bestow on its most holy apostles titles assumed by their most desperate opponents, the 'Heretics' and Gnostics. So we find, for instance, Paul termed the vase of election, *vas electionis*, a title chosen by *Manes*,[494] the greatest heretic of his day in the eyes of the Church, the name Manes meaning, in the Babylonian language, the chosen vessel or receptacle.[495]

So with the Virgin Mary. The Christians were so little gifted with originality, that they copied from the Egyptian and Hindû religions their

---

494. The true name of Manes — who was a Persian by birth — was *Cubricus*. (See Epiph.: *Panar.*: lib. II, tom. II, Haer. LXVI, i.) He was flayed alive at the instance of the Magi, by the Persian King Varanes I. Plutarch says that Manes or Manis means Masses or ANOINTED. The vessel, or vase of election, is, therefore, the vessel full of that light of God, which he pours on one he has selected for his interpreter.

495. C. W. King: *The Gnostics, etc.*, p. 42; 2nd edit.

several apostrophes to their respective Virgin-mothers. The juxta-position of a few examples will make this clear.

Hindú	Egyptian	Roman Catholic
Litany of our Lady Nárí: Virgin (Also Devamátrí)	*Litany of our Lady Isis: Virgin*	*Litany of our Lady of Loretto: Virgin*
1. Holy *Nárí—Mahámáyá*, Mother of perpetual fecundity.	1. Holy Isis, universal mother — *Mut*.	1. Holy Mary, mother of divine grace.
2. Mother of an incarnated God — Vishnu (*Devakí*).	2. Mother of Gods — Hathor.	2. Mother of God.
3. Mother of Krishna.	3. Mother of Horus.	3. Mother of Christ.
4. Eternal Virginity—*Kanyábháva*.	4. *Virgo generatrix*—Neith.	4. Virgin of Virgins.
5. Mother—Pure Essence. *Ákáśa*.	5. Mother-soul of the universe — Anuki (*Ánkhti*).	5. Mother of Divine Grace.
6. Virgin most chaste — *Kanyá*.	6. Virgin sacred earth — Isis.	6. Virgin most chaste.
7. Mother *Tanmátra*, of the *five* virtues or elements.	7. Mother of all the virtues — *Máú*, with the same qualities.	7. Mother most pure. Mother undefiled. Mother inviolate. Mother most amiable. Mother most admirable.
8. Virgin *Triguna* (of the three elements, power or richness, love, and mercy).	8. Illustrious Isis, most powerful, merciful, just. (*Book of the Dead.*)	8. Virgin most powerful. Virgin most merciful. Virgin most faithful.
9. Mirror of Supreme Conscience — *Ahankára.*	9. Mirror of Justice and Truth — *Máú*.	9. Mirror of Justice.
10. Wise Mother — *Sarasatí.*	10. Mysterious mother of the world — *Mut* (secret wisdom).	10. Seat of Wisdom.
11. Virgin of the white Lotus, *Padma* or *Kamalá.*	11. Sacred Lotus.	11. Mystical Rose.
12. Womb of Gold — *Hiraṇyagarbha.*	12. Sistrum of Gold.	12. House of Gold.
13. Celestial Light — *Lakshmí.*	13. Astarte (Syrian), Astaroth (Jewish).	13. Morning Star.
14. Ditto.	14. Argua of the Moon.	14. Ark of the Covenant.
15. Queen of Heaven, and of the universe — *Śakti.*	15. Queen of Heaven, and of the universe — *Sati.*	15. Queen of Heaven.
16. Mother soul of all beings — *Paramátmá.*	16. Model of all mothers — Hathor.	16. *Mater dolorosa.*
·17. *Devamátrí* is conceived without sin, and immaculate herself. (According to the Bráhmanic fancy.)	17. Isis is a Virgin Mother.	17. Mary conceived without sin. (In accordance with later orders.)

If the Virgin Mary has her nuns, who are consecrated to her and bound to live in chastity, so had Isis her nuns in Egypt, as Vesta had hers at Rome, and the Hindû *Nârî*, 'mother of the world,' hers. The virgins consecrated to her *cultus* [*Nârî's*] — the *Devadâsis* of the temples, who were the nuns of the days of old — lived in great chastity, and were objects of the most extraordinary veneration, as the holy women of the goddess. Would the missionaries and some travelers reproachfully point to the modern *Devadâsis*, or Nautch-girls? For all response, we would beg them to consult the official reports of the last quarter century, cited in chapter ii, as to certain discoveries made at the razing of convents, in Austria and Italy. Thousands of infants' skulls were exhumed from ponds, subterranean vaults, and gardens of convents. Nothing to match *this* was ever found in heathen lands.

Christian theology, getting the doctrine of the archangels and angels directly from the Oriental Kabala, of which the Mosaic *Bible* is merely an allegorical screen, ought at least to remember the hierarchy invented by the former for these personified emanations. The hosts of the Cherubim and Seraphim, with which we generally see the Catholic Madonnas surrounded in their pictures, belong, together with the Elohim and Beni-Elohim of the Hebrews, to the *third* kabalistic world, *Yetzirah*. This world is but one remove higher than *Asiah*, the fourth and lowest world, in which dwell the grossest and most material beings — the *qlippoth*, who delight in evil and mischief, and whose chief is *Belial!*

Explaining, in his way, of course, the various 'heresies' of the first two centuries, Irenaeus says: "Our Heretics hold . . . that PROPATOR is known but to the *only-begotten* son, that is, to the *mind*" (the *nous*).[496] It was the Valentinians, the followers of the "profoundest doctor of the Gnosis," Valentinus, who held that "there was a perfect AION, who formerly existed: Bythos" or Bython (the depth) "called Propator." [497] This is again kabalistic, for in the *Zohar* of Shimon ben Yo'hai we read the following: "*Senior occultatus est et absconditus; Microprosopus manifestus est, et non manifestus*" (Rosenroth: *Kabb. den., Lib. myst.*, iv, § 1).

In the religious metaphysics of the Hebrews, the Highest One is an abstraction; he is "without form or being," "with no likeness with anything else." [498] And even Philo calls the Creator the *Logos* who stands next God, "the SECOND God." "The *second* God who is his WISDOM." [499] God is NO-THING, he is nameless, and therefore called *Ain-Soph* — the word *Ain* meaning *nothing*.[500] But if, according to the older Jews, Jehovah is *the* God, and if He manifested Himself several times to Moses

496. *Against Heresies*, I, ii, 1.   497. *Ibid.*, I, i, 1.
498. Franck: *La Kabbale*, II, iii (p. 128).
499. Philo Jud.: *Quaest. et sol. in Gen.*, II, 62.   500. *La Kabbale*, II, iv (pp. 160, sq.)

and the prophets (and the Christian Church anathematized the Gnostics who denied the claim) — how comes it, then, that we read in the fourth gospel that "*No man hath seen God* AT ANY TIME; but the *only-begotten* Son . . . he hath declared him"? (i, 18) The very words of the Gnostics, in spirit and substance. This sentence of St. John — or rather whoever wrote the gospel now bearing his name — floors all the Petrine arguments against Simon Magus, without appeal. The words are repeated and emphasized in chapter vi, 46: "*Not that any man hath seen the Father*, save he which is of God, he [Jesus] hath seen the Father" — the very objection brought forward by Simon in the *Homilies*. These words prove either that the author of the fourth evangel had no idea of the existence of the *Homilies*, or that he was *not* John, the friend and companion of Peter, whom he contradicts point-blank with this emphatic assertion. Be it as it may, this sentence, like many more that might be profitably cited, blends Christianity completely with the Oriental Gnosis, and hence with the KABALA.

While the doctrines, ethical code, and observances of the Christian religion were all appropriated from Brâhmanism and Buddhism, its ceremonials, vestments, and pageantry were taken bodily from Lamaism. The Romish monastery and nunnery are almost servile copies of similar religious houses in Tibet and Mongolia, and interested explorers of Buddhist lands, when obliged to mention the unwelcome fact, have had no other alternative left them but, with an anachronism unsurpassed in recklessness, to charge the offense of plagiarism upon the religious system their own mother Church had despoiled. This makeshift has served its purpose and had its day. The time has at last come when this page of history must be written.

CHAPTER V

"Learn to know all, but keep thyself unknown."— Gnostic Maxim

"There is one God supreme over all gods, diviner than mortals,
Whose form is not like unto man's, and as unlike his nature;
But vain mortals imagine that gods *like themselves are begotten*
With human sensations, and voice, and corporeal members."
— Xenophanes [501]

"Tychiades — Can you tell me the reason, Philocles, why most men desire to lye, and
delight not only to speak fictions themselves, but give busie attention to others who do?
"Philocles — There be many reasons, Tychiades, which compell some to speak lyes,
because they see 'tis profitable."— *A Dialog of Lucian*

"Spartan — Is it to thee, or to God, that I must confess?
"Priest — To God.
"Spartan—Then, man, stand back!"—Plutarch: *Remarkable Lacedemonian Sayings*

WE will now give attention to some of the most important Mysteries of the Kabala, and trace their relations to the philosophical myths of various nations.

In the oldest Oriental Kabala, the Deity is represented as three circles in one, shrouded in a certain smoke or chaotic exhalation. In the preface to the *Zohar*, which transforms the three primordial circles into Three Heads, there is said to be over them an exhalation or smoke, neither black nor white but colorless, and circumscribed within a circle. This is the unknown Essence.[502] The origin of the Jewish image may perhaps be traced to Hermes' *Pymander*, the Egyptian *Logos*, who appears within a cloud of a humid nature, with a smoke escaping from it.[503] In the *Zohar* the highest God is, as we have shown in the preceding chapter and as in the case of the Hindû and Buddhist philosophies, a pure abstraction, whose objective existence is denied by the latter. It is 'Hokhmah, the "Supreme Wisdom, that cannot be understood by reflexion," and that lies within and without the Cranium of Long Face [504] (Sephira), the uppermost of the three "Heads." It is the "boundless and the infinite Ain-Soph," the No-Thing.

The 'three Heads,' superimposed, are evidently taken from the three mystic triangles of the Hindûs, which are also superimposed. The highest 'head' contains the *Trinity in Chaos*, out of which springs the manifested trinity. Ain-Soph, the forever unrevealed, who is bound-

501. Clem. Alex.: *Strom.*, V, xiv.   502. Rosenroth: *Kabb. denudata*, II, p. 242.
503. Champollion-Figeac: *Egypte ancienne*, p. 141.   504. *Idrah Rabbah*, vi, § 58.

less and unconditioned, cannot create, and therefore it seems to us a great error to attribute to him a 'creative thought,' as is commonly done by the interpreters. In every cosmogony this supreme Essence is *passive;* if boundless, infinite, and unconditioned, it can have no *thought* or *idea.* It acts not as the result of volition, but in obedience to its own nature, and *according to the fatality of the law of which it is itself the embodiment.* Thus, with the Hebrew kabalists, Ain-Soph is non-existent אין, for it is incomprehensible to our finite intellects, and therefore cannot exist to our minds. Its first emanation was *Kether,* the Crown, כתר. When the time for an active period had come, then began a natural expansion of this Divine essence from within outwardly, obedient to eternal and immutable law; and from this eternal and infinite light (which to us is darkness) was emitted a spiritual substance.[505] This was the First of the Sephiroth, containing in herself the other nine ספירות, Sephiroth, or intelligences. In their totality and unity they represent the archetypal man, Adam Kadmon, the πρωτόγονος, who in his individuality or unity is yet dual, or bisexual (the Greek *Didumos*), for he is the prototype of all humanity. Thus we obtain three trinities, each contained in a 'head.' In the first head, or face (the three-faced Hindû *Trimûrti*), we find *Kether,* the first androgyne, at the apex of the upper triangle, emitting '*Hokhmah,* or Wisdom, a masculine and active potency — also called *Yah,* יה,— and *Binah,* בינה, or Intelligence, a female and passive potency, represented by the name *Yehovah,* יהוה. These three form the first trinity or 'face' of the Sephiroth. This triad emanated '*Hesed,* חסד, or Mercy, a masculine active potency, also called *Eloah,* from which emanated *Geburah,* גבורה, or Justice, also called *Pa'had,* a feminine passive potency; from the union of these two was produced *Tiphereth,* תפארת, Beauty, Clemency, the Spiritual Sun, known by the divine name *Elohim;* and the second triad, 'face,' or 'head,' was formed. These emanating produced in their turn the masculine potency *Netza'h,* נצח, Firmness, or *Yehovah-Tze'baoth,* who issued the feminine passive potency *Hod,* הוד, Splendor, or *Elohim-Tze'baoth;* from these proceeded *Yesod,* יסוד, Foundation, who is the mighty living one *El'haÿ,* thus yielding the third trinity or 'head.' The tenth Sephira is in fact a duad, and is represented on the diagrams as the lowest circle. It is *Malkhuth* or Kingdom, מלכות, and *Shekhinah,* שכינה, also called Adonaï, and *Cherubim* among the angelic hosts. The first 'Head' is called the Intellectual world; the second 'Head' is the Sensible, or the world of Perception; and the third is the Material or Physical world.

"Before he gave any shape to the universe," says the Kabala, "before

---

505. *Idrah Zutah,* ch. ii.

he produced any form, he was alone, without any form and resemblance to anything else. Who, then, can comprehend him or how he was before the creation, since he was formless? Hence it is forbidden to represent him by any form, similitude, or even by his sacred name, by a single letter, or a single point.[506] . . . The Aged of the Aged, the Unknown of the Unknown, has a form, and yet no form. He has a form whereby the universe is preserved, and yet has no form, because he cannot be comprehended. When he first assumed a form [in Sephira, his first emanation], he caused nine splendid lights to emanate from it." [507]

And now we will turn to the Hindû esoteric Cosmogony and definition of "Him who is, and yet is not."

"From him who is,[508] from this immortal Principle which exists in our minds but cannot be perceived by the senses, is born Purusha, the Divine male and female, who became *Nârâyana*, or the Divine Spirit moving on the water." [509]

Svayambhû, the unknown essence of the Brâhmanas, is identical with Ain-Soph, the unknown essence of the kabalists. As with the latter, the ineffable name could not be pronounced by the Hindûs, under the penalty of death. In the ancient primitive trinity of India, that which may be certainly considered as pre-Vedic, the *germ* which fecundates the *mother-principle*, the mundane egg, or the universal womb, is called *Nara*, the Spirit, or the Holy Ghost, which emanates from the primordial essence. It is like Sephira, the oldest emanation, called the *primordial point*, and the *White Head*, for it is the point of divine light appearing from within the fathomless and boundless darkness. In *Manu* it is "NARA," or the Spirit of God, which moves on "Ayana [Chaos, or place of motion], and is called NÂRÂYANA," or moving on the waters.[509] In Hermes, the Egyptian, we read: "In the beginning of time there was naught in the chaos." But when the *verbum*, issuing from the void like a "colorless smoke," makes its appearance, then "this *verbum* moved on the humid principle." [510] And in *Genesis* we find: "And darkness was upon the face of the deep [chaos]. And the Spirit of God moved upon the face of the waters." In the Kabala, the emanation of the primordial passive principle (Sephira), by dividing itself into two parts, active and passive, emits 'Hokhmah-Wisdom and Binah-Yehovah, and in conjunction with these two acolytes, which complete the trinity, becomes the Creator of the abstract Universe; the physical world being the produc-

---

506. *Zohar*, II, p. 42 b: Amst. ed., 1714.
507. *Ibid.*, III, p. 288 a, (*Idrah Zutah*, ch. i, §§ 41-3).
508. *Ego sum qui sum* (*Exod.*, iii, 14).
509. Jones: *Ordin. of Manu*, ch. i.
510. Champollion-Figeac: *Égypte ancienne*, p. 141.

tion of later and still more material powers.[511]   In the Hindû Cosmogony, *Svayambhû* emits *Nara* and *Nârî*, its bisexual emanation, and dividing its parts into two halves, male and female, these fecundate the mundane egg, within which develops Brahmâ, or rather *Virâj*, the Creator.   "The starting-point of the Egyptian mythology," says Champollion, "is a triad . . . namely, Kneph, Neith, and Phtah; and Ammon, the male, the father; Muth, the female and mother; and Khons, the son."

The ten Sephiroth are copies taken from the ten *Prajâpatis* created by *Virâj*, called the 'Lords of all beings,' and answering to the biblical Patriarchs.

Justin Martyr explains some of the 'heresies' of the day, but in a very unsatisfactory manner. *He shows, however, the identity of all the world-religions at their starting-points.* The first *beginning* opens invariably with the *unknown* and passive deity, producing from himself a certain active power or virtue, 'Rational,' which is sometimes called

---

511. We are fully aware that some Christian kabalists term Ain-Soph the 'Crown'; identify it with Sephira, or Kether; call Ain-Soph 'an emanation from God,' and make the ten Sephiroth comprise 'Ain-Soph' as a unity. They also very erroneously reverse the first two emanations of Sephira — 'Hokhmah and Binah. The greatest kabalists have always held 'Hokhmah (Wisdom) as a male and active intelligence, Yah, יה, and placed it under the No. 2 on the right side of the triangle, whose apex is the Crown, while Binah (Intelligence) or בינה, is under No. 3 on the left hand. But the latter, being represented by its divine name as Yehovah, יהוה, very naturally showed the God of Israel as only a third emanation, as well as a feminine, passive principle. Hence when the time came for the Talmudists to transform their multifarious deities into one living God, they resorted to their Masoretic points and combined to transform Jehovah into Adonai, 'the Lord.' This, under the persecution of the medieval Kabalists by the Church, also forced some of the former to change their female Sephiroth into male, and *vice versa*, so as to avoid being accused of disrespect and blasphemy to Jehovah; whose name, moreover, by mutual and secret agreement they accepted as a *substitute* for Yah, or the mystery name IAO. Alone the *initiated* knew of it, but later it gave rise to a great confusion among the *uninitiated*. It would be worth while — were it not for lack of space — to quote a few of the many passages in the oldest Jewish authorities, such as Rabbi A'qtbah, and in the *Zohar*, which corroborate our assertion. 'Hokhmah-Wisdom is a male principle everywhere, and Binah-Yehovah, a female potency. The writings of Irenaeus, Theodoret, and Epiphanius, teeming with accusations against the Gnostics and 'Heresies,' repeatedly show Simon Magus and Cerinthus making of Binah the feminine divine Spirit which inspired Simon. Binah is Sophia, and the Sophia of the Gnostics is surely not a male potency, but simply the feminine Wisdom, or Intelligence. (See any ancient *Arbor Kabbalistica*, or Tree of the Sephiroth.) Éliphas Lévi, in *Dogme et rituel de la haute magie*, Dogme, ch. x, places 'Hokhmah as No. 2 and as a male Sephira on the right hand of the Tree. In the Kabala the three male Sephiroth — 'Hokhmah, 'Hesed, Netza'h — are known as the Pillar of Mercy; and the three feminine on the left, namely, Binah, Geburah, Hod, are named the Pillar of Judgment; while the four Sephiroth of the center — Kether, Tiphereth, Yesod, and Malkhuth — are called the Middle Pillar. And as Mackenzie in the *Royal Masonic Cyclopaedia* shows, "there is an analogy in these three pillars to the three Pillars of Wisdom, Strength, and Beauty in a Craft Lodge of Masonry, while the Ain-Soph forms the mysterious blazing star, or mystic light of the East" (p. 407).

WISDOM, sometimes the SON, very often God, Angel, Lord, and LOGOS.[512]
The latter is sometimes applied to the very first emanation, but in
several systems it proceeds from the first androgyne or double ray produced at the beginning by the unseen. Philo depicts this wisdom as
male and female.[513] But though its first manifestation had a beginning —
for it proceeded from *Oulam* [514] (Aion, time), the highest of the Aeons
when emitted from the Fathers — it had remained with him *before all
creations*, for it is part of him.[515] Therefore Philo Judaeus calls Adam
Kadmon *'mind'* (the Ennoia of *Bythos* in the Gnostic system). "The
mind, let it be named Adam." [516]

Strictly speaking, it is difficult to view the Jewish *Book of Genesis*
otherwise than as a chip from the trunk of the mundane tree of universal
Cosmogony, rendered in Oriental allegories. As cycle succeeded cycle,
and one nation after another came upon the world's stage to play its brief
part in the majestic drama of human life, each new people evolved from
ancestral traditions its own religion, giving it a local color and stamping it
with its individual characteristics. While each of these religions had its
distinguishing traits by which, were there no other archaic vestiges, the
physical and psychological status of its creators could be estimated, all
preserved a common likeness to one prototype. This parent cult was none
other than the primitive Wisdom-Religion. The Israelitish *Scriptures* are
no exception. The national history of the Israelities — if they can claim
any autonomy before the return from Babylon, and were anything more
than migratory septs of Hindû pariahs — cannot be carried back a day
beyond Moses; and if this ex-Egyptian priest must from theological
necessity be transformed into a Hebrew patriarch, we must insist that
the Jewish nation was lifted with that smiling infant out of the bulrushes
of Lake Moeris. Abraham, their alleged father, belongs to the universal
mythology. Most likely he is but one of the numerous aliases of *Zeruan*
(Saturn), the king of the golden age, who is also called the old man
(emblem of time).[517]

It is now demonstrated by Assyriologists that in the old Chaldaean
books Abraham is called Zeru-an, or Zerb-an — meaning one very rich
in gold and silver, and a mighty prince.[518] He is also called Zarouan
and Zarman — a decrepit old man.[519]

---

512. *Dial. with Trypho*, cxxviii.   513. *De profugis*, § 9.
514. A division indicative of time.
515. Sanchoniathon calls time the oldest Aeon, *Protogonos*, the '*first-born*.'
516. *De cherubim*, part ii, 'Cain,' § 17; also *De mundo*, § 3.
517. Cf. Movers: *Die Phöniz.*, I, p. 86, *sq*. Azrael, angel of death, is also Israel. *Ab-ram*
means father of elevation, high-placed father; for Saturn is the highest or outermost
visible planet.   518. See *Genesis*, xiii, 2.
519. Saturn is generally represented as a very old man, with a sickle in his hand.

The ancient Babylonian legend is that Xisuthrus (Hasisadra of the Tablets,[519a] or Xisuthrus) sailed with his ark to Armenia,[520] and his son Sim became supreme king. Moses of Chorene says that Sim was called Zeruan; and Sim is Shem.[521] In Hebrew, his name writes םש, *Shem* — a sign. Assyria is held by the ethnologists to be the land of Shem, and Egypt called that of Ham. Shem, in the tenth chapter of *Genesis* is made the father of all the children of Eber, of Elam (Oulam or Eilam), and Ashur (Assur or Assyria). The *nephilim*, or fallen men, *Gebers*, mighty men spoken of in *Genesis* (vi, 4), come from *Oulam*, 'men of Shem.' Even Ophir, which is evidently to be sought for in the India of the days of Hiram, is made a descendant of Shem. The records are purposely mixed up to make them fit into the frame of the Mosaic *Bible*. But *Genesis*, from its first verse down to the last, has naught to do with the 'chosen people'; it belongs to the world's history. Its appropriation by the Jewish authors in the days of the so-called *restoration* of the destroyed books of the Israelites by Ezra proves nothing, and until now has been self-propped on an alleged divine revelation. It is simply a compilation of the universal legends of the universal humanity. Bunsen says that in the "Chaldaean tribe immediately connected with Abraham, we find reminiscences of dates disfigured or misunderstood, as genealogies of single men, or indications of epochs. The Abrahamic tribe-recollections go back at least three millenia beyond the grandfather of Jacob." [522]

Eupolemus says that Abraham was born at Kamarina or *Uria*, a city of soothsayers, and *invented astronomy*.[523] Josephus claims the same birthplace for Terah, Abraham's father. The tower of Babel was built as much by the direct descendants of Shem as by those of the 'accursed' Ham and Canaan, for the people in those days were 'one,' and the "whole earth was of one language"; Babel was simply an astrological tower, and its builders were astrologers and adepts of the primitive Wisdom-Religion, or again what we term Secret Doctrine.

The Berosian Sibyl says: Before the Tower, Zeru-an, Titan, and Yapetosthes governed the earth. Zeru-an wished to be supreme, but his two brothers resisted, when their sister, Astlik, intervened and appeased them. It was agreed that Zeru-an should rule, but his male children should be put to death; and strong Titans were appointed to carry this into effect.[524]

Sar (circle, *saros*) is the Babylonian god of the sky. He is also Assaros or Asshur (the son of Shem), and Zero — Zero-ana, the *chakra* or wheel, boundless time. Hence as the first step taken by Zoroaster,

---

519a. Or Atrakhasis; also called Utnapishtim, in the tablets.
520. Berosus in Eusebius: *Chronicon*, I, iii, 2; Abydenus, *ibid.*, I, vii.
521. Cf. Kleuker: *Anh. z. Zend-Avesta*, I, i, p. 189.   522. Bunsen: *Egypt's Place, etc.*, V, p. 85.   523. Euseb.: *Prasp. ev.*, IX.   524. *Berosi frag.*, p. 59; Ritter ed., 1825.

while founding his new religion, was to change the most sacred deities of the Sanskrit *Vedas* into names of evil spirits in his Zend *Scriptures*, and even to reject a number of them, we find no traces in the *Avesta* of Chakra — the symbolic circle of the sky.

Elam, another of the sons of Shem, is *Oulam*, עולם, and refers to an order or cycle of events. In *Ecclesiastes*, iii, 11, it is termed 'world.' In *Ezekiel*, xxvi, 20, 'of old time.' In *Genesis*, iii, 22, the word stands as 'forever'; and in chapter ix, 16, 'eternal.' Finally, the term is completely defined in *Genesis*, vi, 4, in the following words: "There were *nephilim* [giants, fallen men, or Titans] on the earth." The word is synonymous with Aeon, αἰών. In *Proverbs*, viii, 23, it reads: "I was effused from *Oulam*, from *Ras*" (wisdom). By this sentence the wise king-kabalist refers to one of the mysteries of the human spirit — the immortal crown of the man-trinity. While it ought to read as above, and be interpreted kabalistically to mean that the *I* (or my eternal, immortal *Ego*), the spiritual entity, was effused from the boundless and nameless eternity through the creative wisdom of the unknown God, it reads in the canonical translation: "The Lord possessed me in the beginning of his way, before his works of old!" which is unintelligible nonsense, without the kabalistic interpretation. When Solomon is made to say that *I* was "from the beginning . . . while as yet he [the Supreme Deity] had not made the earth nor the highest part of the dust of the world . . . I was there," and "when he appointed the foundations of the earth . . . then I was by him, *as one brought up with him*," what can the kabalist mean by the "*I*" but his own divine spirit, a drop effused from that eternal fountain of light and wisdom — the universal spirit of the Deity?

The thread of glory emitted by Ain-Soph from the highest of the three kabalistic heads, through which "all things shine with light," the thread which makes its exit through Adam *Primus*, is the individual spirit of every man. "I was daily his [Ain-Soph's] delight, rejoicing always before him . . . and my delights were *with the sons of men*," adds Solomon in the same chapter of the *Proverbs*. The immortal spirit delights in the *sons of men* who, without this spirit, are but dualities (physical body and astral soul, or that *life-principle* which animates even the lowest of the animal kingdom). But we have seen that the doctrine teaches that this spirit cannot unite itself with that man in whom matter and the grossest propensities of his animal soul will be ever crowding it out. Therefore Solomon, who is made to speak under the inspiration of his own spirit that possesses him for the time being, utters the following words of wisdom: "Hearken unto me, my son" (the dual man), "blessed are they who keep my ways. . . . Blessed is the man that heareth me, watching daily at my gates. . . . For whoso *findeth me, findeth life*, and shall obtain favor of the Lord. . . . But he that sinneth *against me* wrongeth his *own soul* . . . and loves *death*" (*Proverbs*, ch. viii).

This chapter as interpreted is made by some theologians, like everything else, to apply to Christ, the 'Son of God,' who states repeatedly that he who follows him obtains eternal life, and conquers death. But even in its distorted translation it can be demonstrated that it referred to anything but the alleged Savior. Were we to accept it in this sense, then the Christian theology would have to return, *nolens volens*, to Averroism and Buddhism; to the doctrine of emanation, in short; for Solomon says: "I was effused" from *Oulam* and *Rasit*, both of which are a part of the Deity; and thus Christ would not be, as their doctrine claims, God himself, but only an *emanation* of Him, like the Christos of the Gnostics. Hence the meaning of the personified Gnostic Aeon, the word signifying cycles or determined periods in the eternity, and at the same time representing a hierarchy of celestial beings — spirits. Thus Christ is sometimes termed the 'Eternal Aeon.' But the word 'eternal' is erroneous in relation to the Aeons. Eternal is that which has neither beginning nor end; but the 'Emanations' or Aeons, although having lived as absorbed in the divine essence from the eternity, when once individually emanated, must be said to have a beginning. They may be therefore *endless* in this spiritual life, never eternal.

These endless emanations of the one First Cause, all of which were gradually transformed by the popular fancy into distinct gods, spirits, angels, and demons, were so little considered immortal that all were assigned a limited existence. And this belief, common to all the peoples of antiquity, to the Chaldaean Magi as well as to the Egyptians, and even in our day held by the Brâhmanists and Buddhists, most triumphantly evidences the monotheism of the ancient religious systems. This doctrine calls the life-period of all the inferior divinities, "one day of Parabrahman." After a cycle of four milliards, three hundred and twenty-millions of human years — the tradition says — the trinity itself, with all the lesser divinities, will be annihilated, together with the universe, and cease to exist. Then another universe will gradually emerge from the *pralaya* (dissolution), and men on earth will be enabled to comprehend SVAYAMBHÛ as It is. Alone this primal cause will exist forever, in all Its glory, filling the infinite space. What better proof could be adduced of the deep reverential feeling with which the 'heathen' regard the one Supreme eternal cause of all things visible and invisible?

This is again the source from which the ancient Kabalists derived identical doctrines. If the Christians understood *Genesis* in their own way; and if accepting the texts literally they enforced upon the uneducated masses the belief in a creation of our world out of nothing, and moreover assigned to it a *beginning*, it is surely not the Tanaim, the sole expounders of the hidden meaning contained in the *Bible*, who are to be blamed. No more than any other philosophers had they ever believed either in spontaneous, limited, or *ex nihilo* creations. The Kabala has survived to show that their philosophy was precisely that of the modern Nepal Buddhists, the *Svâbhâvikas*. They believed *in the eternity and the indestructibility of matter*, and hence in many prior creations and destructions of worlds before our own. "There were old worlds which perished." [525] "From this we see that the Holy One, blessed be His name, had successively created and destroyed sundry worlds before he created the present world; and when he created this world he said: 'This pleases me; the previous ones did not please me.' " [526] Moreover, they believed, again like the *Svâbhâvikas*, now termed Atheists, that every thing proceeds (is created) from its own nature, and that once that the first impulse is given by that Creative Force inherent in the 'Self-created substance' or Sephira, everything evolves out of itself, following in pattern the more spiritual prototype which precedes it in the scale of infinite creation. "The indivisible point which has no limit and cannot be comprehended [for it is absolute], expanded from within and formed a brightness which served as a garment [a veil] to the indivisible point. . . . It also expanded from within. . . . Thus *everything originated through* a constant upheaving agitation, and thus finally the world originated." [527]

In the later Zoroastrian books, after Darius had both restored the worship of Ormazd and added to it the purer magianism of the primitive *Secret Wisdom* — חכמות־נסתרה, of which, as the inscription tells us, he was himself a hierophant — we see again reappearing the Zeru-ana, or boundless time, represented by the Brâhmanas in the *chakra*, or a circle, which we see figuring on the uplifted finger of the principal deities. Farther on we will show the relation in which it stands to the Pythagorean mystical numbers — the first and the last —which is a *zero* (O), and to the greatest of the Mystery-Gods IAO. The identity of this symbol alone, in all the old religions, is sufficient to show their common descent from one primitive Faith. [528] This term of 'boundless time,' which can be applied but to the ONE who has neither beginning nor end, is

---

525. *Zohar*, III, p. 292 b, Amst. ed., (*Idrah Zutah*, x, §§ 421, *sq.*).

526. *Beresshith Rabba*, parsha ix.				527. *Zohar*, I, p. 20a.

528. "The Sanskrit *s*," says Max Müller, "is represented by the Zend *h*. . . . Thus the geographical name *hapta hendu*, which occurs in the *Avesta*, becomes intelligible if we retranslate the Zend *h* into the Sanskrit *s*. For *sapta sindhu*, or the seven rivers, is the old Vedic name of India itself" (*Chips, etc.*, I, p. 81). The *Avesta* is the spirit of the *Vedas* — the esoteric meaning made partially known.

called by the Zoroastrians Zeruâna-Akarana, because he has always existed. His glory, they say, is too exalted, his light too resplendent for either human intellect to grasp or mortal eyes to see. His primal emanation is eternal light which, from having been previously concealed in darkness, was called out to manifest itself, and thus was formed Ormazd, 'the King of Life.' He is the first-born of boundless time, but like his own antitype, or pre-existing spiritual idea, has lived within primitive darkness from all eternity. His *Logos* created the pure intellectual world. After the lapse of three grand cycles [529] he created the material world in six periods. The six Amshaspends, or *primitive* spiritual men, whom Ormazd created in his own image, are the mediators between this world and himself. Mithras is an emanation of the Logos and the chief of the twenty-eight *yezidi*, who are the tutelary angels over the spiritual portion of mankind — the souls of men. The *Ferohers* are infinite in number. They are the ideas or rather the ideal conceptions of things which formed themselves in the mind of Ormazd or Ahuramazda before he willed them to assume a concrete form. They are what Aristotle terms 'privations' of forms and substances. The religion of Zarathustra, as he is always called in the *Avesta*, is one from which the ancient Jews have borrowed the most. In one of the *Yaśnas* Ahuramazda, the Supreme, gives to the seer as one of his sacred names *Ahmi*, 'I am'; and in another place, *ahmi yat ahmi*, 'I am that I am,' as Jehovah is alleged to have given it to Moses.

·This Cosmogony, adopted with a change of names in the Rabbinical Kabala, found its way later, with some additional speculations of Manes, the half-Magus, half-Platonist, into the great body of Gnosticism. The real doctrines of the Basilideans, Valentinians, and the Marcionites cannot be correctly ascertained in the prejudiced and calumnious writings of the Fathers of the Church; but rather in what remains of the works of the Bardesanians, known as the Nazarenes. It is next to impossible, now that all their manuscripts and books are destroyed, to assign to any of these sects its due part in dissenting views. But there are a few men still living who have preserved books and direct traditions about the Ophites, although they care little to impart them to the world. Among the unknown sects of Mount Lebanon and Palestine the truth has been concealed for more than a thousand years. And their *diagram* of the Ophite scheme differs from the description of it given by Origen [530] and hence from the *diagram* of J. Matter.[531]

529. What is generally understood in the *Avesta* system as a *thousand* years, means in the esoteric doctrine a cycle of a duration known but to the initiates, and which has an allegorical sense.   530. *Contra Celsum*, VI, xxiv, *sq.*

531. Jacq. Matter: *Histoire critique de gnosticisme*, pl. x: 1828.

The Kabalistic trinity is one of the models of the Christian one. "The ANCIENT whose name be sanctified, is with three heads, but which make only one." [532] *Tria capita exsculpta sunt, unum intra alterum, et alterum supra alterum.* "Three heads are inserted in one another, and one over the other. The first head is the Concealed Wisdom (*Sapientia Abscondita*). Under this head is the ANCIENT [Pythagorean *Monad*], the most hidden of mysteries; a head which is no head [*caput quod non est caput*]; no one can know what that is in this head. No intellect is able to comprehend this wisdom." [533] "This *Senior Sanctissimus* is surrounded by the three heads. He is the eternal LIGHT of the wisdom; and the wisdom is the source from which all the manifestations have begun. These three heads, included in ONE HEAD [which is no head]; and these three are bent down [overshadow] SHORT-FACE [the son] and through them all things shine with light." [534] "Ain-Soph emits a thread from El or *Al* [the highest God of the Trinity], and the light follows the thread and enters, and passing through makes its exit through Adam *Primus* [Kadmon], who is *concealed* until the plan for arranging [*statum dispositionis*] is ready; it threads through him from his head to his feet; and in him [in the concealed Adam] is the figure of A MAN." [535]

"Whoso wishes to have an insight into the sacred unity, let him consider a flame rising from a burning coal or a burning lamp. He will see first a two-fold light — a bright white, and a black or blue light; the white light is *above*, and ascends in a direct light, while the blue, or dark light, is *below*, and seems as the chair of the former, yet both are so intimately connected together that they constitute only one flame. The seat, however, formed by the blue or dark light, is again connected with the burning matter which is *under* it again. The white light never changes its color, it always remains white; but various shades are observed in the lower light, whilst the lowest light, moreover, takes two directions; *above*, it is connected with the white light, and *below* with the burning matter. Now, this is constantly consuming itself, and perpetually ascends to the upper light, and thus everything merges into a single unity." [536]

Such were the ancient ideas of the trinity in the unity, as an abstraction. Man, who is the microcosm of the macrocosm, or of the

---

532. *Idrah Zutah*, ii, § 78; *Zohar*, III, p. 288 b, Amst. ed., 1714.

533. *Idrah Zutah*, ii, §§ 59-63. 534. *Ibid.*, ii, § 63; vii, §§ 177-187.

535. Jam vero quoniam hoc in loco recondita est illa plane non utuntur, et tantum de parte lucis ejus participant quae demittitur et ingreditur intra filum Ain Soph protensum e Persona אל [*Al*, God] deorum: intratque et perrumpit et transit per Adam primum occultum usque in statum dispositionis transitque per eum a capite usque ad pedes ejus: *et in eo est figura hominis* (*Kabbala denudata*, II, p. 246).

536. *Zohar*, I, p. 51a, Amst. ed.

archetypal heavenly man, Adam Kadmon, is likewise a trinity; for he is *body*, *soul*, and *spirit*.

"All that is created by the 'Ancient of the Ancients' can live and exist only by a male and a female," says the *Zohar*.[537] He alone, to whom no one can say, 'Thou,' for he is the spirit of the WHITE-HEAD in whom the THREE HEADS are united, is uncreated. Out of the subtle fire, on one side of the White Head, and of the 'subtle air,' on the other, emanates Shekhinah, his veil (the femininized Holy Ghost). "This air," says *Idrah Rabbah*, "is the most occult [*occultissimus*] attribute of the Ancient of the Days.[538] The Ancient of the Ancient is the *Concealed* of the Concealed.[539] All things are Himself, and Himself is concealed in every way.[540] The *cranium* of the WHITE-HEAD has no beginning, but its end has a shining reflexion and a *roundness* which is our universe." [541]

"They regard," says Kleuker, "the first-born as man and wife, in so far as his light includes in itself all other lights, and in so far as his spirit of life or breath of life includes all other life-spirits in itself." [542] The kabalistic Shekhinah answers to the Ophite Sophia. Properly speaking, Adam Kadmon is the Bythos, but in this emanation-system, where everything is calculated to perplex and place an obstacle to inquiry, he is the *Source* of Light, the first 'primitive man,' and at the same time *Ennoia*, the Thought of Bythos, the Depth, for he is Pymander.

The Gnostics, as well as the Nazarenes, allegorizing on the personification, said that the *First* and *Second* man loved the beauty of Sophia, (Sephira) the first woman, and thus the Father and the Son fecundated the heavenly 'Woman' and from primal darkness procreated the visible light (Sephira is the Invisible, or Spiritual Light), "whom they called the ANOINTED CHRISTUS, or King Messiah." [543] This Christus is the *Adam of Dust* before his fall, with the spirit of the Adonai, his Father, and Shekhinah-Adonai, his mother, upon him; for Adam Primus is Adon, Adonai, or Adonis. The primal existence manifests itself by its wisdom, and produces the *Intelligible* LOGOS (all visible creation). This wisdom was venerated by the Ophites under the form of a serpent. So far we see that the first and second life are the two Adams, or the first and the second man. In the former lies *Eva*, or the yet unborn spiritual Eve, and she is within Adam *Primus*, for she is a part of himself, who is androgyne. The Eva of dust, she who will be called in

---

537. *Idrah Zutah*, viii, § 219; cf. *Zohar*, III, 290 a, Amst. ed.
538. *Idrah Rabbah*, §§ 541-2.   539. *Ibid.*, § 36.   540. *Ibid.*, § 172.
541. *Idrah Zutah*, ii, § 51.   542. *Nat. u. Urspr. d. Emanationslehre, u. s. w.*, p. 11.
543. Irenaeus: *Against Heresies*, I, xxx, § 1.

Genesis "the mother of all that live," is *within* Adam the Second. And now, from the moment of its first manifestation, the LORD MANO, the Unintelligible Wisdom, disappears from the scene of action. It will manifest itself only as Shekhinah, the GRACE; for the CORONA is "the innermost Light of all Lights," and hence it is darkness's own substance.[544]

In the Kabala, *Shekhinah* is the ninth emanation of Sephira, which contains the whole of the ten Sephiroth within herself. *Shekhinah* belongs to the third triad, and is produced together with *Malkhuth* or 'Kingdom,' of which she is the female counterpart. Otherwise she is held to be higher than any of these; for she is the 'Divine Glory,' the 'veil' or 'garment' of Ain-Soph. The Jews, whenever she is mentioned in the *Targumim*, say that she is the glory of Yehovah, which dwelt in the tabernacle, manifesting herself like a visible cloud; the 'Glory' rested over the Mercy-Seat in the *Sanctum Sanctorum*.

In the Nazarene or Bardesanian System, which may be termed the Kabala within the Kabala, the Ancient of Days — *Antiquus Altus* — who is the Father of the Demiurge of the universe, is called the *Third* Life, or *Abatur*; and he is the Father of *Fetahil*, who is the architect of the visible universe, which he calls into existence by the powers of his genii at the order of the 'Greatest'; the Abatur answering to the 'Father' of Jesus in the later Christian theology. These two superior *Lives* then are the crown within which dwells the greatest *Ferho*. "Before any creature came into existence the Lord Ferho existed." [545] This one is the First Life, formless and invisible; in whom the living Spirit of LIFE exists, the Highest GRACE. The two are ONE from eternity, for they are the Light and the CAUSE of the Light. Therefore they answer to the kabalistic concealed *wisdom*, and to the concealed Shekhinah — the Holy Ghost. "This light, which is manifested, is the garment of the Heavenly Concealed," says *Idrah Zutah*.[546] And the 'heavenly man' is the superior Adam. "No one knows his paths except *Macroprosopus*" (Long-face) — the Superior *active* god.[547] Not as I am *written* will I be read; in this world my name will be written Yehovah and read Adonai," [548] say the Rabbins, very correctly. Adonai is the Adam Kadmon; he is FATHER and MOTHER both. By this double mediatorship the Spirit of the 'Ancient of the Ancient' descends upon the *Microprosopus* (Short-face) or the Adam of Eden. And the "Lord God breathes into his nostrils the breath of life."

When the woman separates herself from her androgyne, and becomes

---

544. *Idrah Zutah*, ix, § 353; *Kabb. denudata*, II, p. 364; compare Pythagoras' Monad.
545. *Cod. Naz.*, I, p. 145.   546. *Idrah Zutah*, ix, § 355.   547. *Idrah Rabbah*, viii, §109.
548. *Auszüge aus d. B. Sohar*, p. 11 (Berlin, 1857); *Zohar*, III, p. 230, Amst. ed.

a distinct individuality, the first story is repeated over again. Both the Father and Son, the two Adams, love her beauty; and then follows the allegory of the temptation and fall. It is the same in the Kabala as in the Ophite system, in which both the Ophis and the Ophiomorphos are emanations emblematized as serpents, the former representing Eternity, Wisdom, and Spirit (as in the Chaldaean Magism of Aspic-worship and Wisdom-Doctrine in the olden times), and the latter Cunning, Envy and Matter. Both spirit and matter are serpents; and Adam Kadmon becomes the Ophis who tempts himself — man and woman — to taste of the 'Tree of Good and Evil,' in order to teach them the mysteries of spiritual wisdom. Light tempts Darkness, and Darkness attracts Light, for Darkness is *matter*, and "the *Highest* Light shines not in its *Tenebrae.*" With knowledge comes the temptation of the Ophiomorphos, and he prevails. The dualism of every existing religion is shown forth by the fall. "I have gotten a man from *the Lord*," exclaims Eve, when the Dualism, Cain and Abel — evil and good — is born. "And the Adam knew Hua, his woman (*astu*), and she became pregnant and bore *Kin*, and she said: קינתי איש את יהוה: *Kaniti ais ath* Yava — I have gained or obtained a husband, even *Yava* — Is, Ais — man." "*Cum arbore peccati Deus creavit seculum.*"

And now we will compare this system with that of the Jewish Gnostics — the Nazarenes, as well as with other philosophies.

The Ish Amon, the pleroma, or the boundless circle within which lie 'all forms,' is the THOUGHT of the power divine; it works in SILENCE, and suddenly light is begotten by darkness; it is called the SECOND life; and this one produces, or generates, the THIRD. This third light is 'the FATHER of all things that live,' as EUA is the 'mother of all that live.' He is the Creator who calls inert matter into life, through his vivifying spirit, and, therefore, is called the ancient of the world. Abatur is the 'Father' who creates the first Adam, who creates in his turn the second. Abatur opens a gate and walks to the dark water (chaos), and looking down into it, the darkness reflects the image of Himself . . . and lo! a Son is formed — the Logos or Demiurge; *Fetahil*, who is the builder of the *material* world, is called into existence. According to the Gnostic dogma, this was the *Metatron*, the Archangel Gabriel, or Messenger of Life; or, as the biblical allegory has it, the androgynous Adam-Kadmon again, the SON who, with his Father's spirit, produces the ANOINTED, or Adam before his fall.

When *Svayambhû*, the 'Lord who exists through himself,' feels impelled to manifest himself, he is thus described in the Hindû sacred books:

"Having been impelled to produce various beings from his own divine

substance, he first manifested the waters which developed within themselves a productive seed.

"The seed became a germ bright as gold, blazing like the luminary
with a thousand beams; and in that egg he was born himself, in the
form of BRAHMA, the great principle of all the beings" (*Manu*, I,
slokas 8, 9).

The Egyptian Kneph, or Chnuphis, Divine Wisdom, represented by
a serpent, produces an egg from his mouth, from which issues *Ptah*.
In this case *Ptah* represents the universal germ, as well as Brahma, who
is of the neuter gender, when the final *a* has no accent over it; [549] otherwise it becomes simply one of the names of the Deity. The former was
the model of the THREE LIVES of the Nazarenes, as that of the kabalistic
'Faces,' PARTZUPHIM, which, in its turn, furnished the model for the
Christian Trinity of Irenaeus and his followers. The egg was the primitive matter which served as a material for the building of the visible
universe; it contained, as well as the Gnostic Pleroma, the kabalistic
Shekhinah, the man and wife, the spirit and life, "whose light includes all
other lights" or life-spirits. This first manifestation was symbolized by a
serpent, which is at first *divine* wisdom, but, *falling into generation*,
becomes polluted. *Ptah* is the heavenly man, the Egyptian Adam-
Kadmon, or Christos who, in conjunction with the female Holy Ghost,
the ZOE, produces the five elements, air, water, fire, earth, and ether;
the latter being a servile copy from the Buddhist *Adi*, and his five
Dhyâni-Buddhas, as we have shown in the preceding chapter. The
Hindû *Svâyambhuva-Nara* develops from himself the *mother-principle*,
enclosed within his own divine essence — *Nâri*, the immortal Virgin who,
when impregnated by his spirit, becomes *Tanmâtra*, the mother of the
five elements — air, water, fire, earth, and ether. Thus may be shown
how from the Hindû cosmogony all others proceed.

Knorr von Rosenroth, busying himself with the interpretation of the
Kabala, argues that "In this first state (of secret wisdom), the infinite
God himself can be understood as 'Father' (of the new covenant).
But the *Light*, being let down by the Infinite through a canal into the
'primal Adam' or *Messiah*, and joined with him, can be applied to the
name SON. And the influx emitted down from him [the Son] to the
lower parts [of the universe], can be referred to the character of the Holy
Ghost." [550] Sophia-Achamoth, the half-spiritual, half-material LIFE,
which vivifies the inert matter in the depths of chaos, is the Holy Ghost of
the Gnostics, and the *Spiritus* (female) of the Nazarenes. She is — be it
remembered — the *sister* of *Christos*, the perfect emanation, and both are

---

549. He is the universal and spiritual germ of *all* things.
550. *Adumbratio Kabb. Chr.*, pp. 6, 7.

children or emanations of Sophia, the purely spiritual and intellectual daughter of Bythos, the Depth. For the elder Sophia is Shekhinah, the Face of God, "God's Shekhinah, which is his image." [551]

"The *Son* Zeus-Belus, or Sol-Mithra, is an image of the Father, an emanation from the *Supreme Light*," says Movers. "He passed for Creator." [552]

"Philosophers say the first air is *anima mundi*. But the garment (Shekhinah) is higher than the first air, since it is joined more closely to the Ain-Soph, the Boundless." [553] Thus *Sophia* is Shekhinah, and Sophia-Achamoth the *anima mundi*, the astral light of the kabalists, which contains the spiritual and material germs of all *that is*. For the Sophia-Achamoth, like *Eve*, of whom she is the prototype, is 'the mother of all that live.'

There are three trinities in the Nazarene system as well as in the Hindû philosophy of the ante- and early-Vedic period. While we see the few translators of the Kabala, the Nazarene *Codex*, and other abstruse works, hopelessly floundering amid the interminable pantheon of names, unable to agree as to a system in which to classify them, for the one hypothesis contradicts and overturns the other, we can but wonder at all this trouble, which could be so easily overcome. But even now, when the translation and even the perusal of the ancient Sanskrit has become so easy as a point of comparison, they would never think it possible that every philosophy — whether Semitic, Hamitic, or Turanian (as they call it) — has its key in the Hindû sacred works. Still the facts are there, and facts are not easily destroyed. Thus, while we find the Hindû *trimûrti* triply manifested as

Nara (or Para-Purusha)	Agni	Brahmâ	the Father
Nârî (Mahâmâyâ)	Vâyu	Vishnu	the Mother
Virâj (Brahmâ)	Sûrya	Śiva	the Son

and the Egyptian trinity as follows,

Kneph (or *Amen*)	Osiris	Râ (Horus)	the Father
Maut (or *Mut*)	Isis	Isis	the Mother
Khonsu	Horus	Malouli	the Son [554]

the Nazarene System runs,

Ferho (Iah-Amon)	Mano	Abatur	the Father
Chaos (dark water)	Spiritus (female)	Netubto	the Mother
Fetahil	Lehdoio	Lord Jordan	the Son

The first [trinity of each system] is the concealed or non-manifested trinity — a pure abstraction. The second is the active or the one

551. *Idrah Rabbah*, xliv, § 1122.   552. *Die Phönizier*, I, pp. 265, 550.
553. *Kabb. denud.*, II, p. 236.   554. Champollion-Figeac: *Égypte ancienne.*, pp. 245-6.

revealed in the results of creation, proceeding out of the former — its spiritual prototype. The third is the mutilated image of both the others, crystallized in the form of human dogmas, which vary according to the exuberance of the national materialistic fancy.

The Supreme Lord of splendor and of light, luminous and refulgent, before which no other existed, is called Corona (the crown); Lord Ferho, the unrevealed life which existed in the former from eternity; and Lord Jordan — the spirit, the living water of grace.[555] He is the one through whom alone we can be saved; and thus he answers to the Shekhinah, or the Holy Spirit, the spiritual garment of Ain-Soph. These three constitute the trinity in *abscondito.* The second trinity is composed of the three lives. The first is the similitude of Lord Ferho, through whom he has proceeded forth; and the second Ferho is the King of Light — MANO (*Rex Lucis*). He is the heavenly life and light, and older than the Architect of heaven and earth.[556] The second life is *Ish Amon* [or Iushamin] (Pleroma), the vase of election, containing the visible thought of the *Iordanus Maximus* — the *type* (or its intelligible reflexion), the prototype of the living water, who is the 'spiritual Jordan.'[557] The third life, which is produced by the other two, is ABATUR (*Ab*, the Parent or Father). This is the mysterious and decrepit 'Aged of the Aged,' the "Ancient *Senem sui obtegentem et grandaevum mundi.*" This latter third Life is the Father of the Demiurge Fetahil, the Creator of the world, whom the Ophites call Ilda-Baoth,[558] though Fetahil is the *only-begotten one,* the reflexion of the Father, Abatur, who begets him by looking into the 'dark water';[559] but the Lord Mano, "the Lord of loftiness, the Lord of all genii," is higher than the Father in this kabalistic *Codex* — one is purely spiritual, the other material. So for instance while Abatur's "only-begotten" one is the genius Fetahil, the Creator of the physical world; Lord Mano the 'Lord of Celsitude,' who is the son of Him who is "the Father of all who preach the Gospel," produces also an "only-begotten" one, the Lord Lehdoio, "a just Lord." He is the Christos, the anointed, who pours out the 'grace' of the Invisible Jordan, the Spirit of the *Highest Crown.*

In the Arcanum, "in the assembly of splendor, lighted by MANO, to whom the scintillas of splendor owe their origin," the genii who live in light "arose and went to the visible Jordan and flowing water, where they assembled for a counsel, and called forth the Only-Begotten Son

---

555. *Codex Nazaraeus,* II, pp. 47-57.   556. *Ibid.,* I, p. 145.
557. *Ibid.,* II, p. 211.   558. *Ibid.,* I, p. 309.
559. Sophia Achamoth also begets her son Ilda-Baoth, the *Demiurge,* by looking into chaos or matter, and by coming in contact with it.

of an imperishable image who cannot be conceived by reflexion, Lehdoio
the just Lord, and sprung from Lehdoio the just lord, whom the Life
had produced by his word." [560]

Mano is the chief of the seven Aeons, who are Mano (*Rex Lucis*)
Aiar Zivo, Ignis Vivus, Lux, Vita, Aqua Viva (the living water of baptism, the genius of the Jordan), and Ipsa Vita, the chief of the six
genii, which form with him the mystic *seven*. The Nazarene Mano is
simply the copy of the Hindû first Manu — the emanation of Manu-
Svâyambhuva — from whom evolve in succession the six other Manus,
types of the subsequent races of men. We find them all represented by
the apostle-kabalist John in the "seven lamps of fire" burning before
the throne, which are the seven spirits of God,[561] and in the seven angels
bearing the seven vials. Again in Fetahil we recognise the original of
the Christian doctrine.

In the *Revelation* of Joannes Theologos it is said: "I turned and
saw in the midst of the *seven* candlesticks one like unto the Son of
man . . . his head and his hairs were white like wool, as white as snow;
and his eyes were as a flame of fire; and his feet like unto fine brass,
as if they burned in a furnace" (i, 13, 14, 15). *John* here repeats, as is
well known, the words of Daniel and Ezekiel. "The Ancient of Days
. . . whose hair was white as pure wool . . . etc." And "the appearance of a *man* . . . above the throne . . . and the appearance of fire,
and it had brightness round about" [562] — the fire being "the glory of the
Lord." Fetahil is son of the man, the Third Life, and his upper part
is represented as white as snow, while standing near the throne of the
living fire he has the appearance of a flame.

All these 'apocalyptic' visions are based on the description of the
'white head' of the *Zohar*, in whom the kabalistic trinity is united —
the white head "which conceals in its cranium the spirit," and which is
environed by subtle fire. The "appearance of a man" is that of Adam
Kadmon, through which passes the thread of light represented by the
fire. Fetahil is the *Vir Novissimus* (the newest man), the son of Abatur,[563]
the latter being the 'man,' or the *third* life,[564] now the third personage of
the trinity. *John* sees "one like unto the son of man," holding in his
right hand seven stars, and standing between "seven golden candlesticks" (*Rev.*, i, 13, 16). Fetahil takes his "stand on high," according to
the will of his father, "the highest Aeon who has seven sceptres" and

---

560. *Codex Nazaraeus*, II, pp. 107-9; see *Sôd, the Son of the Man*, p. 60, for translation.
561. *Revelation*, iv, 5.   562. *Ezekiel*, i, 26, 27.   563. *Cod. Naz.*, II, p. 127.
564. The first androgyne duad, being considered a *unit* in all the secret computations,
is therefore the Holy Ghost.

seven genii who astronomically represent the seven planets or "stellars."
He stands "shining in the garment of the Lords, resplendent by the
agency of the genii," [565] He is the Son of his Father, Life, and his mother,
Spirit, or Light. [566] The Logos is represented in the *Gospel according to
John* as one in whom was "*Life*, and the life was the *light* of men" (i, 4).
Fetahil is the Demiurge, and his father created the visible universe of
matter through him. [567] In the *Epistle of Paul to the Ephesians* (iii, 9),
God is said to have "*created all things* by Jesus." In the *Codex Nazaraeus*
the Parent-LIFE says: "Arise, go, our son first-begotten, ordained for all
creatures." [568] "As the living Father hath sent me," says Christ, "God
sent his only-begotten Son that we might live." [569] Finally, having performed his work on earth, Fetahil reascends to his father Abatur. "*Et
qui, relicto quem procreaverat mundo, ad Abatur suum patrem contendit.*" [570]
"My father sent me . . . I go to the Father," repeats Jesus.

Laying aside the theological disputes of Christianity which try to
blend together the Jewish Creator of the first chapter of *Genesis* with
the 'Father' of the *New Testament*, Jesus states repeatedly of his Father
that "He is *in secret*." Surely he would not have so termed the ever-
present 'Lord God' of the Mosaic books, who showed Himself to Moses
and the Patriarchs, and finally allowed all the elders of Israel to look
on Himself. [571] When Jesus is made to speak of the temple at Jerusalem
as of his "Father's house," he does not mean the physical building,
which he maintains he can destroy and then again rebuild in three
days, but of the temple of Solomon the wise Kabalist, who indicates
in his *Proverbs* that every man is the temple of God, or of his own
divine spirit. This term of the "Father who is in secret," we find
used as much in the Kabala as in the *Codex Nazaraeus*, and elsewhere.
No one has ever seen the wisdom concealed in the 'Cranium,' and
no one has beheld the 'Depth' (Bythos). Simon the *Magician* preached
"one Father unknown to all." [572]

We can trace this appellation of a 'secret' God still farther back.
In the Kabala the 'Son' of the *concealed* Father who dwells in light
and glory is the 'Anointed,' the *Ze'ir Anpin*, who unites in himself all
the Sephiroth; he is Christos, or the Heavenly man. It is through
Christos that the Pneuma, or the Holy Ghost, creates 'all things'
(*Ephesians*, iii, 9), and produces the four elements, air, water, fire, and

565. *Codex Nazaraeus*, III, p. 59.   566. *Ibid.*, I, p. 285.   567. *Ibid.*, I, p. 309.
568. *Ibid.*, I, p. 287. See *Sôd, the Son of the Man*, p. 101.
569. *John*, vi, 57; *1 John*, iv, 9.   570. *Codex Nazaraeus*, II, p. 123.
571. "Then went up Moses and Aaron, Nadab and Abihu, and seventy of the elders
of Israel. *And they saw the God of Israel*," *Exodus*, xxiv, 9, 10.
572. *Clement. Homil.*, XVIII, xxii; Irenaeus: *Against Heresies*, II, pref., sq.

earth. This assertion is unquestionable, for we find Irenaeus basing on this fact his best argument for the necessity of there being four gospels. There can be neither more nor fewer than four — he argues. "For as there are four quarters of the world, and four general winds (καθολικὰ πνεύματα) . . . it is right that she [the Church] should have four pillars. . . . From which it is manifest that the Word, *the maker of all*, he *who sitteth upon the Cherubim* . . . as David says, supplicating his advent, 'Thou that sittest between the Cherubim, shine forth!' For the Cherubim also are *four-faced* and their faces are symbols of the working of the Son of God." [573]

We will not stop to discuss at length the special holiness of the four-faced Cherubim, although we might perhaps show their origin in all the ancient pagodas of India, in the *vâhanas* (or vehicles) of their chief gods; as likewise we might easily attribute the respect paid to them to the kabalistic wisdom, which nevertheless the Church rejects with great horror. But we cannot resist the temptation to remind the reader that he may easily ascertain the several significances attributed to these Cherubs by reading the Kabala. "When the souls are to leave their abode," says the *Zohar*, holding to the doctrine of the pre-existence of souls in the world of emanations, "each soul separately appears before the Holy King, dressed in a sublime form, with the features in which it is to appear in this world. It is from this sublime form that the image proceeds." [574] Then it goes on to say that the types or forms of these faces "are four in number — those of the angel or man, of the lion, the bull, and the eagle." Furthermore, we may well express our wonder that Irenaeus should not have re-enforced his argument for the four gospels by citing the whole Pantheon of the four-armed Hindû gods!

Ezekiel in representing his four animals, now called Cherubim, as types of the four symbolical beings which in his visions support the throne of Jehovah, had not far to go for his models. The Chaldaeo-Babylonian protecting genii were familiar to him; the Sed, Alaph or *Kirub* (Cherubim), the bull, with the human face; the Nergal, human-headed lion; Ustur, the Sphinx-man; and the Nattig, with its eagle's head. [574a] The religion of the masters — the idolatrous Babylonians and Assyrians — was transferred almost bodily into the revealed Scripture of the Captives, and from thence came into Christianity.

Already we find Ezekiel addressed by the likeness of the glory of the Lord "as Son of man." This peculiar title is used repeatedly

573. *Against Heresies*, III, xi, § 8.   574. *Zohar*, III, p. 104; Amst. ed.
574a. I. Myer: *Qabbalah*, pp. 227-8: Phila., 1888; A. H. Sayce: *Records of the Past*, III p. 121; J. Kitto: *Cyclop.-Bibl. Lit.*, I, p. 484; F. Lenormant: *Chald. Magic*, pp. 39, 47, 121,

throughout the whole book of this prophet, which is as kabalistic· as the "roll of a book" which the "Glory" causes him to eat. It is written *within* and *without;* and its real meaning is identical with that of the *Apocalypse.* It appears strange that so much stress should be laid on this peculiar appellation, said to have been applied by Jesus to himself, when in the symbolical or kabalistic language a prophet is so addressed. It is as extraordinary to see Irenaeus indulging in such graphic descriptions of Jesus as to show him, "the maker of all, sitting upon a Cherub," [575] unless he identifies him with Shekhinah, whose usual place was among the Charoubs of the Mercy Seat. We also know that the Cherubim and Seraphim are titles of the 'Old Serpent' (the orthodox Devil) the Seraphs being the burning or fiery serpents, in kabalistic symbolism. The ten emanations of Adam Kadmon, called the Sephiroth, have all emblems and titles corresponding to each. So for instance the last two are Victory, or Yehovah-Tze'baoth, whose symbol is the right column of Solomon, the Pillar *Jachin;* while GLORY is the left Pillar, or Boaz, and its name is 'the Old Serpent,' and also 'Seraphim and Cherubim.' [576]

The 'Son of man' is an appellation which could not be assumed by any one but a Kabalist. As shown above, in the *Old Testament* it is used by but one prophet — Ezekiel, the Kabalist. In their mysterious and mutual relations, the Aeons or Sephiroth are represented in the Kabala by a great number of circles, and sometimes by the figure of a MAN, which is symbolically formed out of such circles. This man is Ze'ir Anpin, and the 243 numbers of which his figure consists relate to the different orders of the celestial hierarchy. The original idea of this figure, or rather the model, may have been taken from the Hindû Brahmâ, and the various castes typified by the several parts of his body, as King suggests in his *Gnostics.* In one of the grandest and most beautiful cave-temples at Ellora, Nasak, dedicated to *Viśvakarman*, son of Brahmâ, is a representation of this God and his attributes. To one acquainted with Ezekiel's description of the "likeness of four living creatures," every one of which had four faces and the hands of a man under its wings, etc.,[577] this figure at Ellora must certainly appear absolutely *biblical.* Brahmâ is called the father of 'man,' as well as Jupiter and other highest gods.

It is in the Buddhistic representations of Mount Meru, called by the Burmese *Myé-nmo*, and by the Siamese *Sineru,* that we find one of the originals of the Adam Kadmon, Ze'ir Anpin, the 'heavenly man,' and of all the Aeons, Sephiroth, Powers, Dominions, Thrones, Virtues, and

575. Irenaeus: *Fragments,* lii, liv.
576. C. W. King: *The Gnostics, etc.,* p. 35; 2nd ed.   577. *Ezekiel,* i.

Dignities of the Kabala. Between two pillars, which are connected by an arch, the keystone of the latter is represented by a *crescent*. This is the domain in which dwells the Supreme Wisdom of *Âdi-Buddha*, the Supreme and invisible Deity. Beneath this highest central point comes the circle of the direct emanation of the Unknown — the circle of Brahmâ with some Hindûs, of the first *avatâra* of Buddha, according to others. This answers to Adam Kadmon and the ten Sephiroth. Nine of the emanations are encircled by the tenth, and are occasionally represented by pagodas, each of which bears a name which expresses one of the chief attributes of the manifested Deity. Then below come the seven stages, or heavenly spheres, each sphere being encircled by a sea. These are the celestial mansions of the *devatâs*, or gods, each losing somewhat in holiness and purity as it approaches the earth. Then comes Meru itself, formed of numberless circles within three large ones, typifying the trinity of man; and for one acquainted with the numerical value of the letters in biblical names, like that of the 'Great Beast,' or that of Mithra, μειθρας αβραξας, and others, it is an easy matter to establish the identity of the Meru-gods with the emanations or Sephiroth of the kabalists. Also the genii of the Nazarenes, with their special missions, are all found in this most ancient *mythos*, a most perfect representation of the symbolism of the 'secret doctrine' as taught in archaic ages.

King gives a few hints — though doubtless insufficient to teach anything important, for they are based upon the calculations of Bishop Newton [578]— as to this mode of finding out mysteries in the value of letters. However we find this great archaeologist, who has devoted so much time and labor to the study of Gnostic gems, corroborating our assertion. He shows that the entire theory is Hindû, and points out that the *durgâ*, or female counterpart of each Asiatic god, is what the kabalists term active *Virtue* [579] in the celestial hierarchy, a term which the Christian Fathers adopted and repeated without fully appreciating, and the meaning of which the later theology has utterly disfigured. But to return to Meru.

---

578. *The Gnostics and their Remains*, pp. 253, sq., 262; 2nd edition.

579. "Although this science is commonly supposed to be peculiar to the Jewish Talmudists, there is no doubt that they borrowed the idea from a foreign source, and that from the Chaldaeans, the *founders of magic art*," says King, in *The Gnostics*. The titles *Iao* and *Abraxas*, etc., instead of being recent Gnostic figments, were indeed holy names borrowed from the most ancient formulae of the East. Pliny must allude to them when he mentions the virtues ascribed by the Magi to amethysts engraved with the names of the sun and moon, names not expressed in either the Greek or Latin tongues. (*Nat. Hist.*, xxxviii, § 41). In the '*Eternal Sun*,' the '*Abraxas*,' the '*Adonai*' of these gems, we recognise the very amulets ridiculed by the philosophic Pliny (*The Gnostics etc.*, p. 283; 2nd ed.) — *Virtutes* (miracles) as employed by Irenaeus.

The whole is surrounded by the *Mahâ-Samudra*, or the great sea —
the astral light and ether of the kabalists and scientists; and within the
central circles appears 'the likeness of a man.' He is the Achamoth of
the Gnostics, the twofold unity, or the androgyne man; the heavenly
incarnation, and a perfect representation of *Ze'ir Anpîn* (short-face), the
son of *A'rîkh Anpîn* (long-face).[580] This likeness is now represented in
many lamaseries by Gautama-Buddha, the last of the incarnated avatars.
Still lower, under the Meru, is the dwelling of the great *Nâga*, who is
called *Nâga-Râja*, the king-serpent — the serpent of *Genesis*, the Gnostic
Ophis — and the goddess of the earth, *Bhûmayî-Nârî*, or *Yâmî*, who waits
upon the great dragon, for she is Eve, 'the mother of all that live.' Still
lower is the eighth sphere, the infernal regions. The uppermost regions
of Brahmâ are surrounded by the sun, moon, and planets, the 'seven
stellars' of the Nazarenes, and just as they are described in the *Codex*.

"The seven impostor-Daemons who deceive the sons of Adam. The
name of one is *Sol;* of another *Spiritus Venereus*, Astro . . . ; of the
third *Nebu*, Mercurius, *a false Messiah;* . . . the name of a fourth is *Sin*,
Luna; the fifth is *Kivan* (*Kiun*), Saturnus; the sixth, *Bel*, Zeus; the
seventh, *Nerig*, Mars."[581] Then there are "*Seven Lives* procreated,"
seven good Stellars, "which are from *Kebar-Zivo*, and are those bright
ones who shine in their own form and splendor that pours from on high.
. . . At the gate of the HOUSE OF LIFE the throne is fitly placed for the
Lord of Splendor, . . . and there are THREE habitations."[582] The habitations of the *Trimûrti*, the Hindû trinity, are placed beneath the keystone
— the golden crescent, in the representation of Meru. "And there was
under his feet [of the God of Israel] as it were a paved work of a sapphire-
stone" (*Exod.*, xxiv, 10). Under the crescent is the heaven of Brahmâ,
all paved with sapphires. The paradise of Indra is resplendent with a
thousand suns; that of Śiva (Saturn) is in the northeast; his throne is
formed of lapis-lazuli and the floor of heaven is of fervid gold. "When he
sits on the throne he blazes with fire up to *the loins*." At Hardvâr, during
the fair in which he is more than ever *Mahâdeva* the highest god, the
attributes and emblems sacred to the Jewish 'Lord God' may be recognised one by one in those of Śiva. The Binlang stone,[583] sacred to this
Hindû deity, is an unhewn stone like the Beth-el, consecrated by the
Patriarch Jacob, and set up by him "for a pillar," and like the latter

---

580. So called to distinguish the short-face, who *is exterior*, "from the venerable sacred
ancient" (cf. *Idrah Rabbah*, iii, § 36; v, § 54). *Ze'ir Anpîn* is the 'image of the Father.'
"He that hath seen me hath seen the Father" (*John*, xiv, 9).

581. Norberg: *Codex Nazaraeus*, I, p. 55.   582. *Ibid.*, III, p. 61.

583. This stone, of a sponge-like surface, is found in the Nerbudda river, and is seldom
to be seen in other places.

Binlang is *anointed*. We need hardly remind the student that the *linga*, the emblem sacred to Śiva, and whose temples are modeled after this form, is identical in shape, meaning, and purpose with the 'pillars' set up by the several patriarchs to mark their adoration of the Lord God. In fact, one of these patriarchal *lithoi* might even now be carried in the Śivaitic processions of Calcutta, without its *Hebrew* derivation [?] being suspected. The four arms of Śiva are often represented with appendages like wings; he has *three* eyes and a *fourth* in the crescent, obtained by him at the churning of the ocean, as *Pañcha Mukhti Śiva* has four heads.

In this god we recognise the description given by Ezekiel in the first chapter of his book, in which in his vision he beholds the "likeness of a man" in the four living creatures, who had "four faces, four wings," who had one pair of "straight feet . . . which sparkled like the color *of burnished* brass . . . and their rings were full of eyes round about them four." It is the throne and heaven of Śiva that the prophet describes in saying ". . . and there was the likeness of a throne as the appearance of a sapphire stone . . . and I saw as the color of amber [gold] as the appearance of fire around about . . . from his loins even upward, and from the appearance of his loins even downward, I saw as it were the appearance of fire" (*Ezekiel*, i, 26, 27). "And his feet like unto fine brass, as if they burned in a furnace" (*Revelation*, i, 15). "As for their faces . . . one was the face of a cherub, and the face of a lion . . . they also had the face of *an ox* and the face of an eagle" (*Ezekiel*, i, 10; x, 14). This *fourfold* appearance we find in the two *cherubim* of gold on the two ends of the ark; these symbolic four *faces* being adopted, moreover, later, one for each evangelist, as may be easily ascertained from the pictures of Matthew, Mark, Luke, and John,[584] prefixed to their respective gospels in the Roman Vulgate and Greek *Bibles*.

"Taaut, the great god of the Phoenicians," says Sanchoniathon, "to express the character of Saturn or Kronos, made his image having four eyes . . . two before, two behind, open and closed, and four wings, two expanded, two folded. The eyes denote that the god sees in sleep, and sleeps in waking; the position of the wings that he flies in rest, and rests in flying."[585]

The identity of Saturn with Śiva is corroborated still more when we consider the emblem of the latter, the *damaru*, which is an hour-glass, to show the progress of time, represented by this god in his capacity of a destroyer. The bull *Nandi*, the *vāhana* of Śiva, and the most sacred

---

584. John has an eagle near him; Luke, a bull; Mark, a lion; and Matthew, an angel — the kabalistic quaternary of the Egyptian Tarot.
585. Cf. Cory: *Ancient Fragments*, p. 15; ed. 1832.

emblem of this god, is reproduced in the Egyptian Apis, and in the bull created by Ormazd and killed by Ahriman. The religion of Zoroaster, entirely based upon the 'secret doctrine,' is found held by the people of Eritene [in Bactria]; it was the religion of the Persians when they conquered the Assyrians. From thence it is easy to trace the introduction of this emblem of LIFE represented by the Bull, in every religious system. The college of the Magians had accepted it with the change of dynasty;[586] Daniel is described as a Rabbi, the chief of the Babylonian astrologers and Magi;[587] therefore we see the Assyrian little bulls and thé attributes of Śiva reappearing under a hardly modified form in the cherubs of the Talmudistic Jews, as we have traced the bull Apis in the sphinxes or cherubs of the Mosaic Ark; and as we find it several thousand years later in the company of one of the Christian evangelists, Luke.

Whoever has lived in India long enough to acquaint himself even superficially with the native deities, must detect the similarity between Jehovah and other gods besides Śiva. As Saturn, the latter was always held in great respect by the Talmudists. He was held in reverence by the Alexandrian kabalists as the direct inspirer of the law and the prophets; one of the names of Saturn was Israel, and we will show, in time, his identity in a certain way with Abram, which Movers[588] and others hinted at long since. Thus it cannot be wondered at if Valentinus, Basilides, and the Ophite Gnostics placed the dwelling of their Ilda-Baoth, also a destroyer as well as a creator, in the planet Saturn; for it was he who gave the law in the wilderness and spoke through the prophets. If more proof should be required we shall show it in the testimony of the canonical *Bible* itself. In *Amos* the 'Lord' pours vials of wrath upon the people of Israel. He rejects their burnt-offerings and will not listen to their prayers, but inquires of Amos, "Have ye offered unto *me* sacrifices and offerings in the wilderness forty years, O house of Israel?" "But ye have borne the tabernacles of your Moloch and *Chiun* your images, the *star of your god*" (v, 25, 26). Who are Moloch and *Chiun* but Baal-Saturn-Śiva, and *Chiun*, Kivan, the same Saturn whose star the Israelites had made to themselves? There seems no escape in this case; all these deities are identical.

The same in the case of the numerous Logoi. While the Zoroastrian Sosiosh is framed on the tenth Brâhmanical Avatar, and the fifth Buddha of the followers of Gautama; and while we find the former, after having passed part and parcel into the kabalistic system of king Messiah, reflected in the Apostle Gabriel of the Nazarenes, and Aebel-Zivo, the Legatus, sent on earth by the Lord of Celsitude and Light; all of these —

586. See J. Matter's *Histoire critique de gnosticisme* upon the subject.
587. Cf. *Daniel*, iv, v.   588. *Die Phönizier*, I, p. 396, sq.

Hindû and Persian, Buddhist and Jewish, the Christos of the Gnostics and the Philonean Logos — are found combined in 'the Word made flesh' of the fourth *Gospel*. Christianity includes all these systems, patched and arranged to meet the occasion. Do we take up the *Avesta* — we find there the dual system so prevalent in the Christian scheme. The struggle between Ahriman,[589] Darkness, and Ormazd, Light, has been going on in the world continually since the beginning of time. When the worst arrives and Ahriman will seem to have conquered the world and corrupted all mankind, *then will appear the Savior* of mankind, Sosiosh. He will come seated upon a white horse and followed by an army of good genii, also mounted on milk-white steeds.[590] And this we find faithfully copied in the *Revelation:* "I saw heaven opened, and behold a *white horse;* and he that sat upon him was called Faithful and True. . . . And the armies which were in heaven followed him upon white horses" (*Revelation*, xix, 11, 14). Sosiosh himself is but a later Persian *permutation* of the Hindû Vishnu. The figure of this god may be found unto this day representing him as the Savior, the 'Preserver' (the preserving spirit of God), in the temple of Râma. The picture shows him in his tenth incarnation — the *Kalki-avatâra*, which is yet to come — as an armed warrior mounted upon a white horse. Waving over his head the sword destruction, he holds in his other hand a discus, made up of rings encircled in one another, an emblem of the revolving cycles or great ages,[591] for Vishnu will thus appear but at the end of the *Kaliyuga*, answering to the end of the world expected by our Adventists. "And out of his mouth goeth a sharp sword . . . on his head were many crowns" (*Revelation*, xix, 12, 15). Vishnu is often represented with several crowns superposed on his head. "And I saw an angel standing in the Sun" (17). The *white horse is the horse of the Sun.*[592] Sosiosh, the Persian Savior, is also born of a virgin, and at the end of days he will come as a Redeemer to regenerate the world, but he will be preceded by two prophets, who will come to announce him.[593] Hence the Jews who had Moses and Elias, are now waiting for the Messiah. "Then comes the

---

589. Ahriman, the production of Zoroaster, is so called in hatred of the Arias or Âryas, the Brâhmanas against whose dominion the Zoroastrians had revolted. Although an Ârya (a noble, a sage) himself, Zoroaster, as in the case of the Devas whom he disgraced from gods to the position of *devils*, hesitated not to designate this type of the spirit of evil under the name of his enemies, the Brâhman-Âryas. The whole struggle of Ahura-mazd and Ahriman is but the allegory of the great religious and political war between Brâhmanism and Zoroastrianism.

590. Nork: *Bibl. Mythol.*, II, p. 146.

591. Rev. Dr. Maurice also takes it to mean the cycles; *Hist. of Hindostan*, II, p. 503.

592. Duncker: *Gesch. d. Alterthume*, II, p. 363.

593. Spiegel: *Zend Avesta*, I, pp. 32-7, 244; see also King's synopsis of the *Avesta*, in *The Gnostics*, p. 31; 2nd ed.

general *resurrection*, when the good will immediately enter into this happy abode — the regenerated earth; and Ahriman and his angels (the devils),[594] and the wicked, be purified by immersion in a lake of molten metal. . . . Henceforward all will enjoy unchangeable happiness and, headed by Sosiosh, ever sing the praises of the Eternal One." [595] The above is a perfect repetition of Vishnu in his tenth avatar, for he will then throw the wicked into the infernal abodes in which, after purifying themselves, they will be pardoned — even those devils which rebelled against Brahmâ, and were hurled into the bottomless pit by Śiva; as also the 'blessed ones' will go to dwell with the gods, over the Mount Meru.[596]

Having thus traced the similarity of views respecting the Logos, Metatron, and Mediator, as found in the Kabala and the *Codex* of the Christian Nazarenes and Gnostics, the reader is prepared to appreciate the audacity of the Patristic scheme to reduce a purely metaphysical figure into concrete form, and make it appear as if the finger of prophecy had from time immemorial been pointing down the vista of ages to Jesus as the coming Messiah. A *theomythos* intended to symbolize the coming day, near the close of the great cycle, when the 'glad tidings' from heaven should proclaim the universal brotherhood and common faith of humanity, the day of regeneration — was violently distorted into an accomplished fact.

"Why callest thou me good? there is none good but *one, that is God,*" says Jesus. Is this the language of a God? of the second person in the Trinity, who is identical with the First? And if this Messiah, or Holy Ghost of the Gnostic and Pagan Trinities, had come in his person, what did he mean by distinguishing between himself — the 'Son of man' — and the Holy Ghost? "And whosoever shall speak a word against the Son of man, it shall be forgiven him; but unto him that blasphemeth against the Holy Ghost, it shall not be forgiven," he says.[597] And how account for the marvelous identity of this very language, with the precepts enunciated centuries before by the Kabalists and the 'Pagan' initiates? The following are a few instances out of many.

"No one of the gods, no man or Lord, can be good, but *only God alone,*" says Hermes.[598]

---

594. The *daevas* or devils of the Iranians contrast with the *devas* or deities of India.

595. J. F. Kleuker: *Zend-Avesta*, Bundehesh, § xxxi.

596. See the epistle of Polycrates, bishop of Ephesus, 200 A. D., quoted by Eusebius, *Eccl. Hist.*, III, xxxi; V, xxiv. Origen stoutly maintained the doctrine of eternal punishment to be erroneous. He held that at the second advent of Christ even the devils among the damned would be forgiven. The eternal damnation is a later *Christian* thought. (Cf. Origen: *De princ.*, I, v; II, x; III, vi.)

597. *Luke*, xii, 10.   598. L. Ménard: *Hermès Trismégiste*, pp. 23, 24.

"To be a good man is impossible; God alone possesses this privilege," repeats Plato, with a slight variation.[599]

Six centuries before Christ, the Chinese philosopher Confucius said that his doctrine was simple and easy to comprehend (*Lûn-yû*, chap. v, § 15). To which one of his disciples added: "The doctrine of our Master consists in having an invariable correctness of heart, and in doing toward others as we would that they should do to us." [600]

"Jesus of Nazareth, a man approved of God among you by miracles," [601] exclaims Peter, long after the scene of Calvary. "There was a *man* sent from God, whose name was John," [602] says the fourth *Gospel*, thus placing the Baptist on an equality with Jesus. John the Baptist, in one of the most solemn acts of his life, that of baptizing Christ, thinks not that he is going to baptize a *God*, but uses the word man. "This is he of whom I said, After me cometh a *man*." [603] Speaking of himself, Jesus says, "Ye seek to kill *me*, a *man* that hath told you the truth, which *I have heard of God*." [604] Even the blind man of Jerusalem, healed by the great thaumaturgist, full of gratitude and admiration for his benefactor, in narrating the miracle does not call Jesus God, but simply says, ". . . A *man* that is called Jesus, made clay." [605]

We do not close the list for lack of other instances and proofs, but simply because what we now say has been repeated and demonstrated by others, many times before us. But there is no more incurable evil than blind and unreasoning fanaticism. Few are the men who, like Dr. Priestley, have the courage to write, "This opinion of a *divine ray* . . . attached to the man Jesus . . . appears first in the writings of Justin Martyr (A.D. 141), who, from being a philosopher, became a Christian."[606]

Mohammed appeared nearly six hundred years [607] after the presumed deicide. The Graeco-Roman world was still convulsed with religious dissensions, withstanding all the past imperial edicts and the forcible Christianization. While the Council of Trent was disputing about the *Vulgate*, the unity of God quietly superseded the trinity, and soon the Mohammedans outnumbered the Christians. Why? Because their prophet never sought to identify himself with Allah. Otherwise, it is safe to say, he would not have lived to see his religion flourish. Till the present day Mohammedanism has made and is now making more proselytes than Christianity. Buddha-Siddhârtha came as a simple mortal, centuries before Christ. The religious ethics of this faith [Buddhism] are

---

599. *Protagoras*, §84.   600. Pauthier: *La Chine*, II, p. 375.   601. *Acts*, ii, 22.
602. *John*, i, 6.   603. *Ibid.*, 30.   604. *John*, viii, 40.   605. *Ibid.*, ix, 11.
606. Jos. Priestley, LL. D., F. R. S.: *Gen. Hist. of the Chr. Church*, I, p. 266: Birmingham, 1790. Cf. also his *Hist. of Early Opinions concerning Jesus Christ*, I, p. 92; II, 29, 30, 271; III, 299, 300: Birmingham, 1786.
607. Mohammed was born in 571 A. D.

now found to far exceed in moral beauty anything ever dreamed of by the Tertullians and Augustines.

The true spirit of Christianity can alone be fully found in Buddhism; partially, it shows itself in other 'heathen' religions. Buddha never made of himself a god, nor was he deified by his followers. The Buddhists are now known to far outnumber Christians; they are enumerated at nearly 500,000,000. While cases of conversion [to Christianity] among Buddhists, Brâhmanists, Mohammedans and Jews become so rare as to show how sterile are the attempts of our missionaries, atheism and materialism spread their gangrenous ulcers and gnaw every day deeper at the very heart of Christianity. There are no atheists among heathen populations, and those few among the Buddhists and Brâhmanists who have become infected with materialism may always be found to belong to large cities densely thronged with Europeans, and only among educated classes. Truly says Bishop Kidder: "Were a wise man to choose his religion from those who profess it, perhaps Christianity would be the last religion he would choose!"

In an able little pamphlet from the pen of the popular lecturer, J. M. Peebles, M. D., the author quotes from the London *Athenaeum* an article in which are described the welfare and civilization of the inhabitants of Yarkand and Kashgar, "who seem virtuous and happy." "Gracious Heavens!" fervently exclaims the honest author, who himself was once a Universalist clergyman, "Grant to keep Christian missionaries *away* from 'happy' and heathen Tartary!" [608]

From the earliest days of Christianity, when Paul upbraided the *Church* of Corinth for a crime "as is not so much as named among the Gentiles — that one should have his father's wife"; and for their making a pretext of the 'Lord's Supper' for *debauch* and drunkenness (*1 Corinthians*, v, 1), the profession of the name of Christ has ever been more a pretext than the evidence of holy feeling. However, a correct form of this verse is: "Everywhere the lewd practice among you is heard about, such a lewd practice as is nowhere among the heathen nations — even the having or marrying of the father's wife." The Persian influence would seem to be indicated in this language. The practice existed "nowhere among the nations," except in Persia, where it was esteemed especially meritorious. Hence too the Jewish stories of Abraham marrying his sister, Nahor his niece, Amram his father's sister, and Judah his son's widow, whose children appear to have been legitimate. The Aryan tribes esteemed endogamous marriages, while the Tatars and all barbarous nations required all alliances to be exogamous.

---

608. *Jesus — Man, Myth, or God?*

There was but one apostle of Jesus worthy of that name, and that was Paul. However disfigured were his *Epistles* by dogmatic hands before being admitted into the Canon, his conception of the great and divine figure of the philosopher who died for his idea can still be traced in his addresses to the various Gentile nations. Only — he who would understand him better yet, must study the Philonean *Logos* reflecting now and then the Hindû *Sabda* (logos) of the *Mîmânsâ* school.

As to the other apostles, those whose names are prefixed to the *Gospels* — we cannot well believe in their veracity when we find them attributing to their Master miracles surrounded by circumstances recorded, if not in the oldest books of India, at least in such as antedated Christianity, and in the very phraseology of the traditions. Who, in his days of simple and blind credulity, but marveled at the touching narrative given in the *Gospels according to Mark* and *Luke* of the resurrection of the daughter of Jairus? Who has ever doubted its originality? And yet the story is copied entirely from the *Hari-Purâna*, and is recorded among the miracles attributed to Krishna. We translate it from the French version:

"The King Angashuna caused the betrothal of his daughter, the beautiful Kâlavatî, with the young son of Vâmadeva, the powerful King of Antarvedî, named Govinda, to be celebrated with great pomp.

"But as Kâlavatî was amusing herself in the groves with her companions, she was bitten by a serpent and died. Angashuna tore his clothes, covered himself with ashes, and cursed the day when he was born.

"Suddenly a great rumor spread through the palace, and the following cries were heard, a thousand times repeated: '*Pasya pitaram; pasya gurum!*' 'The Father, the Master!' Then Krishna approached, smiling, leaning on the arm of Arjuna. . . . 'Master!' cried Angashuna, casting himself at his feet, and sprinkling them with his tears, 'See my poor daughter!' and he showed him the body of Kâlavatî, stretched upon a mat. . . .

"'Why do you weep?' replied Krishna, in a gentle voice. '*Do you not see that she is sleeping?* Listen to the sound of her breathing, like the sigh of the night wind which rustles the leaves of the trees. See, her cheeks resuming their color, her eyes, whose lids tremble as if they were about to open; her lips quiver as if about to speak; she is sleeping, I tell you; and hold! see, she moves. *Kâlavatî! Rise and walk!*'

"Hardly had Krishna spoken, when the breathing, warmth, movement and life returned little by little into the corpse, and the young girl, obeying the injunction of the demigod, rose from her couch and rejoined her companions. But the crowd marveled and cried out: 'This is a god, since death is no more for him than sleep?' " [609]

All such parables are enforced upon Christians with the addition of dogmas which, in their extraordinary character, leave far behind them the wildest conceptions of heathenism. The Christians, in order to believe in a Deity, have found it necessary to kill their God, that they themselves should live!

And now the supreme unknown one, the Father of grace and mercy, and his celestial hierarchy are managed by the Church as though they were so many theatrical stars and supernumeraries under salary! Six centuries before the Christian era Xenophanes had disposed of such anthropomorphism by an immortal satire, recorded and preserved by Clement of Alexandria:

> "There is one God Supreme . . . . . .
> Whose form is not like unto man's, and as unlike his nature;
> But vain mortals imagine that gods like themselves are begotten,
> With human sensations, and voice, and corporeal members;
> So if oxen or lions had hands and could work in man's fashion,
> And trace out with chisel or brush their conception of Godhead,
> Then would horses depict gods like horses, and oxen like oxen,
> Each kind the Divine with its own form and nature endowing." [610]

And hear Vyâsa — the poet-pantheist of India who, for all the scientists can prove, may have lived, as Jacolliot has it, some fifteen thousand years ago — discoursing on Mâyâ, the illusion of the senses:

"All religious dogmas only serve to obscure the intelligence of man. . . . Worship of divinities, under the allegories of which is hidden respect for natural laws, drives away truth to the profit of the basest superstitions" (*Vyâsa-Mâyâ*).[611]

It was given to Christianity to paint us God Almighty after the model of the kabalistic abstraction of the 'Ancient of Days.' From old frescos on cathedral ceilings, Catholic missals, and other icons and images, we now find him depicted by the poetic brush of Gustave Doré. The awful, unknown majesty of Him, whom no 'heathen' dared to reproduce in concrete form, is figuring in our own century in *Doré's Illustrated Bible*. Treading upon clouds that float in mid-air, darkness and chaos behind him, and the world beneath his feet, a majestic old man stands, his left hand gathering his flowing robes about him, and his right raised in the gesture of command. He has spoken the Word, and

---

609. Translated from the *Hari-Purâna*, by Jacolliot: *Christna, et le Christ*, pp. 300-1.
610. *Stromata*, V, xiv; translation given in *Supernatural Religion*, part I, iii, § 2.
611. *La genèse de l'humanité*, p. 339: Paris, 1875.

from his towering person streams an effulgence of Light — the Shekhinah. As a poetic conception, the composition does honor to the artist, but does it honor God? Better the chaos behind Him, than the figure itself; for there, at least, we have a solemn mystery. For our part, we prefer the silence of the ancient heathens. With such a gross, anthropomorphic, and, as we conceive, blasphemous representation of the First Cause, who can feel surprised at any iconographic extravagance in the representation of the Christian Christ, the apostles, and the putative Saints? With the Catholics St. Peter becomes quite naturally the janitor of Heaven, and sits at the door of the celestial kingdom — a ticket-taker to the Trinity!

In a religious disturbance which recently occurred in one of the Spanish-American provinces, there were found upon the bodies of some of the killed passports signed by the Bishop of the Diocese and addressed to St. Peter, bidding him "*admit the bearer as a true son of the Church.*" It was subsequently ascertained that these unique documents were issued by the Catholic prelate just before his deluded parishioners went into the fight at the instigation of their priests.

In their immoderate desire to find evidence for the authenticity of the *New Testament*, the best men, the most erudite scholars even among Protestant divines, but too often fall into deplorable traps. We cannot believe that such a learned commentator as Canon Westcott could have left himself in ignorance as to Talmudistic and purely kabalistic writings. How then is it that we find him quoting, with such serene assurance, as presenting "striking analogies to the *Gospel of St. John*," passages from the work of *The Shepherd of Hermas*, which are complete sentences from the kabalistic literature? "The view which Hermas gives of Christ's nature and work is no less harmonious with apostolic doctrine, and it offers striking analogies to the *Gospel of St. John*. . . . He [Jesus] is a 'Rock higher than the mountains, able to hold the whole world; ancient, and yet having a new gate.' . . . He is older than Creation, so that he took counsel with the Father about the creation which he made. . . . No one shall enter in unto him otherwise than by his Son." [612]

Now while — as the author of *Supernatural Religion* well proves — there is nothing in this which looks like a corroboration of the doctrine

---

612. *On the Canon*, pp. 177, *sq.* This work, *The Shepherd of Hermas*, is now considered apocryphal; but it is found in the Sinaitic Codex, and appears among the books in the stichometry of the *Codex Claromontanus*. In the days of Irenaeus it was quoted as Holy Scripture (see *Supern. Rel.*, part II, ch. i, § 3) by the Fathers, held to be divinely inspired, and publicly read in the churches (Irenaeus: *Agst. Heresies*, IV, xx, § 2). When Tertullian became a Montanist he rejected it, after having asserted its divinity (*De oratione*, xvi).

taught in the fourth gospel, he omits to state that nearly everything expressed by the pseudo-Hermas in relation to his parabled conversation with the 'Lord' is a plain quotation, with repeated variations, from the *Zohar* and other kabalistic books. We may as well compare, so as to leave the reader no difficulty in judging for himself.

"God," says Hermas,[613] "planted the vineyard, that is he created the people and gave them to his Son; and the Son . . . himself cleansed their sins, etc."; *i. e.*, the Son washed them in his blood, in commemoration of which Christians drink wine at the communion. In the Kabala it is shown that the Aged of the Aged, or '*Long-Face*,' plants a vineyard, the latter typifying mankind; and a vine, meaning Life. The Spirit of '*King* Messiah' is therefore shown as washing his garments in *the wine* from above, from the creation of the world.[614] Adam, or A-Dam is 'blood.' The life of the flesh is in the blood (*nephesh* — soul).[615] And Adam-Kadmon is the Only-Begotten. Noah also plants a vineyard — the allegorical hot-bed of future humanity. As a consequence of the adoption of the same allegory, we find it reproduced in the Nazarene *Codex*. Seven vines are procreated, which spring from Kebar-Zivo,[616] and Ferho (or Par'ha) Raba waters them. When the blessed will ascend among the creatures of Light, they shall see Iavar-Zivo, *Lord of* Life, and the First Vine![617] These kabalistic metaphors are thus naturally repeated in the *Gospel according to John* (xv, 1): "I am the true vine, and my Father is the husbandman." In *Genesis* (xlix, 10, 11) the dying Jacob is made to say, "The scepter shall not depart from Judah [the lion's whelp], nor a lawgiver from between his feet, until Shiloh (Siloh) come. . . . Binding his foal unto *the vine*, and his ass's colt unto the choice vine, he washed his garments *in wine*, and his clothes *in the blood of grapes*." Shiloh is 'King Messiah,' as well as the Shiloh in Ephraim, which was to be made the capital and the place of the sanctuary. In the *Targum* of Onkelos, the Babylonian, the words of Jacob read: "Until the *King Messiah* shall come."[618] The prophecy has failed in the Christian as well as in the kabalistico-Jewish sense. The scepter has departed from Judah, whether the Messiah has already or will come, unless we believe, with the kabalists, that Moses was the first Messiah, who transferred his soul to Joshua — Jesus.[619]

Says Hermas: "And in the middle of the plain he showed me a great *white* rock which had risen out of the plain, and the rock was

613. *Hermas*, similitude V, § 6.   614. *Zohar*, comm. on *Genesis*, xl, 10.

615. *Levit.*, xvii, 11.   616. *Codex Nazaraeus*, III, p. 61.   617. *Ibid.*, II, p. 281.

618. Nork: *Hundert und ein Frage*, p. 104.

619. We must remind the reader, in this connexion, that Joshua and Jesus are one and the same name. In the Slavonian Bibles Joshua reads — *Iessus* (or Jesus) *Navin*.

higher than the mountains, rectangular, so as to be able to hold the whole world; but that rock was old, having a gate hewn out of it, and the hewing out of the gate seemed to me to be recent." [620]   In the *Zohar* we find: "To 40,000 superior worlds the *white* of the skull of His Head [of the most Sacred Ancient *in absconditu*] is extended.[621] . . . When *Ze'ir* [the first reflexion and image of his Father, the Ancient of the Ancient] will, through the mystery of the seventy names of Metatron, descend into Yetztrah [the third world], he will open a new gate. . . . The Spiritus Decisorius will cut and divide the garment [Shekhinah] into two parts.[622] . . . At the coming of King Messiah, from the sacred cubical stone of the Temple a *white light* will be arising during forty days. This will expand until *it encloses the whole world*. . . . At that time King Messiah will allow himself to be revealed, and will be seen coming out of the gate of the garden of Odan [Eden]. 'He will be revealed in the land Galil.' [623] . . . When 'he has made satisfaction for the sins of Israel, he will lead them on through a *new gate* to the seat of judgment.' [624] At the *Gate of the House of Life*, the throne is prepared for the Lord of Splendor." [625]

Farther on the commentator introduces the following from Hermas: "This *rock* and this *gate* are the Son of God. 'How, lord,' I said, 'is the rock old and the gate new?' 'Listen,' he said, 'and understand, thou ignorant man. The *Son of God is older than all of the creation*, so that he was a councillor with the Father in the work of creation; and for this is he old.' " [626]

Now these two assertions are not only purely kabalistic, without even so much as a change of expression, but Brâhmanical and Pagan likewise. "*Vidi virum excellentem coeli terraeque conditore natu majorem.* . . . I have seen the most excellent [superior] MAN, who is older by birth than the maker of heaven and earth," says the kabalistic *Codex*.[627] The Eleusinian Dionysus, whose particular name was *Iacchos* (Iaccho, Iahoh) [628] — the God from whom the liberation of souls was expected — was considered older than the Demiurge. At the mysteries of the Anthesteria at Limnae (the lakes), after the usual baptism by purification of water, the *Mystae* were made to pass through to another door (gate), and

---

620. *Shepherd of Hermas*, simil. IX, § 2.

621. *Idrah Rabbah*, § 41.

622. Rosenroth: *Kabb. denud.*, II, p. 230; *Book of the Babylonian Companions*, p. 35.

623. *Zohar*, on *Exodus*, p. 11: Sulzbach ed.

624. *Midrash 'Hazitha*.   625. *Codex Nazaraeus*, III, p. 61.

626. Similitude IX, § 12; Westcott: *On the Canon*, pp. 177, *sq.*   627. Vol. II, p. 57.

628. L. Preller: *Griech. Mythol.*, I, p. 486; K. O. Müller: *Hist. Lit. Anct. Greece*, p. 238; F. C. Movers: *Die Phönizier*, I, pp. 547, *sq.*

one particularly for that purpose, which was called 'the gate of Dionysus' and that of 'the *purified.*'

In the *Zohar* the kabalists are told that the work-master, the Demiurge, said to the Lord: "Let us make man after our image." [629] In the original texts of the first chapter of *Genesis*, it stands: "And the *Elohim* [translated as the Supreme God], who are the highest gods or powers, said: Let us make man in *our* [?] image, after *our* likeness." In the *Vedas* Brahmâ holds counsel with Parabrahman as to the best mode to proceed in creating the world.

Canon Westcott, quoting Hermas, shows him asking: " 'And why is the gate *new*, lord?' I said. 'Because,' he replied, 'he was manifested at the last days of the dispensation; for this cause the gate was made new, in order that they who shall be saved might enter by it into the kingdom of God.' " [630] There are two peculiarities worthy of note in this passage. To begin with, it attributes to 'the Lord' a false statement of the same character as that so emphasized by the apostle John, and which brought, at a later period, all the orthodox Christians, who accepted the apostolic allegories as literal, to such inconvenient straits. Jesus, as Messiah, was *not* manifested at the last of the days; for the latter are yet to come, notwithstanding a number of divinely-inspired prophecies, followed by disappointed hopes as a result, to testify to his immediate coming. The belief that the 'last times' had come was natural, when once the coming of King Messiah had been acknowledged. The second peculiarity is found in the fact that the *prophecy* could have been accepted at all, when even its approximate determination is a direct contradiction of Mark, who makes Jesus distinctly state that neither the angels, nor the Son himself, know of that day or that hour. [631] We might add that as the belief undeniably originated with the *Apocalypse*, it ought to be a self-evident proof that it belonged to the calculations peculiar to the kabalists and the Pagan sanctuaries. It was the secret computation of a cycle, which according to their reckoning was ending toward the latter part of the first century. It may also be held as a corroborative proof, that the *Gospel according to Mark*, as well as that ascribed to *John*, and the *Apocalypse*, were written by men of whom not one was sufficiently acquainted with the others. The Logos was first definitely called *petra* (rock) by Philo; the word, moreover, as we have shown elsewhere, means, in Chaldaic and Phoenician, 'interpreter.' Justin Martyr calls him, throughout his works, 'angel,' and makes a clear distinction between the Logos and God the Creator.

629. *Zohar*, I, p. 25; Amst. ed.
630. Simil. IX, § 12; Westcott: *On the Canon*, p. 178.
631. *Mark*, xiii, 32.

"The Word of God is His Son . . . and he is also called Angel and Apostle, for he declares [interprets] whatever we ought to know, and is sent to declare whatever is disclosed." [632]

"Aedan Inferior is distributed into its own paths, into thirty-two sides of paths, yet it is not known to any one but Ze'ir. But no one knows the SUPERIOR AEDAN nor Its paths, except that Long Face" — the Supreme God.[633] Ze'ir is the Nazarene 'genius,' who is called Aebel-Zivo, and Gabriel Legatus — also 'Apostle Gabriel.' [634] The Nazarenes held with the kabalists that even the Messiah who was to come did not know the 'Superior Aedan,' the concealed Deity; no one except the Supreme God; thus showing that above the Supreme Intelligible Deity there is one still more secret and unrevealed. Ze'ir-Anptn is the third God, while 'Logos,' according to Philo Judaeus, is the second one.[635] This is distinctly shown in the Codex. "The false Messias shall say: I am Deus, son of Deus; my Father sent me here. . . . I am the first Legate, I am Aebel-Zivo, I am come from on high! But distrust him; for he will not be Aebel-Zivo. Aebel-Zivo will not permit himself to be seen in this age." [636] Hence the belief of some Gnostics that it was not Aebel-Zivo (Archangel Gabriel) who 'overshadowed' Mary, but Ilda-Baoth, who formed the material body of Jesus; Christos uniting himself with him only at the moment of baptism in the Jordan.

Can we doubt Nork's assertion that "the Bereshîth Rabba, the oldest part of the Midrash Rabboth, was known to the Church Fathers in a Greek translation"? [637]

But if on the one hand they were sufficiently acquainted with the different religious systems of their neighbors to have enabled them to build a new religion alleged to be distinct from all others, their ignorance of the Old Testament itself, let alone the more complicated questions of Grecian metaphysics, is now found to have been deplorable. "For instance, in Matthew, xxvii, 9 f, the passage from Zechariah, xi, 12, 13, is attributed to Jeremiah," says the author of Supernatural Religion.[638] "In Mark, i, 2, a quotation from Malachi, iii, 1, is as-

632. First Apol., lxiii.   633. Idrah Rabbah, viii, §§ 107-109.
634. Codex Nazaraeus, I, pp. 23, 181.

635. Quaest. et solut. in Gen., II, § 62. Philo says that the Logos is the interpreter of the highest God, and argues, "that he must be the God of us imperfect beings" (Leg. alleg., III, § 73). According to his opinion man was not made in the likeness of the most High God, the Father of all, but in that of the second God who is his word — Logos" (Philo: Fragmenta, 1; ex Euseb.: Praepar. evang., VIII, 13).

636. Codex Nazaraeus, I, p. 57; Dunlap: Sôd, the Son of the Man, p. 59.

637. Nork: Hundert und ein Frage, p. xvii; Sôd, the Son of the Man, p. 87, in which the author quotes Nork (op. cit., pp. xiv, xvii) to the effect that parts of the Midrashim, and the Targum of Onkelos antedate the New Testament.

638. Part III, ch. i.

cribed to Isaiah. In *1 Corinthians*, ii, 9, a passage is quoted as *Holy Scripture*, which is not found in the *Old Testament* at all, but which is taken, as Origen and Jerome state, from an apocryphal work, *The Revelation of Elias* (Origen: *Tract.*, xxxv, § 17, *in Matt.*), and the passage is similarly quoted by the so-called *Epistle of Clement to the Corinthians* (xxxiv)." How reliable are the pious Fathers in their explanations of divers heresies may be illustrated in the case of Epiphanius, who mistook the Pythagorean sacred Tetrad, called in the Valentinian *Gnosis*, Kol-Arbas, for a *heretic leader*.[639] What with the involuntary blunders and deliberate falsifications of the teachings of those who differed in views with them; the canonization of the mythological Aura Placida (gentle breeze) into a pair of Christian martyrs — St. Aura and St. Placida;[640] the deification of a *spear* and a *cloak*, under the names of SS. Longimus and Amphibolus;[641] and the Patristic quotations from prophets, of what was never in those prophets at all — one may well ask in blank amazement whether the so-called religion of Christ has ever been other than an incoherent dream since the death of the Great Master.

So malicious do we find the holy Fathers in their unrelenting persecution of pretended '*heresies*,'[642] that we see them telling without hesitation the most preposterous untruths, and inventing entire narratives, the better to impress their own otherwise unsupported arguments upon ignorance. If the mistake in relation to the Tetrad had at first originated as a simple consequence of an unpremeditated blunder of Hippolytus, the explanations of Epiphanius and others who fell into the same absurd error[643] have a less innocent look. When Hippolytus gravely denounces the great heresy of the Tetrad, Kol-Arbas, and states that the imaginary Gnostic leader is "Colarbasus, who endeavors to explain

639. Writing upon Ptolemaeus and Heracleon, the author of *Supernatural Religion* (part II, ch. x) says that "the inaccuracy of the Fathers keeps pace with their want of critical judgment," and then proceeds to illustrate this particularly ridiculous blunder committed by Epiphanius, in common with Hippolytus, Tertullian, and Philastrius. "Mistaking a passage of Irenaeus, *Agst. Her.*, I, xiv, regarding the Sacred Tetrad (Kol-Arbas), Hippolytus supposes Irenaeus to refer to another heretic leader." He at once treats the Tetrad as such a leader named 'Colarbasus,' and after dealing with the doctrines of Secundus, and Ptolemaeus, and Heracleon, he proposes to show, "what are the opinions held by Marcus and *Colarbasus*," these two being, according to him, the successors of the school of Valentinus (cf. Bunsen: *Hippolytus and his Age*, p. 54, *sq.*; Hippol.: *Refut. of all Heresies*, IV, xiii; VI, xxxiii, *sq.*; VI, l.

640. See Godfrey Higgins: *Anacalypsis*.

641. Inman: *Ancient Pagan and Modern Christian Symbolism*, p. 84.

642. Meaning — holding up of *different views*.

643. "This absurd mistake," remarks the author of *Supernatural Religion*, (part II, ch. x) "shows how little these writers knew of the Gnostics of whom they wrote, and how the one ignorantly follows the other."

religion by measures and numbers," [644] we may simply smile. But when
Epiphanius, with abundant indignation, elaborates upon the theme,
"which is Heresy XV," and pretending to be thoroughly acquainted with
the subject, adds: "A certain Heracleon follows after Colarbasus,
which is Heresy XVI," [645] then he lays himself open to the charge of
deliberate falsification.

If this zealous *Christian* can boast so unblushingly of having caused
"*by his information* seventy women, even of rank, to be sent into exile,
through the seductions of some in whose number he had himself been
drawn into joining their sect," he has left us a fair standard by which to
judge him. C. W. King remarks, very aptly, on this point, that "it may
reasonably be suspected that this worthy renegade had in this case saved
himself from the fate of his fellow-religionists by turning evidence against
them, on the opening of the persecution." [646]

And thus, one by one, perished the Gnostics, the only heirs to whose
share had fallen a few stray crumbs of the unadulterated truth of primitive Christianity. All was confusion and turmoil during these first centuries, till the moment when all these contradictory dogmas were finally
forced upon the Christian world, and examination was forbidden. For
long ages it was made a sacrilege, punishable with severe penalties, often
death, to seek to comprehend that which the Church had so conveniently
elevated to the rank of *divine* mystery. But since biblical critics have
taken upon themselves to 'set the house in order,' the cases have become
reversed. Pagan creditors now come from every part of the globe to claim
their own, and Christian theology begins to be suspected of complete
bankruptcy. Such is the sad result of the fanaticism of the 'orthodox'
sects, who, to borrow an expression of the author of *The Decline and Fall
of the Roman Empire*, never were, like the Gnostics, "the most polite, the
most learned, and most wealthy of the Christian name." And if not all
of them "smelt garlic," as Renan will have it, on the other hand few of
these Christian saints have ever shrunk from spilling their neighbors'
blood, if the views of the latter did not agree with their own.

And so all our philosophers were swept away by the ignorant and
superstitious masses. The Philaletheians, the lovers of truth, and their
eclectic school, perished; and there, where the young Hypatia had taught
the highest philosophical doctrines; and where Ammonius Saccas had
explained that "the *whole which Christ had in view* was to reinstate and
restore to its primitive integrity the wisdom of the ancients — to reduce

---

644. *Refutation of all Heresies*, IV, xiii.

645. Epiph.: *Panar.*, lib. I, tom. III, Haer. XXXVI, i (quoted in *Supernatural Religion*).
See Volkmar's *Die Colarbasus-gnosis* in Niedner's *Zeitschr. Hist. Theol.;* 1855.

646. *The Gnostics and their Remains*, p. 409; 2nd ed.

within bounds the universally prevailing dominion of superstition . . .
and to exterminate the various errors that had found their way into the
different popular religions" [647]— there, we say, freely raved the οἱ πολλοί
of Christianity. No more precepts from the mouth of the "God-taught
philosopher," but others expounded by the incarnation of a most cruel,
fiendish superstition.

"If thy father," wrote St. Jerome, "lies down across thy threshold, if
thy mother uncovers to thine eyes the bosom which suckled thee, trample
on thy father's lifeless body, trample on thy mother's bosom, and, with
eyes unmoistened and dry, fly to the Lord who calleth thee"!!

This sentence is equaled, if not outrivaled, by this other, pronounced
in a like spirit. It emanates from another Father of the early Church, the
eloquent Tertullian, who hopes to see all the "philosophers" in the
gehenna fire of Hell. "What shall be the magnitude of that scene! . . .
How shall I laugh! How shall I rejoice! How shall I triumph when I
see so many illustrious kings who were said to have mounted into heaven,
groaning with Jupiter, their god, in the lowest darkness of hell! Then
shall the governors who have persecuted the name of Christ burn in more
cruel fire than any they had kindled for the saints!" [648]

These murderous expressions illustrate the spirit of Christianity to
this day. But do they illustrate the teachings of Christ? By no means.
As Éliphas Lévi says, "The God in the name of whom we would trample
on our mother's bosom we must see in the hereafter, a hell gaping widely
at his feet, and an exterminating sword in his hand. . . . Moloch burned
children but a few seconds; it was reserved to the disciples of a god who
is alleged to have died to redeem humanity on the cross, to create a new
Moloch whose burning stake is eternal!"

That this spirit of true 'Christian love' has safely crossed nineteen
centuries and rages now in America, is fully instanced in the case of the
rabid Moody, the revivalist, who exclaims: "I have a son, and no one
but God knows how I love him; but I would see those beautiful eyes dug
out of his head tonight, rather than see him grow up to manhood and go
down to the grave without Christ and without hope"!!

To this an American paper of Chicago very justly responds: "This
is the spirit of the Inquisition, which we are told is dead. If Moody in
his zeal would 'dig out' the eyes of his darling son, to what lengths may
he not go with the sons of others, whom he may love less? It is the
spirit of Loyola, gibbering in the nineteenth century, and prevented from
lighting the fagot-flame and heating red-hot the instruments of torture
only by the arm of law."

---

647. Mosheim: *An Eccl. Hist.*, cent. II, part II, ch. i, § 8: Dublin, 1767.
648. Tertullian: *De spectaculis*, xxx.

CHAPTER VI

"The curtains of Yesterday drop down, the curtains of Tomorrow roll up; but Yesterday and Tomorrow both *are*."— *Sartor Resartus:* Natural Supernaturalism

"May we not then be permitted to examine the authenticity of the Bible, which since the second century has been put forth as the criterion of scientific truth? To maintain itself in a position so exalted, it must challenge human criticism."
— *Conflict between Religion and Science,* ch. vii

"One kiss of Nara upon the lips of Nârî and all Nature wakes."
— VINA-SNATI (A Hindû Poet)

WE must not forget that the Christian Church owes its present canonical *Gospels,* and hence its whole religious dogmatism, to the *Sortes Sanctorum.* Unable to agree as to which were the most divinely-inspired of the numerous gospels extant in its time, the mysterious Council of Nicaea concluded to leave the decision of the puzzling question to miraculous intervention. This Nicene Council may well be called mysterious. There was a mystery, first, in the mystical number of its 318 bishops, on which Barnabas [649] lays such a stress; added to this, there is no agreement among ancient writers as to the time and place of its assembly, nor even as to the bishop who presided.[650] Notwithstanding the grandiloquent eulogium of Constantine,[651] Sabinus, the Bishop of Heraclea, affirms that "except Constantine, the emperor, and Eusebius Pamphili, these bishops were a set of *illiterate, simple creatures, that understood nothing*"; [652] which is equivalent to saying that they were a set of fools. Such was apparently the opinion entertained of them by Pappus, who tells us of the bit of magic resorted to, so as to decide which were the *true* gospels. In his *Synodicon* to that Council Pappus says that, having "promiscuously put all the books that were referred to the Council for determination under a communion-table in a church, they [the bishops] besought the Lord that the *inspired* writings might get upon the table, while the spurious ones remained underneath, and *it happened accordingly.*" [652a] But we are not told who kept the keys of the council-chamber over night!

On the authority of ecclesiastical eye-witnesses, therefore, we are at liberty to say that the Christian world owes its 'Word of God' to a

---

649. *Epistle of Barnabas,* viii, 11-13 (Hone edit.): London, 1820.
    650. Mosheim: *Eccl. Hist.,* cent. IV, part II, ch. v, § 12.
651. Socrates: *Eccl. Hist.,* I, ix.   652. *Ibid.,* I, viii.
    652a. Fabric.: *Bibl. graeca,* lib. VI, iii, § viii, 'Synodus Nicaena.'

method of divination, for resorting to which the Church subsequently condemned unfortunate victims as conjurers, enchanters, magicians, witches, and vaticinators, and burnt them by thousands! In treating of this truly divine phenomenon of the self-sorting manuscripts, the Fathers of the Church say that God himself presides over the *Sortes*. As we have shown elsewhere, Augustine confesses that he himself used this sort of divination. But opinions, like revealed religions, are liable to change. That which for nearly fifteen hundred years was imposed on Christendom as a book, of which every word was written under the direct supervision of the Holy Ghost; of which not a syllable, nor a comma could be changed without sacrilege, is now being retranslated, revised, corrected, and clipped of whole verses, in some cases of entire chapters. And yet, as soon as the new edition is out, its doctors would have us accept it as a new 'Revelation' of the nineteenth century, with the alternative of being held as an infidel. Thus we see that no more *within* than *without* its precincts is the infallible Church to be trusted more than would be reasonably convenient. The forefathers of our modern divines found authority for the *Sortes* in the verse where it is said: "The lot is cast into the lap, but the whole disposing thereof is of the Lord"; [653] and now, their direct heirs hold that "the whole disposing thereof is of the Devil." Perhaps they are unconsciously beginning to endorse the doctrine of the Syrian Bardesanes, that the actions of God, as well as of man, *are subject to necessity?*

It was no doubt, also, according to strict 'necessity' that the Neo-Platonists were so summarily dealt with by the Christian mob. In those days the doctrines of the Hindû naturalists and antediluvian Pyrrhonists were forgotten, if they ever had been known at all to any but a few philosophers; and Mr. Darwin, with his modern *discoveries*, had not even been mentioned in the prophecies. In this case the law of the survival of the fittest was reversed; the *Neo-Platonists were doomed to destruction from the day when they openly sided with Aristotle.*

At the beginning of the fourth century crowds began gathering at the door of the academy where the learned and unfortunate Hypatia expounded the doctrines of the divine Plato and Plotinus, and thereby impeded the progress of Christian proselytism. She too successfully dispelled the mist, hanging over the religious 'mysteries' invented by the Fathers, not to be considered dangerous. This alone would have been sufficient to imperil both herself and her followers. It was precisely the

---

653. *Proverbs*, xvi, 33. In ancient Egypt and Greece, and among Israelites, small sticks and balls called the 'sacred divining lots' were used for this kind of oracle in the temples. According to the figures which were formed by the accidental juxtaposition of the latter, the priest interpreted the will of the gods.

teachings of this Pagan philosopher, which had been so freely borrowed by the Christians to give a finishing touch to their otherwise incomprehensible scheme, that had seduced so many into joining the new religion; and now the Platonic light began shining so inconveniently bright upon the pious patchwork, as to allow every one to see whence the 'revealed' doctrines were derived. But there was a still greater peril. Hypatia had studied under Plutarch, the head of the Athenian school, and had learned all the secrets of theurgy. While she lived to instruct the multitude, no 'divine miracles' could be produced before one who could divulge the natural causes by which they took place. Her doom was sealed by Cyril [of Alexandria], whose eloquence she eclipsed, and whose authority, built on degrading superstitions, had to yield before hers which was erected on the rock of immutable natural law. It is more than curious that Cave, the author of the *Lives of the Fathers*, should find it incredible that Cyril sanctioned her murder on account of his "general character." A saint who will sell the gold and silver vessels of his church, and then, after spending the money, lie at his trial, as he did, may well be suspected of anything.[654] Besides, in this case the Church had to fight for her life, to say nothing of her future supremacy. Alone, the hated and erudite Pagan scholars, and the no less learned Gnostics, held in their doctrines the hitherto concealed wires of all these theological marionettes. Once the curtain should be lifted, the connexion between the old Pagan and the new Christian religions would be exposed; and then, what would have become of the 'mysteries' into which it is sin and blasphemy to pry? With such a coincidence of the astronomical allegories of various Pagan myths with the dates adopted by Christianity for the nativity, crucifixion, and resurrection, and such an identity of rites and ceremonies, what would have been the fate of the new religion, had not the Church under the pretext of serving Christ got rid of the too-well-informed philosophers? To guess what, if the *coup d'état* had then failed, might have been the prevailing religion in our own century would indeed be a hard task. But in all probability the state of things which made of the Middle Ages a period of intellectual darkness, which degraded the nations of the Occident, and lowered the European of those days almost to the level of a Papuan savage — could not have occurred.

The fears of the Christians were only too well founded, and their pious zeal and prophetic insight was rewarded from the very first. In the demolition of the Serapeum, after the bloody riot between the Christian mob and the Pagan worshipers had ended with the interference of the emperor, a Latin cross, of a perfect Christian shape, was discovered

---

654. [This description applies to Cyril of Jerusalem, not to Cyril of Alexandria. See footnote 113, *supra.*]

hewn upon the granite slabs of the adytum. This was a lucky discovery, indeed; and the monks did not fail to claim that the cross had been hallowed by the Pagans in a 'spirit of prophecy.' At least Sozomen,[655] with an air of triumph, records the fact. But archaeology and symbolism, those tireless and implacable enemies of clerical false pretences, have found in the hieroglyphics of the legend running around the design at least a partial interpretation of its meaning.

According to King and other numismatists and archaeologists, the cross was placed there as the symbol of eternal life. Such a Tau, or Egyptian cross, was used in the Bacchic and Eleusinian Mysteries. Symbol of the dual generative power, it was laid upon the breast of the initiate, after his 'new birth' was accomplished, and the Mystae had returned from their baptism in the sea. It was a mystic sign that his spiritual birth had regenerated and united his astral soul with his divine spirit, and that he was ready to ascend in spirit to the blessed abodes of light and glory — the Eleusinia. The Tau was a magic talisman at the same time as a religious emblem. It was adopted by the Christians through the Gnostics and Kabalists, who used it largely, as their numerous gems testify, and who had the Tau (or handled cross) from the Egyptians, and the Latin cross from the Buddhist missionaries, who brought it from India (where it can be found even now), two or three centuries B. C. The Assyrians, Egyptians, ancient Americans, Hindûs, and Romans had it in various, but very slight, modifications of shape. Till very late in the medieval ages, it was considered a potent spell against epilepsy and demoniacal possession; and the "signet of the living God," brought down in St. John's vision by the angel ascending from the east to "seal the servants of our God in their foreheads," was but the same mystic Tau — the Egyptian cross. In the painted glass of St. Dionysus (France) this angel is represented as stamping this sign on the forehead of the elect; the legend reads, SIGNVM TAY. In King's *Gnostics* the author reminds us that "this mark is commonly borne by St. Anthony, an *Egyptian* recluse."[656] What the real meaning of the Tau was, is explained to us by the Christian St. John, the Egyptian Hermes, and the Hindû Brâhmanas. It is quite evident that, with John at least, it meant the 'Ineffable Name,' as he calls this "signet of the living God" a few chapters farther on[657] the "*Father's name written in their foreheads.*"

---

655. *Eccl. Hist.*, VII, xv. Another untrustworthy, untruthful, and ignorant writer and ecclesiastical historian of the fifth century. His alleged history of the strife between the Pagans, Neo-Platonics, and the Christians of Alexandria and Constantinople, which extends from the year 324 to 439, dedicated by him to Theodosius, the younger, is full of deliberate falsifications. Edition of Reading, Cantab., 1720. Translated. Pion frères, Paris. Cf. also Socrates: *Eccl. Hist.*, V, xvii.

656. Vol. I, p. 135 (first edition).   657. *Revelation*, vii, 2, 3; xiv, 1.

The *Brahmâtma*, the chief of the Hindû initiates, had on his head-gear two keys, symbol of the revealed mystery of life and death, placed cross-like; and in some Buddhist pagodas of Tatary and Mongolia the entrance of a chamber within the temple, generally containing the staircase which leads to the inner *dâgoba*,[658] and the porticos of some *Prachidas*[659] are ornamented with a cross formed of two fishes, and as found on some of the zodiacs of the Buddhists. We should not wonder at all at learning that the sacred device in the tombs of the Catacombs, at Rome, the *vesica piscis*, was derived from the said Buddhist zodiacal sign. How general must have been that geometrical figure in the world-symbols, may be inferred from the fact that there is a Masonic tradition that Solomon's temple was built on three foundations, forming the 'triple Tau,' or three crosses.

In its mystical sense the Egyptian cross owes its origin, as an emblem, to the realization by the earliest philosophy of an androgynous dualism in every manifestation in nature, which proceeds from the abstract ideal of a likewise androgynous deity; while the Christian emblem is simply due to chance. Had the Mosaic law prevailed, Jesus should have been lapidated.[660] The crucifix was an instrument of torture, and quite as common among the Romans as it was unknown among Semitic nations. It was called the 'Tree of Infamy.' It was only later that it was adopted as a Christian symbol; but during the first two decades the apostles looked upon it with horror.[661] It is certainly not the Christian Cross that John had in mind when speaking of the "signet of the living God," but the *mystic* Tau — the Tetragrammaton, or mighty name — which on the most ancient kabalistic talismans was represented by the four Hebrew letters composing the Holy Word.

The famous Lady Ellenborough, known among the Arabs of Damascus, and in the desert, after her last marriage, as *Hanoum Medjouyé*, had a talisman in her possession, presented to her by a 'Druze' ['Hamza-ite] from Mount Lebanon. It was recognised by a certain sign on its left corner to belong to that class of gems known in Palestine as '*Messianic*' amulets of the second or third century, B.C. It is a green stone of a pentagonal form; at the bottom is engraved a fish; higher, Solomon's seal;[662]

---

658. *Dâgoba* is a small temple of globular form, in which are preserved the relics of Gautama.   659. *Prachidas* are buildings of all sizes and forms, like our mausoleums, and are sacred to votive offerings to the dead.

660. The Talmudistic records claim that, after having been hanged, he was lapidated and buried under the water at the junction of two streams. *Mishnah Sanhedrin*, vi, 4; *Talmud* of Babylon, same article, 43 a, 67 a. (Cited by E. Renan.)

661. *Coptic Legends of the Crucifixion*, MSS. xi.

662. The engraving represents the talisman as of twice the natural size. We are at a loss to understand why King, in his 'Gnostic Gems,' represents Solomon's seal as a five-pointed star, whereas it is six-pointed, and is the signet of Vishnu, in India (*The Gnostics, etc.*, p. 388; 2nd ed.).

and still higher, the four Chaldaic letters — Yod, He, Vau, He, IAHO, which form the name of the Deity. These are arranged in quite an unusual way, running from below upward, in reversed order, and forming the Egyptian Tau. Around these there is a legend which, as the gem is not our property, we are not at liberty to give. The Tau, in its mystical sense, as well as the *cruz ansata*, is the *Tree of Life*.

It is well known that the earliest Christian emblems — before it was ever attempted to represent the bodily appearance of Jesus — were the Lamb, the Good Shepherd, and *the Fish*. The origin of the latter emblem, which has so puzzled the archaeologists, thus becomes comprehen-

sible. The whole secret lies in the easily-ascertained fact that, while in the Kabala the King Messiah is called 'Interpreter,' or Revealer of the mystery, and shown to be the *fifth* emanation, in the *Talmud* — for reasons we will now explain — the Messiah is very often designated as 'DAG,' or the Fish. This is an inheritance from the Chaldaeans, and relates — as the very name indicates — to the Babylonian Dagon, the man-fish, who was the instructor and interpreter of the people to whom he appeared. Abarbanel explains the name, by stating that the sign of his (Messiah's) coming "is the conjunction of Saturn and Jupiter in the sign *Pisces*." [663] Therefore, as the Christians were intent upon identifying their Christos with the Messiah of the *Old Testament*, they adopted it so readily as to forget that its true origin might be traced still farther back than the Babylonian Dagon. How eagerly and closely the ideal of Jesus was united, by the early Christians, with every imaginable kabalistic and Pagan tenet, may be inferred from the language of Clement of Alexandria, addressed to his brother co-religionists.

When they were debating upon the choice of the most appropriate symbol to remind them of Jesus, Clement advised them in the following words: "Let the engraving upon the gem of your ring be either *a dove*, or *a ship running before the wind* [the Argha], or *a fish*." [664] Was the good father, when writing this sentence, laboring under the recollection of Joshua, son of Nun (called *Jesus* in the Greek and Slavonian versions)? or had he forgotten the real interpretation of these Pagan symbols?

663. King (*The Gnostics*, 1st edit.) gives the figure of a Christian symbol, very common during the Middle Ages, of three fishes interlaced into a triangle, and having the FIVE letters (a most sacred Pythagorean number) I X Θ T Σ engraved on it. The number five relates to the same kabalistic computation.   664. *Paedagogus*, III, xi.

Joshua, son of Nun, or Nave (*Navis*), could have with perfect propriety adopted the image of a *ship*, or even of a fish, for Joshua means Jesus, son of the fish-god; but it was really too hazardous to connect the emblems of Venus, Astarte, and all the Hindû goddesses — the *argha*, *dove*, and *fish* — with the 'immaculate' birth of their god! This looks very much as if in the early days of Christianity but little distinction was made between Christ, Bacchus, Apollo, and the Hindû Krishna, the incarnation of Vishnu, with whose first avatar this symbol of the fish originated.

In the *Hari-Purâna*, in the *Bhâgavata-Purâna*, as well as in several other books, the god Vishnu is shown as having assumed the form of a fish with a human head in order to reclaim the *Vedas* lost during the deluge. Having enabled Vaivasvata to escape with all his tribe in the ark, Vishnu, pitying weak and ignorant humanity, remained with them for some time. It was this god who taught them to build houses, cultivate the land, and to thank the unknown Deity whom he represented, by building temples and instituting a regular worship; and as he remained half-fish, half-man all the time, at every sunset he used to return to the ocean wherein he passed the night.

"It is he," says the sacred book, "who taught men, after the diluvium, all that was necessary for their happiness.

"One day he plunged into the water and returned no more, for the earth had covered itself again with vegetation, fruit, and cattle.

"But he had taught the Brâhmanas the secret of all things" (*Hari-Purâna*).

So far, we see in this narrative the *double* of the story given by the Babylonian Berosus about Oannes, the fish-man, who is no other than Vishnu — unless, indeed, we have to believe that it was Chaldaea which civilized India!

We say again, we desire to give nothing on our sole authority. Therefore we cite Jacolliot who, however criticized and contradicted on other points, and however loose he may be in the matter of chronology (though even in this he is nearer right than those scientists who would have all Hindû books written since the Council of Nice), at least cannot be denied the reputation of a good Sanskrit scholar. And he says, while analysing the word *Oan*, or Oannes, that *O* in Sanskrit is an interjection expressing an invocation, as O Svayambhû! O God! etc.; and *Ana* is a radical, signifying in Sanskrit a spirit, a being, and we presume what the Greeks meant by the word *Daimon*, a semi-god.

"What an extraordinary antiquity," he remarks, "this fable of Vishnu, disguised as a fish, gives to the sacred books of the Hindûs; especially in presence of the fact that the *Vedas* and *Manu* reckon more *than twenty-five thousand years of existence*, as proved by the most serious as the most authentic documents. Few peoples, says the learned Halled, have their annals more authentic or serious than the Hindûs." [665]

We may, perhaps, throw additional light upon the puzzling question of the fish-symbol by reminding the reader that according to *Genesis* the first created of living beings, the first type of animal life, was the fish. "And the Elohim said: 'Let the waters bring forth abundantly the moving creature that *hath life*' . . . and God created great whales . . . and the morning and the evening were the *fifth day*." [666] Jonah is swallowed by a big fish, and is cast out again three days later. This the Christians regard as a premonition of the three days' sepulture of Jesus which preceded his resurrection — though the statement of the three days is as fanciful as much of the rest, and adopted to fit the well-known threat to destroy the temple and rebuild it again in *three* days. Between his burial and alleged resurrection there intervened but *one day* — the Jewish Sabbath — as he was buried on Friday evening and rose to life at dawn on Sunday. However, whatever other circumstance may be regarded as a prophecy, the story of Jonah cannot be made to answer the purpose.

'Big Fish' is Cetus, the latinized form of Ketos (κῆτος), and Ketos is Dagon, Poseidon, the feminine form of it being Keton Atar-gatis — the Syrian goddess, and Venus, of Askalon. [667] The figure or bust of Der-Ketos, or Astarte, was generally represented on the prow of the ships. Jonah (Hebrew, for *dove;* a bird sacred to Venus) fled to Jaffa, where the god Dagon, the man-fish, was worshiped, and dared not go to Nineveh, *where the dove was revered.* Hence some commentators believe that when Jonah was thrown overboard and was swallowed by a fish, we must understand that he was picked up by one of these vessels, on the prow of which was the figure of *Ketos*. But the kabalists have another legend, to this effect: they say that Jonah was a run-away priest from the temple of the goddess where the dove was worshiped, and that he desired to abolish idolatry and institute monotheistic worship. That, caught near Jaffa, he was held prisoner by the devotees of Dagon in one of the prison-cells of the temple, and that it is the strange form of the cell which gave rise to the allegory. In the collection of Mose de Garcia, a Portuguese kabalist, there is a drawing representing the interior of the temple of Dagon. In the middle stands an immense idol, the upper portion of whose body is human, and the lower fish-like. Between the belly and the tail is an aperture which can be closed like the door of a closet. In it the transgressors against the local deity were shut up until further disposal. The drawing in question was made from an old tablet covered with curious drawings and inscriptions in old Phoenician characters describing

---

665. *La genèse de l'humanité*, pp. 80, 81.   666. *Genesis*, i, 20-23.
667. Pliny: *Nat. Hist.*, V, xix; Diod. Sicul.: *Bibl. hist.*, II, iv.

this Venetian *oubliette* of biblical days. The tablet itself was found in an excavation a few miles from Jaffa. Considering the extraordinary tendency of Oriental nations for puns and allegories, is it not barely possible that the 'big fish' by which Jonah was swallowed was simply the cell within the belly of Dagon?

It is significant that this double appellation of 'Messiah' and 'Dag' (fish) of the Talmudists should so well apply to the Hindû Vishnu, the 'Preserving' Spirit, and the second personage of the Brâhmanic trinity. This deity, having already manifested itself, is still regarded as the future Savior of humanity, and is the selected Redeemer, who will appear at its tenth incarnation or *avatâra*, like the Messiah of the Jews, to lead the blessed onward, and restore to them the primitive *Vedas*. At his first avatar, Vishnu is alleged to have appeared to humanity in form like a fish. In the temple of Râma there is a representation of this god which answers perfectly to the description of Dagon, as given by Berosus. He has the body of a man issuing from the mouth of a fish, and holds in his hands the lost *Veda*. Vishnu, moreover, is the water-god, in one sense, the Logos of the Parabrahman, for as the three persons of the manifested god-head constantly interchange their attributes, we see him in the same temple represented as reclining on the seven-headed serpent, Ananta (eternity), and moving, like the *Spirit* of God, on the face of the primeval waters.

Vishnu is evidently the Adam Kadmon of the kabalists, for Adam is the Logos or the first Anointed, as Adam Second is the King Messiah.

Lakhmi, or *Lakshmî*, the passive or feminine counterpart of Vishnu, the creator and the preserver, is also called Âdi-Mâyâ. She is the 'Mother of the World,' *Dhâtrî*, the Venus-Aphrodite of the Greeks; also Isis and Eve. While Venus is born from the sea-foam, Lakshmî springs out from the water at the churning of the sea; when born, she is so beautiful that all the gods fall in love with her. The Jews, borrowing their types wherever they could get them, made their first woman after the pattern of Lakshmî. It is curious that Viracocha, the Supreme Being in Peru, means, literally translated, 'foam of the sea.'

Eugène Burnouf, the great authority of the French school, announces his opinion in the same spirit: "We must learn one day," he observes, "that all ancient traditions disfigured by emigration and legend belong to the history of India." Such is the opinion of Colebrooke, Inman, King, Jacolliot, and many other Orientalists.

We have said above that according to the secret computation peculiar to the students of the hidden science, Messiah is the fifth emanation or potency. In the Jewish Kabala, where the ten Sephiroth emanate from Adam Kadmon (placed below the crown), he comes fifth. So in

the Gnostic system; so in the Buddhistic, in which the fifth Buddha —
Maitreya, will appear at his last advent to save mankind before the final
destruction of the world. If Vishnu is represented in his forthcoming
and last appearance as the *tenth* avatar or incarnation, it is only because
every unit held as an androgyne manifests itself doubly. The Buddhists
who reject this dual-sexed incarnation reckon but five. Thus, while
Vishnu is to make his last appearance in his tenth, Buddha is said to do
the same in his fifth incarnation.[668]

The better to illustrate the idea, and show how completely the real
meaning of the avatars, known only to the students of the secret doctrine, was misunderstood by the ignorant masses, we elsewhere give
the diagrams of the Hindû and Chaldaeo-Kabalistic avatars and emanations.[669] This basic and true fundamental stone of the secret cycles
shows on its very face that far from taking their revealed *Vedas* and
Bible literally, the Brâhman-pandits and the Tanaim — the scientists
and philosophers of the pre-Christian epochs — speculated on the creation and development of the world quite in a Darwinian way, both anticipating him and his school in regard to the natural selection of species,
their gradual development and transformation.

We advise every one tempted to enter an indignant protest against
this affirmation to read more carefully the books of Manu, even in the
incomplete translation of Sir William Jones, and the more or less care-
less one of Jacolliot. If we compare the Sanchoniathon-Phoenician
Cosmogony and the record of Berosus with the *Bhâgavata-Purâna* and
Manu, we shall find enunciated exactly the same principles as those now
offered as the latest developments of modern science. We have quoted
from the Chaldaean and Phoenician records in our first volume; we will
now glance at the Hindû books.

"When this world had issued out of darkness, the subtile elementary
principles produced the vegetal seed which animated first the plants;
from the plants life passed into fantastical bodies which were born *in the
ilus of the waters;* then, through a series of forms and various animals,
it reached MAN." [670]

"He [man, before becoming such] will pass successively through
plants, worms, insects, fish, serpents, tortoises, cattle, and wild animals;
such is the inferior degree."

"Such, from Brahmâ down to the vegetables, are declared the transmigrations which take place in this world." [671]

---

668. The Kabalistic Sephiroth are also ten in number, or five pairs.
669. An avatar is a descent from on high upon earth of the Deity in some manifest shape.
670. *Bhâgavata-Purâna.*   671. *Manu,* I, 50; XII, 42.

In the Sanchoniathonian Cosmogony, men are also evolved out of the ilus of the chaos,[672] and the same evolution and transformation of species are shown.

And now we will leave the rostrum to Mr. Darwin: "I believe that animals have descended from at most only four or five progenitors." [673]

Again: "I should infer from analogy that probably all the organic beings which have ever lived on this earth, have descended from some one primordial form.[674] . . . I view all beings, not as special creations, but as the lineal descendants of some few beings which lived long *before the first bed of the Silurian system was deposited.*" [675]

In short, they lived in the Sanchoniathonian chaos, and in the *ilus* of Manu. Vyâsa and Kapila go still farther than Darwin and Manu. "They see in Brahmâ but the name of the universal germ; *they deny the existence of a First Cause;* and pretend that everything in nature found itself developed only in consequence of material and fatal forces," says Jacolliot.[676]

Correct as may be this latter quotation from Kapila, it demands a few words of explanation. Jacolliot repeatedly compares Kapila and Veda-Vyâsa with Pyrrho and Littré. We have nothing against such a comparison with the Greek philosopher, but we must decidedly object to any with the French Comtist; we find it an unmerited fling at the memory of the great Aryan sage. Nowhere does this prolific writer state the repudiation by either ancient or modern Brâhmanas of God — the 'unknown,' universal Spirit; nor does any other Orientalist accuse the Hindûs of the same, however perverted the general deductions of our savants about Buddhistic atheism. On the contrary, Jacolliot states more than once that the learned Pandits and educated Brâhmanas have never shared the popular superstitions; and affirms their unshaken belief in the unity of God and the soul's immortality, although most assuredly neither Kapila, nor the initiated Brâhmanas, nor the followers of the Vedânta school, would ever admit the existence of an anthropomorphic creator, a 'First Cause' in the Christian sense. Jacolliot, in his *Indo-European and African Traditions*, is the first to make an onslaught on Professor Müller, for remarking that the Hindû gods were "masks without actors . . . names without being, and not beings without names." [677] Quoting, in support of his argument, numerous verses from the sacred Hindû books, Jacolliot adds: "Is it possible to refuse to the author of these stanzas a definite and clear conception of the divine

672. See Cory: *Ancient Fragments*, p. 3; ed. 1832.
673. *On the Origin of Species*, first edition, p. 484.   674. *Ibid.*, p. 484.
675. *Ibid.*, pp. 488, 489.   676. *La genèse de l'humanité*, p. 338.
677. *Les traditions indo-européennes et africaines*, p. 291.

force, of the Unique Being, Sovereign-master and Creator of the Universe? . . . Were the altars then built to a metaphor?" [678]

The latter argument is perfectly just, so far as Max Müller's negation is concerned. But we doubt whether the French rationalist understands Kapila's and Vyâsa's philosophy better than the German philologist does the "theological twaddle," as the latter terms the *Atharva-Veda*. Professor Müller and Jacolliot may have ever so great claims to erudition, and be ever so familiar with Sanskrit and other ancient Oriental languages, but both lack the key to the thousand and one mysteries of the old secret doctrine and its philosophy. Only, while the German philologist does not even take the trouble to look into this magical and "theological twaddle," we find the French Indianist never losing an opportunity to investigate. Moreover he honestly admits his incompetency ever to fathom this ocean of mystical learning. In its existence he not only firmly believes, but throughout his works he incessantly calls the attention of science to its unmistakable traces at every step in India. Still, though the learned Pandits and Brâhmanas — his revered "masters of the pagodas of Villenoor and Chelambrum in the Carnatic," [679] as it seems, positively refused to reveal to him the mysteries of the magical part of the *Agrushada-Parikshai*,[680] and of Brahmâtma's triangle,[681] he persists in the honest declaration that everything is possible in Hindû metaphysics, even to the Kapila and Vyâsa systems having been hitherto misunderstood.

M. Jacolliot weakens his assertion immediately afterward with the following contradiction:

"We were one day inquiring of a Brâhmana of the pagoda of Chelambrum, who belonged to the *skeptical school of the naturalists of Vyâsa*, whether he believed in the existence of God. He answered us, smiling: '*Aham eva param-Brahma*' — I am myself a god.

"'What do you mean by that?'

"'I mean that every being on earth, however humble, is an immortal portion of immortal substance.'" [682]

The answer is one which would suggest itself to every ancient philosopher, Kabalist and Gnostic, of the early days. It contains the very spirit of the Delphic and Kabalistic commandment, for esoteric philosophy solved ages ago the problem of what man was, is, and will be. If per-

678. *Les traditions indo-européennes et africaines*, pp. 293, *sq.*

679. *Les Fils de Dieu*, p. 32.   680. *Le spiritisme dans le monde*, p. 78, and others.

681. *Les Fils de Dieu*, p. 272. While not at all astonished that Brâhmanas should have refused to satisfy M. Jacolliot's curiosity, we must add that the meaning of this sign is known to the superiors of every Buddhist lamasery, and not alone to the Brâhmanas.

682. *La genèse de l'humanité*, p. 339.

sons believing the *Bible* verse which teaches that the "Lord God formed man of the dust of the ground, and breathed into his nostrils the breath of life," reject at the same time the idea that every atom of this dust, as every particle of this 'living soul,' contains 'God' within itself, then we pity the logic of such Christians. They forget the verses which precede the one in question. God blesses equally every beast of the field and every living creature, in the water as in the air, and He endows them all with *life*, which is a breath of His own Spirit, and the *soul* of the animal. Humanity is the Adam Kadmon of the 'Unknown,' His microcosm, and His only representative on earth, and every man is a god on earth.

We would ask this French scholar, who seems so familiar with every *śloka* of the books of Manu, and other Vedic writers, the meaning of this sentence so well known to him:

"Plants and vegetation reveal a multitude of forms because of their precedent actions; they are surrounded by darkness, but are nevertheless endowed with an interior soul, and feel equally pleasure and pain" (*Manu*, I, 48-9).

If the Hindû philosophy teaches the presence of a degree of *soul* in the lowest forms of vegetable life, and even in every atom in space, how is it possible that it should deny the same immortal principle to man? And if it once admits the immortal spirit in man, how can it logically deny the existence of the parent source — I will not say the first, but the eternal Cause? Neither rationalists nor sensualists, who do not comprehend Indian metaphysics, should estimate the ignorance of Hindû metaphysicians by their own.

The grand cycle, as we have heretofore remarked, includes the progress of mankind from its germ in the primordial man of spiritual form to the deepest depth of degradation he can reach — each successive step in the descent being accompanied by a greater strength and grossness of the physical form than its precursor — and ends with the Flood. But while the grand cycle, or age, is running its course, seven minor cycles are passed, each marking the evolution of a new race out of the preceding one, on a new world. And each of these races, or grand types of humanity, breaks up into subdivisions of families, and they again into nations and tribes — as we see the earth's inhabitants subdivided today into Mongols, Caucasians, Indians, etc.

Before proceeding to show by diagrams the close resemblance between the esoteric philosophies of all the ancient peoples, however geographically remote from each other, it will be useful to explain briefly the real ideas which underlie all those symbols and allegorical representations that have hitherto so puzzled the uninitiated commentators. Better than anything, it may show that religion and science were closer knit than

twins in days of old; that they were one in two and two in one from the
very moment of their conception. With mutually convertible attributes,
science was spiritual and religion was scientific. Like the androgyne man
of the first chapter of *Genesis* — 'male and female,' passive and active;
created in the image of the Elohim. Omniscience developed omnipo-
tency, the latter called for the exercise of the former, and thus the giant
had dominion given him over all the four kingdoms of the world. But,
like the second Adam, these androgynes were doomed to 'fall and lose
their powers' as soon as the two halves of the duality separated. The
fruit of the Tree of Knowledge gives death without the fruit of the Tree
of Life. Man must know *himself* before he can hope to know the ultimate
genesis even of beings and powers less developed in their inner nature
than himself. So with religion and science; united two in one, they
were infallible, for the spiritual intuition was there to supply the limita-
tions of physical senses. Separated, exact science rejects the help of the
inner voice, while religion becomes merely dogmatic theology — each is
but a corpse without a soul.

The esoteric doctrine, then, teaches, like Buddhism and Brâhmanism,
and even the persecuted Kabala, that the one infinite and unknown Essence exists from all eternity, and in regular and harmonious successions
is either passive or active. In the poetical phraseology of *Manu* these
conditions are called the 'day' and the 'night' of Brahma. The latter is
either 'awake' or 'asleep.' The *Svâbhâvikas*, or philosophers of the
oldest school of Buddhism (which still exists in Nepal), speculate only
upon the active condition of this 'Essence,' which they call *Svabhâva*,
and deem it foolish to theorize upon the abstract and 'unknowable'
power in its passive condition. Hence they are called atheists by both
Christian theology and modern science; for neither of the two is able
to understand the profound logic of their philosophy. The former will
allow of no other God than the personified *secondary* powers which have
blindly worked out the visible universe, and which became with them the
anthropomorphic God of the Christians — the Jehovah, roaring amid
thunder and lightning. In its turn rationalistic science greets the Buddhists and the *Svâbhâvikas* as the 'positivists' of the archaic ages. If
we take a one-sided view of the philosophy of the latter, our materialists
may be right in their own way. The Buddhists maintain that there is *no*
Creator, but an infinitude of *creative powers*, which collectively form the
one eternal substance, the *essence* of which is inscrutable — hence not a
subject for speculation for any true philosopher. Socrates invariably
refused to argue upon the mystery of universal being, yet no one would
ever have thought of charging him with atheism, except those who were
bent upon his destruction. Upon inaugurating an active period, says the

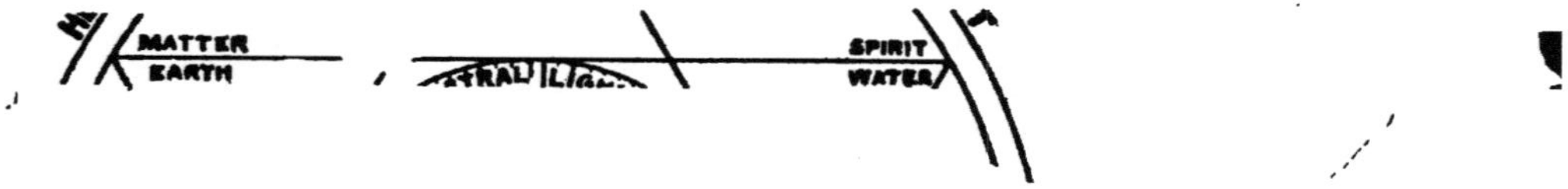
MATTER
EARTH
SPIRIT
WATER

Secret Doctrine, an expansion of this Divine essence, *from within outwardly,* occurs in obedience to eternal and immutable law, and the phenomenal or visible universe is the ultimate result of the long chain of cosmical forces thus progressively set in motion. In like manner, when the passive condition is resumed, a contraction of the Divine essence takes place, and the previous work of creation is gradually and progressively undone. The visible universe becomes disintegrated, its material dispersed; and 'darkness,' solitary and alone, broods once more over the face of the 'deep.' To use a metaphor which will convey the idea still more clearly, an outbreathing of the 'unknown essence' produces the world; and an inhalation causes it to disappear. *This process has been going on from all eternity, and our present universe is but one of an infinite series which had no beginning and will have no end.*

Thus we are enabled to build our theories solely on the visible manifestations of the Deity, on its objective natural phenomena. To apply to these creative principles the term 'God' is puerile and absurd. One might as well call by the name of Benvenuto Cellini the fire which fuses the metal, or the air that cools it when it is run in the mold. If the inner and ever-concealed spiritual, and to our minds abstract, Essence within these forces can ever be connected with the creation of the physical universe, it is but in the sense given to it by Plato. IT may be termed, at best, the framer of the abstract universe which developed gradually in the Divine Thought within which it had lain dormant.

In Chapter VIII we will attempt to show the esoteric meaning of *Genesis,* and its complete agreement with the ideas of other nations. The six days of creation will be found to have a meaning little suspected by the multitude of commentators, who have exercised their abilities to the full extent in attempting to reconcile them by turns with Christian theology and un-Christian geology. Disfigured as the *Old Testament* is, yet in its symbolism is preserved enough of the original in its principal features to show the family likeness to the cosmogonies of older nations than the Jews.

We here give the diagrams of the Hindû and the Chaldaeo-Jewish cosmogonies. The antiquity of the diagram of the former may be inferred from the fact that many of the Brâhmanical pagodas are designed and built on this figure, called the *Srî-antara.*[683] And yet we find the highest honors paid to it by the Jewish and medieval kabalists, who call it 'Solomon's seal.' It will be quite an easy matter to trace it to its origin, once we are reminded of the history of the king-kabalist and his transactions with King Hiram and Ophir — the country of peacocks, gold, and ivory — for which land we have to search in old India.

---

683. See *Journal of the Royal Asiatic Society,* XIII, p. 79.

EXPLANATION OF THE TWO DIAGRAMS

REPRESENTING THE

CHAOTIC AND THE FORMATIVE PERIODS, BEFORE AND AFTER OUR UNIVERSE BEGAN TO BE EVOLVED

FROM THE ESOTERIC BRÂHMANIC, BUDDHISTIC, AND CHALDÆAN
STANDPOINTS, WHICH AGREE IN EVERY RESPECT WITH THE
EVOLUTIONARY THEORY OF MODERN SCIENCE

The Hindû Doctrine
The Upper Triangle

Contains the Ineffable Name. It is the AUM — to be pronounced only mentally, under penalty of death. The Unrevealed Parabrahman, the Passive-Principle; the absolute and unconditioned *mukta*, which cannot enter into the condition of a Creator, as the latter, in order to *think, will,* and *plan,* must be bound and conditioned (*baddha*); hence, in one sense, be a finite being. "This (Parabrahman) was absorbed in the non-being, imperceptible, without any distinct attribute, non-existent for our senses. He was absorbed in his (to us) eternal, (to himself) periodical sleep," for it was one of the 'Nights of Brahma.' Therefore he is not the *First* but the Eternal Cause. He is the Soul of Souls, whom no being can comprehend in this state. But "he who studies the secret Mantras and comprehends the *Vâch*" (the Spirit or hidden voice of the Mantras, the active manifestation of the latent Force) will learn to understand him in his 'revealed' aspect.

The Chaldæan Doctrine
The Upper Triangle

Contains the Ineffable Name. It is Ain-Soph, the Boundless, the Infinite, whose name is known to no one but the initiated, and could not be pronounced aloud under the penalty of death.

No more than Parabrahman can Ain-Soph create, for he is in the same condition of non-being as the former; he is אין non-existent so long as he lies in his latent or passive state within *Oulam* (the boundless and termless time); as such he is not the Creator of the visible universe, neither is he the *Aor* (Light). He will become the latter when the period of creation shall have compelled him to expand the Force within himself, according to the Law of which he is the embodiment and essence.

"Whosoever acquaints himself with ה the *Merkabah,* and the *la'hash* (secret speech or incantation) [684] will learn the secret of secrets."

684. *La'hash* is nearly identical in meaning with *Vâch,* the hidden power of the Mantras.

Both 'This' and Ain-Soph, in their first manifestation of Light, emerging from within Darkness, may be summarized in the Svabhâvat, the Eternal and the uncreated Self-existing Substance which produces all; while everything which is of its essence produces itself out of its own nature.

The Space Around the Upper Triangle

When the 'Night of Brahma' was ended, and the time came for the Self-Existent to manifest *Itself* by revelation, it made its glory visible by sending forth from its Essence an active Power, which, female at first, subsequently becomes

The Space Around the Upper Triangle

When the active period had arrived, Ain-Soph sent forth from within his own eternal essence Sephira, the active Power, called the Primordial Point, and the Crown, *Kether.* It is only through her that the 'Un-bounded Wisdom' could

androgyne. It is *Aditi*, the 'Infinite,'[685] the Boundless, or rather the 'Unbounded.' *Aditi* is the 'mother' of all the gods, and *Aditi* is the Father and the Son.[686] "Who will give us back to the great Aditi, that I may see father and mother?"[687] It is in conjunction with the latter female, Force, that the Divine but latent Thought produces the great 'Deep' — water. "Water is born from a transformation of light . . . and from a *modification* of the water is born the earth," says *Manu* I, *śloka* 78).

"Ye are born of Aditi from the water, you who are born of the earth, hear ye all my call."[688]

In this water (or primeval chaos) the 'Infinite' androgyne, which, with the Eternal Cause, forms the first abstract Triad, rendered by AUM, deposited the germ of universal life. It is the Mundane Egg, in which took place the gestation of *Puruṣha*, or the manifested Brahmā. The germ which fecundated the *Mother* Principle (the water) is called *Nara*, the Divine Spirit or Holy Ghost,[689] and the waters themselves are an emanation of the former, *Nārī*, while the Spirit which brooded over it is called *Nārāyana*.[690]

"In that egg, the great Power sat inactive a whole *year [of the Creator]*, at the close of which, by his thought alone, he caused the egg to divide itself."[691] The upper half became heaven, the lower, the

give a concrete form to his abstract Thought. Two sides of the upper triangle, the right side and the base, are composed of unbroken lines; the third, the left side, is dotted. It is through the latter that emerges Sephira. Spreading in every direction, she finally encompasses the whole triangle. In this emanation of the female active principle from the left side of the mystic triangle, is foreshadowed the creation of Eve from Adam's left rib. Adam is the Microcosm of the Macrocosm, and is created in the image of the Elohim. In the Tree of Life עץ חיים the triple triad is disposed in such a manner that the three male Sephiroth are on the right, the three female on the left, and the four uniting principles in the center. From the Invisible Dew falling from the Higher 'Head' Sephira creates primeval water, or chaos taking shape. It is the first step toward the solidification of Spirit, which through various modifications will produce earth.[692] "*It requires earth and water to make a living soul*," says Moses.

When Sephira emerges like an active power from within the latent Deity, she is female; when she assumes the office of a creator, she becomes a male; hence, she is androgyne. She is the 'Father and Mother Aditi' of the Hindū Cosmogony.

685. In *Rig-Veda Sanhitā* the meaning is given by Max Müller as the Absolute, "for it is derived from '*diti*,' bond, and the negative particle *A*."

686. 'Hymns to the Maruts,' I, 89, 10.

687. *Ibid.*, I, 24, 1. 688. *Ibid.*, X, 63, 2.

689. Thus is it that we find in all the philosophical theogonies the Holy Ghost female. The numerous sects of the Gnostics had Sophia; the Jewish kabalists and Talmudists, Shekhinah (the garment of the Highest), which descended between the two cherubim upon the Mercy Seat; and we find even Jesus made to say, in an old text, "My *Mother*, the Holy Ghost, took me." *Gosp. of Hebrews*, see Origen: *Comm. in Johann.*, p. 59, ed. Huet.

"The waters are called *nārā*, because they were the production of *Nara*," the Spirit of God (*Ordinances of Manu*, I, 10).

690. Nārāyana, that which moves on the waters.

691. *Manu*, I, 12.

692. George Smith (ch. v) gives the first verses of the Akkadian *Genesis* as found in the Cuneiform Texts on the *laterae coctiles*. There, also, we find *Anu*, the passive deity or Ain-Soph; *Bel*, the Creator, the Spirit of God (Sephira) moving on the face of the waters, hence water itself; and *Hea*, the Universal Soul or wisdom of the three combined.

The first eight verses read thus:

1. When above, were not raised the heavens;

2. and below on the earth a plant had not grown up.

3. The abyss had not broken its boundaries.

4. The chaos [or water] Tiamat [the sea] was the producing mother of the whole of them. [This is the Cosmical Aditi and Sephira.]

5. Those waters at the beginning were ordained but

6. a tree had not grown, a flower had not unfolded.

7. When the gods had not sprung up, any one of them;

8. a plant had not grown, and order did not exist. This was the chaotic or ante-genesis period.

earth (both yet in their ideal, not their manifested form).

Thus this second triad, only another name for the first one (never pronounced aloud), and which is the real pre-Vedic and primordial *secret* Trimûrti, consisted of

Nara, Father-Heaven,

Nârî, Mother-Earth,

Virâj, the Son — or Universe.

The Trimûrti, comprising Brahmâ, the Creator, Vishnu, the Preserver, and Siva, the Destroyer and Regenerator, belongs to a later period. It is an anthropomorphic afterthought, invented for the more popular comprehension of the uninitiated masses. The *Dîkshita*, the initiate, knew better. Thus also, the profound allegory under the colors of a ridiculous fable, given in the *Aitareya-Brâhmanam*,[693] which resulted in the representations in some temples of Brahmâ-Nara, assuming the form of a bull, and his daughter, Aditi-Nârî, that of a heifer, contains the same metaphysical idea as the 'fall of man,' or that of the Spirit into generation — matter. The All-pervading Divine Spirit embodied under the symbols of Heaven, the Sun, and Heat (fire) — the correlation of cosmic forces — fecundates Matter or Nature, the daughter of Spirit. And Brahmâ himself has to submit to and bear the penance of the curses of the other gods (Elohim) for such an incest. (See corresponding column.) According to the immutable, and therefore fatal law, both Nara and Nârî are mutually Father and Mother, as well as Father and Daughter.[694] Matter, through infinite transformation, is the gradual product of Spirit. The unification of one Eternal Supreme Cause required such a correlation; and if nature be

After brooding over the 'Deep,' the 'Spirit of God' produces its own image in the water, the Universal Womb, symbolised in *Manu* by the Golden Egg. In the kabalistic Cosmogony, Heaven and Earth are personified by Adam Kadmon and the second Adam. The first Ineffable Triad, contained in the abstract idea of the 'Three Heads,' was a 'mystery name.' It was composed of Ain-Soph, Sephira, and Adam Kadmon, the Protogonos, the latter being identical with the former, when bisexual.[695] In every triad there is a male, a female, and an androgyne. Adam-Sephira is the Crown (Kether). It sets itself to the work of creation by first producing 'Hokhmah, Male Wisdom, a masculine active potency, represented by יה, yah, or the Wheels of Creation, אופנים, from which proceeds Binah, Intelligence, female and passive potency, which is *Yehovah*, יהוה, whom we find in the *Bible* figuring as the Supreme. But this Yehovah is not the kabalistic Yod-heva. The *binary* is the fundamental corner-stone of *Gnosis*. As the binary is the Unity multiplying itself and self-creating, the kabalists show the 'Unknown' passive Ain-Soph as emanating from himself Sephira, which, becoming visible light, is said to produce Adam Kadmon. But, in the hidden sense, Sephira and Adam are one and the same light, only latent and active, invisible and visible. The second Adam, as the human tetragram, produces in his turn Eve, out of his side. It is this second triad, with which the kabalists have hitherto dealt, hardly hinting at the Supreme and Ineffable One, and never committing anything to writing. All knowledge concerning the latter was imparted orally. It is the *second* Adam, then, who is the unity represented by *Yod*, emblem of the kabalistic male principle, and, at the same time, he is 'Hokhmah, *Wisdom*, while *Binah* or Yehovah is Eve; the first,

---

693. See Haug's translation: III, iii, 33.

694. The same transformations are found in the cosmogony of every important nation. Thus we see in the Egyptian mythology, Isis and Osiris, sister and brother, man and wife; and Horus, the Son of both, becoming the husband of his mother, Isis, and producing a son, *Malouli*. (Champollion-Figeac: *Egypte ancienne*, p. 245.)

695. When a female power, she is Sephira; when male, he is Adam Kadmon; for, as the former contains in herself the other nine Sephiroth, so, in their totality, the latter, including Sephira, is embodied in the Archetypal Kadmon, the πρωτόγονος.

the product or effect of that Cause, in its turn it has to be fecundated by the same divine Ray which produced nature itself. The most absurd cosmogonical allegories, if analysed without prejudice, will be found built on strict and logical necessarianism.

"Being was born from not-being," says a verse in the *Rig-Veda*.[696] The first being had to become androgyne and finite, by the very fact of its creation as a being. And thus even the sacred Trimûrti, containing Brahmâ, Vishnu, and Śiva, will have an end when the 'night' of Parabrahman succeeds the present 'day,' or period of universal activity.

The second, or rather the first, triad — as the highest one is a pure abstraction — is the intellectual world. The *Vâch* which surrounds it is a more definite transformation of Aditi. Besides its occult significance in the secret Mantra, Vâch is personified as the active power of Brahmâ proceeding from him. In the *Vedas* she is made to speak of herself as the supreme and universal soul. "I bore the Father on the head of the universal mind, and *my origin is in the midst of the ocean;* and therefore do I pervade all beings. . . . Originating all beings, I pass like the breeze [Holy Ghost]. I am above this heaven, beyond this earth; and *what is the Great One that am I.*"[697] Literally, Vâch is speech, the power of awakening, through the metrical arrangement contained in the number and syllables of the Mantras,[698] corresponding powers in the invisible world. In the sacrificial Mysteries Vâch stirs up the Brahma (*Brahma jinvati*), or the power lying latent at the bottom of every magical operation. It existed from eternity as the *Yajña* (its latent form), lying dormant in Brahma from 'no-beginning,' and proceeded forth from him as Vâch (the active power). It is the key to the '*Trai-*

'Hokhmah, issuing from Kether, or the androgyne, Adam Kadmon, and the second, Binah, from 'Hokhmah. If we combine with *Yod* the three letters which form the name of Eve, we shall have the divine tetragram pronounced IEVO-HEVAH, Adam and Eve, יהוה, Jehovah, male and female, or the idealization of humanity embodied in the first man. Thus is it that we can prove that, while the Jewish kabalists, in common with their initiated masters, the Chaldaeans and the Hindûs, adored the Supreme and Unknown God in the sacred silence of their sanctuaries, the ignorant masses of every nation were left to adore something which was certainly less than the Eternal Substance of the Buddhists, the so-called Atheists. As Brahmâ, the deity manifested in the mythical Manu, or the first man (born of *Svayambhû*, or the Self-existent One), is finite, so Jehovah, embodied in Adam and Eve, is but a *human* god. He is the symbol of humanity, a mixture of good with a portion of unavoidable evil; of spirit fallen into matter. In worshiping Jehovah, we simply worship nature, as embodied in man, half-spiritual and half-material, at best: we are Pantheists, when not fetish worshipers, like the idolatrous Jews, who sacrificed on high places, in groves, to the personified male and female principle, ignorant of IAO, the Supreme 'Secret Name' of the Mysteries.

Shekhinah is the Hindû Vâch, and praised in the same terms as the latter. Though shown in the kabalistic Tree of Life as proceeding from the ninth Sephiroth, yet Shekhinah is the 'veil' of Ain-Soph and the 'garment' of Jehovah. The 'veil' — for it succeeded for long ages in concealing the real supreme God, the universal Spirit, and masking Jehovah the exoteric deity — made the Christians accept him as the 'father' of the initiated Jesus. Yet the kabalists, as well as the Hindû *Dîkshita*, know the power of the Shekhinah or Vâch, and call it the 'secret wisdom,' חכמה-נסתרה.

The triangle played a prominent part in the religious symbolism of every great nation; for everywhere it represented the

696. *Mandala* I, *Sûkta* 166; Max Müller.

697. *Asiatic Researches*, VIII, p 403; Colebrooke's translation.

698. As in the Pythagorean numerical system every number on Earth, or the world of the effects, corresponds to its invisible prototype in the world of causes.

vidyâ,' the thrice sacred science which teaches the *Yajus* (the sacrificial Mysteries).[698]

Having done with the unrevealed triad, and the first triad of the Sephiroth, called the 'intellectual world,' little remains to be said. In the great geometrical figure which has the double triangle in it, the central circle represents the world within the universe. The double triangle belongs to one of the most important, if it is not in itself the most important, of the mystic figures in India. It is the emblem of the Trimûrti, three in one. The triangle with its apex upward indicates the male principle, downward the female; the two typifying at the same time spirit and matter. This world within the infinite universe is the microcosm within the macrocosm, as in the Jewish Kabala. It is the symbol of the womb of the universe, the terrestrial egg, whose archetype is the golden mundane egg. It is from within this spiritual bosom of mother nature that proceed all the great saviors of the universe — the avatars of the invisible Deity.

"Of him who is and yet is not, from the not-being, Eternal Cause, is born the being Purusha," says Manu, the legislator. Purusha is the 'divine male,' the *second* god, and the avatar, or the Logos of Parabrahman and his divine son, who in his turn produced Virâj, the son, or the ideal type of the universe. "Virâj begins the work of creation by producing the ten *Prajâpatis*, 'the lords of all beings'" (*Manu*, I, 11, *sq.*, 33, *sq.*).

According to the doctrine of *Manu*, the universe is subjected to a periodical and never-ending succession of creations and dissolutions, which periods of creation are named *Manvantaras*.

"It is the germ [which the Divine Spirit produced from its own substance] which never perishes in the being, for it becomes the soul of Being, and at the period of *pralaya* [dissolution] it returns to absorb itself again *into the Divine Spirit, which itself* rests from all eternity within

three great principles — spirit, force, and matter; or the active (male), passive (female), and the dual or correlative principle which partakes of both and binds the two together. It was the *Arba* or mystic 'four,'[700] the mystery-gods, the Kabiri, summarised in the unity of one supreme Deity. It is found in the Egyptian pyramids, whose equal sides tower up until lost in one crowning point. In the kabalistic diagram the central circle of the Brâhmanical figure is replaced by the cross; the celestial perpendicular and the terrestrial horisontal base-line.[701] But the idea is the same: Adam Kadmon is the type of humanity as a collective totality within the unity of the creative God and the universal spirit.

699. See initial chap., vol i, p. xliii, word *Yajna.*

700. Eve is the trinity of nature, and Adam the unity of spirit; the former the created material principle, the latter the ideal organ of the creative principle, or, in other words, this androgyne is both the principle and the Logos, for ‎‏נ‏‎ is the male, and ‎‏ר‏‎ the female; and, as Lévi expresses it, this first letter of the holy language, Aleph, represents a man pointing with one hand toward the sky, and with the other toward the ground. It is the macrocosm and the microcosm at the same time, and explains the double triangle of the Masons and the five-pointed star. While the male is active, the female principle is passive, for it is *spirit* and *matter*, the latter word meaning *mother* in nearly every language. The columns of Solomon's temple, Jachin and Boaz, are the emblems of the androgyne; they are also respectively male and female, white and black, square and round; the male a unity, the female a binary. In the later kabalistic treatises, the active principle is pictured by the sword ‎‏זכר‏‎, the passive by the sheath ‎‏נקבה‏‎. See *Dogme et rituel de la haute magie*, Dogme, i, ii.

701. The vertical line being the male principle, and the horisontal the female, out of the union of the two at the intersection point is formed the *cross*; the oldest symbol in the Egyptian history of gods. It is the key of Heaven in the rosy fingers of Neith, the celestial virgin, who opens the gate at dawn for the exit of her first-begotten, the radiant sun. It is the Stauros of the Gnostics, and the philosophical cross of the high-grade Masons. We find this symbol ornamenting the *tee* of the umbrella-shaped oldest pagodas in Tibet, China, and India, as we find it in the hand of Isis, in the shape of the 'handled cross.' In one of the Chaitya caves, at Ajunta, it surmounts the three umbrellas in stone, and forms the center of the vault.

Svayambhû, the 'Self-Existent One'"
(*Ordinances of Manu*, I).

As we have shown, neither the *Svâbhâvikas*, Buddhist philosophers — nor the Brâhmanas believe in a creation of the universe *ex nihilo*, but both believe in the *Prakriti*, the indestructibility of matter.

The evolution of species, and the successive appearance of various new types is very distinctly shown in *Manu*.

"From earth, heat, and water, are born all creatures, whether animate or inanimate, produced by the germ which the Divine Spirit drew from its own substance. Thus has Brahma established the series of transformations from the plant up to man, and from man up to the primordial essence." . . . "Among them each succeeding being [or element] acquires the quality of the preceding; and in as many degrees as each of them is advanced, with so many properties is it said to be endowed" (*Manu*, I, *śloka* 20).[702]

This, we believe, is the veritable theory of the modern evolutionists.

---

702. "When this world had emerged from obscurity, the subtle elementary principles produced the vegetable germ which at first animated the plants; from the plants, life passed through the fantastic organisms which were born in the ilus (*bous*) of the waters; then through a series of forms and different animals, it at length reached man" (*Manu*, I; and *Bhâgavata-Purana*).

Manu is a convertible type, which can by no means be explained as a personage. Manu means sometimes humanity, sometimes man. The Manu who emanated from the uncreated *Svayambhû* is, without doubt, the type of Adam Kadmon. The Manu who is progenitor of the other six Manus is evidently identical with the Rishis, or seven primeval sages who are the forefathers of the post-diluvian races. He is — as we shall show in chapter viii — Noah, and his 'six sons,' or subsequent generations, who are the originals of the post-diluvian and mythical patriarchs of the Bible.

"Of him who is formless, the non-existent (also the eternal, but *not* First Cause), is born the heavenly man." But after he created the form of the heavenly man אָדָם עִלָּאָה, he "used it as a vehicle wherein to descend," says the Kabala. Thus Adam Kadmon is the avatar of the concealed power. After that the heavenly Adam creates or engenders by the combined power of the Sephiroth, the earthly Adam. The work of creation is also begun by Sephira in the creation of the ten Sephiroth (who are the Prajâpatis of the Kabala, for they are likewise the Lords of all beings).

The *Zohar* asserts the same. According to the kabalistic doctrine there were old worlds (*Zohar*, III, p. 292 b; Amsterdam ed.). Everything will return some day to that from which it first proceeded. "All things of which this world consists, spirit as well as body, will return to their principal, and the roots from which they proceeded" (*Zohar*, II, p. 218 b). The kabalists also maintain the indestructibility of matter, albeit their doctrine is shrouded still more carefully than that of the Hindûs. The creation is eternal, and the universe is the 'garment,' or 'the veil of God' — Shekhinah; and the latter is immortal and eternal as Him within whom it has ever existed. Every world is made after the pattern of its predecessor, and each more gross and material than the preceding one. In the Kabala all were called sparks (*Zohar*, III, p. 292 b). Finally, our present grossly materialistic world was formed.

In the Chaldaean account of the period which preceded the Genesis of our world, Berosus speaks of "a time when there existed nothing but darkness, and an abyss of waters, filled with hideous monsters, produced of a two-fold principle. . . . There were creatures in which were combined the limbs of every species of animals. In addition to these, fishes, reptiles, serpents, with other monstrous animals which assumed each other's shape and countenance." [703]

---

703. Cory: *Ancient Fragments*, p. 23, *sq.*

In the first book of Manu we read: "Know that the sum of 1000 divine ages composes the totality of one day of Brahman; and that one night is equal to that day." One thousand divine ages is equal to 4,320,000,000 of human years, in the Brâhmanical calculations.

"At the expiration of each night, Brahman, who has been asleep, awakes, and [through the sole energy of the motion] causes to emanate from himself the spirit, which in its essence *is*, and yet is not."

"Prompted by the desire to create, the Spirit [first of the emanations] operates the creation and gives birth to ether, which the sages consider as having the faculty of transmitting sound.

"Ether begets air whose property is tangible [and which is necessary to life].

"Through a transformation of the air, light is produced.

"From [air and] light [which begets heat], water is formed [and the water is the womb of all the living germs]." [704]

Throughout the whole immense period of progressive creation, covering 4,320,000,000 years, ether, air, water and fire (heat) are constantly forming matter under the never-ceasing impulse of the Spirit, or the *unrevealed* God who fills up the whole creation, for he is in all, and all is in him. This computation, which was secret and which is hardly hinted at even now, led Higgins into the error of dividing every ten ages into 6000 years. Had he added a few more ciphers to his sums he might have come nearer to a correct explanation of the neroses, or secret cycles.[705]

In the *Sepher Yetzirah*, the kabalistic Book of Creation, the author has evidently repeated the words of Manu. In it the Divine Substance is represented as having alone existed from the eternity, boundless and absolute; and it emitted from itself the Spirit. "One is the Spirit of the living God, blessed be His Name, who liveth for ever! Voice, Spirit, and Word, this is the Holy Spirit"; [706] and this is the kabalistic abstract Trinity, so unceremoniously anthropomorphized by the Fathers. From this triple ONE emanated the whole Cosmos. First from ONE emanated number TWO, or Air, the creative element; and then number THREE, *Water*, proceeded from the air; *Ether* or *Fire* complete the mystic four, the Arba-il.[707] "When the Concealed of the Concealed wanted to reveal Himself, he first made a point [primordial point, or the first Sephira, air or Holy Ghost], shaped it into a sacred form [the ten Sephiroth, or the Heavenly man], and covered it with a rich and splendid garment, *that is the world*." [708] "He maketh the Wind his messengers, flaming Fire his

---

704. *Manu*, I, 72-78.   705. See I, i, pp. 32-34 of this work.
            706. *Sepher Yetzirah*, ch. i, mishnah 9.
    707. *Ibid.*, mishnah 10.   708. *Zohar*, I, 2 a.

servants," quotes the *Yetzirah*, showing the cosmical character of the later personified angels, [709] and that the Spirit permeates every minutest atom of the Cosmos.[710]

When the cycle of creation is run down, the energy of the manifested word is weakening. He alone, the Unconceivable, is unchangeable (ever latent), but the Creative Force, though also eternal, as it has been in the former from 'no beginning,' yet must be subject to periodical cycles of activity and rest; as it had a *beginning* in one of its aspects, when it first emanated, therefore it must also have an end. Thus the evening succeeds the day, and the night of the deity approaches. Brahmâ is gradually falling asleep. In one of the books of the *Zohar* we read the following:

"As Moses was keeping a vigil on Mount Sinai, in company with the Deity, who was concealed from his sight by a cloud, he felt a great fear overcome him and suddenly asked: 'Lord, where art Thou . . . sleepest thou, O Lord?' And the *Spirit* answered him: 'I never sleep; were I to fall asleep for a moment *before my time*, all the Creation would crumble into dissolution in one instant.' " And Vâmadeva-Modelyar describes the 'Night of Brahma,' or the second period of the Divine Unknown existence, thus:

"Strange noises are heard, proceeding from every point. . . . These are the precursors of the Night of Brahma; *dusk rises at the horizon* and the Sun passes away behind the thirtieth degree of *Makara* (sign of the zodiac), and will reach no more the sign of the *Mîna* (zodiacal *pisces*, or fishes). The *gurus* of the pagodas appointed to watch the *râśi-chakra* [Zodiac] may now break their circle and instruments, for they are henceforth useless.

"Gradually light pales, heat diminishes, uninhabitable spots multiply on the earth, the air becomes more and more rarefied; the springs of waters dry up, the great rivers see their waves exhausted, the ocean shows its sandy bottom, and plants die. Men and animals decrease in size daily. Life and motion lose their force, planets can hardly gravitate in space; they are extinguished one by one, like a lamp which the hand of the *chokra* [servant] neglects to replenish. *Sûrya* (the Sun) flickers and goes out, matter falls into dissolution (*pralaya*), and Brahmâ merges back into *Dyaus*, the Unrevealed God, and his task being accomplished, he falls asleep. Another day is passed, night sets in and continues until the future dawn."

---

709. *Sepher Yetzirah*, i, 10; *Psalms*, civ, 4.

710. It is interesting to recall *Hebrews*, i, 7, in connexion with this passage. "Who maketh his angels [messengers] spirits, and his ministers [servants, those who minister] a flame of fire." The resemblance is too striking for us to avoid the conclusion that the author of *Hebrews* was as familiar with the Kabala as adepts usually are.

"And now again re-enter into the golden egg of His Thought the germs of all that exist, as the divine Manu tells us. During His peaceful rest the animated beings, endowed with the principles of action, cease their functions, and all feeling (*manas*) becomes dormant. When they are all absorbed in the SUPREME SOUL, this Soul of all the beings sleeps in complete repose till the day when it resumes its form and awakes again from its primitive darkness." [711]

If we now examine the ten mythical avatars of Vishnu, we find them recorded in the following progression:

1. *Matsya-Avatâra:* as a fish. It will also be his tenth and last avatar, at the end of the Kali-yuga.

2. *Kûrma-Avatâra:* as a tortoise.

3. *Varâha:* as a boar.

4. *Nâra-Sinha:* as a *man-lion;* last animal stage.

5. *Vâmana:* as a dwarf; first step toward the human form.

6. *Parašu-Râma:* as a hero, but yet an imperfect man.

7. *Râma-Chandra:* as the hero of *Râmâyana.* Physically a perfect man; his next of kin, friend and ally, Hanumân the monkey-god. *The monkey endowed with speech.*[712]

8. *Krishna-Avatâra:* the Son of the Virgin *Devanâgî* (or *Devakî*) one formed by God, or rather by the manifested Deity Vishnu, who is identical with Adam Kadmon.[713] Krishna is also called *Kaneya,* the Son of the Virgin.

9. Gautama-Buddha, *Siddhârtha,* or *Šâkya-muni.* (The Buddhists reject this doctrine of their Buddha being an incarnation of Vishnu.)

10. This avatar has not yet occurred. It is expected in the future, like the Christian Advent, the idea of which was undoubtedly copied from the Hindû. When Vishnu appears for the last time he will come as a 'Savior.' According to the opinion of some Brâhmanas he will appear himself under the form of the horse *Kalki.* Others maintain that he will be mounting it. This horse is the envelope of the spirit of evil, and Vishnu will mount it, invisible to all, till he has conquered it for the last time. The *Kalki-Avatâra,* or the last incarnation, divides Brâhmanism into two sects. That of the Vaishnava refuses to recognise

---

711. Cf. Jacolliot: *The Sons of God*, pp. 229, 230.

712. May it not be that Hanumân is the representative of that link of beings half-men, half-monkeys, which, according to the theories of Messrs. Hovelacque and Schleicher, were arrested in their development, and fell, so to say, into a retrogressive evolution?

713. The Primal or Ultimate Essence has *no name* in India. It is indicated some-times as 'That' and 'This.' "This [universe] was not originally anything. There was neither heaven, nor earth, nor atmosphere. That being non-existent resolved 'Let me be.'" (Dr. John Muir: *Original Sanskrit Texts*, V, p. 366.)

the incarnations of their god Vishnu in animal forms literally. They claim that these must be understood as allegorical.

In this list of avatars we see traced the gradual evolution and transformation of all species out of the ante-Silurian mud of Darwin and the *ilus* of Sanchoniathon and Berosus. Beginning with the Azoic time, corresponding to the *ilus* in which Brahmâ implants the creative germ, we pass through the Palaeozoic and Mesozoic times, covered by the first and second incarnations as the fish and tortoise; and the Cenozoic, which is embraced by the incarnations in the animal and semi-human forms of the boar and man-lion; and we come to the fifth and crowning geological period, designated as the "era of mind, or age of man," whose symbol in the Hindû mythology is the dwarf — the first attempt of nature at the creation of man. In this list we should follow the main idea, not judge the degree of knowledge of the ancient philosophers by the literal acceptance of the popular form in which it is presented to us in the grand epic poem of *Mahâbhârata* and its chapter the *Bhagavad-Gîtâ*.

Even the four ages of the Hindû chronology contain a far more philosophical idea than appears on the surface. It defines them according to both the psychological, or mental, and the physical states of man during their period. Krita-yuga, the golden age, the 'age of joy,' or spiritual innocence of man; Tretâ-yuga, the age of silver, or that of fire—the period of supremacy of man and of giants and of the sons of God; Dvâpara-yuga, the age of bronze — a mixture already of purity and impurity (spirit and matter), the age of doubt; and at last our own, the Kali-yuga, or age of iron, of darkness, misery and sorrow. In this age Vishnu had to incarnate himself in Krishna, in order to save humanity from the goddess *Kali*, consort of Śiva, the all-annihilating — the goddess of death, destruction and human misery. *Kali* is the best emblem to represent the 'fall of man'; the falling of spirit into the degradation of matter, with all its terrific results. We have to rid ourselves of *Kali* before we can ever reach *Moksha*, or Nirvâna, the abode of blessed Peace and Spirit.

With the Buddhists the last incarnation is the fifth. When Maitreya-Buddha comes, then our present world will be destroyed; and a new and a better one will replace it. The four arms of every Hindû Deity are the emblems of the four preceding manifestations of our earth from its invisible state, while its head typifies the fifth and last *Kalki-Avatâra*, when this would be destroyed, and the power of Bodhi — Wisdom (with the Hindûs, of Brahmâ), will be again called into requisition to manifest itself — as a *Logos* — to create the future world.

In this scheme the male gods typify Spirit in its deific attributes, while their female counterparts — the *Śaktis* — represent the active energies of these attributes. The *Durgá* (active virtue) is a subtle invisible force, which answers to Shekhinah — the garment of Ain-Soph. She is the *Sakti* through which the passive 'Eternal' calls forth the visible universe from its first ideal conception. All three personages of the exoteric Trimûrti are shown using their *Saktis* as *Váhanas* (vehicles). Each of them is for the time being the form which sits upon the mysterious wagon of Ezekiel.

Nor do we see less clearly carried out in this succession of avatars the truly philosophical idea of a simultaneous spiritual and physical evolution of creatures and man. From a fish the progress of this dual transformation carries on the physical form through the shape of a tortoise, a boar, and a man-lion; and then, appearing in the dwarf of humanity, it shows *Parasu-Ráma* physically a perfect, spiritually an undeveloped entity, until it carries mankind, personified by one god-like man, to the apex of physical and spiritual perfection — a god on earth. In Krishna and the other Saviors of the world we see the philosophical idea of the progressive dual development understood and as clearly expressed in the *Zohar*. The 'Heavenly man,' who is the Protogonos, Tikkun, the first-born of God, or the universal Form and Idea, engenders Adam. Hence the latter is god-born in humanity, and endowed with the attributes of all the ten Sephiroth. These are: Wisdom, Intelligence, Justice, Love, Beauty, Splendor, Firmness, etc. They make him the Foundation or basis, '*the mighty living one*,' אל חי, and the crown of creation, thus placing him as the Alpha and Omega to reign over the 'kingdom' — Malkhuth. ."Man is both the import and the highest degree of creation," says the *Zohar*. "As soon as man was created, everything was complete, including the upper and nether worlds, for everything is comprised in man. He unites in himself all forms." [714]

But this does not relate to our degenerated mankind; it is only occasionally that men are born who are the types of what man should be, and yet is not. The first races of men were spiritual, and their protoplastic bodies were not composed of the gross and material substances of which we see human bodies composed nowadays. The first men were created with all the faculties of the Deity, and powers far transcending those of the angelic host; for they were the direct emanations of Adam Kadmon, the primitive man, the Macrocosm; while the present humanity is several degrees removed even from the earthly Adam, who was the Microcosm, or 'the little world.' Ze'ir Anptn, the mystical figure of the Man, consists of 243 numbers, and we see in the circles which follow each other that it is the angels which emanated from the 'Primi-

---

714. *Zohar*, III, p. 48 a; Amsterdam ed.

tive Man,' not the Sephiroth from angels. Hence man was intended from the first to be a being of both a progressive and retrogressive nature. Beginning at the apex of the divine cycle, he gradually began receding from the center of Light, acquiring at every new and lower sphere of being (worlds each inhabited by a different race of human beings) a more solid physical form, and losing a portion of his *divine* faculties.

In the 'fall of Adam' we must see, not the personal transgression of man, but simply the law of the dual evolution. Adam, or 'Man,' begins his career of existences by dwelling in the garden of Eden "dressed in the celestial garment, which *is a garment of heavenly light*" (*Zohar*, II, p. 229 b); but when expelled he is "clothed" by God, or the eternal law of Evolution or necessarianism, with "coats of skin." But even on this earth of material degradation — in which the divine spark (Soul, a corruscation of the Spirit) was to begin its physical progression in a series of imprisonments from a stone up to a man's body — if he but exercise his WILL and call his deity to his help, man can transcend the powers of the angel. "Know ye not that we shall judge angels?" asks Paul (*1 Corinthians*, vi, 3). "The real man is the Soul" (Spirit), teaches the *Zohar*. "The mystery of the earthly man is after the mystery of the heavenly man . . . the wise can read the mysteries in the human face" (II, p. 76 a).

This is still another of the many sentences by which Paul must be recognised as an initiate. For reasons fully explained, we give far more credit for genuineness to certain Epistles of the apostles, now dismissed as apocryphal, than to many suspicious portions of the *Acts*. And we find corroboration of this view in the *Epistles of Paul to Seneca, and Seneca to Paul.*[714a] In one message Paul styles Seneca "most respected master," while Seneca terms the apostle simply "brother."

The true religion of Judaic philosophy can no more be judged by the absurdities of the exoteric *Bible*, than we have any right to form an opinion of Brâhmanism and Buddhism from their nonsensical and some-times disgusting popular forms. If we only search for the true essence of the philosophy of both *Manu* and the Kabala, we shall find that Vishnu, as well as Adam Kadmon, is the expression of the universe itself; and that his incarnations are but concrete and various embodi-ments of the manifestations of this 'Stupendous Whole.' "I am the Soul, O Arjuna. I am the Soul which exists in the heart of all beings; and I am the beginning and the middle, and also the end of existing things," says Krishna to his disciple, in the *Bhagavad-Gîtâ* (ch. x).

"I am Alpha and Omega, the beginning and the ending . . . I am the first and the last," says the Lord to John (*Rev.*, i, 8, 17).

714a. Hone: *Apocr. N. T.*, pp. 95, 97: London, 1820.

Brahmâ, Vishnu, and Śiva are a trinity in a unity, and, like the
Christian trinity, they are mutually convertible. In the esoteric doctrine they are one and the same manifestation of him "whose name is too
sacred to be pronounced, and whose power is too majestic and infinite to
be imagined." Thus by describing the avatars of one, all others are
included in the allegory, with a change of form but not of substance. It
is out of such manifestations that emanated the many worlds that were,
and that will emanate the one — which is to come.

Coleman, followed in this by other Orientalists, presents the seventh
avatar of Vishnu in the most caricatured way.[715] Apart from the fact
that the *Râmâyana* is one of the grandest epic poems in the world — the
source and origin of Homer's inspiration — this avatar conceals one of
the most scientific problems of our modern day. The learned Brâhmanas
of India never understood the allegory of the famous war between men,
giants, and monkeys otherwise than in the light of the transformation of
species. It is our firm belief that were European academicians to seek
for information from some learned native Brâhmanas, instead of unanimously and incontinently rejecting their authority, and were they, like
Jacolliot — against whom they have nearly all arrayed themselves — to
seek for light in the oldest documents scattered about the country in
pagodas, they might learn strange but not useless lessons. Let any one
inquire of an *educated* Brâhmana the reason for the respect shown to monkeys — the origin of which feeling is indicated in the story of the valorous
feats of Hanumân, the generalissimo and faithful ally of the hero of the
Râmâyana,[716] and he would soon be disabused of the erroneous idea that
the Hindûs accord deific honors to a monkey-*god*. He would, perhaps,
learn — were the Brâhmana to judge him worthy of an explanation —
that the Hindû sees in the ape but what Manu desired he should: the
transformation of species most directly connected with that of the human
family — a bastard branch engrafted on their own stock before the final
perfection of the latter.[717] He might learn, further, that in the eyes of the

---

715. Coleman: *Mythology of the Hindus*, pp. 22, *sq.*

716. The siege and subsequent surrender of Lankâ (Isle of Ceylon) to Râma is placed
by the Hindû chronology — based upon the Zodiac — at 7500 to 8000 years B. C., and
the following or eighth incarnation of Vishnu at 4800 B. C. (from the *Book of the Historical
Zodiacs* of the Brâhmanas).

717. A Hanoverian scientist has recently published a work entitled *Über die Auflösung
der Arten durch natürliche Zuchtwahl*, in which he shows, with great ingenuity, that
Darwin was wholly mistaken in tracing man back to the ape. On the contrary he
maintains that it is the ape which has evolved from man. That in the beginning mankind was morally and physically the type and prototype of our present race and of
human dignity, in beauty of form, regularity of feature, cranial development, nobility
of sentiments, heroic impulses, and grandeur of ideal conceptions. This is a purely
Brâhmanic, Buddhistic, and kabalistic philosophy. His book is copiously illustrated

educated 'heathen' the spiritual or *inner* man is one thing, and his terrestrial, physical casket another. That *physical* nature, the great combination of physical correlations of forces, ever creeping on toward perfection, has to avail herself of the material at hand; she models and remodels as she proceeds, and finishing her crowning work in man, presents him alone as a fit tabernacle for the overshadowing of the Divine Spirit. But the latter circumstance does not give man the right of life and death over the animals lower than himself in the scale of *nature*, or the right to torture them. Quite the reverse. Besides being endowed with a soul — of which every animal, and even plant, is more or less possessed — man has his immortal *rational* soul, or *nous*, which ought to make him at least equal in magnanimity to the elephant, who treads so carefully, lest he should crush weaker creatures than himself. It is this feeling which prompts Brâhmanist and Buddhist alike to construct hospitals for sick animals and even insects, and to prepare refuges wherein they may finish their days. It is this same feeling, again, which causes the Jaina sectarian to sacrifice one-half of his life-time in brushing away from his path the helpless, crawling insects, rather than recklessly deprive the smallest of life; and it is again from this sense of highest benevolence and charity toward the weaker, however abject the creature may be, that they [the Jainas] honor one of the natural modifications of their own dual nature, and that later the popular belief in metempsychosis arose. No trace of the latter is to be found in the *Vedas;* and the true interpretation of the doctrine, discussed at length in *Manu* and the Buddhistic sacred books, having been confined from the first to the learned sacerdotal castes, the false and foolish popular ideas concerning it need occasion no surprise.

Upon those who, in the remains of antiquity, see evidence that modern times can lay small claim to originality, it is common to charge a disposition to exaggerate and distort facts. But the candid reader will scarcely aver that the above is an example in point. There were evolutionists before the day when the mythical Noah is made, in the *Bible*, to float in his ark; and the ancient scientists were better informed, and had their theories more logically defined than the modern evolutionists.

Plato, Anaxagoras, Pythagoras, the Eleatic schools of Greece, as well as the old Chaldaean sacerdotal colleges, all taught the doctrine of the dual evolution; the doctrine of the transmigration of souls referring only

---

with diagrams, tables, etc. He says that the gradual debasement and degradation of man, morally and physically, can be readily traced throughout the ethnological transformations down to our times. And as one portion has already degenerated into apes, so the civilised man of the present day will at last, under the action of the inevitable law of necessity, be also succeeded by like descendants. If we may judge of the future by the actual present, it certainly does seem possible that so unspiritual and materialistic a body as our physical scientists should end as *simiae* rather than as seraphs,

to the progress of man from world to world, after death here. Every philosophy worthy of the name taught that the *spirit* of man, if not the *soul*, was pre-existent. "The Essenes," says Josephus, "believed that the souls were immortal, and that they descended from the ethereal spaces to be chained to bodies." [718] In his turn Philo Judaeus says the "air is full of them [of souls]; those which are nearest the earth, descending to be tied to mortal bodies, παλινδρομοῦσιν αὖθις, return to other bodies, being desirous to live in them." [719] In the *Zohar* the soul is made to plead her freedom before God: "Lord of the Universe! I am happy in this world, and do not wish to go into another world, where I shall be a handmaid, and be exposed to all kinds of pollutions." [720] The doctrine of fatal necessity, the everlasting immutable Law, is asserted in the answer of the Deity: "Against thy will thou becomest an embryo, and against thy will thou art born." [721] Light would be incomprehensible without darkness, to make it manifest by contrast; good would be no good without evil, to show the priceless nature of the boon; and so personal virtue could claim no merit, unless it had passed through the furnace of temptation. Nothing is eternal and unchangeable, save the Concealed Deity. Nothing that is finite — whether because it had a beginning, or must have an end — can remain stationary. It must either progress or recede; and a soul which thirsts after a reunion with its spirit, which alone confers upon it immortality, must purify itself through cyclic transmigrations onward toward the only Land of Bliss and Eternal Rest, called in the *Zohar* 'The Palace of Love,' היכל אהבה; [722] in the Hindû religion, *Moksha;* among the Gnostics, the 'Pleroma of eternal Light'; and by the Buddhists, Nirvâna. The Christian calls it the 'Kingdom of Heaven,' and claims to have alone found the truth, whereas he has but invented a new name for a doctrine which is coeval with man.

The proof that the transmigration of the soul does not relate to man's condition on this earth *after* death, is found in the *Zohar*, notwithstanding the many incorrect renderings of its translators. "All souls which have alienated themselves in heaven from the Holy One — blessed be His Name — have thrown themselves into an abyss at their very existence, and have anticipated the time when they are to descend on earth. [723] . . . Come and see when the soul reaches the Treasury of Life. . . . The soul could not bear this light, but for the luminous mantle which she puts on. For just as the soul, when sent to this earth, puts on an earthly garment

718. *Jewish War*, II, viii, 11.   719. *De somniis*, I, § 22; *De gigant.*, § 2, sq.
        720. *Zohar*, II, p. 96 a; Amst. ed.
721. *Mishnah Pirke Aboth*, IV, § 29; cf. Mackensie: *Royal Masonic Cyclopaedia*, p. 413.
722. *Zohar*, II, p. 97 a.   723. *Ibid.*, III, p. 61 b.

to preserve herself here, so she receives above a shining garment, in order to be able to look without injury into the mirror whose light proceeds from the Lord of Light." [724] Moreover, the *Zohar* teaches that the soul cannot reach the abode of bliss unless she has received the "holy kiss, or the reunion of the soul *with the substance from which she emanated*" — spirit.[725] All souls are dual, and while the soul is a feminine principle, the spirit is masculine. While imprisoned in body, man is a trinity, unless his pollution is such as to have caused his divorce from the spirit. "Woe to the soul which prefers to her divine husband [spirit] the earthly wedlock with her terrestrial body," records a text of the *Book of the Keys*.[726] ✓

These ideas on the transmigrations and the trinity of man were held by many of the early Christian Fathers. It is the jumble made by the translators of the *New Testament* and of ancient philosophical treatises, between soul and spirit, that has occasioned the many misunderstandings. This is also one of the many reasons why Buddha, Plotinus, and so many other initiates are now accused of having longed for the total extinction of their souls — 'absorption into the Deity,' or 'reunion with the universal soul,' meaning, according to modern ideas, annihilation. The animal soul must, of course, be disintegrated [dispossessed] of its [material] particles before it is able to link its purer essence forever with the immortal spirit. But the translators of both the *Acts* and the *Epistles*, who laid the foundation of the *Kingdom of Heaven*, and the modern commentators on the Buddhist *Sûtra of the Foundation of the Kingdom of Righteousness*, have muddled the teaching of the great apostle of Christianity, as of the great reformer of India. The former have smothered the word ψυχικός, so that no reader imagines it to have any relation with *soul;* and with this confounding together of *soul* and *spirit*, *Bible* readers get only a perverted sense of anything on the subject; while the interpreters of the *Sûtra* have failed to understand the meaning and object of the Buddhistic four degrees of *Dhyâna*.[726a]

In the writings of Paul the entity of man is divided into a trine — flesh, psychical existence or *soul*, and the overshadowing and at the same time interior entity or SPIRIT. His phraseology is very definite when he teaches the *anastasis*, or the continuation of life of those who have died. He maintains that there is a *psychical* body which is sown in the corruptible, and a spiritual body that is raised in incorruptible substance. "The first man is of the earth earthy, the second man from heaven."

---

724. *Zohar*, I, pp. 65 b, 66 a.   725. *Ibid.*, II, p. 97 a; I, p. 168 a.
726. A Hermetic work.   726a. E. Burnouf: *Le lotus de la bonne loi*, p. 801 *sq.;*
Lalita-Vistara, xxii; T. W. Rhys Davids: *Buddhism*, p. 176; *Sacred Books of the East*, X, XIII, XIX, XXXV, Oxford; Hardy: *A Manual of Budhism;* etc., etc.

Even James (iii, 15) identifies the soul by saying that its wisdom "descendeth not from above" but is terrestrial, *psychical, demoniacal* (see Greek text). Plato, speaking of the Soul (*psuche*), observes that "when she allies herself to the *nous* [divine substance, a god, as *psuche* is a goddess], she does everything aright and felicitously; but the case is otherwise when she attaches herself to *anoia*." What Plato calls *nous*, Paul terms the *Spirit;* and Jesus makes the *heart* what Paul says of the *flesh.* The natural condition of mankind was called in Greek ἀποστασία; the new condition ἀνάστασις. In Adam came the former (death), in Christ the latter (resurrection), for it is he who first publicly taught mankind the 'Noble Path' to Eternal life, as Gautama pointed the same Path to Nirvâna. To accomplish this end there was but one way, according to the teachings of both. "Poverty, chastity, contemplation or inner prayer, contempt for wealth and the illusive joys of this world."

"Enter on this Path and put an end to sorrow; verily the Path has been preached by me, who have found how to quench the darts of grief. You yourselves must make the effort; *the Buddhas are only preachers.* The thoughtful who enter the Path are freed from the bondage of the Deceiver (*Mâra*).[727] .

"Enter ye in at the strait gate: for wide is the gate, and broad is the way, that leadeth to destruction. . . . Follow me . . . Every one that heareth these sayings of mine, and doeth them not, shall be likened unto a foolish man" (*Matthew*, vii, 13, 26). "*I can of mine own self do nothing*" (*John*, v, 30). "The care of this world, and the deceitfulness of riches, choke the word" (*Matthew*, xiii, 22), say the Christians; and it is only by shaking off all delusions that the Buddhist enters on the 'Path' which will lead him "away from the restless tossing waves of the ocean of life," and take him "to the calm City of Peace, to the real joy and rest of Nirvâna."

The Greek philosophers are alike made misty instead of mystic by their too learned translators. The Egyptians revered the Divine Spirit, the One-Only One, as NUT. It is most evident that it is from that word that Anaxagoras borrowed his denominative *nous*, or as he calls it, Νοῦς αὐτοκρατής — the Mind or Spirit self-potent, the ἀρχέτης κινήσεως. "All things," says he, "were in chaos; then came Νοῦς and introduced order."[728] He also denominated this Νοῦς the One that ruled the many. In his idea *Nous* was God; and the *Logos* was man, the emanation of the former. The external powers perceived *phenomena;* the *nous* alone recognised *noumena* or subjective things. This is purely Buddhistic and esoteric. Here Socrates took his clew and followed it, and Plato after him,

---

727. *Dhammapada, slokas* 275-6.   728. Diog. Laert.: *Vita Anaxag.,* § 1.

with the whole world of interior knowledge. Whereas the old Ionico-Italian world culminated in Anaxagoras, the new world began with Socrates and Plato. Pythagoras made the *Soul* a self-moving unit, with three elements, the *nous*, the *phrēn* and the *thumos;* the latter two, shared with the brutes; the first, alone, being his essential *self*. So the charge that he taught transmigration is refuted; he taught no more than Gautama-Buddha did, whatever the popular superstition of the Hindū rabble made of it [Gautama's teaching] after his death. Whether Pythagoras borrowed from Buddha, or Buddha from somebody else, matters not; the esoteric doctrine is the same.

The Platonic School is even more distinct in enunciating all this.

The real selfhood was at the basis of all. Socrates therefore taught that he had a δαιμόνιον (*daimonion*), a spiritual something which put him on the road to wisdom. He himself knew nothing, but this put him in the way to learn all.

Plato followed him with a full investigation of the principles of being. There was an *Agathon*, Supreme God, who produced in his own mind a *paradeigma* of all things.

He taught that in man was "the immortal principle of the soul," a mortal body, and a "separate mortal kind of soul," which was placed in a separate receptacle of the body from the other; the immortal part was in the head (*Timaeus,* § xix), the other in the trunk (xliv).

Nothing is plainer than that Plato regarded the interior man as constituted of two parts — one always the same, formed of the same essence as Deity, and one mortal and corruptible.

"Plato and Pythagoras," says Plutarch, "distribute the soul into two parts, the rational (noëtic) and irrational (*agnoia*); they say that part of the soul of man which is rational, is eternal; for though it be not God, yet it is the product of an eternal deity; but that part of the soul which is divested of reason (*agnoia*) dies." [729]

"Man," says Plutarch, "is compound; and they are mistaken who think him to be compounded of two parts only. For they imagine that the understanding is a part of the soul, but they err in this no less than those who make the soul to be a part of the body, for the understanding (*nous*) as far exceeds the soul, as the soul is better and diviner than the body. Now this composition of the soul (ψυχή) with the understanding (νοῦς) makes reason; and with the body, passion; of which the one is the beginning or principle of pleasure and pain, and the other of virtue and vice. Of these three parts conjoined and compacted together, the earth has given the body, the moon the soul, and the sun the understanding to the generation of man.

---

729. Plutarch: *Sentiments Concerning Nature*, IV, iv, vii.

"Now of the deaths we die, *the one makes man two of three*, and the other, *one* of [out of] two. The former is in the region and jurisdiction of Demeter, whence the name given to the Mysteries, τελεταί, resembled that given to death, τελευτή. The Athenians also heretofore called the deceased sacred to Demeter. As for the *other death*, it is in the moon or region of Persephone. And as with the one the terrestrial, so with the other the celestial Hermes doth dwell. This suddenly and with violence plucks the soul from the body; but Proserpina mildly and in a long time disjoins the understanding from the soul. For this reason she is called *Monogenes, only-begotten*, or rather *begetting one alone;* for the better part of man becomes alone when it is separated by her. Now both the one and the other happen thus according to nature. It is ordained by Fate that every soul, whether with or without understanding (νοῦς), when gone out of the body, should wander for a time, though not all for the same, in the region lying between the earth and moon. For those that have been unjust and dissolute suffer there the punishment due to their offences; but the good and virtuous are there detained till they are purified, and have by expiation purged out of them all the infections they might have contracted from the contagion of the body, as if from foul health, living in the mildest part of the air, called the Meadows of Hades, where they must remain for a certain prefixed and appointed time. And then, as if they were returning from a wandering pilgrimage or long exile into their country, they have a taste of joy such as they principally receive who are initiated into Sacred Mysteries, mixed with trouble, admiration, and each one's proper and peculiar hope." [730]

The *daimonion* of Socrates was this νοῦς, mind, spirit, or divine understanding. "The νοῦς of Socrates," says Plutarch, "was pure and mixed itself with the body no more than necessity required. . . . Every soul hath some portion of νοῦς, reason; a man cannot be a man without it; but as much of each soul as is mixed with flesh and appetite is changed and through pain or pleasure becomes irrational. Every soul doth not mix herself after one sort; some plunge themselves into the body, and so in this life their whole frame is corrupted by appetite and passion; others are mixed as to some part, but the purer part [*nous*] still remains *without the body*. It is not drawn down into the body, but it swims above and touches [overshadows] the extremest part of the man's head; it is like a cord to hold up and direct the subsiding part of the soul, as long as it proves obedient and is not overcome by the appetites of the flesh. The part that is plunged into the body is called *soul*. But the incorruptible part is called the *nous* and *the vulgar think it is within them*, as they likewise imagine the image reflected from a glass to be in that glass.

---

730. *On the Orb of the Moon*, § 28.

But the more intelligent, who know it to be without, call it a Daemon" (a god, a spirit).[731]

"The soul, like to a dream, flies quickly away, which it does not immediately, as soon as it is separated from the body, but afterward, when it is alone and divided from the understanding (νοῦς). . . . The soul being moulded and formed by the understanding (νοῦς), and itself moulding and forming the body by embracing it on every side, receives from it an impression and form; so that although it be separated both from the understanding and the body, it nevertheless so retains still its figure and resemblance for a long time, that it may with good right be called its image.

"And of these souls the moon is the element, because souls resolve into her, as the bodies of the deceased do into earth. Those, indeed, who have been virtuous and honest, living a quiet and philosophical life, without embroiling themselves in troublesome affairs, are quickly resolved; because being left by the *nous*, understanding, and no longer using the corporeal passions, they incontinently vanish away." [732]

We find even Irenaeus, that untiring and mortal enemy of every Grecian and 'heathen' heresy, explaining his belief in the trinity of man. The perfect man according to his views consists of *flesh*, *soul*, and *spirit*. ". . . carne, anima, spiritu, altero quidem figurante, spiritu, altero quod formatur, carne. Id vero quod inter haec est duo, est anima, quae aliquando subsequens spiritum elevatur ab eo, aliquando autem consentiens carni in terrenas concupiscentias." [733]

And Origen, in his *Sixth Epistle to the Romans*, says: "There is a threefold partition of man, the body or flesh, the lowest part of our nature, on which the old serpent by original sin inscribed the law of sin, and by which we are tempted to vile things, and as oft as we are overcome by temptations are joined fast to the Devil; the spirit, in or by which we express the likeness of the divine nature in which the very Best Creator, from the archetype of his own mind, engraved with his finger [that is, his spirit], the eternal law of honesty; by this we are joined [conglutinated] to God and made one with God. In the third, the soul mediates between these, which, as in a factious republic, cannot but join with one party or the other, is solicited this way and that and is at liberty to choose the side to which it will adhere. If, renouncing the flesh, it betakes itself to the party of the spirit, it will itself become spiritual; but if it cast itself down to the cupidities of the flesh, it will degenerate itself into body."

Plato defines *soul* as "the motion that is able to move itself." "Soul is the most ancient of all things, and the commencement of motion."

---

731. *On the Daemon of Socrates*, §§ 20, 21.
732. Plutarch: *On the Orb of the Moon*, § 30.   733. *Agst. Heresies*, V, ix.

"Soul was generated prior to body, and body is posterior and secondary, as being, according to nature, ruled over by the ruling soul." "The soul which administers all things that are moved in every way, administers likewise the heavens."

"Soul then leads everything in heaven, and on earth, and in the sea, by its movements — the names of which are, to will, to consider, to take care of, to consult, to form opinions true and false, to be in a state of joy, sorrow, confidence, fear, hate, love, together with all such primary movements as are allied to these . . . being a goddess herself, she ever takes as an ally Nous, a god, and disciplines all things correctly and happily; but when with *anoia* — not-*nous* — it works out everything the contrary." [734]

In this language, as in the Buddhist texts, the negative is treated as essential existence. *Annihilation* comes under a similar exegesis. The positive state is essential being, but no manifestation as such. When the spirit, in Buddhistic parlance, entered *nirvâna*, it lost objective existence but retained subjective. To objective minds this is becoming absolute nothing; to subjective, NO-thing, nothing to be displayed to sense.

These rather lengthy quotations are necessary for our purpose. Better than anything else they show the agreement between the oldest 'Pagan' philosophies — not "assisted by the light of divine revelation," to use the curious expression of Laboulaye in relation to Buddha [734a] — and the early Christianity of some Fathers. Both Pagan philosophy and Christianity, however, owe their elevated ideas on the soul and spirit of man and the unknown Deity to Buddhism and the Hindû Manu. No wonder that the Manichaeans maintained that Jesus was a permutation of Gautama; that Buddha, Christ, and Mani were one and the same person,[735] for the teachings of the former two were identical. It was the doctrine of old India that Jesus held to when preaching the complete renunciation of the world and its vanities in order to reach the kingdom of Heaven, Nirvâna, where "men neither marry nor are given in marriage, but live like the angels."

It is the philosophy of Siddhârtha-Buddha again, that Pythagoras expounded when asserting that the *ego* (νοῦς) was eternal with God, and that the soul only passed through various stages (Hindû *Rûpa-lokas*) to arrive at the divine excellence; meanwhile the *thumos* returned to the earth, and even the *phrēn* was eliminated. Thus the *metempsychosis* was only a succession of disciplines through refuge-heavens (called by the Buddhists *Zion*),[736] to work off the exterior mind, to rid the *nous* of the

---

734. Plato: *The Laws*, X, vii, viii.   734a. See footnote 873.

735. Neander: *Gen. Hist. Chr. Rel. and Church*, § IV, appx., *s. v.* 'Manichaeans.'

736. It is from the highest *Zion* that Maitreya-Buddha, the Savior to come, will descend on earth; and it is also from *Zion* that comes the Christian Deliverer (*Romans*, xi, 26).

phrēn, or soul, the Buddhist *Viññâna-skandha, that principle that lives* from *Karma* and the *Skandhas* (groups). It is the latter, the metaphysical personations of the 'deeds' of man, whether good or bad, which after the death of his body incarnate themselves, so to say, and form their many invisible but never-dying compounds into a new body, or rather into an ethereal being, the *double* of what man was *morally*. It is the astral body of the kabalist and the 'incarnated deeds,' which form the new sentient self as its *Ahankâra* (the ego, self-consciousness), given to it by the sovereign Master (the breath of God), and which can never perish, for it is immortal *per se*, as a spirit; hence the sufferings of the newly-born *self*, till it rids itself of every earthly thought, desire and passion.

We now see that the 'four mysteries' of the Buddhist doctrine have been as little understood and appreciated as the 'wisdom' hinted at by Paul, and spoken "among them that are *perfect*" (initiated), the 'mystery-wisdom' which "none of the *Archons* of this world" knew.[737] The fourth degree of the Buddhist *Dhyâna*, the fruit of *Samâdhi*, which leads to the utmost perfection, to *Viśodhana*, a term correctly rendered by Burnouf as the verb "*perfected*,"[738] is wholly misunderstood by others, as well as by himself. Defining the condition of *Dhyâna*, St.-Hilaire argues thus:

"Finally, having attained the fourth degree, the ascetic possesses no more this feeling of beatitude, however obscure it may be; he has also lost all memory; . . . he has reached impassibility, as near a neighbor of Nirvâna as can be. . . . However, this absolute impassibility does not hinder the ascetic from acquiring, at this very moment, *omniscience and the magical power; a flagrant contradiction, about which the Buddhists* no more disturb themselves than about so many others."[739]

And why should they, when these contradictions are, in fact, no contradictions at all? It ill behooves us to speak of contradictions in other peoples' religions, when those of our own have bred, besides the three great conflicting bodies of Romanism, Protestantism, and the Eastern Church, a thousand and one most curious smaller sects. However it may be, we have here a term applied to one and the same thing by the Buddhist holy 'mendicants' and by Paul the apostle. When the latter says: "If so be that I might attain the *resurrection* from among the dead [the Nirvâna], not as though I had already attained, or were already *perfect*" (initiated),[740] he uses an expression common among the initiated Buddhists. When a Buddhist ascetic has reached the 'fourth degree,' he is considered a *rahat*. He produces every kind of phenomena by the

---

737. *1 Cor.*, ii, 6, 7, 8.   738. *Le lotus de la bonne loi*, p. 806.

739. *Le Bouddha et sa religion*, p. 137: Paris, 1860.   740. *Philippians*, iii, 11, 12

sole power of his freed spirit. A *rahat*, say the Buddhists, is one who has acquired the power of flying in the air, becoming invisible, commanding the elements and working all manner of wonders — commonly and erroneously called *meipo* (miracles). He is a *perfect* man, a demi-god. A god he will become when he reaches Nirvâna; for, like the initiates of both Testaments, the worshipers of Buddha know that they "are gods."

"Genuine Buddhism, overleaping the barrier between finite and infinite mind, urges its followers to aspire, *by their own efforts*, to that divine perfectibility of which it teaches that man is capable, and by attaining which man becomes *a god*," says Brian Houghton Hodgson.[741]

Dreary and sad were the ways, and blood-covered the tortuous paths by which the world of the Christians was driven to embrace the Irenaean and Eusebian Christianity. And yet, unless we accept the views of the ancient Pagans, what claim has our generation to having solved any of the mysteries of the 'kingdom of heaven'? What more does the most pious and learned of Christians know of the future destiny and progress of our immortal spirits than the heathen philosopher of old, or the modern 'Pagan' beyond the Himâlaya? Can he even boast that he knows as much, although he works in the full blaze of 'divine' revelation? We have seen a Buddhist holding to the religion of his fathers, both in theory and practice; and, however blind may be his faith, however absurd his notions on some particular doctrinal points, later engraftings of an ambitious clergy, yet in practical works his Buddhism is far more Christ-like in deed and spirit than the average life of our Christian priests and ministers. The fact alone that his religion commands him to "honor his own faith, but never slander that of other people,"[742] is sufficient. It places the Buddhist lama immeasurably higher than any priest or clergyman who deems it his sacred duty to curse the 'heathen' to his face, and sentence him and his religion to 'eternal damnation.' Christianity becomes every day more and more a religion of pure emotionalism. The doctrine of Buddha is entirely based on practical works. A general love of all beings, human and animal, is its nucleus. A man who knows that unless he toils for himself he has to starve, and understands that he has no scapegoat to carry the burden of his iniquities for him, is ten times more likely to become a better man than one who is taught that murder, theft, and profligacy can be washed in one instant as white as snow, if he but believes in a God who, to borrow an expression of Volney, "once took food upon earth, and is now himself the food of his people."

---

741. *The Mahâvansa*, I, Introduction.   742. From the Five Articles of Faith.

CHAPTER VII

"Of the tenets of the Druzes, nothing authentic has ever come to light; the popular belief amongst their neighbors is that they adore an idol in the form of a calf."
— KING: *The Gnostics and their Remains* (2nd ed.)

"O ye Lords of Truth without fault, who are forever cycling for eternity . . . save me from the annihilation of this Region of the *Two Truths*." [742a]

"Pythagoras correctly regarded the 'Ineffable Name' of God . . . as the Key to the Mysteries of the universe."
— PANCOAST: *Blue and Red Light*

IN the next two chapters we shall notice the most important of the Christian secret sects — the so-called 'Heresies' which sprang into existence between the first and fourth centuries of our era.

Glancing rapidly at the Ophites and Nazareans, we shall pass to their scions which yet exist in Syria and Palestine under the name of Druzes ['Hamza-ites] [742b] of Mount Lebanon; and near Basra or Bassorah, in Persia, under that of Mendaeans, or Disciples of St. John. All these sects have an immediate connexion with our subject, for they are of kabalistic parentage, and at one time held to the secret 'Wisdom-Religion,' recognising as the One Supreme, the Mystery-God of the *Ineffable Name*. Noticing these numerous secret societies of the past, we shall bring them into direct comparison with several of the modern. We shall conclude with a brief survey of the Jesuits, and of that venerable nightmare of the Roman Catholic Church — modern Freemasonry. All of these modern as well as ancient fraternities — present Freemasonry excepted — were and are more or less connected with magic, practically, as well as theoretically; and every one of them — Freemasonry *not* excepted — was and still is accused of demonolatry, blasphemy and licentiousness.

Our object is not to write the history of any of them; but only to compare these sorely-abused communities with the Christian sects, past and present, and then, taking historical facts for our guidance, to defend the secret science, as well as the men who are its students and champions, against any unjust imputation.

One by one the tide of time engulfed the sects of the early centuries, until of the whole number only one survived in its primitive integrity. That one still exists, still teaches the doctrine of its founder, still exem-

---

742a. De Rougé: *Rituel funéraire des anciens Égyptiens*.   742b. See footnote 795.

plifies its faith in works of power. The quicksands which swallowed up
every other outgrowth of the religious agitation of the times of Jesus,
with its records, relics, and traditions, proved firm ground for this.
Driven from their native land, its members found refuge in Persia, and
today the anxious traveler may converse with the direct descendants of
the 'Disciples of John,' who listened, on the Jordan's shore, to the 'man
sent from God' and were baptized, and believed. This curious people,
numbering 30,000 or more, are miscalled 'Christians of St. John,' but
in fact should be known by their old name of Nazareans, or their new one
of Mendaeans.

.To term them Christians is wholly unwarranted. They neither believe in Jesus as Christ, nor accept his atonement, nor adhere to his
Church, nor revere its 'Holy Scriptures.' Neither do they worship
the Jehovah-God of the Jews and Christians, a circumstance which
of course proves that their founder, John the Baptist, did not worship
him either. And if not, what right has he to a place in the *Bible*, or in
the portrait-gallery of Christian saints? Still further, if Ferho was his
God, and he was 'a man sent by God,' he must have been sent by
Lord Ferho, and in his name baptized and preached. Now, if Jesus
was baptized by John, the inference is that he was baptized according
to his own faith; therefore, Jesus too, was a believer in Ferho, or Faho,
as they call him; a conclusion that seems the more warranted by his
silence as to the name of his 'Father.' And why should the hypothesis
that *Faho* is but one of the many corruptions of Fho or Fo, as the
Tíbetans and Chinese call Buddha, appear ridiculous? In the North
of Nepal, Buddha is more often called *Fo* than *Buddha*. The Book of
Mahâvansa shows how early the work of Buddhistic proselytism began
in Nepal; and history teaches that Buddhist monks crowded into
Syria [743] and Babylon in the century preceding our era, and that

---

743. Not only did the Buddhist missionaries make their way to the Mesopotamian
Valley, but they even went so far west as Ireland. The Rev. Dr. Lundy, in his work
Monumental Christianity, p. 255, referring to an Irish Round Tower, observes: "Henry
O'Brien explains this Round Tower crucifixion as that of Buddha; the animals as the
elephant and the bull sacred to Buddha, and into which his soul entered after death;
the two figures standing beside the cross as Buddha's virgin mother, and Kama, his
favorite disciple. The whole picture bears a close likeness to the crucifixion in the cemetery of Pope Julius, except the animals, which are conclusive proof that it cannot be
Christian. It came ultimately from the far East to Ireland with the Phoenician colonists,
who erected the Round Towers as symbols of the Life-giving and Preserving Power
of man and nature, and how that universal life is produced through suffering and death"
(*The Round Towers of Ireland*, p. 301; 1st ed.).

When a Protestant clergyman is thus forced to confess the pre-Christian existence
of the crucifix in Ireland, its Buddhistic character, and the penetration of the missionaries
of that faith even to that then remote portion of the earth, we need not wonder that
in the minds of the Nazarean contemporaries of Jesus and their descendants he should

Boodhasp (*Bodhisattva*), the alleged Chaldaean, was the founder of Sabaeanism or *baptism*.[744]

What the actual Baptists, *el-Mogtasilah*, or Nazaraeans, do believe, is fully set forth in other places, for they are the very Nazarenes of whom we have spoken so much, and from whose *Codex* we have quoted. Persecuted and threatened with annihilation, they took refuge in the Nestorian body, and so allowed themselves to be arbitrarily classed as Christians, but as soon as opportunity offered, they separated, and now for several centuries have not even nominally deserved the appellation. That they are, nevertheless, so called by ecclesiastical writers, is perhaps not very difficult to comprehend. They know too much of early Christianity to be left outside the pale, to bear witness against it with their traditions without the stigma of heresy and backsliding being fastened upon them to weaken confidence in what they might say.

But where else can science find so good a field for biblical research as among this too-neglected people? No doubt of their inheritance of the Baptist's doctrine; their traditions are without a break. What they teach now, their forefathers taught at every epoch where they appear in history. They are the disciples of that John who is said to have foretold the advent of Jesus, baptized him, and declared that the latchet of his shoe he (John) was not worthy to unloose. As they two — the Messenger and the Messiah — stood in the Jordan, and the elder was consecrating the younger — his own cousin, too, humanly speaking — the heavens opened and God Himself, in the shape of a dove, descended in a glory upon his 'Beloved Son'! How then, if this tale be true, can we account for the strange infidelity which we find among these surviving Nazaraeans? So far from believing Jesus the Only-Begotten Son of God, they actually told the Persian missionaries, who in the seventeenth century first discovered them to Europeans, that the Christ of the *New Testament* was "a false teacher," and that the Jewish system, as well as that of Jesus (?), came from the realm of darkness! Who knows better than they? Where can more competent living witnesses be found? Christian

---

not have been associated, in the character of a Redeemer, with that universally known and archaic emblem.

In noticing this admission of Dr. Lundy, Mr. Charles Sotheran remarked, in a lecture before the American Philological Society, that both legends and archaeological remains unite in proving beyond question "that Ireland, like every other nation, once listened to the propagandists of Siddhârtha-Buddha."

744. "The religion of multiplied baptisms, the scion of the still existent sect named the 'Christians of St. John,' or Mendaeans, whom the Arabs call *el-Mogtasilah*, the Baptists. The Aramaean verb *seba*, origin of the name *Sabian*, is a synonym of βαπτίζω" — Renan: *La Vie de Jésus*, ch. vi. Cf. Chwolsohn: *Die Ssabier u. d. Ssabismus*, I, p. 798.

ecclesiastics would force upon us an anointed Savior heralded by John,
and the disciples of this very Baptist, from the earliest centuries, have
stigmatized this ideal personage as an impostor, and his putative Father,
Jehovah, "a spurious God," the Ilda-Baoth of the Ophites! Unlucky for
Christianity will be the day when some fearless and honest scholar shall
persuade their elders to let him translate the contents of their secret
books and compile their hoary traditions! It is a strange delusion that
makes some writers think that the Nazaraeans have no other sacred
literature, no other literary relics than four doctrinal works and that
curious volume full of astrology and magic which they are bound to
peruse at the sunset hour on every Sol's day (Sunday).

This search after truth leads us, indeed, into devious ways. Many are
the obstacles that ecclesiastical cunning has placed in the way of our finding the primal source of religious ideas. Christianity is on trial, and has
been, ever since science felt strong enough to act as Public Prosecutor.
A portion of the case we are drafting in this book. What of truth is there
in this Theology? Through what sects has it been transmitted? *Whence
was it primarily derived?* To answer, we must trace the history of the
World Religion, alike through the secret Christian sects as through those
of other great religious subdivisions of the race; *for the Secret Doctrine is
the Truth*, and that religion is nearest divine that has contained it with
least adulteration.

Our search takes us hither and thither, but never aimlessly do we
bring sects widely separated in chronological order into critical juxta-
position. There is one purpose in our work to be kept constantly in
view — the analysis of religious beliefs, and the definition of their descent
from the past to the present. What has most blocked the way is Roman
Catholicism; and not until the secret principles of this religion are
uncovered can we comprehend the iron staff upon which it leans to
steady its now tottering steps.

We shall begin with the Ophites, Nazaraeans, and the modern Druzes.
The personal views of the author, as they will be presented in the
schemes, will be most decidedly at variance with the prejudiced speculations of Irenaeus, Theodoret, and Epiphanius (the sainted renegade,
who sold his brethren), inasmuch as they will reflect the ideas of certain
Kabalists in close relation with the mysterious Druzes of Mount Lebanon. The Syrian *okhals*, or Spiritualists, as they are sometimes termed,
are in possession of a great many ancient manuscripts and gems bearing
upon our present subject.

The first *scheme* — that of the Ophites — from the very start, as we
have shown, varies from the description given by the Fathers, inasmuch
as it makes Bythos, or depth, a female emanation, and assigns her a place

answering to that of Pleroma, only in a far superior region; whereas, the Fathers assure us that the Gnostics gave the name of Bythos to the First Cause. As in the kabalistic system, it represents the boundless and infinite void within which is concealed in darkness the Unknown Primal motor of all. It envelops HIM like a veil: in short we recognise again the 'Shekhinah' of the Ain-Soph. Alone the name of IAΩ, Iao, marks the upper center, or rather the presumed spot where the Unknown One may be supposed to dwell. Around the Iao runs the legend, CEMEC EIΛAM ABPAΣAH, "the eternal Sun-Abrasax" (the Central Spiritual Sun of all the Kabalists, represented in some diagrams of the latter by the circle of Tiphereth).

From this region of unfathomable Depth issues forth a circle formed of spirals; which in the language of symbolism means a grand cycle, κύκλος, composed of smaller ones. Coiled within, so as to follow the spirals, lies the serpent — emblem of wisdom and eternity — the Dual Androgyne: the cycle representing *Ennoia*, or the Divine mind, and the Serpent — the Agathodaimon, the Ophis — the Shadow of the Light. Both were the *Logoi* of the Ophites; or the unity as *Logos* manifesting itself as a double principle of good and evil; for according to their views these two principles are immutable, and existed from all eternity, as they will ever continue to exist.

This symbol accounts for the adoration by this [the Ophite] sect of the Serpent, as the Savior, coiled around either the Sacramental loaf, or a Tau. As a unity, Ennoia and Ophis are the *Logos;* when separated, one is the Tree of Life (Spiritual); the other, the Tree of Knowledge of Good and Evil. Therefore we find Ophis urging the first human couple — the material production of Ilda-Baoth, but which owed its spiritual principle to Sophia-Achamoth — to eat of the forbidden fruit, although Ophis represents Divine Wisdom.

The Serpent, the Tree of Knowledge of Good and Evil, and the Tree of Life, are all symbols transplanted from the soil of India. The *Arasa-Maram*, the banyan tree, so sacred with the Hindûs, since Vishnu during one of his incarnations reposed under its mighty shade, and there taught humanity philosophy and sciences, is called the Tree of Knowledge and the Tree of Life. Under the protective umbrage of this king of the forest, the Gurus teach their pupils their first lessons on immortality and initiate them in the mysteries of life and death. The *Java*-ALEIM of the Sacerdotal College are said, in the Chaldaean tradition, to have taught the sons of men to become like one of them. To the present day Foh-tchou,[745] who lives in his *Foh-Maëyu*, or temple of Buddha, on the

---

745. Foh-Tchou, literally, in Chinese, meaning Buddha's lord, or the teacher of the doctrines of Buddha — Foh.

top of *Kuen-lun-shan*,[746] the great mountain, produces his greatest religious miracles under a tree called in Chinese *Sung-Ming-Shŭ*, or the Tree of Knowledge and the Tree of Life, for ignorance is death, and knowledge alone gives immortality. This marvelous display takes place every three years, when an immense concourse of Chinese Buddhists assemble in pilgrimage at the holy place.

Ilda-Baoth, the 'Son of Darkness' and the creator of the material world, was made to inhabit the planet Saturn, which identifies him still further with the Jewish Jehovah, who was Saturn himself, according to the Ophites, and is by them denied his Sinaitic name. From Ilda-Baoth emanate six spirits, who respectively dwell with their father in the seven planets. These are *Saba* — or Mars; *Adonai* — Sol, or the Sun;[747] *Ievo* — the Moon; *Eloi* — Jupiter; *Astaphoi* — Mercury (spirit of water); and *Ouraïos* — Venus, spirit of fire.[748]

In their functions and description as given, these seven planets are identical with the Hindû *Sapta-Lokas*, the seven places or spheres, or the superior and inferior worlds; for they represent the kabalistic seven spheres. With the Ophites, they belong to the lower spheres. The monograms of these Gnostic planets are also Buddhistic, the latter differing, albeit slightly, from those of the usual astrological 'houses.' In the explanatory notes which accompany the scheme, the names of Cerinthus (the disciple of Simon Magus), of Menander, and of certain other Gnostics, whose names are not to be met with in the Patristic writings, are often mentioned; such as Par'ha (Ferho), for instance.[749]

The author of the scheme claims, moreover, for his sect the greatest antiquity, bringing forward as a proof that their 'forefathers' were the builders of all the 'Dracontia' temples, even of those beyond 'the great waters.' He asserts that the 'Just One,' who was the mouth-piece of the Eternal Aeon (Christos), himself sent his disciples into the world, placing them under the double protection of Sigē (Silence, the Logos), and Ophis, the Agathodaimon. The author alludes, no doubt, to the favorite expression of Jesus, "be wise as serpents, and harmless

---

746. This mountain is situated south-west of China, almost between China and Tibet.

747. SOL, being situated in this scheme exactly in the center of the solar system (of which the Ophites appear to have been cognisant) — hence, under the direct vertical ray of the Higher Spiritual Sun — showers his brightness on all other planets.

748. Speaking of Venus, Placidus the astrologer always maintained that "her bluish luster denotes heat." As to Mercury, it was a strange fancy of the Ophites to represent him as a spirit of water, when, astrologically considered, he is as "a cold, dry, earthy and melancholy star."

749. The name which Norberg translates, in his *Onomasticon* to the *Codex Nazaraeus*, as Ferho, stands in the original *Par'ha Rabba*. In the *Life of Manes*, given by Epiphanius, in his *Panaria*, lib. II, tom. II, Haer. LXVI, iii, is mentioned a certain priest of Mithras, a friend of the great Heresiarch Manes, named Parchus.

as doves." In the scheme Ophis is represented as the Egyptian Cnuphis or Kneph, called Dracontia. He appears as a serpent standing erect on its tail, with a lion's head, crowned and radiate, and bearing on the point of each ray one of the seven Greek vowels — symbol of the seven celestial spheres. This figure is quite familiar to those who are acquainted with the Gnostic gems,[750] and is borrowed from the Egyptian *Hermetic books*. The description given in the *Revelation*, of one "like unto the Son of Man," with his seven stars, and who is the Logos, is another form of Ophis.

The Nazarene scheme, except in a change of names, is identical with that of the Gnostics, who evidently borrowed their ideas from it, adding a few appellations from the Basilidean and Valentinian systems. To avoid repetition, we will now simply present the the two in parallel.

Thus, we find that in the Nazarene Cosmogony the names of their powers and genii stand in the following relations to those of the Gnostics:

NAZARENE

First Trinity

Lord FERHO — the Life which is no Life — the Supreme God. The *Cause* which produces the Light, or the Logos *in abscondito*. The water of Jordanus Maximus — the water of Life, or Ajar, the feminine principle. Unity in a Trinity, enclosed within the ISH AMON.

Second Trinity

(The manifestation of the first)

1. Lord MANO — the King of Life and Light — *Rex Lucis*. First LIFE, or the primitive man.
2. Lord Jordan — manifestation or emanation of Jordan Maximus — the waters of grace. Second LIFE.
3. The Superior Father — Abatur. Third LIFE.

This Trinity produces also a duad — Lord Lehdoio, and Fetahil, the genius (the former, a perfect emanation; the latter, imperfect).

GNOSTIC-OPHITE

First Unity in a Trinity

IAO — the Ineffable Name of the Unknown Deity — Abraxas, and the 'Eternal Spiritual Sun.' Unity enclosed within the Depth, Bythos, feminine principle — the boundless circle, within which lie all ideal forms. From this Unity emanates the

Second Trinity

(Idem)

1. Ennoia — mind.

2. Ophis, the Agathodaimon.

3. Sophia Androgyne — wisdom; who, in her turn — fecundated with the Divine Light — produces

Christos and Sophia-Achamoth (one perfect, the other imperfect), as an emanation.

---

750. Its description is found in one of the magic books of the Egyptian King Nechepso, or *Nekau*, and its use prescribed on green jasper stones, as a potent amulet. Galen mentions it (*Galeni op.*—'De simpl. med. fac.,' IX; cf. King: *The Gnostics, etc.*, p. 220, 2nd ed.).

Lord Jordan — 'the Lord of all Jordans,'   Sophia-Achamoth emanates Ilda-Baoth —
manifests Netubto (Faith *without*   the Demiurge, who produces material
Works).[751]   and soulless creation. 'Works *with-
                                                          out* Faith' (or grace).[752]

Moreover, the Ophite seven planetary genii, who emanated one from
the other, are found again in the Nazarene religion under the name of
the "seven impostor-daemons," or stellars, who "will deceive all the
sons of Adam." These are *Sol; Spiritus Venereus* (Holy Spirit, in her
material aspect),[752] the mother of the "seven badly-disposed stellars,"
answering to the Gnostic Achamoth; *Nebu*, or Mercury, "a false Messiah, who will deprave the ancient worship of God";[753] Sin (or Luna,
or Shuril); Kiun (Kivan, or Saturn); Bel-Jupiter; and the seventh,
Nerig, Mars (*Codex Nazaraeus*, I, p. 55).

The Christos of the Gnostics is the chief of the seven Aeons, St.
John's seven spirits of God; the Nazarenes have also their seven genii
or good Aeons, whose chief is *Rex Lucis*, Mano, their Christos. The
Sapta-Rishis, the seven sages of India, inhabit the *Sapta-Puras*, or the
seven celestial cities.

What less or more do we find in the Universal Ecclesia, until the days
of the Reformation, and in the Roman Popish Church after the separation? We have compared the relative values of the Hindû Cosmogony,
the Chaldaean, Zoroastrian, Jewish Kabala, and that of the so-termed
Heretics. A correct plan of the Judaico-Christian religion — to enforce which on the heathen who have furnished it are expended such
great sums every year — would still better prove the identity of the two;
but we lack space, and are also spared the necessity of proving what is
already thoroughly demonstrated.

In the Ophite gems of King (*Gnostics*), we find the name of Iao repeated, and often confounded with that of Ievo, while the latter simply
represents one of the genii antagonistic to Abraxas. In order that these
names may not be taken as identical with the name of the Jewish Jehovah we will at once explain this word. It seems to us surpassingly strange
that so many learned archaeologists should have so little insisted that
there was more than one Jehovah, and disclaimed that the name origin-

---

751. Consider those two diametrically-opposed doctrines — the Catholic and the
Protestant; the one preached by Paul, the semi-Platonist, and the other by James, the
orthodox Talmudist.

752. The material, bad side of Sophia-Achamoth, who emanates from herself Ilda-
Baoth and his six sons.

753. See Norberg's translation of *Codex Nazaraeus*, Preface. This proves once more
the identification of Jesus with Gautama-Buddha in the minds of the Nazarene Gnostics,
as *Nebu* or Mercury is the planet sacred to the Buddhas.

ated with Moses. Iao is certainly a title of the Supreme Being, and belongs *partially* to the Ineffable Name; but it neither originated with nor was it the sole property of the Jews. Even if it had pleased Moses to bestow the name upon the tutelar 'Spirit,' the alleged protector and national deity of the 'chosen people of Israel,' there is yet no possible reason why other nationalities should receive Him as the Highest and One-living God. But we deny the assumption altogether. Besides, there is the fact that Yaho or Iao was a 'mystery name' from the beginning, for יהוה and וה never came into use before King David. Anterior to his time few or no proper names were compounded with *iah* or *yah*. It looks rather as though David, being a sojourner among the Tyrians and Philistines (*2 Samuel*), brought thence the name of Jehovah. He made Zadok high-priest, from whom came the Zadokites or Sadducees. He lived and ruled first at Hebron חברון, 'Habir-on or Kabir-town, where the rites of the four (mystery-gods) were celebrated. Neither David nor Solomon recognised either Moses or the law of Moses. They aspired to build a temple to יהוה, like the structures erected by Hiram to Hercules and Venus, Adon and Astarte.

Says Fürst: "The very ancient name of God, Yaho, written in the Greek Iαω, appears, apart *from its derivation*, to have been an old mystic name of the Supreme deity of the Shemites. [Hence it was told to Moses when initiated at HOR-EB — the *cave*, under the direction of Jethro, the Kenite or Cainite priest of Midian.] In an old religion of the Chaldaeans, whose remains are to be found amongst the Neo-Platonists, the highest divinity enthroned above the seven heavens, representing the Spiritual Light-Principle (*nous*) [754] and also conceived as the Demiurgus,[755] was called Iαω, who was, like the Hebrew Yaho, יהו, mysterious and unmentionable, and whose name was communicated to the initiated. The Phoenicians had a Supreme God whose name was triliteral and *secret*, and he was Iαω." [756]

But while Fürst insists that the name has a Semitic origin, there are other scholars who trace it farther back than he does, and look beyond the classification of the Caucasians.

In Sanskrit we have *Jah* and *Jaya*, or *Jaa* and *Jagad*, and this throws light on the origin of the famous festival of the car of *Jagan-nâtha*, commonly called Jaggernâth. *Javhe* means 'he who is,' and Dr. Spiegel traces even the Persian name of God, *Ahura*, to the root *ah*,[757] which

---

754. *Nous*, the designation given by Anaxagoras to the Supreme Deity, was taken from Egypt, where he was styled NUT.
755. By very few though, for the creators of the material universe were always considered as subordinate deities to the Most High God.
756. Lydus: *De mensibus*, IV, 38, 74; Cedrenus: *Compendium historiarum*, I, p. 296.
757. *Erân das Land zwischen dem Indus und Tigris*: Berlin, 1863; *Avesta*, I, p. 9

in Sanskrit is pronounced *as*, to breathe, to be, and *asu*, became, therefore, in time, synonymous with 'Spirit.' [758] Rawlinson strongly supports
the opinion of an Aryan or Vedic influence on the early Babylonian
mythology. We have given, a few pages back, the strongest possible
proofs of the identity of Vishnu with Dag-on. The same may be adduced
for the title of Iaω, and its Sanskrit root traced in every country. Jυ or
Jovis is the oldest Latin name for God. "As male he is Ju-*piter*, or *Ju*,
the father, *pitri* being Sanskrit for father; as feminine, Ju-*no* or Ju, the
comforter — נוח being the Phoenician word for rest and comfort." [759]
Professor Max Müller shows that although *Dyaus*, sky, does not occur as
a masculine in the ordinary Sanskrit, yet it does occur in the *Veda*, "and
thus bears witness to the early Aryan worship of Dyaus, the Greek
Zeus". ('The Veda,' in *Chips, etc.*, I, p. 78).

To grasp the real and primitive sense of the term IAΩ, and the reason
for its becoming the designation of the most mysterious of all deities, we
must search for its origin in the figurative phraseology of all the primitive people. We must first of all go to the most ancient sources for our
information. In one of the *Books of Hermes*, for instance, we find him
saying that the number TEN is the mother of the soul, and that the *life*
and *light* are therein united. For "the number 1 (one) is born from the
spirit, and the number 10 (ten) from matter"; [760] "the unity has made
the TEN, the TEN the unity." [761]

The kabalistic *gematria* — one of the methods for extracting the hidden meaning from letters, words, and sentences — is arithmetical. It
consists in applying to the letters of a word the sense they bear as numbers, in *outward* shape as well as in their individual sense. Moreover,
by the *Temura* (another method used by the kabalists) any word could
be made to yield its mystery out of its anagram. Thus we find the author
of *Sepher Yetzirah* saying, one or two centuries before our era: [762] "ONE,
the spirit of the *Alahim* of Lives." [763] So again, in the oldest kabalistic
diagrams, the *ten* Sephiroth are represented as wheels or circles, and
Adam Kadmon, the primitive man, as an *upright* pillar. "Wheels and

---

758. *Asi* means, moreover, 'Thou art,' in Sanskrit, and also 'sword,' *Asi*, without
the accent on the first vowel.

759. Professor A. Wilder.

760. These sacred anagrams were called *Zeruph*.

761. *Book of Numbers*, or *Book of the Keys*.

762. The *Sepher Yetzirah*, or book of the creation, was written by Rabbi A'qíbah, who
was the teacher and instructor of Shimon ben Yo'hai, called the prince of the Kabalists,
who wrote the *Zohar*. Franck asserts that the *Yetzirah* was written in the first century A. D.
(*La Kabbale*, I, i; 3rd ed.), but other and as competent judges make it far older. At all
events it is now proved that Shimon ben Yo'hai lived *before* the second destruction of
the temple.   763. *Sepher Yetzirah*, i, § 9.

seraphim and the holy creatures (*'hayyoth*)," says Rabbi A'qîbah.[764] In another system of the same branch of the symbolical Kabala, called *Albath* — which arranges the letters of the alphabet by pairs in three rows — all the couples in the first row bear the numerical value *ten;* and in the system of Shimon ben Shetah [765] the uppermost couple, the most sacred of all, is preceded by the Pythagorean cipher, one and a nought, or zero — 10.

If we can once appreciate the fact that among all the peoples of the highest antiquity the most natural conception of the First Cause manifesting itself in its creatures, and that to this they could not but ascribe the creation of all, was that of an androgyne deity; that the male principle was considered the vivifying invisible spirit, and the female, mother nature; we shall be enabled to understand how that mysterious cause came at first to be represented (in the picture-writings, perhaps) as the combination of the Alpha and Omega of numbers, a decimal, then as IAO, a triliteral name, containing in itself a deep allegory.

IAO, in such a case, would — etymologically considered — mean the 'Breath of Life,' generated or springing forth between an upright male and an egg-shaped female principle of nature; for, in Sanskrit, *as* means 'to be,' 'to live or exist'; and originally it meant 'to breathe.' "From it," says Max Müller, "in its original sense of breathing, the Hindûs formed '*asu*,' breath, and '*asura*,' the name of God, whether it meant the breathing one or the giver of breath." [766] It certainly meant the latter. In Hebrew 'Ah' and 'Iah' mean life. Cornelius Agrippa, in his treatise on the *Pre-eminence of Woman*,[766a] shows that "the word Eve suggests comparison with the mystic symbols of the kabalists, the name of the woman having affinity with the ineffable Tetragrammaton, the most sacred name of the divinity." Ancient names were always consonant with the things they represented. In relation to the mysterious name of the Deity in question, the hitherto inexplicable hint of the kabalists as to the efficacy of the letter H, "which Abram took away from his wife Sarah" and "put *into the middle of his own name*," becomes clear.

It may perhaps be argued, by way of objection, that it is not ascertained as yet at what period of antiquity the *nought* occurs for the first time in Indian manuscripts or inscriptions. Be that as it may, the case presents circumstantial evidence of too strong a character not to carry a conviction of probability with it. According to Max Müller "the two words 'cipher' and 'zero,' which are in reality but one, would almost in

---

764. *Sepher Yetzirah,* i, § 10. See the constancy with which Ezekiel in his vision sticks to the '*wheels*' of the 'living creatures' (ch. i, *passim*).

765. He was an Alexandrian Neo-Platonist under the first of the Ptolemies.

766. *Chips, etc.,* I, p. 156.   766a. *De nobilitate et praecellentia feminei sexus.*

themselves be sufficient to prove that our figures are borrowed from the
Arabs.[767] 'Cipher' is the Arabic 'cifron,' which means *empty*, a translation of the Sanskrit name of the nought, '*śûnya*,' " he says. The Arabs
had their figures from Hindûstân, and never claimed the discovery for
themselves.[768] As to the Pythagoreans, we need but turn to the ancient
manuscripts of Boethius' *Geometry*, composed in the sixth century, to find
in the Pythagorean numerals [769] the 1 and the *nought*, as the first and final
cipher. And Porphyry, who quotes from the Pythagorean Moderatus,[770]
says that the numerals of Pythagoras were "hieroglyphical symbols, by
means whereof he explained ideas concerning the nature of things."

Now if the most ancient Indian manuscripts show as yet no trace of
decimal notation in them — and Max Müller states very clearly that
until now he has found but nine letters (the initials of the Sanskrit numerals) in them — on the other hand we have records as ancient to supply
the needed proof. We speak of the sculptures and the sacred imagery in
the most ancient temples of the far East. Pythagoras derived his knowledge from India; and we find Professor Max Müller corroborating this
statement, at least so far as allowing the *Neo*-Pythagoreans to have been
the first teachers of 'ciphering' among the Greeks and Romans; that
"they, at Alexandria, or in Syria, became acquainted with the Indian
figures, and adapted them to the Pythagorean abacus" (our figures).
This cautious admission implies that Pythagoras himself was acquainted
with only *nine* figures. But we might reasonably answer that although
we possess no certain proof that the decimal notation was known to
Pythagoras, who lived at the very close of the archaic ages,[771] we yet
have sufficient evidence to show that the full numbers, as given by
Boethius, were known to the Pythagoreans, even before Alexandria was
built.[772] This evidence we find in Aristotle, who says that "some philosophers hold that ideas and numbers are of the same nature, and amount
to TEN in all." [773] This, we believe, will be sufficient to show that the
decimal notation was known among them at least as early as four
centuries B. C., for Aristotle does not seem to treat the question as an
innovation of the 'Neo-Pythagoreans.'

Besides, as we have remarked above, the representations of the
archaic deities, on the walls of the temples, are of themselves quite suggestive enough. So, for instance, Vishnu is represented in the *Kûrmâva-
târa* (his second avatar) as a tortoise sustaining a circular pillar, on which
the semblance of himself (*Mâyâ*, or the illusion) sits with all his attributes.[774] While one hand holds a flower, another a club, the third a shell,

---

767. *Chips, etc.*, II, p. 284.   768. *Ibid.*   769. King: *The Gnostics*, p. 370; 2nd ed.
770. *Pythagoras vita.*   771. 608 B. C.   772. This city was built 332 B. C.
773. *Metaphys.*, XII, viii; XIII, viii.   774. See pl. IX in Maurice: *Hist. of Hindostan*, I.

the fourth, generally the upper one, or at the right, holds on his forefinger, extended as the cipher 1, the *chakra*, or discus, which resembles a ring or a wheel, and might be taken for the nought. In his first avatar, the *Matsyâvatâra*, when emerging from the fish's mouth, he is represented in the same position.[775] The ten-armed *Durgâ* of Bengal; the ten-headed *Râvana* the giant; *Pârvatî* — as *Durgâ, Indra and Indrânî* — are found with this attribute, which is a perfect representation of the May-pole.[776]

The holiest of the temples among the Hindûs are those of Jagan-nâtha. This deity is worshiped equally by all the sects of India, and *Jagan*-nâtha is named 'The Lord of the World.' He is the god of the Mysteries, and his temples, which are most numerous in Bengal, are all of a pyramidal form.

There is no other deity-name which affords such a variety of etymologies as Iaho, nor one which can be so variously pronounced. It is only by associating it with the Masoretic points that the later Rabbins succeeded in making Jehovah read 'Adonai' — or Lord. Philo Byblius [777] spells it in Greek letters IEYΩ — IEVO. Theodoret [778] says that the Samaritans pronounced it *IABE* (*Yahve*) and the Jews *AIA*. Diodorus [779] states that "among the Jews they relate that Moses called the God IAΩ," which would make it as we have shown I-ah-O. It is on the authority of the *Bible* itself, therefore, that we maintain that before his initiation by Jethro, his father-in-law, Moses had never known the word Iaho. The future Deity of the sons of Israel calls out from the burning bush and gives His name as "I am that I am," and specifies carefully that He is the "Lord God of the Hebrews" (*Exod.*, iii, 18), not of the other nations. Judging him by his own acts throughout the Jewish records, we doubt whether Christ himself, had he appeared in the days of the *Exodus*, would have been welcomed by the irascible Sinaitic Deity. However, 'The Lord God,' who becomes, on His own confession, Jehovah only in the 6th chapter of *Exodus* (verse 3) finds his veracity put to a startling test in *Genesis*, xxii, 14, in which *revealed* passage Abraham builds an altar to *Jehovah-jireh*.

It would seem therefore only natural to draw a distinction between the mystery-God-name Iaω, adopted from the highest antiquity by all who participated in the esoteric knowledge of the priests, and its phonetic counterparts which we find treated with so little reverence by the Ophites and other Gnostics. Once having burdened themselves, like the Azazel

---

775. See drawings from the Temple of Râma, pl. III, Coleman's *Mythology of the Hindus:* New York, J. W. Bouton, publisher.

776. See Hargrave Jennings: *The Rosicrucians*, II, p. 34; 3rd ed.

777. Philo Bybl. in Euseb.: *Praep. ev.*, X, xi.   778. Theod.: *Quaest.* xv in *Exod.*

779. Diod. Sic.: *Bibl. hist.*, I, 94. Cf. Gesenius: *A Hebr. and Engl. Lexicon, s. v.* יהוה.

of the wilderness, with the sins and iniquities of the Jewish nation, it now appears hard for the Christians to have to confess that those whom they thought fit to consider the 'chosen people' of God — and their sole predecessors in monotheism — were, till a very late period, as idolatrous and polytheistic as their neighbors. The shrewd Talmudists have escaped the accusation for long centuries by screening themselves behind the Masoretic invention. But, as in everything else, truth was at last brought to light. We know now that Ihoh, יהוה, must be read Iahoh and Iah, not Jehovah. Iah of the Hebrews is plainly the Iacchos (Bacchus) of the Mysteries; the God "from whom the liberation of souls was expected — Dionysus, Iacchos, Iahoh, Iao." [780] Aristotle then was right when he said: "Joh יהוה was Oromasdes and Ahriman Pluto, for the God of heaven, Ahura-mazda, rides on a chariot which the *Horse of the Sun* follows." [781] And Dunlap quotes *Psalms*, lxviii, 4, which reads:

> "Praise him by his name Iach (יה),
> Who rides upon the heavens, as on a horse,"

and then shows that "the Arabs represented Iauk (Ia'h) by a horse — the Horse of the Sun (Dionysus)." [782] "Iah is a softening of Iach," he explains. "ח *ch* and ה *h* interchange; so *s* softens to *h*. The Hebrews express the idea of LIFE both by a *ch* and an *h;* as *chiah,* to be, *hiah,* to be; Iach, God of Life, Iah, 'I *am.*' " Well then may we repeat these lines of Ausonius (*Epig.* xxv):

> "Ogygia calls me Bacchus; Egypt thinks me Osiris;
> The Musians name me Phanax; the Indi consider me Dionysus;
> The Roman Mysteries call me Liber; the Arabian race Adonis!"

And the chosen people Adoni and Jehovah — we may add.

How little the philosophy of the old secret doctrine was understood is illustrated in the atròcious persecutions of the Templars by the Church, and in the accusation against them of worshiping the Devil under the shape of the goat — Baphomet! Without going into the old Masonic mysteries, there is not a Mason — of those we mean who *do know something* — but has an idea of the true relation that Baphomet bore to Azazel, the scapegoat of the wilderness, [783] whose character and meaning are entirely perverted in the Christian translations. " 'This terrible and

---

780. K. O. Müller: *A Hist. of the Lit. of Anct. Greece,* p. 238; Movers: *Die Phönisier,* I, pp. 547-53; Dunlap: *Söd, the Myst. of Adoni,* p. 21.

781. *A Universal History,* V, p. 301: London, 1747-66 (64 vols.).

782. Dunlap: *The Spirit-History of Man,* pp. 64, 67, 78.

783. See *Leviticus,* xvi, 8, 10, and other verses relating to the biblical goat in the original texts.

venerable name of God,' says Lanci, librarian to the Vatican, 'through
the pen of biblical glossers, has been a *devil*, a mountain, a *wilderness*, and
a *he-goat*' "— quotes Mackenzie in the *Royal Masonic Cyclopaedia;* and
he very correctly remarks that "this word should be divided into Azaz
and El," for "it signifies God of Victory, but is here used in the sense of
author of Death, in contrast to Jehovah, the *author of Life;* the latter received a dead goat as an offering." [784] The Hindû Trinity is composed of
three personages, which are convertible into one. The *Trimûrti* is one,
and in its abstraction indivisible, and yet we see a metaphysical division
taking place from the first, and while Brahmâ, though collectively representing the three, remains behind the scenes, Vishnu is the Life-Giver, the
Creator, and the Preserver, and Śiva is the *Destroyer* and the *Death-
giving* deity. "Death to the *Life-giver*, life to the *Death-dealer*. The
symbolical antithesis is grand and beautiful," says Gliddon.[785] '*Deus est
Daemon inversus*' of the kabalists now becomes clear. It is but the
intense and cruel desire to crush out the last vestige of the old philosophies by perverting their meaning, for fear that her own dogmas should
not be rightly fathered on her, which impels the Catholic Church to
carry on such a systematic persecution in regard to Gnostics, Kabalists,
and even the comparatively innocent Masons.

Alas, alas! How little has the divine seed, scattered broadcast by
the hand of the meek Judaean philosopher, thrived or brought forth fruit!
He who himself had shunned hypocrisy, warned against public prayer,
showing contempt for useless exhibition of the same, could he but
cast his sorrowful glance on the earth from the regions of eternal bliss,
would see that this seed fell neither on sterile rock nor by the wayside.
Nay, it took deep root in the most prolific soil; one enriched even
to plethora with lies and human gore!

"For if the truth of God hath more abounded *through my lie* unto his
glory; why yet am I also judged as a sinner?" naïvely inquires Paul, the
best and sincerest of all the apostles, after saying, "I speak as a man."
And he then adds, "and not rather [then say] (as we be *slanderously
reported*, and as some affirm that we say), 'Let us do evil that good may
come' — *whose damnation is just*." (*Rom.*, iii, 5, 7, 8.) In spite of this
distinct repudiation of the hypothetical travesty on right ethics, the
travesty itself was misread as a direct inspiration from God! This explains, if it does not excuse, the maxim adopted later by the Church [786]
that "it is an act of virtue to deceive and lie, when by such means
the interests of *the Church* might be promoted." A maxim applied

---

784. Article 'Goat,' p. 257.   785. Nott and Gliddon: *Types of Mankind*, p. 600;
Royal Masonic Cyclopaedia, loc. cit.   786. Mosheim: *An Ecclesiastical History*,
cent. IV, part II, iii, § 16. Read the whole section to appreciate the doctrine in full.

in its fullest sense by that accomplished professor in forgery, the Armenian Eusebius; or again, by that innocent-looking bible-kaleidoscopist — Irenaeus. And these men were followed by a whole army of pious assassins, who in the meanwhile had improved upon the system of deceit by proclaiming that it was lawful even to kill, when by murder they could enforce the new religion. Theophilus, "that perpetual enemy of peace and virtue," as the famous bishop was called; Cyril of Alexandria, Athanasius, the murderer of Arius, and a host of other canonized 'Saints,' were all only too worthy successors of *Saint* Constantine, who drowned his wife in boiling water, butchered his little nephew, murdered with his own pious hand two of his brothers-in-law, killed his own son Crispus, bled to death several men and women, and smothered in a well an old monk. However, we are told by Eusebius that this Christian Emperor was rewarded by a *vision* of Christ himself, bearing his cross, who instructed him to march to other triumphs, inasmuch as he would always protect him!

It is under the shade of the Imperial standard, with its famous sign, '*In hoc signo vinces*,' that '*visionary*' Christianity, which had crept on since the days of Irenaeus, arrogantly proclaimed its rights in the full blaze of the sun. The Labarum had most probably furnished the model for the *true* cross, which was 'miraculously,' and agreeably to the Imperial will, found a few years later. Nothing short of such a remarkable vision, impiously doubted by some severe critics — Dr. Lardner for one — and a fresh miracle to match, could have resulted in the finding of a cross where there had never been one before. Still, we have either to believe the phenomenon or dispute it at the risk of being treated as infidels; and this notwithstanding that upon a careful computation we should find that the fragments of the 'true Cross' had multiplied themselves even more miraculously than the five loaves in the invisible bakery, and the two fishes. In all cases like this, where miracles can be so conveniently called in, there is no room for dull fact. History must step out, that fiction may step in.

If the alleged founder of the Christian religion is now, after the lapse of nineteen centuries, preached — more or less unsuccessfully however — in every corner of the globe, we are at liberty to think that the doctrines attributed to him would astonish and dismay him more than any one else. A system of deliberate falsification was adopted from the first. How determined Irenaeus was to crush truth and build up a Church of his own on the mangled remains of the seven primitive churches mentioned in the *Revelation*, may be inferred from his quarrel with Ptolemaeus. And this is again a case of evidence against which no blind faith can prevail. Ecclesiastical history assures us that Christ's ministry was but of three years' duration. There is a decided discrepancy on this point between the first three synoptics and the fourth gospel; but it was left for Irenaeus to show to Christian posterity that so early as A. D. 180 — the probable time when this Father wrote his works against heresies — even such pillars of the Church as himself either knew nothing certain about it, or deliberately lied and falsified dates to support their own views. So anxious was the worthy Father to meet every possible objection against his plans, that no falsehood, no sophistry, was too much for him. How are we to understand the following; and who is the falsifier in this case? The argument of Ptolemaeus was that Jesus was too young to have taught anything of much importance; adding that "Christ preached for *one year only*, and then suffered in the twelfth month." In this Ptolemaeus was very little at variance with the gospels. But Irenaeus, carried by his object far beyond the limits of prudence, from a mere discrepancy between one and three years, makes it *ten* and even twenty years! "Destroying his [Christ's] whole work, and *robbing him of that age* which is *both more necessary* and more honorable than any other; that more advanced age, I mean, during which also, as a teacher, he excelled all others." And then, having no certain data to furnish, he throws himself back on *tradition*, and claims that Christ preached for over TEN years! [787] In another place he makes Jesus fifty years old.

But we must proceed in our work of showing the various origins of Christianity, as also the sources from which Jesus derived his own ideas of God and humanity.

The Koinobioi lived in Egypt, where Jesus passed his early youth. They were usually confounded with the Therapeutae, who were, however, only a branch of this widely-spread society. Such is the opinion of Godfrey Higgins and Dr. Rebold. After the downfall of the principal sanctuaries, which had already begun in the days of Plato, the many different sects, such as the Gymnosophists and the Magi — from whom Clearchus very erroneously derives the former — the Pythagoreans, the Sufis, and the Rishis of Kashmir, instituted a kind of international and universal Freemasonry among their esoteric societies. "These Rishis," says Higgins, "are the Essenians, Carmelites, or Nazarites of the temple." [788] "That occult science known by ancient priests under the name of *regenerating fire*," says Dr. Rebold, ". . . is a science that for more than 3000 years was the peculiar possession of the [Indian and Egyptian] priesthood, into the knowledge of which Moses was initiated at Heliopolis, where he was educated; and Jesus among the Essenian

---

787. *Against Heresies*, II, xxii, §§ 4, 5.   788. *Anacalypsis*.

priests of [Egypt or] Judaea; and by which these two great reformers, *particularly the latter*, wrought many of the miracles mentioned in the *Scriptures.*" [789]

Plato [according to Ammianus] states that the mystic Magian religion, known under the name of *Machagistia*, is the least corrupted form of worship of things divine. Later, the Mysteries of the Chaldaean sanctuaries were added to it by one of the Zoroasters and Darius Hystaspes.[790] The latter completed and perfected it still more with the help of the knowledge obtained by him from the learned ascetics of India, whose rites were identical with those of the initiated Magi.[791] Ammianus, in his history of Julian's Persian expedition, gives the story by stating that one day "Hystaspes, as he was boldly penetrating into the unknown regions of Upper India, came upon a certain wooded solitude, the tranquil recesses of which were occupied by those exalted sages, the Brachmanes [or Shamans]. Instructed by their teachings in the science of *the motions of the* world and of the heavenly bodies, and in *pure religious rites* . . . he infused a portion into the minds of the Magi. The latter, coupling these doctrines with their *own peculiar science of foretelling the future*, have handed down the whole through their descendants to succeeding ages." [790] It is from these descendants that the Sufis, chiefly composed of Persians and Syrians, acquired their profound knowledge of astrology, medicine, and the esoteric doctrine of the ages. "The Sufi doctrine," says C. W. King, "involved the grand idea of one universal creed which could be secretly held under any profession of an outward faith; and in fact took virtually the same view of religious systems as that in which the ancient philosophers had regarded such matters." [792] The mysterious Druzes of Mount Lebanon are the descendants of all these. Solitary Copts, earnest students scattered hither and thither throughout the sandy solitudes of Egypt, Arabia Petraea, Palestine, and the impenetrable forests of Abyssinia, though rarely met with, may sometimes be seen. Many and various are the nationalities to which belong

789. E. Rebold: *A General History of Free-Masonry*, pp. 30-1.
790. Amm. Marcell.: *Rom. Hist.*, XXIII, vi, 32, 33.
791. We hold to the idea — which becomes self-evident when the Zoroastrian imbroglio is considered — that there were, even in the days of Darius, two distinct sacerdotal castes of Magi: the initiated, and those who were allowed to officiate only in the popular rites. We see the same in the Eleusinian Mysteries. Belonging to every temple there were attached the 'hierophants' of the *inner* sanctuary, and the secular clergy who were not even instructed in the Mysteries. It was against the absurdities and superstitions of the latter that Darius revolted, and "crushed them," for the inscription on his tomb shows that he was a 'hierophant' and a Magian himself. It is also merely the exoteric rites of this class of Magi which descended to posterity; for the great secrecy in which were preserved the 'Mysteries' of the true Chaldaean Magi was never violated, however much guess-work may have been expended on them.
792. *The Gnostics and their Remains*, p. 415; 2nd ed.

the disciples of that mysterious school, and many the side-shoots of that one primitive stock. The secrecy preserved by these sub-lodges, as well as by the one and supreme great lodge, has ever been proportionate to the activity of religious persecutions; and now, in the face of the growing materialism, their very existence is becoming a mystery.[793]

But it must not be inferred, on that account, that such a mysterious brotherhood is but a fiction, not even *a name*, though it remains unknown to this day. Whether its affiliates are called by an Egyptian, Hindû, or Persian name, it matters not. Persons belonging to one of these sub-brotherhoods have been met by trustworthy and not unknown persons, besides the present writer, who states a few facts concerning them, by the special permission of one *who has a right to give it*. In a recent and very valuable work on secret societies, K. R. H. Mackenzie's *Royal Masonic Cyclopaedia*, we find the learned author himself, an honorary member of the Canongate Kilwinning Lodge, No. 2 (Scotland), and a Mason not likely to be imposed upon, stating the following, under the head, 'Hermetic Brothers of Egypt':

"An occult fraternity, which has endured from very ancient times, having a hierarchy of officers, secret signs, and passwords, and a peculiar method of instruction in science, moral philosophy and religion. . . . If we may believe those who at the present time profess to belong to it, *the philosopher's stone, the elixir of life, the art of invisibility*, and the power of communication directly with the ultramundane life, are parts of the inheritance they possess. The writer has met with only three persons who maintained the actual existence of this body of religious philosophers, and who hinted that they themselves were actually members. There was no reason to doubt the good faith of these individuals — apparently unknown to each other, and men of moderate competence, blameless lives, austere manners, and almost ascetic in their habits.

---

793. These are truths which cannot fail to impress themselves upon the minds of earnest thinkers. While the Ebionites, Nazarites, Haemerobaptists, Lampseans, Sabaeans, and many other sects of the earliest days, wavered later between the varying dogmas suggested to them by the *esoteric* and misunderstood parables of the Nazarene teacher, whom they justly regarded as a prophet — there were men, for whose names we might vainly search history, who preserved the secret doctrines of Jesus as pure and unadulterated as they had been received. And still, even all these above-mentioned and conflicting sects were far more orthodox in their Christianity, or rather Christism, than the Churches of Constantine and Rome. "It was a strange fate that befell these unfortunate people" (the Ebionites), says Lord Amberley, "when, overwhelmed by the flood of heathenism that had swept into the Church, they were condemned as heretics. Yet there is no evidence that they had ever swerved from the doctrines of Jesus, or of the disciples who knew him in his lifetime. Jesus himself had been circumcised, . . . reverenced the temple at Jerusalem as 'a house of prayer for all nations.' . . . But the torrent of progress swept past the Ebionites, and left them stranded on the shore" (*An Analysis of Religious Belief*, by Viscount Amberley, I, p. 446).

They all appeared to be men of forty to forty-five years of age, and evidently of vast erudition . . . their knowledge of languages not to be doubted. . . . They never remained long in any one country, but passed away without creating notice." [794]

Another of such sub-brotherhoods is the sect of the Pitris in India. Known by name, now that Jacolliot has brought it into public notice, it is still more arcane, perhaps, than the brotherhood that Mr. Mackenzie names the 'Hermetic Brothers.' What Jacolliot learned of it, was from fragmentary manuscripts delivered to him by Brâhmanas, who had their reasons for doing so, we must believe. The *Agrushada Parikshai* gives certain details about the association, as it was in days of old, and when explaining mystic rites and magical incantations explains nothing at all, so that the mystic *L'om, L'Rhum, Sh'krum,* and *Sho'rhim Ramaya-Namaha* remain, for the mystified writer, as much a puzzle as ever. To do him justice, though, he fully admits the fact, and does not enter upon useless speculations. (*Le Spiritisme, etc.*, p. 78.)

Whoever desires to assure himself that there now exists a religion which has baffled, for centuries, the impudent inquisitiveness of missionaries, and the persevering inquiry of science, let him violate, if he can, the seclusion of the Syrian Druzes. He will find them numbering over 80,000 warriors, scattered from the plain east of Damascus to the western coast. They covet no proselytes, shun notoriety, keep friendly — as far as possible — with both Christians and Mohammedans, respect the religion of every other sect or people, but will never disclose their own secrets. Vainly do the missionaries stigmatize them as infidels, idolaters, brigands, and thieves. Neither threat, bribe, nor any other consideration will induce a Druze to become a convert to dogmatic Christianity. We have heard of two in fifty years, and both have finished their careers in prison, for drunkenness and theft. They proved to be "real *Druzes,*" [795]

---

794. What will perhaps still more astonish American readers, is the fact that in the United States a mystical fraternity now exists, which claims an intimate relationship with one of the oldest and most powerful of Eastern Brotherhoods. It is known as the Brotherhood of Luxor, and its faithful members have the custody of very important secrets of science. Its ramifications extend widely throughout the great Republic of the West. Though this brotherhood has been long and hard at work, the secret of its existence has been jealously guarded. Mackensie describes it as having "a Rosicrucian basis, and numbering many members" (*Royal Masonic Cyclopaedia*, p. 461). But in this the author is mistaken; it has no Rosicrucian basis. The name Luxor is primarily derived from the ancient Beluchistan city of Luksur, which lies between Bela and Kedgee, and also gave its name to the Egyptian city.

795. These people do not accept the name of Druses, but regard the appellation as an insult. They call themselves the 'disciples of 'Hamsa,' their Messiah, who came to them, in the eleventh century, from the 'Land of the Word of God,' and, together with his disciple, Mokhtana Boha-eddin, committed this *Word* to writing, and entrusted it

said one of their chiefs, in discussing the subject. There never was a case of an *initiated* Druze becoming a Christian. As to the uninitiated, they are never allowed even to see the sacred writings, and none of them have the remotest idea where these are kept. There are missionaries in Syria who boast of having in their possession a few copies. The volumes alleged to be correct expositions of these secret books (such as the translation by Pétis de la Croix, in 1701, from the works presented by Nasr-Allah to the French king), are nothing more than a compilation of 'secrets' known more or less to every inhabitant of the southern ranges of Lebanon and Anti-Libanus. They were the work of an apostate Dervish, who was expelled from the sect Hanafi for improper conduct — the embezzlement of the money of widows and orphans. The *Exposé de la Religion des Druzes*, in two volumes, by Silvestre de Sacy (1838), is another network of hypotheses. A copy of this work was to be found, in 1870, on the window-sill of one of their principal *Holowés*, or places of religious meeting. To the inquisitive question of an English traveler as to their rites, the *Okhal*,[796] a venerable old man who spoke English as well as French, opened the volume of de Sacy, and, offering it to his interlocutor, remarked, with a benevolent smile: "Read this instructive and truthful book; I could explain to you neither better nor more correctly the secrets of God and our blessed 'Hamza, than it does." The traveler understood the hint.

Mackenzie says they settled at Lebanon about the tenth century, and "seem to be a mixture of Kurds, Mardi-Arabs, and other semi-civilized tribes. Their religion is compounded of Judaism, Christianity, and Mohammedanism. They have a regular order of priesthood and *a kind of hierarchy* . . . there is a regular system of passwords and signs. . . .Twelve month's probation, to which either sex is admitted, precedes initiation."

We quote the above only to show how little even persons as trustworthy as Mr. Mackenzie really know of these mystics.

Mosheim,[797] who knows as much, or we should rather say as little, as any others, is entitled to the merit of candidly admitting that their religion is peculiar to themselves, and is involved in some mystery. We should say it is — rather!

That their religion exhibits traces of Magianism and Gnosticism is natural, as the whole of the Ophite esoteric philosophy is at the bottom of it. But the characteristic dogma of the Druzes is the absolute unity

---

to the care of a few initiates, with the injunction of the greatest secrecy. They are usually called Unitarians.

796. The Okhal (from the Arabic *akl* — intelligence or wisdom) are the initiated, or wise men of this sect. They hold in their mysteries the same position as the hierophant of old, in the Eleusinian and others.   797. *Eccl. Hist.*, cent. XVI, pt. III, ii, 19.

of God. He is the essence of life, and, although incomprehensible and invisible, is to be known through *occasional manifestations in human form.*[798] Like the Hindûs, they hold that he has incarnated more than once on earth. 'Hamza was the *precursor*, not the inheritor, of Hakem, the last manifestation (the tenth avatar),[799] who is yet to come. 'Hamza was the personification of the 'Universal Wisdom.' Bohaeddin in his writings calls him Messiah. The whole number of his disciples, or those who at different ages of the world have imparted wisdom to mankind, which the latter as invariably have forgotten and rejected in course of time, is one hundred and sixty-four (164, the kabalistic *s d k*). Therefore their stages or degrees of promotion after initiation are five; the first three degrees are typified by the "three feet of the candlestick of the inner Sanctuary, which holds the light of the *five* elements"; the last two degrees, the most important and terrifying in their solemn grandeur, belong to the highest orders; and together the five degrees emblematically represent the said five mystic Elements. The "three feet are the holy *Application*, the *Opening*, and the *Phantom*," says one of their books; on man's inner and outer soul, and his body, a phantom, a passing shadow. The body, or matter, is also called the 'Rival,' for "he is the minister of sin, the Devil ever creating dissensions between the Heavenly Intelligence [spirit] and the soul, which he tempts incessantly." Their ideas on transmigration are Pythagorean and kabalistic. The spirit, or Temeami (the divine soul), was in Elijah and John the Baptist; and the soul of Jesus was that of 'Hamza; that is to say, of the same degree of purity and sanctity. Until their resurrection, by which they understand the day when the spiritual bodies of men will be absorbed into God's own essence and being (the Nirvâna of the Hindûs), the souls of men will keep their astral forms, except the few chosen ones who from the moment of their separation from their bodies begin to exist as pure spirits. The life of man they divide into soul, body, and intelligence, or mind. It is the latter which imparts and communicates to the soul the divine spark from its 'Hamza (Christos).

They have seven great commandments which are imparted equally to all the uninitiated; and yet even these well-known articles of faith have been so mixed up in the accounts of outside writers that, in one of the best Cyclopaedias of America (Appleton's), they are garbled after the fashion that may be seen in the comparative tabulation below; the spurious and the true order parallel:

---

798. This is the doctrine of the Gnostics, who held Christos to be the individual immortal Spirit in man.

799. The ten Messiahs or avatars remind us again of the five Buddhistic and ten Brâhmanic avatars of Buddha and Krishna.

CORRECT VERSION OF THE COMMANDMENTS AS IMPARTED ORALLY BY THE TEACHERS [800]	GARBLED VERSION REPORTED BY THE CHRISTIAN MISSIONARIES AND GIVEN IN PRETENDED EXPOSITIONS [801]
1. *The unity of God,* or the infinite oneness of Deity.	1. (2) "'Truth in words,' meaning in practice, *only truth to the religion and to the initiated; it is lawful to act and to speak falsehood to men of another creed.*" [802]
2. *The essential excellence of Truth.*	2. (7) "Mutual help, watchfulness, and protection."
3. Toleration; right given to all men and women to freely express their opinions on religious matters, and make the latter subservient to reason.	3. (?) "To renounce all other religions." [803]
4. Respect to all men and women according to their character and conduct.	4. (?) "To be separate from infidels of every kind, not externally but only in heart." [804]
5. Entire submission to God's decrees.	5. (1) "Recognise God's eternal unity."
6. Chastity of body, mind, and soul.	6. (5) "Satisfied with God's acts."
7. Mutual help under all conditions.	7. (5) "Resigned to God's will."

As will be seen, the only *exposé* in the above is that of the great ignorance, perhaps malice, of the writers who, like Silvestre de Sacy, undertake to enlighten the world upon matters concerning which they know nothing.

"Chastity, honesty, meekness, and mercy," are thus the four theological virtues of all Druzes, besides several others demanded from the initiates; "murder, theft, cruelty, covetousness, slander," the five sins, to which several other sins are added in the sacred tablets, but which we must abstain from giving. The morality of the Druzes is strict and

---

800. See, farther on, a letter from an 'Initiate.'

801. In this column the first numbers are those given in the article on the 'Druzes' in the *New American Cyclopaedia* (Appleton's), VI, p. 631. The numbers in parentheses show the sequence in which the commandments would stand were they given correctly.

802. This pernicious doctrine belongs to the old policy of the Catholic Church, but is certainly false as regards the Druzes. They maintain that it is right and lawful to *withhold the truth* about their own tenets, no one outside their own sect having a right to pry into their religion. The *okhals* never countenance deliberate falsehood in any form, although the laymen have many a time got rid of the spies sent by the Christians to discover their secrets, by deceiving them with sham initiations. (See the letter of Prof. Rawson to the author, p. 313.)

803. This commandment does not exist in the Lebanon teaching.

804. There is no such commandment, but the practice thereof exists by mutual agreement, as in the days of the Gnostic persecution.

uncompromising. Nothing can tempt one of these Lebanon Unitarians
to go astray from what he is taught to consider his duty. *Their ritual
being unknown to outsiders*, their would-be historians have hitherto denied
them one. Their 'Thursday meetings' are open to all, but no inter-
loper has ever participated in the rites of initiation which take place
occasionally on Fridays in the greatest secrecy. Women are admitted
to them as well as men, and play a part of great importance at the
initiation of men. The probation, unless some extraordinary exception
is made, is long and severe. Once in a certain period of time a solemn
ceremony takes place, during which all the elders and the initiates of
the highest two degrees start out for a pilgrimage of several days to a
certain place in the mountains. They meet within the safe precincts of
a monastery said to have been erected during the earliest times of the
Christian era. Outwardly one sees but old ruins of a once grand edifice,
used, says the legend, by some Gnostic sects as a place of worship during
the religious persecutions. The ruins above ground, however, are but
a convenient mask, the subterranean chapel, halls, and cells covering
an area of ground far greater than the upper building; while the rich-
ness of ornamentation, the beauty of the ancient sculptures, and the
gold and silver vessels in this sacred resort, appear like "a dream of
glory," according to the expression of an initiate. As the lamaseries
of Mongolia and Tïbet are visited upon grand occasions by the holy
shadow of 'Lord Buddha,' so here, during the ceremonial, appears the
resplendent ethereal form of 'Hamza, the Blessed, which instructs the
faithful. The most extraordinary feats of what would be termed magic
take place during the several nights that the convocation lasts; and one
of the greatest mysteries — faithful copy of the past — is accomplished
within the discreet bosom of our mother earth; not an echo, nor the
faintest sound, not a glimmer of light betrays without the grand secret
of the initiates.

'Hamza, like Jesus, was a mortal man, and yet ' 'Hamza ' and
'Christos' are synonymous terms as to their inner and hidden meaning.
Both are symbols of the *Nous*, the divine and higher soul of man — his
spirit. The doctrine taught by the Druzes on that particular question
of the duality of spiritual man, consisting of one soul mortal, and
another immortal, is identical with that of the Gnostics, the older Greek
philosophers, and other initiates.

Outside the East we have met one initiate (and only one) who, for
some reasons best known to himself, does not make a secret of his initiation into the Brotherhood of Lebanon. It is the learned traveler and
artist, Professor A. L. Rawson, of New York City. This gentleman has
passed many years in the East, four times visited Palestine, and has

traveled to Mecca. It is safe to say that he has a priceless store of facts about the beginnings of the Christian Church, which none but one who had had free access to repositories closed against the ordinary traveler could have collected. Professor Rawson, with the true devotion of a man of science, noted down every important discovery he made in the Palestinian libraries, and every precious fact orally communicated to him by the mystics he encountered, and some day they will see the light. He has most obligingly sent us the following communication, which, as the reader will perceive, fully corroborates what is above written, from our personal experience, about the strange fraternity *incorrectly* styled the Druzes:

"34 BOND ST., NEW YORK, June 6, 1877

". . . Your note, asking me to give you an account of my initiation into a secret order among the people commonly known as Druzes, in Mount Lebanon, was received this morning. I took, as you are fully aware, an obligation at that time to conceal within my own memory the greater part of the 'mysteries,' with the most interesting parts of the 'instructions'; so that what is left may not be of any service to the public. Such information as I can rightfully give, you are welcome to have and use as you may have occasion.

"The probation in my case was, by *special dispensation*, made one month, during which time I was 'shadowed' by a priest, who served as my cook, guide, interpreter, and general servant, that he might be able to testify to the fact of my having strictly conformed to the rules in diet, ablutions, and other matters. He was also my instructor in the text of the ritual, which we recited from time to time for practice, in dialogue or in song, as it may have been. Whenever we happened to be near a Druze village, on a Thursday, we attended the 'open' meetings, where men and women assembled for instruction and worship, and to expose to the world generally their religious practices. I was never present at a Friday 'close' meeting before my initiation, nor do I believe any one else, man or woman, ever was, except by collusion with a priest, and that is not probable, for a false priest forfeits his life. The practical jokers among them sometimes 'fool' a too curious 'Frank' by a sham initiation, especially if such a one is suspected of having some connexion with the missionaries at Beirut or elsewhere.

"The initiates include both women and men, and the ceremonies are of so peculiar a nature that both sexes are required to assist in the ritual and 'work.' The 'furniture' of the 'prayer-house' and of the 'vision-chamber' is simple, and except for convenience may consist of but a strip of carpet. In the 'Gray Hall' (the place is never named, and is underground, *not far* from Bayt-ed-Deen) there are some rich decorations and valuable pieces of ancient furniture, the work of Arab silversmiths five or six centuries ago, inscribed and dated. The day of initiation must be a continual fast from daylight to sunset in winter, or six o'clock in summer, and the ceremony is from beginning to end a series of trials and temptations, calculated to test the endurance of the candidate under physical and mental pressure. It is seldom that any but the young man or woman succeeds in 'winning' all the 'prizes,' since *nature will sometimes exert itself* in spite of the most stubborn will, and the neophyte fail of passing some of the tests. In such a case the probation is extended another year, when another trial is had.

"Among other tests of the neophyte's self-control are the following: Choice pieces

of cooked meat, savory soup, pilau, and other appetizing dishes, with sherbet, coffee, wine,
and water, are set, as if accidentally, in his way, and he is left alone for a time with the
tempting things. To a hungry and fainting soul the trial is severe. But a more difficult
ordeal is when the seven priestesses retire, all but one, the youngest and prettiest, and the
door is closed and barred on the outside, after warning the candidate that he will be left
to his 'reflections,' for half an hour. Wearied by the long-continued ceremonial, weak
with hunger, parched with thirst, and a sweet reaction coming after the tremendous strain
to keep his animal nature in subjection, this moment of privacy and of temptation is
brimful of peril. The beautiful young vestal, timidly approaching, and with glances which
lend a double magnetic allurement to her words, begs him in low tones to 'bless her.'
Woe to him if he does! A hundred eyes see him from secret peep-holes, and only to the
ignorant neophyte is there the appearance of concealment and opportunity.

"There is no infidelity, idolatry, or other really bad feature in the system. They
have the relics of what was once a grand form of nature-worship, which has been contracted under a despotism into a secret order, hidden from the light of day, and exposed
only in the smoky glare of a few burning lamps, in some damp cave or chapel under
ground. The chief tenets of their religious teachings are comprised in seven 'tablets,'
which are these, to state them in general terms:

"1. The unity of God, or the infinite oneness of deity.

"2. The essential excellence of truth.

"3. The law of toleration as to all men and women in opinion.

"4. Respect for all men and women as to character and conduct.

"5. Entire submission to God's decrees as to fate.

"6. Chastity of body and mind and soul.

"7. Mutual help under all conditions.

"These tenets are not printed or written. Another set is printed or written to mislead
the unwary, but with these we are not concerned.

"The chief results of the initiation seemed to be a kind of mental illusion or sleep-
waking, in which the neophyte saw, or thought he saw, the images of people who were
known to be absent, and in some cases thousands of miles away. I thought (or perhaps
it was my mind at work) I saw friends and relatives that I knew at the time were in
New York State, while I was then in Lebanon. How these results were produced I cannot
say. They appeared in a dark room, when the 'guide' was talking, the 'company' singing
in the next 'chamber,' and near the close of the day, when I was tired out with fasting,
walking, talking, singing, robing, unrobing, seeing a great many people in various conditions as to dress and undress, and with great mental strain·in resisting certain physical
manifestations that result from the appetites when they overcome the will, and in paying
close attention to the passing scenes, hoping to remember them — so that I may have
been unfit to judge of any new and surprising phenomena, and more especially of those
apparently magical appearances which have always excited my suspicion and distrust.
I know the various uses of the magic-lantern, and other apparatus, and took care to
examine the room where the 'visions' appeared to me the same evening, and the next day
and several times afterwards, and knew that, in my case, there was no use made of any
machinery or other means besides the voice of the 'guide and instructor.' On several
occasions afterward, when at a great distance from the 'chamber,' the same or similar
visions were produced, as, for instance, in Hornstein's Hotel at Jerusalem. A daughter-in-

law of a well-known Jewish merchant in Jerusalem is an initiated 'sister,' and can produce the visions almost at will on any one who will live strictly according to the rules of the Order for a few weeks, more or less, according to their nature, as gross or refined, etc.

"I am quite safe in saying that the initiation is so peculiar that it could not be printed so as to instruct one who had not been 'worked' through the 'chamber.' So it would be even more impossible to make an *exposé* of them than that of the Freemasons. The real secrets are acted and not spoken, and require several initiated persons to assist in the work.

"It is not necessary for me to say how some of the notions of that people seem to perpetuate certain beliefs of the ancient Greeks — as, for instance, the idea that a man has two souls, and many others — for you probably were made familiar with them in your passage through the 'upper' and 'lower chamber.' If I am mistaken in supposing you an 'initiate,' please excuse me. I am aware that the closest friends often conceal that 'sacred secret' from each other; and even husband and wife may live — as I was informed in Dayr-el-Kamar was the fact in one family there — for twenty years together and yet neither know anything of the initiation of the other. You, undoubtedly, have good reasons for keeping your own counsel.

"Yours truly,

"A. L. RAWSON"

Before we close the subject we may add that if a stranger ask for admission to a 'Thursday' meeting he will never be refused. Only, if he be a Christian, the *okhal* will open a *Bible* and read from it; and if a Mohammedan, he will hear a few chapters of the *Korân*, and the ceremony will end with this. They will wait until he is gone, and then, shutting well the doors of their convent, take to their own rites and books, passing for this purpose into their subterranean sanctuaries.[805] "The Druzes remain, even more than the Jews, a peculiar people," says Colonel Churchill, one of the few fair and strictly impartial writers. "They marry within their own race; they are rarely if ever converted; they adhere tenaciously to their traditions, and they baffle all efforts to discover their cherished secrets. . . . The bad name of that caliph whom they claim as their founder is fairly compensated by the pure lives of many whom they honor as saints, and by the heroism of their feudal leaders."

And yet the Druzes may be said to belong to one of the least esoteric of secret societies. There are others far more powerful and learned, the existence of which is not even suspected in Europe. There are many branches belonging to the great 'Mother Lodge' which, mixed up with certain communities, may be termed secret sects within other sects. One of them is the sect commonly known as that of the *Langhana-sâstra*. It reckons several thousand adepts who are scattered about in small groups in the south of the Dekhan, India. In the popular superstition, this sect is dreaded on account of its great reputation for magic and sorcery. The

---

805. Cf. Col. Churchill: *Mount Lebanon*, II, pp. 255-6: London, 1853.

Brâhmanas accuse its members of atheism and sacrilege, for none of them will consent to recognise the authority of either the *Vedas* or *Manu*, except so far as they conform to the versions in their possession, and which they maintain are professedly the only original texts; the *Langhana-śástra* have neither temples nor priests, but twice a month every member of the community has to absent himself from home for three days. Popular rumor, originated among their women, ascribes such absences to pilgrimages performed to their places of fortnightly resort. In some secluded mountainous spots, unknown and inaccessible to other sects, hidden far from sight among the luxurious vegetation of India, they keep their bungalows, which look like small fortresses, encircled as they are by lofty and thick walls. These, in their turn, are surrounded by the sacred trees called *assonata*, and in Tamil *arassa maram*. These are the 'sacred groves,' the originals of those of Egypt and Greece, whose initiates also built their temples within such 'groves' inaccessible to the profane.[806]

It will not be found without interest to see what Mr. John Yarker, Jr., has to say on some modern secret societies among the Orientals. "The nearest resemblance to the Brâhmanical Mysteries is probably found in the very ancient '*Paths*' of the Dervishes, which are usually governed by twelve officers, the oldest 'Court' superintending the others by right of seniority. Here the Master of the 'Court' is called '*Sheik*,' and has his deputies, 'Caliphs,' or successors, of which there may be many (as, for instance, in the brevet degree of a Master Mason). The order is divided into at least four columns, pillars, or degrees. The first step is that of 'Humanity,' which supposes attention to the written law, and 'annihilation in the *Sheik*.' The second is that of the 'Path,' in which the '*Murid*,' or disciple, attains spiritual powers and 'self-annihilation' into the 'Peer' or founder of the 'Path.' The third stage is called 'Knowledge,' and the '*Murid*' is supposed to become inspired, called 'annihilation into the Prophet.' The fourth stage leads him even to God, when he becomes a part of the Deity and sees him in all things. The first and second stages have received modern subdivisions, as 'Integrity,' 'Virtue,' 'Temperance,' 'Benevolence.' After this the *Sheik* confers upon him the grade of 'Caliph,' or Honorary Master, for in their mystical language, 'the man must die before the saint can be born.' It will be seen that this kind of mysticism is applicable to Christ as founder of a 'Path.' "

To this statement, the author adds the following on the Bektash Dervishes, who "often initiated the Janizaries. They wear *a small marble*

---

806. Every temple in India is surrounded by such belts of sacred trees. And like the Kounboum of Kansu (Mongolia) no one but an initiate has a right to approach them.

cube spotted with blood. Their ceremony is as follows: Before reception a year's probation is required, during which false secrets are given to test the candidate; he has two godfathers *and is divested of all metals and even clothing;* from the wool of a sheep a cord is made for his neck, and a girdle for his loins; he is led into the center of a square room, presented as a slave, and seated upon a large stone with twelve escallops; his arms are crossed upon his breast, his body inclined forwards, his right toes extended over his left foot; after various prayers he is placed in a particular manner, with his hand in a peculiar way in that of the Sheik, who repeats a verse from the *Korān:* 'Those who on giving thee their hand swear to thee an oath, swear it to God, the hand of God is placed in their hand; whoever violates this oath, will do so to his hurt, and to whoever remains faithful God will give a magnificent reward.' Placing the hand below the chin is their sign, perhaps in memory of their vow. All use the double triangles. The Brahmins inscribe the angles with their trinity, and they possess also the Masonic sign of distress as used in France." [807]

From the very day when the first mystic found the means of communication between this world and the worlds of the invisible host, between the sphere of matter and that of pure spirit, he concluded that to abandon this mysterious science to the profanation of the rabble was to lose it. An abuse of it might lead mankind to speedy destruction; it was like surrounding a group of children with explosive batteries and furnishing them with matches. The first self-made adept initiated but a select few, and kept silence with the multitudes. He recognised his God and felt the great Being within himself. The 'Ātman,' the Self,[808] the mighty Lord and Protector, once that man knew him

807. *Scientific and Religious Mysteries of Antiquity*, pp. 7, 8: New York, 1878.

808. This 'Self,' which the Greek philosophers called *Augoeides*, the 'Shining One,' is impressively and beautifully described in Max Müller's lecture on the *Veda*. Showing the *Veda* to be the first book of the Aryan nations, the professor adds that "we have in it a period of the intellectual life of man to which there is no parallel in any other part of the world. In the hymns of the *Veda* we see man left to himself to solve the riddle of this world. . . . He invokes them [the gods], he praises, he worships them. But still with all these gods around him, beneath him, and above him, the early poet seems ill at rest within himself. There, too, in his own breast, he has discovered a power . . . that is never mute when he prays, never absent when he fears and trembles. It seems to inspire his prayers, and yet to listen to them; it seems to live in him, and yet to support him and all around him. The only name he can find for this mysterious power is 'Brāhman'; for *brāhman* meant originally force, will, wish, and the propulsive power of creation. But this impersonal *brāhman*, too, as soon as it is named, grows into something strange and divine. It ends by being one of many gods, one of the great triad, worshiped to the present day. And still the thought within him has no real name; that power which is nothing but itself, which supports the gods, the heavens, and every living being, floats before his mind, conceived but not expressed. At last he calls it 'Ātman,' for *ātman*, originally breath or spirit, comes to mean Self,

as the '*I am,*' the '*Ego Sum,*' the '*Ahmi,*' showed his full power to him who could recognise the "*still small voice.*" From the days of the primitive man described by the first Vedic poet, down to our modern age, there has not been a philosopher worthy óf that name who did not carry in the silent sanctuary of his heart the grand and mysterious truth. If initiated, he learnt it as a sacred science; if otherwise, then, like Socrates repeating to .himself, as well as to his fellow-men, the noble injunction, "O man, know thyself," he succeeded in recognising his God within himself. "Ye are gods," the king-psalmist tells us, and we find Jesus reminding the scribes that the expression, "Ye are gods," was addressed to other mortal men, claiming for himself the same privilege without any blasphemy.[809] And, as a faithful echo, Paul, while asserting that we are all "the temple of the living God,"[810] cautiously adds, that, after all, these things are only for the 'wise,' and it is 'unlawful' to speak of them.

Therefore we must accept the reminder, and simply remark that even in the tortured and barbarous phraseology of the *Codex Nazaraeus* we detect throughout the same idea. Like an undercurrent, rapid and clear, it runs without mixing its crystalline purity with the muddy and heavy waves of dogmatism. We find it in the *Codex,* as well as in the *Vedas,* in the *Avesta,* as in the *Abhidharma,* and in Kapila's *Sánkhya-Sútras* not less than in the *Fourth Gospel.* We cannot attain the 'Kingdom of Heaven' unless we unite ourselves indissolubly with our *Rex Lucis,* the Lord of Splendor and of Light, our Immortal God. We must first conquer immortality and "take the Kingdom of Heaven by violence," offered to our material selves. "The first man is of the earth, earthy; the *second* man *is from heaven.* . . . Behold, I show you a *mystery,*" says Paul (*1 Corinthians,* xv, 47, 51). In the religion of Sâkya-Muni, which learned commentators have delighted so much of late to set down as purely *nihilistic,* the doctrine of immortality is very clearly defined, notwithstanding the European, or rather Christian, ideas about Nirvâna. In the sacred Jaina books of Patuna, the dying Gautama-

---

and Self alone; *Self,* whether Divine or human; Self, whether creating or suffering; . Self, whether one or all; but always Self, independent and free. 'Who has seen the first-born,' says the poet, 'when he who has no bones (*i. e.* form) bore him that had bones? Where was the life, the blood, the Self of the world? Who went to ask this from any one that knew it?' (*Rig-Veda,* I, 164, 4). This idea of a divine Self once expressed, everything else must acknowledge its supremacy; '*Self* is the Lord of all things. Self is the King of all things. As all the spokes of a wheel are contained in the nave and the circumference, all things are contained in this Self; all Selves are contained in this Self. Brâhman itself is but Self' (*Brihadâranyaka-Upanishad,* IV, 5, 15, p. 487, ed. Roer; *Ibid.,* p. 478; *Chhândogya-Upanishad,* VIII, 3, 3, 4.)"— *Chips from a German Workshop,* I, pp. 67-69.

809. *John,* x, 34, 35.   810. *2 Corinthians,* vi, 16.

Buddha is thus addressed: "Arise into *Nirvi* (Nirvâna) from this decrepit body into which thou hast been sent. Ascend into *thy former abode*, O blessed Avatar!" This seems to us the very opposite of Nihilism. If Gautama is invited to reascend into his "former abode," and this abode is Nirvâna, then it is incontestable that Buddhistic philosophy does *not* teach final annihilation. As Jesus is alleged to have appeared to his disciples after death, so to the present day is Gautama believed to descend from Nirvâna. And if he has an existence there, then this state cannot be equivalent to *annihilation*.

Gautama, no less than all other great reformers, had a doctrine for his 'elect' and another for the outside masses, though the main object of his reform consisted in initiating all, so far as it was permissible and prudent to do, without distinction of castes or wealth, to the great truths hitherto kept so secret by the selfish Brâhmanical class. Gautama-Buddha it was whom we see the first in the world's history, moved by that generous feeling which locks the whole of humanity within one embrace, inviting the 'poor,' the 'lame,' and the 'blind' to the King's festival table, from which he excluded those who had hitherto sat alone, in haughty seclusion. It was he who with a bold hand first opened the door of the sanctuary to the pariah, the fallen one, and all those "afflicted by men" clothed in gold and purple, often far less worthy than the outcast to whom their finger was scornfully pointing. All this did Siddhârtha six centuries before another reformer, as noble and as loving, though less favored by opportunity, in another land. If both, aware of the great danger of furnishing an uncultivated populace with the double-edged weapon of *knowledge which gives power*, left the innermost corner of the sanctuary in the profoundest shade, who that is acquainted with human nature can blame them for it? But while one was actuated by prudence, the other was forced into such a course. Gautama left the esoteric and most dangerous portion of the 'secret knowledge' untouched, and lived to the ripe old age of eighty, with the certainty of having taught the essential truths, and having converted to them one-third of the world; Jesus promised his disciples the knowledge which confers upon man the power *of producing far greater miracles than he ever did himself*, and he died, leaving but a few faithful men, only half way to knowledge, to struggle with the world to which they could impart but what they *half*-knew themselves. Later, their followers disfigured truth still more than they themselves had done.

It is not true that Gautama never taught anything concerning a future life, or that he denied the immortality of the soul. Ask any intelligent Buddhist his ideas on Nirvâna, and he will unquestionably express himself, as the well-known Wong-Chin-Fu the Chinese orator, now traveling in this country, did in a recent conversation with us about *Niepang* (Nirvâna). "This condition," he remarked, "we all understand to mean a final reunion with God, coincident with the perfection of the human spirit by its ultimate disembarrassment of matter. It is the very opposite of personal annihilation."

Nirvâna means the certitude of personal immortality in *Spirit*, not in *Soul*, which, as a finite emanation, must certainly disintegrate its particles — a compound of human sensations, passions, and yearning for some objective kind of existence — before the immortal spirit of the *Ego* is quite freed, and henceforth secure against further transmigration in any form. And how can man ever reach this state so long as the *Upâdâna*, that state of longing for *life*, more life, does not disappear from the sentient being, from the *Ahankâra* clothed, however, in a sublimated body? It is the 'Upâdâna' or the intense desire which produces WILL, and it is *will* which develops *force*, and the latter generates *matter*, or an object having form. Thus the disembodied *Ego*, through this sole undying desire in him, unconsciously furnishes the conditions of his successive self-procreations in various forms, which depend on his mental state and *Karma*, the good or bad deeds of his preceding existence, commonly called 'merit and demerit.' This is why the 'Master' recommended to his mendicants the cultivation of the four degrees of *Dhyâna*, the noble 'Path of the Four Truths,' *i. e.*, that gradual acquirement of stoical indifference for either life or death; that state of spiritual self-contemplation during which man utterly loses sight of his physical and dual individuality, composed of soul and body; and uniting himself with his third and higher immortal self, the *real and heavenly man*, merges, so to say, into the divine Essence whence his own spirit proceeded like a spark from the common hearth. Thus the Arhat, the holy mendicant, can reach Nirvâna while yet on earth; and his spirit, totally freed from the trammels of the "psychical, terrestrial, *devilish* wisdom," as James calls it, and being in its own nature omniscient and omnipotent, can on earth, through the sole power of his *thought*, produce the greatest of phenomena.

"It is the missionaries in China and India, who first started this falsehood about Niepang, or Niepana (Nirvâna)," says Wong-Chin-Fu. Who can deny the truth of this accusation after reading the works of the Abbé Dubois, for instance? A missionary who passes forty years of his life in India, and then writes that the "Buddhists admit of no other God but the body of man, and have no other object but the satisfaction of their senses," utters an untruth which can be proved on the testimony of the laws of the Talapoins of Siam and Burmah; laws which prevail unto this very day and which sentence a *sahân*, or *punghi* (a learned man: from the Sanskrit *pandit*), as well as a simple Talapoin, to death by decapitation for the crime of unchastity. No foreigner can be admitted into their *Kyums*, or *Vihâras* (monasteries); and yet there are French writers, otherwise impartial and fair, who, speaking of the great severity of the rules to which the Buddhist monks are subjected in these communities, and without possessing one single fact to corroborate their skepticism, bluntly say, that "notwithstanding the great laudations bestowed upon them (Talapoins) by certain travelers, merely on the *strength of appearances,* I do not believe at all in their chastity." [811]

Fortunately for the Buddhist *talapoins, lamas, sahâns, upasampadas,* [812] and even *sâmanêras,* [813] they themselves have popular records and facts which are weightier than the unsupported personal opinion of a Frenchman, born in Catholic lands, whom we can hardly blame for having lost all faith in clerical virtue. When a Buddhist monk becomes guilty (which does not happen once in a century, perhaps) of criminal conversation, he has neither a congregation of tender-hearted members, whom he can move to tears by an eloquent confession of his guilt, nor a Jesus, on whose overburdened, long-suffering bosom are flung, as in a common Christian dust-box, all the impurities of the race. No Buddhist transgressor can comfort himself with visions of a Vatican, within whose sin-encompassing walls black is turned into white, murderers into sinless saints, and where golden or silvery lotions can be bought at the confessional to cleanse the tardy penitent of greater or lesser offenses against God and man.

Except a few impartial archaeologists, who trace a direct Buddhistic element in Gnosticism as in all the early short-lived systems, we know of very few authors who, in writing upon primitive Christianity, have accorded to this subject its due importance. Have we not facts enough to suggest at least some interest in that direction? Do we not learn that, as early as in the days of Plato, there were 'Brachmans' — read Buddhist, Samanean, Saman, or Shaman missionaries — in Greece, and that at one time they had overflowed the country? Does not Pliny show them established on the shores of the Dead Sea for "thousands of ages"? After making every necessary allowance for the exaggeration we still have several centuries B. C. left as a margin. And is it possible that their influence should not have left deeper traces in all these sects than is generally thought? We know that the Jaina sect claims Buddhism as derived from its tenets — that Buddhism existed before Siddhârtha,

---

811. Jacolliot: *Voyage au pays des éléphants,* p. 252.

812. Buddhist chief priests at Ceylon.

813. *Sâmanêra* is one who studies to obtain the high office of an *Upasampada.* He is a disciple and is looked upon as a son by the chief priest. We suspect that the Catholic seminarist must look to the Buddhists for the parentage of his title.

better known as Gautama-Buddha. The Hindû Brâhmanas who, by
the European Orientalists, are denied the right of knowing anything
about their own country, or of understanding their own language and
records better than those who have never been in India, on the same
principle as the Jews are forbidden, by the Christian theologians, to
interpret their own Scriptures — the Brâhmanas, we say, have authentic
records. And these show the incarnation from the Virgin Avany of the
first Buddha — *divine light* — as having taken place more than some
thousands of years B. C., on the island of Ceylon. The Brâhmanas
reject the claim that it was an avatar of Vishnu, but admit the appearance of a reformer of Brâhmanism at that time. The story of the Virgin
Avany and her divine son, *Sâkya-muni*, is recorded in one of the sacred
books of the Singhalese Buddhists — the *Nirdhasa;* and the Brâhmanic
chronology fixes the great Buddhistic revolution and religious war, and
the subsequent spread of Sâkya-muni's doctrine in Tibet, China, Japan,
and other places at 4620 years B. C.[814]

It is clear that Gautama-Buddha, the son of the King of Kapilavastu,
and the descendant of the first *Sâkya*, through his father, who was of the
Kshatriya, or warrior-caste, did not invent his philosophy. Philanthropist by nature, his ideas were developed and matured while under the
tuition of *Tîrthankara*, the famous guru of the Jaina sect. The latter [the
Jainas] claim the present Buddhism as a diverging branch of their own
philosophy, and themselves as the only followers of the first Buddha who
were allowed to remain in India after the expulsion of all other Buddhists,
probably because they had made a compromise, and admitted some of
the Brâhmanic notions. It is, to say the least, curious that three dissenting and inimical religions, like Brâhmanism, Buddhism, and Jainism,
should agree so perfectly in their traditions and chronology as to Buddhism, and that our scientists should give a hearing but to their own unwarranted speculations and hypotheses. If the birth of Gautama may,
with some show of reason, be placed at about 600 B. C., then the preceding Buddhas ought to have some place allowed them in chronology.
The Buddhas are not gods, but simply individuals overshadowed by the
spirit of *Buddha* — the divine ray. Or is it because, unable to extricate
themselves from the difficulty by the help of their own researches only,
our Orientalists prefer to obliterate and deny the whole, rather than accord to the Hindûs the right of knowing something of their own religion
and history? Strange way of discovering truths!

The common argument adduced against the Jaina claim of having
been the source of the restoration of ancient Buddhism, that the principal

---

814. Jacolliot: *Les Fils de Dieu*, pp. 349, 352, in which he declares that he copied these
dates from the *Book of the Historical Zodiacs*, preserved in the pagoda of Vilenur.

tenet of the latter religion is opposed to the belief of the Jainas, is not a sound one. Buddhists, say our Orientalists, deny the existence of a Supreme Being; the Jainas admit one, but protest against the assumption that the 'He' can ever interfere in the regulation of the universe. We have shown in the preceding chapter that the Buddhists do not deny any such thing. But if any disinterested scholar could study carefully the Jaina literature, in their thousands of books preserved — or shall we say hidden — in Rajputana, at Jesalmir, Pattan, and other places; [815] and especially if he could but gain access to the oldest of their sacred volumes, he would find a perfect identity of philosophical thought, if not of popular rites, between the Jainas and the Buddhists. The *Ádi-Buddha* and *Ádinátha* (or *Ádíśvara*) are identical in essence and purpose. And now if we trace the Jainas back, with their claims to the ownership of the oldest cave-temples (those superb specimens of Indian architecture and sculpture), and their records of an almost incredible antiquity, we can hardly refuse to view them in the light which they claim for themselves. We must admit that in all probability they are the only true descendants of the primitive owners of old India, dispossessed by those conquering and mysterious hordes of white-skinned Bráhmanas, whom in the twilight of history we see appearing at the first as wanderers in the valleys of Jumna and Ganges. The books of the *Srávakas* — the only descendants of the *Arhatas* or earliest Jainas, the naked forest-hermits of the days of old — might perhaps throw some light on many a puzzling question. But will our European scholars, so long as they pursue their own policy, ever have access to the *right* volumes? We have our doubts about this. Ask any trustworthy Hindû how the missionaries have dealt with those manuscripts which unluckily fell into their hands, and then see if we can blame the natives for trying to save from desecration the 'gods of their fathers.'

To maintain their ground Irenaeus and his school had to fight hard with the Gnostics. Such also was the lot of Eusebius, who found himself hopelessly perplexed to know how the Essenes should be disposed of. The ways and customs of Jesus and his apostles exhibited too close a resemblance to this sect to allow the fact to pass unexplained. Eusebius tried to make people believe that the Essenes were the first Christians. His efforts were thwarted by Philo Judaeus, who wrote his historical account of the Essenes and described them with the minutest care as they were long before there had appeared a single Christian in Palestine. But if there were no *Christians*, there were Chrestians long before the era of Christianity; and the Essenes belonged to the latter as well as to all other

---

815. We were told that there were nearly 20,000 of such books.

initiated brotherhoods, without even mentioning the Krishna-ites of
India. Lepsius shows that the word *Nofer* means *Chrēstos*, 'good,' and
that one of the titles of Osiris, "Onnofer" (*Un-nefer*) must be translated
"the goodness of God made manifest." [816] "The worship of Christ was
not universal at this early date," explains Mackenzie, "by which I mean
that Christolatry had not been introduced; but the worship of *Chrēstos*—
the Good Principle — had preceded it by many centuries, and even survived the general adoption of Christianity, as shown on monuments still
in existence. . . . Again, we have an inscription which is pre-Christian on
an epitaphial tablet (Spon: *Misc. erud. ant.*, X, xviii, 2). Ιακωβι
Λαρισαιων Δημοσιι Ηρως Χρηστε Χαιρε, and De Rossi (*La Roma Sotteranea
Cristiana*, I, tav. xxi) gives us another example from the catacombs —
'Aelia Chreste, in Pace.' " [817] And *Kris*, as Jacolliot shows, means in
Sanskrit 'sacred.' [818]

The meritorious stratagems of the trustworthy Eusebius [819] thus
proved lost labor. He was triumphantly detected by Basnage, [820] who,
says Gibbon, "examined with the most critical accuracy the curious
treatise of Philo, [821] which describes the Therapeutae. By proving it was
composed as early as the time of Augustus, he has demonstrated, in
spite of Eusebius and a crowd of modern Catholics, that the Therapeutae were neither Christians nor monks." [822]

As a last word — the *Christian* Gnostics sprang into existence toward
the beginning of the second century, and just at the time when the Essenes most mysteriously faded away, which indicated that they were the
identical Essenes, and moreover pure *Christists*, viz., they believed, and
were those who best understood, what one of their own brethren had
preached. In insisting that the letter Iota, mentioned by Jesus in
Matthew (v, 18), indicated a secret doctrine in relation to the ten aeons,
it is sufficient to demonstrate to a Kabalist that Jesus belonged to the
Freemasonry of those days; for I, which is Iota in Greek, has other
names in other languages; and is, as it was among the Gnostics of those
days, a pass-word, meaning the SCEPTER of the FATHER, in Eastern
brotherhoods which exist to this very day.

But in the early centuries these facts, if known, were purposely
ignored, and not only withheld from public notice as much as possible,
but vehemently denied whenever the question was forced upon discus-
sion. The denunciations of the Fathers were rendered bitter in proportion to the truth of the claim which they endeavored to refute.

"It comes to this," writes Irenaeus, complaining of the Gnostics,

816. Lepsius: *Königsbuch*, b. 11, tal. i. dyn. 5, h. p. In *1 Peter*, ii, 3, Jesus is called
the Lord 'Crestos.'   817. *Royal Masonic Cyclopaedia*, pp. 206-7.
818. *Christna, etc.*, p. 357.   819. *Eccl. Hist.*, II, xvii.   820. *Hist. des Juifs*, II, ch.20-23.
821. *De vita contempl.*   822. *Decline and Fall, etc.*, ch. xv, note 162.

"they neither consent to Scripture nor tradition." [823]   And why should we wonder at that, when even the commentators of the nineteenth century, with nothing but fragments of the Gnostic manuscripts to compare with the voluminous writings of their calumniators, have been enabled to detect fraud on nearly every page of the latter?   How much more clearly must the polished and learned Gnostics, with all their advantages of personal observation and knowledge of fact, have realized the stupendous scheme of fraud that was being consummated before their very eyes! Why should they [the Christians] accuse Celsus of maintaining that their religion was all based on the speculations of Plato, with the difference that his doctrines were far more pure and rational than theirs, when we find Sprengel, seventeen centuries later, writing the following? — "Not only did they [the Christians] think to discover the dogmas of Plato in the books of Moses, but, moreover, they fancied that, by introducing Platonism into Christianity, they would *elevate the dignity of this religion and make it more popular among the nations.*" [824]

They introduced it so well, that not only was the Platonic philosophy selected as a basis for the trinity, but even the legends and mythical stories which had been current among the admirers of the great philosopher — for in the eyes of his posterity a time-honored custom required such an allegorical homage to every hero worthy of deification — were revamped and used by the Christians.   Without going so far as India, did they not have a ready model for the 'miraculous conception' in the legend about Perictione, Plato's mother? [825]   In her case it was also maintained by popular tradition that she had immaculately conceived him, and that the god Apollo was his father.   Even the annunciation by an angel to Joseph "in a dream," the Christians copied from the message of Apollo to Ariston, Perictione's husband, that the child to be born from her was the offspring of that god.   So too, Romulus was said to be the son of Mars by the virgin Rhea Sylvia.

It is generally held by all the symbolical writers that the Ophites were found guilty of practising the most licentious rites during their religious meetings.   The same accusation was brought against the Manichaeans, the Carpocratians, the Paulicians, the Albigenses — in short against every Gnostic sect which had the temerity to claim the right to think for itself.   In our modern days the 160 American sects and the 125 sects of England are not so often troubled with such accusations; times are changed, and even the once all-powerful clergy have to either bridle their tongues or prove their slanderous accusations.

We have carefully looked over the works of such authors as Payne

---

823. *Against Heresies*, III, ii, 2.   824. *Gesch. d. Arzneikunde*, II, p. 200.
825. Diog. Laert.: *Lives, etc.*, 'Plato,' § 1; Plutarch: *Sympos.*, viii, 1.

Knight, C. W. King, and Olshausen, which treat of our subject; we have reviewed the bulky volumes of Irenaeus, Tertullian, Sozomen, Theodoret; and in none but those of Epiphanius have we found any accusation based upon direct evidence of an eye-witness. 'They say'; '*Some* say'; 'We have heard' — such are the general and indefinite terms used by the patristic accusers. Alone Epiphanius, whose works are invariably referred to in all such cases, seems to chuckle with delight whenever he couches a lance. We do not mean to take upon ourselves to defend the sects which inundated Europe in the eleventh century, and which introduced the most wonderful creeds; we limit our defense merely to those Christian sects whose theories were usually grouped under the generic name of *Gnosticism*. These are those which appeared immediately after the alleged crucifixion, and lasted till they were nearly exterminated under the rigorous execution of the Constantinian law. The greatest guilt of these were their syncretistic views, for at no other period of the world's history had truth a poorer prospect of triumph than in those days of forgery, lying, and deliberate falsification of facts.

But before we are forced to believe the accusations, may we not be permitted to inquire into the historical characters of their accusers? Let us begin by asking, upon what ground does the Church of Rome build her claim for the supremacy of her doctrines over those of the Gnostics? Apostolic succession, undoubtedly. The succession *traditionally* instituted by the apostle Peter. But what if this prove a fiction? Clearly, the whole superstructure supported upon this one imaginary stilt would fall in a tremendous crash. And when we do inquire carefully, we find that we must take the word of Irenaeus *alone* for it — of Irenaeus, who did not furnish one single valid proof of the claim which he so audaciously advanced, and who resorted for that to endless forgeries. He gives authority neither for his dates nor his assertions. This Smyrniote worthy has not even the brutal but sincere faith of Tertullian, for he contradicts himself at every step, and supports his claims solely on acute sophistry. Though he was undoubtedly a man of the shrewdest intellect and great learning, he fears not in some of his assertions and arguments even to appear an idiot in the eyes of posterity, so long as he can 'carry the situation.' Twitted and cornered at every step by his not less acute and learned adversaries, the Gnostics, he boldly shields himself behind blind faith, and in answer to their merciless logic falls back upon imaginary tradition invented by himself.[826] Reber wittily remarks: "As we read his misapplications of words and sentences, we should conclude that he was a lunatic if we did not know that he was something else." [827]

---

826. Irenaeus: *Agst. Her.*, III, iii, 3.   827. *The Christ of Paul*, p. 188: N. Y., 1876.

So boldly mendacious does this 'holy Father' prove himself in many instances, that he is even contradicted by Eusebius, more cautious if not more truthful than himself. Eusebius is driven to that course in the face of unimpeachable evidence. So for instance Irenaeus asserts that Papias, Bishop of Hierapolis, was a direct "hearer of St. John"; [828] and Eusebius is compelled to show that Papias never made any such claim, but simply stated that he had received his *doctrine from those who had known John.*[829]

In one point the Gnostics had the best of Irenaeus. They drove him, through mere fear of inconsistency, to the recognition of their kabalistic doctrine of atonement; unable to grasp it in its allegorical meaning, Irenaeus presented, with Christian theology as we find it in its present state of 'original sin *versus* Adam,' a doctrine which would have filled Peter with pious horror if he had been still alive.

The next champion for the propagation of Apostolic Succession is Eusebius himself. Is the word of this Armenian Father any better than that of Irenaeus? Let us see what the most competent critics say of him. And before we turn to modern critics at all, we might remind the reader of the scurrilous terms in which Eusebius is attacked by George Syncellus, the Vice-Patriarch of Constantinople (eighth century), for his audacious falsification of the Egyptian Chronology.[830] The opinion of Socrates, a historian of the fifth century, is no more flattering. He fearlessly charges Eusebius with perverting historical dates in order to please the Emperor Constantine.[831] In his chronographic work, before proceeding to falsify the synchronistic tables *himself*, in order to impart to Scriptural chronology a more trustworthy appearance, Syncellus covers Eusebius with the choicest of monkish Billingsgate. *Baron Bunsen has verified the justness, if not justified the politeness, of this abusive indictment.* His elaborate researches in the rectification of the *Egyptian List of Chronology* by Manetho led him to perceive that throughout his work the Bishop of Caesarea had undertaken, "in a very *unscrupulous* and arbitrary spirit," to mutilate history. "Eusebius," he says, "is the originator of that systematic theory of synchronisms which has so often subsequently maimed and mutilated history in its Procrustean bed."[830] To this the author of the *Intellectual Development of Europe* adds: "Among those who have been guilty of this literary offense, the name of the celebrated Eusebius, the Bishop of Caesarea . . . should be designated!"[832]

It will not be amiss to remind the reader that it is the same Eusebius who is charged with the interpolation of the famous paragraph concerning

828. *Against Heresies*, V, xxxiii, § 4.   829. *Eccles. Hist.*, III, xxxix.
830. Bunsen: *Egypt's Place, etc.*, I, pp. 83, 206; II, 438, *sq.*; 1st ed.
831. Socrates: *Eccl. Hist.*, I, i.   832. Draper: *Op. cit.*, ch. vi.

Jesus which was so miraculously found, in his time, in the writings of
Josephus,[833] the sentence in question having till that time remained perfectly unknown. Renan in his *Life of Jesus* expresses a contrary opinion.
"I believe," says he, "the passage respecting Jesus to be authentic. *It
is perfectly in the style of Josephus;* and, *if* this historian had made
mention of Jesus, it is *thus* that he must have spoken of him."

Begging this eminent scholar's pardon, we must contradict him.
Laying aside his cautious "*if*," we shall merely show that though the
short paragraph may possibly be genuine, and "perfectly in the style of
Josephus," its several parentheses are most palpably later forgeries; and
"*if*" Josephus had made any mention of Christ at all, it is *not* thus that he
would "have spoken of him." The whole paragraph consists of but a few
lines, and reads: "At this time was *Iesous,* a 'WISE MAN,' [834] if at least *it
is right to call him a man!* [ἄνδρα] for he was a doer of surprising works,
and a teacher of such men as receive 'the truths' with pleasure. . . .
This was the ANOINTED [!!]. And on an accusation by the first men
among us, having been condemned by Pilate to the cross, they did not
stop loving him who loved them. For *he appeared to them on the third
day alive,* as the divine prophets had said these and many other wonderful things concerning him."

This paragraph (of sixteen lines in the original) has two unequivocal
assertions and one qualification. The latter is expressed in the following sentence: "If at least it is right to call him a man." The unequivocal
assertions are contained in the words, "This was the ANOINTED," and in
the statement that Jesus "appeared to them *on the third day alive.*"
History shows us Josephus as a thoroughly uncompromising, stiff-necked,
orthodox Jew, though he wrote for 'the Pagans.' It is well to observe the
false position in which these sentences would have placed a true-born
Jew, if they had really emanated from him. Their 'Messiah' was then
and is still expected. The Messiah is the *Anointed,* and *vice versa.* And
Josephus is made to admit that the "first men" among them have
accused and crucified *their* Messiah and Anointed!! No need to comment any further upon such a preposterous incongruity,[835] even though
supported by so ripe a scholar as Renan.

As to that patristic fire-brand Tertullian, whom Des Mousseaux
apotheosizes in company with his other demi-gods, he is regarded by
Reuss, Baur, and Schwegler in quite a different light. The untrust-

---

833. *Antiquities,* XVIII, iii, 3; Renan: *La vie de Jésus,* introd.
834. 'Wise man' always meant with the ancients a kabalist. It means astrologer and
magician (Jost: *The Israelite Indeed,* III, p. 206). '*Hakim* [Arabic] is a physician.
835. Dr. Lardner rejects it as spurious, and gives *nine* reasons for rejecting it (cf.
The Credibility of the Gospel History).

worthiness of statement and inaccuracy of Tertullian, says the author of *Supernatural Religion*,[836] are often apparent. Reuss [837] characterizes his Christianism as "*âpre, insolent, brutal, ferrailleur*. It is without unction and without charity, sometimes even *without loyalty*, when he finds himself confronted with opposition. . . . If in the second century all parties except certain Gnostics were intolerant, Tertullian was the most intolerant of all!"

The work begun by the early Fathers was achieved by the sophomorical Augustine. His supra-transcendental speculations on the Trinity; his imaginary dialogs with the Father, Son, and the Holy Spirit, and the *disclosures* about, and covert allusions to, his ex-brethren, the Manichaeans, have led the world to load Gnosticism with opprobrium, and have thrown into a deep shadow the insulted majesty of the one God, worshiped in reverential silence by every 'heathen.'

And thus is it that the whole pyramid of Roman Catholic dogmas rests not upon proof, but upon assumption. The Gnostics had cornered the Fathers too cleverly, and *the only salvation of the latter was a resort to forgery.* For nearly four centuries the great historians, some nearly contemporary with Jesus, had not taken the slightest notice either of his life or death. Christians wondered at such an unaccountable omission of what the Church considered the greatest events in the world's history. Eusebius saved the battle of the day. Such are the men who have slandered the Gnostics.

The first and most unimportant sect we hear of is that of the *Nicolaitans*, of whom John, in the *Apocalypse*, makes the voice in his vision say that he hates their doctrine.[838] These Nicolaitans were the followers, however, of Nicolas of Antioch, one of the "seven" chosen by the "twelve" to make distribution from the common fund to the proselytes at Jerusalem (*Acts* ii, 44, 45; vi, 1-5), hardly more than a few weeks, or perhaps months, after the crucifixion;[839] and a man "of honest report, *full of the Holy Ghost and wisdom*" (verse 3). Thus it would appear that the "Holy Ghost and wisdom" from on high were no more a shield against the accusation of 'heresy' than though they had never overshadowed the 'chosen· ones' of the apostles.

It would be but too easy to detect what kind of 'heresy' it was that offended, even had we not other and more authentic sources of information in the kabalistic writings. The accusation [against the Nicolaitans] and the precise nature of the 'abomination' are stated in the second chapter of the book of *Revelation*, verses 14, 15. The sin was merely—*marriage*.

---

836. Part II, vii.
838. *Revelation*, ii, 6, 15.
837. *Rev. de Théol.*, xv, p. 67, *sq.*: 1857.
839. Philip, the first martyr, was one of the seven, and he was stoned about the year A. D. 34.

John was a 'virgin'; several of the Fathers assert the fact on the authority of tradition. Even Paul, the most liberal and high-minded of them all, finds it difficult to reconcile the position of a married man with that of a faithful servant of God. "There is difference also between a wife and a virgin." [840] The latter cares "for the things of the Lord," and the former only for "how she may please her husband." "If any man think that he behaveth himself uncomely toward his virgin . . . let them marry. Nevertheless, he that standeth stedfast in his heart," and "hath power over his own will, and hath so decreed . . . that he will keep *his virgin*, doeth well." So that he who marries "doeth well . . . but he that giveth her not in marriage *doeth better*." "Art thou loosed from a wife?" he asks, "seek not a wife" (27). And remarking that according to his judgment, both will be happier if they do not marry, he adds, as a weighty conclusion: "And I think also that I have the spirit of God" (40). Far from this spirit of tolerance are the words of John. According to his vision there are "but the hundred and forty and four thousand, which were *redeemed* from the earth," and "these are they which were not defiled with women; for *they are virgins*." [841] This seems conclusive; for except Paul there is not one of these primitive *Nazari*, there 'set apart' and vowed to God, who seemed to make a great difference between 'sin,' within the relationship of legal marriage, and the 'abomination' of adultery.

With such views and such narrow-mindedness, it was but natural that these fanatics should have begun by casting this *iniquity* as a slur in the faces of brethren, and then 'bearing on progressively' with their accusations. As we have already shown, it is only Epiphanius whom we find giving such minute details as to the Masonic 'grips' and other signs of recognition among the Gnostics. He had once belonged to their number, and therefore it was easy for him to furnish particulars. Only how far the worthy Bishop is to be relied upon is a very grave question. One need fathom human nature but very superficially to find that there seldom yet has been a traitor or a renegade who in a moment of danger turned 'State's evidence,' who would not lie as remorselessly as he had betrayed. Men never forgive, or relent toward, those whom they injure. We hate our victims in proportion to the harm we do them. This is a truth as old as the world. On the other hand it is preposterous to believe that such persons as the Gnostics, who according to Gibbon [842] were the wealthiest, proudest, most polite, as well as the most learned "of the Christian name," were guilty of the disgusting, libidinous actions of which Epiphanius delights to accuse them. Were they even like that "set of

---

840. *1 Corinthians*, vii, 34.   841. *Revelation*, xiv, 3, 4.
                    842. *Decline and Fall, etc.*, I, xv.

tatterdemalions, almost naked, with fierce looks," that Lucian describes as Paul's followers,[843] we should hesitate to believe such an infamous story. How much less probable then that men who were Platonists as well as Christians should have ever been guilty of such preposterous rites.

Payne Knight seems never to suspect the testimony of Epiphanius. He argues that "if we make allowance for the willing exaggerations of religious hatred, and consequent popular prejudice, the general conviction that these sectarians had rites and practices of a licentious character appears too strong to be entirely disregarded."[844] If he draws an honest line of demarcation between the Gnostics of the first three centuries and those medieval sects whose doctrines "rather closely resembled modern communism," we have nothing to say. Only, we would beg every critic to remember that if the Templars were accused of that most 'abominable crime' of applying the 'holy kiss' to the root of Baphomet's tail,[845] St. Augustine is also suspected, and on very good grounds too, of having allowed his community to go somewhat astray from the primitive way of administering the 'holy kiss' at the feast of the Eucharist. The holy Bishop seems quite too anxious as to certain details of the ladies' toilet for the 'kiss' to be of a strictly orthodox nature.[846] Wherever there lurks a true and sincere religious feeling, there is no room for worldly details.

Considering the extraordinary dislike exhibited from the first by Christians to all manner of cleanliness, we cannot enough wonder at such a strange solicitude on the part of the holy Bishop for his female parishioners, unless, indeed, we have to excuse it on the ground of a lingering reminiscence of Manichaean rites!

It would be hard, indeed, to blame any writer for entertaining such suspicions of immorality as those above noticed, when the records of many historians are at hand to help us to make an impartial investigation. 'Heretics' are accused of crimes in which the Church has more or less openly indulged even down to the beginning of our century. In 1232 and 1233 Pope Gregory IX issued two bulls against the Stedingers "for various *heathen* and magical practices," [847] and the latter, as a matter of course, were slaughtered in the name of Christ and his Holy Mother. In 1282 a parish priest of Inverkeithing, named John, performed rites on Easter day by far worse than 'magical.' Collecting a crowd of young girls, he forced them to enter into "divine ecstasies" and Bacchanalian

843. Philopatrix, in R. Taylor's *The Diegesis, etc.*, p. 376: Boston, 1832.
844. *Worship of Priapus, the Mystic Theol. of the Ancients*, pp. 175-6; ed. 1865.
845. King: *The Gnostics and their Remains*, p. 420, note; 2nd ed.
846. *Sermones*, clii. See Payne Knight, *op. cit.*, p. 107.
847. Baronius: *Annales Ecclesiastici*, XXI, p. 89: Antwerp, 1610.

fury, dancing the old Amazonian circle-dance around the figure of the heathen 'god of the gardens.' Notwithstanding that upon the complaint of some of his parishioners he was cited before his bishop, he retained his benefice because he proved that *such was the common usage of the country.*[848] The Waldenses, those 'earliest Protestants,' were accused of the most unnatural horrors, burned, butchered, and exterminated for calumnies heaped upon them by their accusers. Meanwhile the latter, in open triumph, formed their heathen processions of 'Corpus Christi,' with emblems modeled on those of Baal-Peor and 'Osiris,' in every city in Southern France, carrying in yearly processions on Easter days loaves and cakes fashioned like the so-much-decried emblems of the Hindû Sivites and Vishnites, as late as 1825![849]

Deprived of their old means for slandering other Christian sects whose religious views differ from their own, it is now the turn of the 'heathen,' Hindûs, Chinese, and Japanese, to share with the ancient religions the honor of having cast in their teeth denunciations of their 'libidinous religions.'

Without going far for proofs of equal if not greater immorality, we would remind Roman Catholic writers of certain *bas-reliefs* on the doors of St. Peter's Cathedral. They are as brazen-faced as the door itself; but less so than any author, who knowing all this feigns to ignore historical facts. A long succession of Popes have rested their pastoral eyes upon these brazen pictures of the vilest obscenity through those many centuries, without ever finding the slightest necessity for removing them. Quite the contrary; for we might name certain Popes and Cardinals who made it a life-long study to copy these heathen suggestions of 'nature-gods,' in practice as well as in theory.

In Polish Podolia there was some years ago in a Roman Catholic Church a statue of Christ in black marble. It was reputed to perform miracles on certain days, such as having its hair and beard grow in the sight of the public, and exhibiting other *less* innocent wonders. This show was finally prohibited by the Russian Government. When in 1585 the Protestants took Embrun (Department of the Upper Alps), they found in the churches of this town relics of such a character that, as the *Chronicle* expresses it, "old Huguenot soldiers were seen to blush, several weeks after, at the bare mention of the discovery." In a corner of the Church of St. Fiacre, near Monceaux in France, there was — and it is still there, if we mistake not — a seat called 'the chair of St. Fiacre,'

---

848. *Chron. de Lanercost;* Stevenson ed.
849. Dulaure: *Histoire abrégée des différents cultes,* II, p. 285;
          Martezzi: *Pagani e Christiani,* p. 78.

which had the reputation of conferring fecundity upon barren women. A rock in the vicinity of Athens, not far from the so-called 'Tomb of Socrates,' is said to be possessed of the same virtue. When some twenty years since Queen Amelia [of Greece], perhaps in a merry moment, was said to have tried the experiment, there was no end of most insulting abuse heaped upon her by a Catholic Padre on his way through Syra to some mission. The Queen, he declared, was a "superstitious heretic!" "an abominable witch!" "Jezebel using magic arts." Much more the zealous missionary would doubtless have added, had he not, while in the midst of his vituperations, found himself landed in a pool of mud outside the window. The virtuous elocutionist was forced to this unusual transit by the strong arm of a Greek officer who happened to enter the room at the right moment.

There never was a great religious reform that was not pure at the beginning. The first followers of Buddha, as well as the disciples of Jesus, were all men of the highest morality. The aversion felt by the reformers of all ages to vice under any shape, is proved in the cases of Sâkya-muni, Pythagoras, Plato, Jesus, St. Paul, Ammonius Saccas. The great Gnostic leaders — if less successful — were not less virtuous in practice nor less morally pure. Marcion, Basilides, Valentinus,[850] were renowned for their ascetic lives. The Nicolaitans, who if they did not belong to the great body of the Ophites were numbered among the small sects which were absorbed in it at the beginning of the second century, owe their origin, as we have shown, to Nicolas of Antioch, "a man of honest report, full of the Holy Ghost and wisdom." How absurd the idea that such men would have instituted "libidinous rites." As well accuse Jesus of having promoted the similar rites which we find practised so extensively by the medieval *orthodox* Christians behind the secure shelter of monastic walls.

If however we are asked to credit such an accusation against the Gnostics, an accusation transferred with tenfold acrimony, centuries later, to the unfortunate heads of the Templars, why should we not believe the same of the orthodox Christians? Minucius Felix states that the first Christians were accused by the world of inducing, during the ceremony of the 'Perfect Passover,' each neophyte on his admission to plunge a knife into an infant concealed under a heap of flour; the body then serving for a banquet to the whole congregation. After they had become the dominant party they (the Christians) transferred this charge to their own dissenters.[851]

The real crime of heterodoxy is plainly stated by John in his *Epistles*

---

850. Valentinus is termed by Tertullian a Platonist (*De praescr. haer.*, vii).
851. Cf. King: *The Gnostics and their Remains*, p. 197, 1st ed.; pp. 124, 334, 2nd ed.

and *Gospel.* "He that confesseth not that Jesus Christ is come in the flesh . . . is a deceiver and *an antichrist*" (*2 John*, 7). In his previous *Epistle*, he teaches his flock that there are *two* trinities (v, 7, 8) — in short, the Nazarene system.

The inference to be drawn from all this is that the made-up and dogmatic Christianity of the Constantinian period is simply an offspring of the numerous conflicting sects, half-castes themselves, born of Pagan parents. Each of these could claim representatives converted to the so-called *orthodox* body of Christians. And as every newly-born dogma had to be carried out by the majority of votes, every sect colored the main substance with its own hue till the moment when the emperor enforced this *revealed* olla-podrida, of which he evidently did not himself understand a word, upon an unwilling world as the *religion of Christ.* Wearied in the vain attempt to sound this fathomless bog of international speculations, unable to appreciate a religion based on the pure spirituality of an ideal conception, Christendom gave itself up to the adoration of brutal force as represented by a Church backed up by Constantine. Since then, among the thousand rites, dogmas, and ceremonies copied from Paganism, the Church can claim but one invention as thoroughly original with her, namely, the doctrine of eternal damnation; and one custom, that of the anathema. The Pagans rejected both with horror. "An execration is a fearful and grievous thing," says Plutarch. "Wherefore, the priestess at Athens was commended for refusing to curse Alcibiades [for desecration of the Mysteries] when the people required her to do it; *for*, she said, *that she was a priestess of prayers and not of curses.*" [852]

"Deep researches would show," says Renan,[852a] "that nearly everything in Christianity . . . is mere baggage brought from the Pagan Mysteries. . . . The primitive Christian worship was nothing but a mystery. The whole interior police of the Church, the degrees of initiation, the command of silence, and a crowd of phrases in the ecclesiastical language, have no other origin. The revolution which overthrew Paganism *seems* at first glance . . . an absolute rupture with the past . . . but *the popular faith saved its most familiar symbols from shipwreck.* Christianity introduced at first so little change into the habits of private and social life, that with great numbers in the fourth and fifth centuries it remains uncertain whether they were Pagans or Christians; many seem even to have pursued an irresolute course between the two worships." Speaking further of *Art*, which formed an essential part of the ancient religion, he says that "*it had to break with scarce one of its traditions.* Primitive Christian art is really nothing but Pagan art in its decay, or in its lower departments.

---

852. Plutarch: *Alcibiades,* § 22; *Roman Questions,* § 44.
852a. In *Les religions d'antiquité.*

The Good Shepherd of the catacombs in Rome is a copy from the Aristeus, or from the Apollo Nomius, which figures in the same posture on the Pagan sarcophagi, and still carries the flute of Pan, in the midst of the four half-naked Seasons. On the Christian tombs of the Cemetery of St. Calixtus, Orpheus charms the animals. Elsewhere, the Christ as Jupiter-Pluto, and Mary as Proserpina, receive the souls that Mercury — wearing the broad-brimmed hat, and carrying in his hand the rod of the soul-guide (*psychopompos*) — brings to them in presence of the three Fates. Pegasus, the symbol of the apotheosis; Psyche, the symbol of the immortal soul; Heaven personified by an old man, the river Jordan; and Victory — figure on a host of Christian monuments."

As we have elsewhere shown, the primitive Christian community was composed of small groups scattered about and organized in secret societies, with passwords, grips and signs. To avoid the relentless persecutions of their enemies, they were obliged to seek safety and hold meetings in deserted catacombs, the fastnesses of mountains, and other safe retreats. Like disabilities were naturally encountered by each religious reform at its inception. From the very first appearance of Jesus and his twelve disciples, we see them congregating apart, having secure refuges in the wilderness, and among friends in Bethany, and elsewhere. Were Christianity not composed of '*secret communities*' from the start, history would have more *facts* to record of its founder and disciples than it has.

How little Jesus had impressed his personality upon his own century, is calculated to astound the inquirer. Renan shows that Philo, who died toward the year 50, and who was born many years earlier than Jesus, living all the while in a Jewish community [852b] while the 'glad tidings' were being preached all over Palestine, according to the *Gospels*, had never heard of him! Josephus the historian, who was born three or four years after the death of Jesus, mentions his execution in a short sentence, and even those few words were altered "by a *Christian hand*," says the author of the *Life of Jesus*.[853] Writing at the close of the first century when Paul, the learned propagandist, is said to have founded so many churches, and Peter is alleged to have established the apostolic succession, which the Irenaeo-Eusebian chronology shows to have already included three bishops of Rome,[854] Josephus, the painstaking enumerator and careful historian of even the most unimportant sects, entirely ignores the existence of a Christian sect. Suetonius, secretary of Hadrian, writing in the first quarter of the second century, knows so little of Jesus or his history as to say that the Emperor Claudius "banished all the Jews, who were

---

852b. On at least one occasion Philo visited Jerusalem, although his chief residence was in Alexandria, long "a favorite abode of the learned Jews" (Yonge: *The Works of Philo Judaeus*, preface).   853. Introd.; also ch. xxviii.   854. Linus, Anacletus, and Clement.

continually making disturbances, at the instigation of one *Chrestus*,"
meaning Christ, we must suppose.[855] The Emperor Hadrian himself,
writing still later, was so little impressed with the tenets or importance of
the new sect, that in a letter to Servianus he shows that he believes the
Christians to be worshipers of Serapis.[856] "In the second century," says
C. W. King, "the syncretistic sects that had sprung up in Alexandria,
the very hot-bed of Gnosticism, found out in Serapis a prophetic type of
Christ as the Lord and Creator of all, and Judge of the living and the
dead." Thus, while the 'Pagan' philosophers had never viewed Serapis,
or rather the abstract idea which was embodied in him, as otherwise than
a representation of the Anima Mundi, the Christians anthropomorphized
the 'Son of God' and his 'Father,' finding no better model for him than
the idol of a Pagan myth! "There can be no doubt," remarks the same
author, "that the head of Serapis, marked, as the face is, by a grave and
pensive majesty, supplied the first idea for the conventional portraits
of the Savior." [857]

In the notes taken by a traveler — whose episode with the monks
on Mount Athos we have mentioned elsewhere — we find that, during
his early life, Jesus had frequent intercourse with the Essenes belonging
to the Pythagorean school, and known as the Koinobioi. We believe it
rather hazardous on the part of Renan to assert so dogmatically, as he
does, that Jesus "ignored the very name of Buddha, of Zoroaster, of
Plato"; that he had never read a Greek or a Buddhistic book, "although he had more than one element in him, which unawares to himself proceeded from Buddhism, Parsism, and the Greek wisdom." [858] This
is conceding half a miracle, and allowing as much to chance and coincidence. It is an abuse of privilege, when an author, who claims to write
historical facts, draws convenient deductions from hypothetical pre-
misses, and then calls it a biography — a *Life* of Jesus. No more than
any other compiler of legends concerning the problematical history of the
Nazarene prophet has Renan one inch of secure foothold upon which to
maintain himself; nor can any one else assert a claim to the contrary,
except on inferential evidence. And yet, while Renan has not one
solitary fact to show that Jesus had never studied the metaphysical tenets
of Buddhism and Parsism, or heard of the philosophy of Plato, his oppo-

---

855. *Lives of the Caesars* — 'Claudius,' § 25.   856. "Illi, qui Serapin colunt,
Christiani sunt, et devoti sunt Serapi, qui se Christi episcopos dicunt."— Vopiscus:
Vita Saturnini, in *Script. hist. August.*, p. 245.
857. *The Gnostics and their Remains*, pp. 161-2; 2nd ed. (p. 68, 1st ed.). In Payne
Knight's *Symbol. Lang. of Ancient Art and Mythology*, Serapis is represented as wearing
his hair long, "formally turned back and disposed in ringlets falling down upon his breast
and shoulders like that of women. His whole person, too, is always enveloped in drapery
reaching to his feet" (§ 145.) This is the conventional picture of Christ.
858. *La vie de Jésus*, ch. xxxviii.

nents have the best reasons in the world to suspect the contrary. When they find that — 1, all his sayings are in a Pythagorean spirit, when not *verbatim* repetitions; 2, his code of ethics is purely Buddhistic; 3, his mode of action and walk in life, Essenean; and 4, his mystical mode of expression, his parables, and his ways, those of an initiate, whether Grecian, Chaldaean, or Magian (for the 'Perfect,' who spoke the *hidden* wisdom, were of the same school of archaic learning the world over), it is difficult to escape from the logical conclusion that he belonged to that same body of initiates. It is a poor compliment paid the Supreme, this forcing upon Him four gospels, in which, contradictory as they often are, there is not a single narrative, sentence, or peculiar expression, whose parallel may not be found in some older doctrine or philosophy. Surely, the Almighty — were it but to spare future generations their present perplexity — might have brought down with Him, at His *first and only* incarnation on earth, something original — something that would trace a distinct line of demarcation between Himself and the score or so of incarnate Pagan gods, who had been born of virgins, had all been saviors, and were either killed, or otherwise sacrificed themselves for humanity.

Too much has already been conceded to the emotional side of the story. What the world needs is a less exalted, but more faithful view of a personage, in whose favor nearly half of Christendom has dethroned the Almighty. It is not the erudite, world-famous scholar, whom we question for what we find in his *Vie de Jésus*, nor is it one of his *historical* statements. We simply challenge a few unwarranted and untenable assertions that have found their way past the emotional narrator, into the otherwise beautiful pages of the work — a life built altogether on mere probabilities, and yet that of one who, if accepted as a historical personage, has far greater claims upon our love and veneration, fallible as he is with all his greatness, than if we figure him as an omnipotent God. It is but in the latter character that Jesus must be regarded by every reverential mind as a failure.

Notwithstanding the paucity of old philosophical works now extant, we could find no end of instances of perfect identity between Pythagorean, Hindû, and *New Testament* sayings. There is no lack of proofs upon this point. What is needed is a Christian public that will examine what will be offered, and show common honesty in rendering its verdict. Bigotry has had its day, and done its worst. "We need not be frightened," says Professor Müller, "if we discover traces of truth, traces even of Christian truth, among the sages and lawgivers of other nations." [858a]

After reading the following philosophical aphorisms, who can believe that Jesus and Paul had never read the Grecian and Indian philosophers?

[858a] *Chips from a German Workshop*, I, p. 53.

SENTENCES FROM SEXTUS, THE PYTHAGO-REAN, AND OTHER HEATHEN	VERSES FROM THE NEW TESTAMENT [859]
1. "Possess not treasures, but those things which no one can take from you" (Sextus: *Adv. Math.*).	1. "Lay not up for yourselves treasures upon earth, where moth and rust doth corrupt, and where thieves break through and steal" (*Matthew*, vi, 19).
2. "It is better for a part of the body which contains purulent matter, and threatens to infect the whole, *to be burnt*, than to continue so in *another state* [life]" (Iamblichus: *Protrept.*).	2. "And if thy hand offend thee, cut it off; it is better for thee to enter *into life* maimed, than . . . go into hell," etc. (*Mark*, ix, 43).
3. "You have in yourself something *similar to God*, and therefore use yourself *as the temple of God*" (Sextus).	3. "Know ye not ye are *the temple of God*, and that the Spirit of God dwelleth in you?" (*1 Corinthians*, iii, 16).
4. "The greatest honor which can be paid to God, is to know and imitate his *perfection*" (Sextus).[860]	4. "That ye may be the children of your Father which is in heaven: . . . Be ye therefore perfect, even as your *Father* which is in heaven *is perfect*" (*Matthew*, v, 45-48).
5. "What I do not wish men to do to me, I also wish not to do to men" (*Analects of Confucius*, ch. v, xv; see Max Müller's *Chips, etc.*, xiii).	5. "Whatsoever ye would that men should do to you, do ye even so to them" (*Matthew*, vii, 12).
6. "The moon shines even in the house of the wicked" (*Manu*).	6. "He maketh his sun to rise on the evil and on the good, and sendeth rain on the just and on the unjust" (*Matthew*, v, 45).
7. "They who give, have things given to them; those who withhold, have things taken from them" (*Ibid.*).	7. "Whosoever hath, to him shall be given . . . but whosoever hath not, from him shall be taken away even that he hath" (*Matthew*, xiii, 12).
8. "Purity of mind alone sees God" (*Ibid.*)— still a popular saying in India.	8. "Blessed are the pure in heart: for they shall see God" (*Matthew*, v, 8).

Plato did not conceal the fact that he derived his best philosophical doctrines from Pythagoras, and that he himself was merely the first to reduce them to systematic order, occasionally interweaving with them metaphysical speculations of his own. But Pythagoras himself got his recondite doctrines, first from the descendants of Mochus, and later from the Bráhmanas of India. He was also initiated into the Mysteries among the hierophants of Thebes, and the Persian and Chaldaean Magi. Thus step by step do we trace the origin of most of our Christian doctrines to Middle Asia. Drop out from Christianity the personality of Jesus,

---

859. See *Mishnah Pirke Aboth;* a Collection of Proverbs and Sentences of the old Jewish Teachers, in which many New Testament sayings are found (ed. Strack, Karlsruhe, 1882).
860. Iamblichus: *Life of Pythagoras, or Pythagoric Life*, pp. 269, *sq.*; ed. T. Taylor.

so sublime because of its unparalleled simplicity, and what remains? History and comparative theology echo back the melancholy answer, "A crumbling skeleton formed of the oldest Pagan myths!"

While the mythical birth and life of Jesus are a faithful copy of those of the Brâhmanical Krishna, his historical character of a religious reformer in Palestine is the true type of Buddha in India. In more than one respect their great resemblance in philanthropic and spiritual aspirations, as well as external circumstances, is truly striking. Though the son of a king (while Jesus was but a carpenter), Buddha was not of the high Brâhmanical caste by birth. Like Jesus, he felt dissatisfied with the dogmatic spirit of the religion of his country, the intolerance and hypocrisy of the priesthood, their outward show of devotion, and their useless ceremonials and prayers. As Buddha broke violently through the traditional laws and rules of the Brâhmanas, so did Jesus declare war against the Pharisees and the proud Sadducees. What the Nazarene did as a consequence of his humble birth and position, Buddha did as a voluntary penance. He traveled about as a beggar; and — again like Jesus — later in life he sought by preference the companionship of "publicans and sinners." Each aimed at a social as well as at a religious reform; and giving a death-blow to the old religions of their respective countries, each became the founder of a new one.

"The reform of Buddha," says Max Müller, "had originally much more of a social than of a religious character. . . . The most important element of the Buddhist reform has always been its social and moral code, not its metaphysical theories. *That moral code is one of the most perfect which the world has ever known* . . . and he whose meditations had been how to deliver the soul of man from misery and the fear of death, had delivered the people of India from a degrading thraldom and from priestly tyranny." Further, the lecturer adds that were it otherwise, "Buddha might have taught whatever philosophy he pleased, and we should hardly have heard his name. The people would not have minded him, and his system would only have been a drop in the ocean of philosophic speculation, by which India was deluged at all times." [861]

The same with Jesus. While Philo, whom Renan calls Jesus's elder brother, Hillel, Shammai, and Gamaliel are hardly mentioned — Jesus has become a God! And still, pure and divine as was the moral code taught by Christ, it never could have borne comparison with that of Buddha, but for the tragedy of Calvary. That which helped forward the deification of Jesus was his dramatic death, the voluntary sacrifice of his life, alleged to have been made for the sake of mankind, and the later

---

861. *Chips from a German Workshop,* 'Buddhism,' pp. 216-7.

convenient dogma of the atonement, invented by the Christians. In India, where life is valued as of no account, the crucifixion would have produced little effect, if any. In a country where — as all the Indianists are well aware — religious fanatics set themselves to dying by inches, in penances lasting for years; where the most fearful macerations are self-inflicted by fakirs; where young and delicate widows, in a spirit of bravado against the government, as much as out of religious fanaticism, mount the funeral pile with a smile on their face; where, to quote the words of the great lecturer, "men in the prime of life throw themselves under the car of Jaggernâth, to be crushed to death by the idol they believe in; where the plaintiff who cannot get redress starves himself to death at the door of his judge; where the philosopher who thinks he has learned all which this world can teach him, and who longs for absorption into the Deity, quietly steps into the Ganges in order to arrive at the other shore of existence,"[862] in such a country even a voluntary crucifixion would have passed unnoticed. In Judaea, and even among braver nations than the Jews — the Romans and the Greeks — where every one clung more or less to life, and most people would have fought for it with desperation, the tragical end of the great Reformer was calculated to produce a profound impression. The names of even such minor heroes as Mutius Scaevola, Horatius Cocles, the mother of the Gracchi, and others, have descended to posterity; and, during our school-days, as well as later in life, their histories have awakened our sympathy and commanded a reverential admiration. But, can we ever forget the scornful smile of certain Hindûs, at Benares, when an English lady, the wife of a clergyman, tried to impress them with the greatness of the sacrifice of Jesus, in giving *his* life for us? Then, for the first time the idea struck us how much the pathos of the great drama of Calvary had to do with subsequent events in the foundation of Christianity. Even the unimaginative Renan was moved by this feeling to write in the last chapter of his *Vie de Jésus* a few pages of singular and sympathetic beauty.[863]

---

862. Max Müller: 'Christ and other Masters,' in *Chips, etc.*, I, p. 57.

863. The *Life of Jesus* by Strauss, which Renan calls "*un livre, commode, exact, spirituel et consciencieux*" (a handy, exact, witty, and conscientious book), rude and iconoclastic as it is, is nevertheless in many ways preferable to the *Vie de Jésus* of the French author. Laying aside the intrinsic and historical value of the two works — with which we have nothing to do, we now simply point to Renan's distorted outline-sketch of Jesus. We cannot think what led Renan into such an erroneous delineation of character. Few of those who, while rejecting the divinity of the Nazarene prophet, still believe that he is no myth, can read the work without experiencing an uneasy and even angry feeling at such a psychological mutilation. He makes of Jesus a sort of sentimental ninny, a theatrical simpleton, enamored of his own poetical divagations and speeches, wanting every one to adore him, and finally caught in the snares of his

Apollonius, a contemporary of Jesus of Nazareth, was like him an enthusiastic founder of a new spiritual school. Perhaps less metaphysical and more practical than Jesus, less tender and perfect in his nature, he nevertheless inculcated the same quintessence of spirituality, and the same high moral truths. His great mistake was in confining them too closely to the higher classes of society. While to the poor and the humble Jesus preached "Peace on earth and good will to men," Apollonius was the friend of kings, and moved with the aristocracy. He was born among the latter, and was himself a man of wealth, while the 'Son of man,' representing the people, "had not where to lay his head"; nevertheless, the two 'miracle-workers' exhibited striking similarity of purpose. Still earlier than Apollonius had appeared Simon Magus, called "the great Power of God." His 'miracles' are both more wonderful, more varied, and better attested than those either of the apostles or of the Galilean philosopher himself. Materialism denies the fact in both cases, but history affirms. Apollonius followed both; and how great and renowned were his miraculous works in comparison with those of the alleged founder of Christianity, as the kabalists claim, we have history again, and Justin Martyr, to corroborate.[864]

Like Buddha and Jesus, Apollonius was the uncompromising enemy of all outward show of piety, all display of useless religious ceremonies and hypocrisy. If, like the Christian Savior, the sage of Tyana had by preference sought the companionship of the poor and humble; and if instead of dying comfortably, at over one hundred years of age, he had been a voluntary martyr, proclaiming divine Truth from a cross,[865] his

---

enemies. Such was not Jesus, the Jewish philanthropist, the adept and mystic of a school now forgotten by the Christians and the Church — if it ever was known to her; the hero, who preferred even to risk death, rather than withhold some truths which he believed would benefit humanity. We prefer Strauss, who openly names him an impostor and a pretender, occasionally calling in doubt his very existence; but who at least spares him that ridiculous color of sentimentalism in which Renan paints him.

864. See chapter iii, p. 97 of the present volume.

865. In a recent work, called *The World's Sixteen Crucified Saviors* (by Mr. Kersey Graves) which attracted our notice by its title, we were indeed startled, as we were forewarned on the title-page we should be, by *historical* evidences to be found neither in history nor tradition. Apollonius, who is represented in it as one of these sixteen "saviors," is shown by the author as finally "*crucified* . . . having risen from the dead . . . appearing to his disciples after his resurrection, and" — like Christ again — "convincing a *Tommy* [?] Didymus" by getting him to feel the print of the nails on his hands and feet (see note, p. 268). To begin with, neither Philostratus, the biographer of Apollonius, nor history says any such thing. Though the precise time of his death is unknown, no disciple of Apollonius ever said that he was either crucified, or appeared to them. So much for one "Savior." After that we are told that Gautama-Buddha, whose life and death have been so minutely described by several authorities — Barthélemy St.-Hilaire included — was also "*crucified* by his enemies near the foot of the

blood might have proved as efficacious for the subsequent dissemination of spiritual doctrines as that of the Christian Messiah.

The calumnies set afloat against Apollonius were as numerous as they were false. So late as eighteen centuries after his death he was defamed by Bishop Douglas in his work against miracles. In this the Right Reverend bishop crushed himself against historical facts. If we study the question with a dispassionate mind, we shall soon perceive that the ethics of Gautama-Buddha, Plato, Apollonius, Jesus, Ammonius Saccas and his disciples, were all based on the same mystic philosophy; that all worshiped one God, whether they considered Him as the 'Father' of humanity, who lives in man as man lives in Him, or as the Incomprehensible Creative Principle; and that all led God-like lives. Ammonius, speaking of his philosophy, taught that the Platonic school dated from the days of Hermes, who brought his wisdom from India. It was the same mystical contemplation throughout, as that of the Yogins: the communion of the Brâhmana with his own luminous Self — the 'Âtman.' And this Hindû term is again kabalistic, *par excellence*. Who is Self? is asked in the *Rig-Veda;* "Self is the Lord of all things . . . all things are contained in this Self; all selves are contained in this Self. Brâhman itself is but Self," [866] is the answer. Says the *Idrah Rabbah:* "All things are Himself, and Himself is *concealed* on every side." [867] The "Adam Kadmon of the kabalists contains in himself all the souls of the Israelites, and he is himself in every soul," says the *Zohar.* [868] The groundwork of the Eclectic School was thus identical with the doctrines of the Yogins, the Hindû mystics, and the earlier Buddhism of the disciples of Gautama.

Nepal mountains" (see p. 107); while the Buddhist books, history, and scientific research tell us, through the lips of Max Müller and a host of Orientalists, that Gautama-Buddha, (Sâkya-muni) died near the Ganges. "He had nearly reached the city of *Kusinâgara,* when his vital strength began to fail. He halted in a forest, and while sitting under a *sâl* tree he gave up the ghost" (Max Müller: *Chips from a German Workshop,* I, p. 213). The references of Mr. Graves to Higgins and Sir W. Jones, in some of his hazardous speculations, prove nothing. Max Müller (p. 219) shows some antiquated authorities writing elaborate books "in order to prove that Buddha had been in reality the Thoth of the Egyptians, that he was Mercury, or Wodan, or Zoroaster, or Pythagoras. Even Sir. W. Jones . . . identified Buddha first with Odin and afterwards with Shishak." We are in the nineteenth century, not in the eighteenth; and though to write books on the authority of the earliest Orientalists may in one sense be viewed as a mark of respect for old age, it is not always safe to try the experiment in our times. Hence this highly instructive volume lacks one important feature which would have made it still more interesting. The author should have added to the list, after Prometheus the "Roman," and Alcides the "*Egyptian god*" (p. 266), a seventeenth "crucified Savior" — "Venus, god of the war," introduced to an admiring world by Mr. Artemus Ward the 'showman'!

866. *Chhândogya-Upanishad,* viii, 3, 4; Max Müller: *Chips, etc.,* I, p. 69.

867. *Idrah Rabbah,* § 172.

868. Rosenroth: *Kabbala denudata,* II, p. 304, *sq.*

And when Jesus assured his disciples that "the spirit of truth, whom the world cannot receive because *it seeth Him not*, neither knoweth Him," dwells *with* and *in* them, who "are in Him and He in them," [869] he but expounded the same tenet that we find running through every philosophy worthy of that name.

St.-Hilaire, the learned and skeptical French savant, does not believe a word of the miraculous portion of Buddha's life; nevertheless he has the candor to speak of Gautama as being *only second to* Christ in the great purity of his ethics and personal morality. For both of these opinions he is respectfully rebuked by Des Mousseaux. Vexed at this scientific contradiction of his accusations of demonolatry against Gautama-Buddha, he assures his readers that "ce savant distingué n'avait point étudié cette question." [870]

"I do not hesitate to say," remarks Barthélemy St.-Hilaire, "that, except Christ alone, there is not among the founders of religions a figure either more pure or more touching than that of Buddha. His life is spotless. His constant heroism equals his conviction; . . . He is the perfect model of all the virtues he preaches; his abnegation, his charity, his unalterable sweetness of disposition, do not fail him for one instant; he abandoned, at the age of twenty-nine, his father's court to become a monk and a beggar; . . . and when he dies in the arms of his disciples, it is with the serenity of a sage who practised virtue all his life, and who dies convinced of having found the truth." [871] This deserved panegyric, which occasioned Des Mousseaux's wrath, is no stronger than the one which Laboulaye himself pronounced.[872] "It is more than difficult," wrote the latter, "to understand how men not assisted by revelation could have soared so high and approached so near the truth." [873] Curious that there should be so many lofty souls "not assisted by revelation"!

And why should any one feel surprised that Gautama could die with philosophical serenity? As the kabalists justly say, "Death does not exist, and man never steps outside of universal life. Those whom we think dead live still in us, as we live in them.[874] . . . The more one lives for his kind, the less need he fear to die." And we might add that he who *lives* for humanity does even more than he who dies for it.

The *Ineffable name*, in the search for which so many kabalists — unacquainted with any Oriental or even European adept — vainly consume their knowledge and lives, dwells latent in the heart of every man. This

869. *John*, xiv, 17.   870. *Les hauts phénomènes de la magie*, p. 74.
871. J. Barthélemy St.-Hilaire: *Le Bouddha et sa religion*, p. v; Paris, 1860.
872. Cf. Max Müller: *Chips, etc.*, I, p. 217.   873. *Journal des Débats*, Avril, 1853.
874. Éliphas Lévi: *Dogme et rituel de la haute magie*, Rituel, ch. xiii.

mirific name which, according to the most ancient oracles, "rushes into
the infinite worlds, ἀχομήτω στροφάλιγγι,"[875] can be obtained in a twofold
way: by regular initiation, and through the 'small voice' which Elijah
heard in the cave of Horeb, the mount of God. And "when Elijah
heard it he wrapped his *face in his mantle*, and stood in the entering of
the cave. And behold there came *the* voice."

When Apollonius of Tyana desired to hear the 'small voice,' he used
to wrap himself up entirely in a mantle of fine wool, on which he placed
both his feet, after having performed certain magnetic passes, and pronounced not the 'name' but an invocation well known to every adept.
Then he drew the mantle over his head and face, and his translucent or
astral spirit was free. On ordinary occasions he wore wool no more than
the priests of the temples. The possession of the secret combination of
the 'name' gave the hierophant supreme power over every being, human
or otherwise, inferior to himself in soul-strength. Hence, when Max
Müller [876] tells us of the Quiché "Hidden majesty which was never to be
opened by human hands," the kabalist perfectly understands what was
meant by the expression, and is not at all surprised to hear even this most
erudite philologist exclaim: "What it was we do not know!"

We cannot too often repeat that it is only through the doctrines of
the more ancient philosophies that the religion preached by Jesus can be
understood. It is through Pythagoras, Confucius, and Plato, that we can
comprehend the idea which underlies the term 'Father' in the *New Testament*. Plato's ideal of the Deity, whom he terms the one everlasting,
invisible God, the Fashioner and Father of all things,[877] is rather the
'Father' of Jesus. This Divine Being, of whom the Grecian sage says
that He can neither be envious nor the originator of evil, for He can produce nothing but what is good and just,[878] is certainly not the Mosaic
Jehovah, the "*jealous* God," but the God of Jesus, who "alone is good."
He extols His all-embracing, divine power [879] and His omnipotence, but
at the same time intimates that, as He is unchangeable, He can never
desire to change his laws, *i. e.*, to extirpate evil from the world through a
miracle.[880] He is omniscient, and nothing escapes His watchful eye.[881]
His justice, which we find embodied in the law of compensation and
retribution, will leave no crime without punishment, no virtue without its
reward; [882] and therefore he declares that the only way to honor God is to
cultivate moral purity. He utterly rejects not only the anthropomorphic

875. Proclus: *On the Cratylus of Plato.*   876. *Chips, etc.,* I, p. 336.
877. Plato: *Timaeus,* §§ 9, 16, etc.; *Polit.,* § 13: Bohn's Libr. ed.
878. *Timaeus,* § 10; *Phaedrus,* § 56; *Repub.,* II, xviii.   879. *Laws,* IV, vii; X, x.
880. *Repub.,* II, xx; *Theaet.* §§ 84, 85.   881. *Laws,* X, xi.
882. *Laws,* IV, vii; *Repub.,* II, viii; X, xii.

idea that God could have a material body,[883] but "rejects with disgust those fables which ascribe passions, quarrels, and crimes of all sorts to the minor gods." [884] He indignantly denies that God allows Himself to be propitiated, or rather bribed, by prayers and sacrifices.[885]

The *Phaedrus* of Plato displays all that man once was, and that which he may yet become again. "Before man's spirit sank into sensuality and was embodied with it through the loss of his wings, he lived among the gods in the airy [spiritual] world where everything is true and pure." In the *Timaeus* he intimates that there was a time when mankind did not perpetuate itself, but lived as pure spirits. In the future world, says Jesus, "they neither marry nor are given in marriage," but "are as the angels which are in heaven."

The researches of Laboulaye, Anquetil-Duperron, Colebrooke, Barthélemy St.-Hilaire, Max Müller, Spiegel, Burnouf, Wilson, and so many other linguists, have brought some of the truth to light. And now that the difficulties of the Sanskrit, the Tibetan, the Singhalese, the Zend, the Pahlavi, the Chinese, and even of the Burmese, are partially conquered, and the *Vedas*, and the Zend *Avesta*, the Buddhist texts, and even Kapila's *Sûtras* are translated, a door is thrown wide open, which, once passed, must close forever behind any speculative or ignorant calumniators of the old religions. Even till the present time the clergy have, to use the words of Max Müller — "generally appealed to the devilries and orgies of heathen worship . . . but they have seldom, if ever, endeavored to discover the true and original character of the strange forms of faith and worship which they call the work of the devil." [886] When we read the true history of Buddha and Buddhism, by Müller, and the enthusiastic opinions of both expressed by Barthélemy St.-Hilaire and Laboulaye; and when, finally, a Popish missionary, an eye-witness, and one who least of all can be accused of partiality to the Buddhists — the Abbé Huc, we mean — finds occasion for nothing but admiration for the high individual character of these 'devil-worshipers'; we must consider Śâkya-muni's philosophy as something more than the religion of fetishism and atheism, which the Catholics would have us believe it. Huc was a missionary, and it was his first duty to regard Buddhism as no better than an outgrowth of the worship of Satan. The poor Abbé was struck off the list of missionaries at Rome,[887] after his

---

883. *Phaedrus*, § 55.   884. E. Zeller: *Plato and the Older Academy*: London.

885. *Laws*, X, xiii.   886. Max Müller: *Chips, etc.*, I, p. 182.

887. Of the Abbé Huc, Max Müller thus wrote in his *Chips from a German Workshop*, I, p. 187: "The late Abbé Huc pointed out the similarities between the Buddhist and Roman Catholic ceremonials with such *naïveté*, that to his surprise he found his delightful *Travels in Tartary, Thibet, etc.* placed on the 'Index.' 'One cannot fail

book of travels was published. This illustrates how little we may expect to learn the truth about the religions of other people through missionaries, when their accounts are first revised by the superior ecclesiastical authorities, and the former severely punished for telling the truth.

When these men who have been and still are often termed "the obscene ascetics," the devotees of different sects of India in short, generally termed Yogins, were asked by Marco Polo, "how it comes that they are not ashamed to go stark naked as they do?" they answered the inquirer of the thirteenth century as a missionary of the nineteenth was answered. "We go naked," they say, "because naked we came into the world, and we desire to have nothing about us that is of this world. Moreover, we have no sin of the flesh to be conscious of, and therefore, we are not ashamed of our nakedness, any more than you are to show your hand or your face. You who are conscious of the sins of the flesh, do well to have shame, and to cover your nakedness." [888]

One could make a curious list of the excuses and explanations of the clergy to account for similarities daily discovered between Romanism and heathen religions. Yet the summary would invariably lead to one sweeping claim: The doctrines of Christianity were plagiarized by the Pagans the world over! Plato and his older Academy stole the ideas from the Christian revelation — said the Alexandrian Fathers!! The Brâhmanas and Manu borrowed from the Jesuit missionaries, and the *Bhagavad-Gîtâ* was the production of Father Calmet, who transformed Christ and John into Krishna and Arjuna to fit the Hindû mind!! The trifling fact that Buddhism and Platonism both antedated Christianity, and that the *Vedas* had already degenerated into Brâhmanism before the days of Moses, makes no difference. The same with regard to Apollonius of Tyana. Although his thaumaturgical powers could not be denied in the face of the testimony of emperors, their courts, and the populations of several cities; and although few of these had ever heard of the Nazarene prophet whose 'miracles' had been witnessed by a few apostles only, whose very individualities remain to this day a problem in history, yet Apollonius has to be accepted as the "monkey of Christ."

---

being struck,' he writes, 'with their great resemblance to Catholicism. The bishop's crosier, the mitre, the dalmatic, the round hat that the great lamas wear in travel, . . . the mass, the double choir, the psalmody, the exorcisms, the censer with five chains to it, opening and shutting at will, the blessings of the lamas, who extend their right hands over the head of the faithful ones, the rosary, the celibacy of the clergy, the penances and retreats, the cultus of the Saints, the fasting, the processions, the litanies, the holy water; such are the similarities of the Buddhists with ourselves.' He might have added the tonsure, relics, and the confessional."

888. *Travels of Marco Polo*, II, p. 301; J. Crawfurd: *Journal of an Embassy to the Courts of Siam, etc.*, p. 182: 1830.

If many really pious, good, and honest men are yet found among the Catholic, Greek, and Protestant clergy, whose sincere faith has the best of their reasoning powers, and who, having never been among heathen populations, are unjust only through ignorance, it is not so with the missionaries. The invariable subterfuge of the latter is to attribute to demonolatry the really Christ-like life of the Hindû and Buddhist ascetics and many of the lamas. Years of sojourn among 'heathen' nations, in China, Tatary, Tíbet, and Hindûstân have furnished them with ample evidence how unjustly the so-called idolators have been slandered. The missionaries have not even the excuse of sincere faith to give the world that they mislead; and with very few exceptions one may boldly paraphrase the remark made by Garibaldi, and say that: "*A priest knows himself to be an impostor, unless he be a fool, or have been taught to lie from boyhood.*"